D1210118

"It's all too easy to relegate the beautif. cy of our faith and leave its intricate politics and theology and, yes, future, to the scholars. But beyond the pilgrimages, photo tours, and souvenirs is a land and people favored by almighty God and pivotal in history from Abraham to Armageddon. When you're ready to move past the beauty of its topography and dig into the intricacies of God's plan for his chosen people, here is a your travelogue from experts who have made it their mission to make the trip remarkably accessible."

Jerry B. Jenkins, coauthor of the Left Behind Series

"This book deals with one of the most complex issues in biblical studies as well as modern politics. It is must reading for anyone who hopes to grasp what the Scriptures have to say about Israel in our day and in the future."

Richard Pratt, President, Third Millennium Ministries

"As a participant in dialogue with Palestinian Christian scholars and Messianic Jewish scholars, I am very happy to discover a volume that deals with the important issues of Israel and the land promises, based on biblical interpretation, theology and exegesis. This book is an important contribution to the dialogue and a strong case against both supersession in general and the spiritualizing of the promises of the land to the Jewish people."

Daniel Juster, Director, Tikkun International

"Few subjects have provoked as much controversy or been dealt with in such a cavalier fashion as that of the significance of Israel. The editors and authors redress this imbalance, giving clear and detailed consideration to all aspects of the topic. This single volume is a rich resource for anyone wanting to study carefully what the Bible has to say about the Jewish people and the land. It provides relevant and practical teaching on the Jewish people in Scripture, theology, and today's world. With a high view of Scripture and a firm confidence in God's ongoing purposes for the Jewish people, this book adds a vital and well-articulated contribution to the present-day political and theological debate, and challenges the reader to take seriously God's faithfulness to his people."

Richard Harvey, Senior Researcher, Jews for Jesus

"With conflicts in Israel and the Middle East so often in the news, it is important for believers to understand God's plan for Israel, its relationship to the church, and its relationship to the rest of the people in the Middle East. Believers who read *The People, the Land, and the Future of Israel* will have the tools to think about and discuss the future of Israel in a compassionate, biblically informed way."

Robert Jeffress, Pastor, First Baptist Church, Dallas, Texas

"As followers of Christ, what should be our position on the Jewish state and on the land of Israel? Is Israel merely like any other nation or are they a fulfillment of ancient Scriptures from ancient prophets? Should the church support Israel or not? *The People, the Land, and the Future of Israel* is an indispensable tool and resource that I believe has arrived just in the nick of time. The Israel question is dividing the church. That is why this book of biblical theology is needed now. I am going to give it to every pastor I know. I pray that God will use this book to enlighten the body of Christ and heal the division that has split the church over the nation of Israel."

Tom Doyle, author and Vice President of e3 Partners

"This immensely practical biblical theology of Israel and the Jewish people has been written by prominent scholars who skillfully and faithfully communicate God's message. Through the lens of Scripture, the reader is introduced to the importance of the nation of Israel, to God's love for Israel, to his plan for his chosen people, and to the extraordinary ways in which biblical prophecy is coming to pass in this generation. Read the volume; study its truths; answer its inductive review questions; watch videos of the original platform presentations. This volume indeed is one for such a time as this!"

Dorothy Kelley Patterson, Professor of Theology in Women's Studies, Southwestern Baptist Theological Seminary

"In a time of increasing anti-semitism and anti-Israelism in the world, it is absolutely critical for the church to be very clear about the ongoing significance of the people Israel to the unfolding of God's purposes in the world. This book offers theological clarity for an increasingly complex situation."

Alan Hirsch, missiologist and cofounder of Future Travelers

(Go to the end of this book for more endorsements.)

THE PEOPLE, THE LAND, AND THE FUTURE OF ISRAEL

ISRAEL AND THE JEWISH PEOPLE IN THE PLAN OF GOD

EDITORS

DARRELL L. BOCK AND MITCH GLASER

Kregel
Publications

CONTENTS

Practical Theology

CONTRIBUTORS

Craig A. Blaising, Ph.D., serves as Executive Vice President and Provost as well as Professor of Theology at Southwestern Baptist Theological Seminary, a position he has held since joining Southwestern in 2002. He is a contributing author of *Progressive Dispensationalism*, and *Three Views on the Millennium and Beyond*.

Darrell L. Bock, Ph.D., is Executive Director of Cultural Engagement at Center for Christian Leadership and Senior Research Professor of New Testament Studies at Dallas Theological Seminary. He is the author of several books, including the bestseller *Breaking the Da Vinci Code* and numerous works in New Testament studies, including *Jesus According to Scripture* and *Truth Matters*.

Michael L. Brown, Ph.D., is the Founder and President of FIRE School of Ministry and serves as a professor at The King's University, Gordon-Conwell Theological Seminary (Charlotte), Southern Evangelical Seminary, and Denver Theological Seminary. He is the author of twenty-five books, including the highly acclaimed five-volume series *Answering Jewish Objections to Jesus* and the Jeremiah volume in the *Expositor's Biblical Commentary* (revised edition), and he is a contributor to the *Oxford Dictionary of Jewish Religion,* the *Theological Dictionary of the Old Testament,* and other scholarly publications.

Robert B. Chisholm, Th.D., is Department Chair and Professor of Old Testament Studies at Dallas Theological Seminary. He is a translator and the senior Old Testament editor of the NET Bible. He is the author of several books, including *A Commentary on Judges and Ruth, Interpreting the Historical Books, Handbook on the Prophets,* and *A Workbook for Intermediate Hebrew.*

Pastor David Epstein has served as the Senior Pastor of the historic Calvary Baptist Church in New York City since 1997, where he is also the Chancellor and a faculty member of the New York School of the Bible, which is affiliated with Lancaster Bible College. He is the author of *A Time for Hope: One New York Pastor's Biblical Response to 9/11, Terrorism and Islam.*

Craig A. Evans, Ph.D., D.Habil., is the Payzant Distinguished Professor of New Testament at Acadia Divinity College in Nova Scotia, Canada. He is the author of several books, including *Jesus and His Contemporaries, Fabricating Jesus, Jesus and His World: The Archaeological Evidence,* and *From Jesus to the Church: The First Christian Generation.*

John S. Feinberg, Ph.D., is Chair of the Department of Biblical and Systematic Theology and Professor of Biblical and Systematic Theology at Trinity Evangelical Divinity School. He is the author of several books, including *The Many Faces of Evil, Ethics for a Brave New World,* and *Continuity and Discontinuity*

Mitch Glaser, Ph.D., is President of Chosen People Ministries. He is the co-editor of *To the Jew First: The Case for Jewish Evangelism in Scripture and History* and *The Gospel According to Isaiah 53.* He is also the author of *Isaiah 53 Explained.*

Gregory Hagg, Ph.D., Professor of Bible Exposition at Talbot School of Theology, is the Program Director and Professor in the Charles L. Feinberg Center, which offers an accredited Master of Divinity in Messianic Jewish Studies from Talbot School of Theology, which has partnered with Chosen People Ministries to provide excellent theological training for those who are reaching out to the Jewish people.

Walter C. Kaiser, Jr., Ph.D., is President Emeritus and Colman M. Mockler Distinguished Professor of Old Testament at Gordon-Conwell Theological Seminary. He is the author of several books, including *The Uses of the Old Testament in the New, Revive Us Again: Biblical Insights for Encouraging Spiritual Renewal,* and *Mission in the Old Testament: Israel as a Light to the Nations*

Barry R. Leventhal, Ph.D., is Distinguished Senior Professor, Former Provost, Former Academic Dean at Southern Evangelical Seminary. He has published numerous pieces on the Holocaust.

Eugene H. Merrill, Ph.D., is currently an independent scholar, having retired from Dallas Theological Seminary in June 2013 as Distinguished Professor of Old Testament Studies (Emeritus). He was on the faculty there for thirty-eight years. He is the author of several books, including *An Historical Survey of the Old Testament, 1 & 2 Chronicles,* and *Kingdom of Priests: A History of Old Testament Israel.*

Joel C. Rosenberg, *New York Times* best-selling author with nearly three million copies of his books in print and founder of The Joshua Fund, mobilizing Christians to "bless Israel and her neighbors."

Michael Rydelnik, DMiss., is Professor of Jewish Studies at Moody Bible Institute in Chicago, Illinois. He is the author of *Understanding the Arab Israeli Conflict, The Messianic Hope: Is the Hebrew Bible Really Messianic?* and co-editor of and contributor to *The Moody Bible Commentary.*

Mark R. Saucy, Ph.D., is Professor of Systematic Theology at Talbot School of Theology. He is the author of *The Kingdom of God and the Teaching of Jesus: In 20th Century Theology.*

Michael Vanlaningham, Ph.D., is Professor of Bible at the Moody Bible Institute in Chicago, Illinois, where he served formerly as interim chairman of the Bible Department. He is the author of *Christ, the Savior of Israel: An Evaluation of the Dual Covenant and Sonderweg Interpretations of Paul's Letters.*

Michael J. Vlach, Ph.D., is Associate Professor of Theology at The Master's Seminary. He is the author of several books, including *Has the Church Replaced Israel?: A Theological Evaluation, The Church as a Replacement of Israel: An Analysis of Supersessionism,* and *Dispensationalism: Essential Beliefs and Common Myths.*

Michael J. Wilkins, Ph.D., is Dean of the Faculty and Distinguished Professor of New Testament at Talbot School of Theology, he specializes in New Testament theology, Christology, and discipleship. He is the author of several books, including *Matthew (NIVAC), Following the Master: Biblical Theology of Discipleship, "Matthew" (ZIBBC), In His Image: Reflecting Christ in Everyday Life,* and *Discipleship in the Ancient World*

FOREWORD

JOEL C. ROSENBERG

The nations of the world are turning against Israel and the Jewish people. Will the church do so, as well?

In October 2013, a group of pastors, theologians and biblical scholars from over the U.S. and Canada gathered in the historic Calvary Baptist Church in New York City for a conference to consider "The People, the Land, and the Future of Israel." This could not have been a more timely subject, for Israel and the Jewish people face extraordinary peril—existential threats—on a magnitude equal to, and perhaps greater than, any the Jewish State has faced since 1948.

In the pages ahead, you will read the extraordinary and compelling work of these scholars. They examine vitally important historical, theological, and contemporary issues related to Israel and the Jewish people from numerous angles. They came together to affirm what the Scriptures teach about God's deep and enduring love and plan for Israel, while simultaneously affirming God's great love for the Palestinian people, and all of the Arab, Persian, Turkish, and other people of the region, according to the Abrahamic Covenant. In so doing, they have created a book that is the first of a kind, and one that is immensely practical for anyone trying both to understand these issues—not through the lens of politics, but through the lens of Scripture—and to communicate these biblical truths to others.

Indeed, many pastors, ministry leaders, seminary students, and lay people have not taken the time to carefully study what the Scriptures have to say on these subjects. As events in the Middle East heat up, they are looking for sound, credible resources to help them better understand God's heart on these subjects, and how to communicate these truths to others. This is why I am so deeply grateful to Dr. Mitch Glaser, the leadership of Chosen People Ministries, and the folks at Kregel, for loving Israel and the Jewish people and the church enough to have called together such fine scholars to share their wisdom, based on years of careful research, and create such a book.

That said, before we to work our way through all these key issues, it is useful to understand all of these issues in the context of our times. This was what I was asked to do at the conference, and I believe it remains a helpful place to start.

The Stakes Are High

In some ways, the modern State of Israel has never been more secure. It has won numerous wars against its enemies since 1948 and is widely perceived to have the strongest and most effective ground forces and air forces in the region. It has short and long-range ballistic missiles, the most advanced missile- and rocket-defense system on the planet, and (allegedly) possesses nuclear weapons, as well. Israel has a strong and growing economy, an increasingly high-tech business sector, excellent colleges and universities, and a robust and growing tourism industry.

However, the security situation around Israel is rapidly deteriorating. Consider recent developments.

In Egypt, we have watched millions of Arabs take to the streets calling for revolution and the dramatic fall from power of the Mubarak regime. We have seen the terrifying rise of the Muslim Brotherhood—and its leader Mohamed Morsi—to power, determined to impose Sharia law and end the peace treaty with Israel. Then we witnessed a stunning reversal as 22 million Egyptians signed a petition calling for the end of the Morsi regime, and created historic unrest in the streets, after which the military arrested Morsi, removed the leadership of the Brotherhood, and seized power.

In Syria, we seem to be watching the implosion of a modern Arab state. Tragically, more than 140,000 Syrians have been killed in a bloody civil war, including men, women, and children who have been murdered by their own government with chemical weapons. More than two million Syrians have fled the country. Some five million more Syrians have become "internally displaced"—that is, they have not fled their country but they have fled their homes and villages and are on the run for their lives. Who but the Lord can foretell where it will all lead?

In Lebanon, we are witnessing a modern Arab Sunni state steadily being hijacked from within by an Iranian, Shia-backed terrorist movement known as Hezbollah.

By God's grace, the Hashemite Kingdom of Jordan has been stable for several decades, and a peace treaty between Jordan and Israel is in place. But radical Islamists would like nothing more than to blow up that peace process, topple King Abdullah II, and create an Islamist regime on Israel's eastern flank.

The peace process between the Israelis and Palestinians has repeatedly foundered, raising the possibility of further violence between two noble peoples that have already suffered so much.

And then there is Iran, the only state in human history ruled by an apocalyptic, genocidal death cult. Its regime is driven by Shia Islamic end times theology. Its mullahs are feverishly building intercontinental ballistic missiles, and feverishly building the scientific and technological infrastructure to build not just one nuclear warhead, but an arsenal of several dozen warheads. They have defied one UN Security Resolution after another, and are working hand-in-glove with North Korea, which not long ago tested its third nuclear warhead.

Make no mistake: The stakes are high. If the Ayatollah Khamenei and his regime are able to build nuclear warheads and attach them to high-speed ballistic missiles, they could do in about six minutes what it took Adolf Hitler nearly six years to do: kill six million Jews. That's how many Jews live in Israel today, and this is who the regime in Tehran has vowed to "wipe off the map."

Yet Israel is not Khamenei's main target. Israel, in Shia eschatology, is merely the "Little Satan." The United States is the "Great Satan" for the mullahs. Yet over the last decade or so, most leaders in Washington and at the U.N. have seemed unable or unwilling to take decisive steps to neutralize the Iranian nuclear threat.

"In our time, the biblical prophecies are being realized."

Just days before we met at the Manhattan conference, Israeli Prime Minister Benjamin Netanyahu arrived in the US. He met with President Obama and Vice President Biden and their top advisors at the White House, and later with Secretary Kerry at the State Department. Later that day, the Prime Minister met with top Congressional leaders as well.

The following day, the Prime Minister delivered the final address to the leaders of the world gathered for the opening Fall Session of the United Nations General Assembly. It was a powerful and sobering speech, focused primarily on the steadily rising Iranian nuclear threat and the inability of the world, thus far, to neutralize that threat. Mr. Netanyahu warned world leaders not to be beguiled by the election of the new Iranian President Hassan Rouhani, whom he described as a "wolf in sheep's clothing." He also warned that Israel would be willing to take decisive action against Iran alone, if necessary, to prevent the ayatollahs from acquiring nuclear warheads.

It was a fascinating speech, and at times, quite personal. But the Prime Minister concluded his address with a sentence I have never heard coming from the lips of an Israeli leader in the modern era.

"In our time the biblical prophecies are being realized," Mr. Netanyahu declared. "As the prophet Amos said, 'They shall rebuild ruined cities and inhabit them. They shall plant vineyards and drink their wine. They shall till gardens and eat their fruit. And I will plant them upon their soil never to be uprooted again.' Ladies and gentlemen, the people of Israel have come home never to be uprooted again."

How extraordinary—an Israeli Prime Minister telling the leaders of the world that Bible prophecies are coming to pass in our lifetime. How many pastors and theologians in our day even believe this, much less are proclaiming it to be so?

Mr. Netanyahu was correct. The miraculous rebirth of the State of Israel—and the dramatic re-gathering of Jews back to the Holy Land from all over the world —are central examples of End Times prophecies found in the Bible being fulfilled. What's more, the Prime Minister also alluded in his speech to the biblical prophecies of a Persian king named "Cyrus" who would rise up one day and set the Jewish people free from captivity.

"The Jewish people's odyssey through time has taught us two things: Never give up hope, always remain vigilant. Hope charts the future. Vigilance protects it," Mr. Netanyahu said. "Today our hope for the future is challenged by a nuclear-armed Iran that seeks our destruction. But I want you to know, that wasn't always the case. Some 2,500 years ago the great Persian king Cyrus ended the Babylonian exile of the Jewish people. He issued a famous edict in which he proclaimed the right of the Jews to return to the land of Israel and rebuild the Jewish temple in Jerusalem. That's a Persian decree. And thus began an historic friendship between the Jews and the Persians that lasted until modern times."

It was the Hebrew prophet Isaiah who foretold the rise of a great Persian king named "Cyrus" who would emerge one day to bless the Jewish people, release them from captivity, send them back to the land of Israel, and rebuild the city of Jerusalem. (See Isaiah 44:28 through 45:13.) And sure enough, a Persian king named "Cyrus" did, in fact, emerge to fulfill Isaiah's startling prophecies, as we read in 2 Chronicles 36 and Ezra 1.

Mr. Netanyahu's interest in the Scriptures has been growing significantly in recent years, and is increasingly an element in his public statements. At a speech at the Auschwitz death camp in 2009, for example, he **declared** that the prophecies of Ezekiel 37—the dry bones of the Jewish people coming back together miraculously to form the State of Israel—had come to pass in his lifetime.

> "The most important lesson of the Holocaust is that a murderous evil must be stopped early, when it is still in its infancy and before it can carry out its designs," noted Mr. Netanyahu. "The enlightened nations of

the world must learn this lesson. We, the Jewish nation, who lost a third of our people on Europe's blood-
soaked soil, have learned that the only guarantee for
defending our people is a strong State of Israel and the
army of Israel. We have learned to warn the nations of
the world of impending danger but at the same time,
to prepare to defend ourselves. As the head of the Jewish state, I pledge to you today: We will never again
permit evil to snuff out the life of our people and the
life of our own country...."

"After the Holocaust," he continued, "the Jewish people rose from ashes and destruction, from a terrible
pain that can never be healed. Armed with the Jewish
spirit, the justice of man, and the vision of the prophets, we sprouted new branches and grew deep roots.
Dry bones became covered with flesh, a spirit filled
them, and they lived and stood on their own feet. As
Ezekiel prophesied: 'Then He said unto me: "These
bones are the whole House of Israel. They say, 'Our
bones are dried up, our hope is gone; we are doomed.'
Prophesy, therefore, and say to them: Thus said the
Lord God: I am going to open your graves and lift you
out of your graves, O My people, and bring you to the
land of Israel.'" I stand here today on the ground where
so many of my people perished—and I am not alone.
The State of Israel and all the Jewish people stand with
me. We bow our heads to honor your memory and lift
our heads as we raise our flag—a flag of blue and white
with a Star of David in its center. And everyone sees.
And everyone hears. And everyone knows—that our
hope is not lost."

The question for Israelis and for people everywhere now is this: If
the prophecies of Ezekiel 37 have largely come to pass in our lifetime,
is it not possible that other major Bible prophecies will come true in
our lifetime as well?

A Landmark Survey of American Jews
On the very same day as the Prime Minister's address to the United
Nations, a landmark survey of the American Jewish community was
released with startling new insights.

"The first major survey of American Jews in more than 10 years
finds a significant rise in those who are not religious, marry outside
the faith and are not raising their children Jewish—resulting in rapid

assimilation that is sweeping through every branch of Judaism except the Orthodox," reported *The New York Times*.

The survey was conducted by the Pew Research Center's Religion & Public Life Project. Excerpts from the *Times* article:

- The intermarriage rate, a bellwether statistic, has reached a high of fifty-eight percent for all Jews, and seventy-one percent for non-Orthodox Jews—a huge change from before 1970 when only seventeen percent of Jews married outside the faith.
- Two-thirds of Jews do not belong to a synagogue.
- One-fourth do not believe in God.
- One-third had a Christmas tree in their home last year.
- "It's a very grim portrait of the health of the American Jewish population in terms of their Jewish identification," said Jack Wertheimer, a professor of American Jewish history at the Jewish Theological Seminary, in New York.
- Sixty-nine percent say they feel an emotional attachment to Israel.
- But only forty percent believe that the land that is now Israel was "given to the Jewish people by God."

Perhaps the most striking finding of the survey, the *Times* reported, was that "34 percent said you could still be Jewish if you believe that Jesus was the Messiah." It was an extraordinary question to be asked, and an extraordinary result. One in three American Jews now believe you can believe in Jesus as Messiah and still be Jewish. Consider the implications of that fact. Out of an estimated six million American Jews, some two million people no longer believe it is an act of betrayal to the Jewish people for a Jewish person to embrace Jesus as the long-awaited Messiah and hope of Israel.

The full report, which was a mixed offering of bad news and good, should be studied carefully. The implications of the findings must be properly analyzed. But let us consider the possibility that the report offers us clues that we may be approaching the dawn of the greatest spiritual awakening in the modern history of the Jewish people and that the Lord is about to open the eyes of many to the truth of who Yeshua really is. This, in turn, would suggest that if Jewish and Gentile believers in Jesus will commit themselves to faithfully sharing the Gospel with the Jewish people in the US, Israel and around the world in the years ahead—and do so in a loving, gentle, winsome manner, not with the unconscionable coercion and insensitivity of previous ages—millions of Jewish people may be more ready to hear and receive than at any epoch since the first century. How exciting that would be! Is the church ready for such a season of dramatic evangelism and discipleship among God's chosen people? Let us hope so.

Reasons for Hope

In a world that is lost and dark and getting darker, there are reasons for hope.

Yes, evil is on the march. But the Lord God Almighty is holy and sovereign, and He, too, is on the move. In our own lifetime, we have seen the dramatic rebirth of the State of Israel, and the return of millions of Jewish people to the Holy Land, and the rebuilding of the ancient ruins in Israel, all in fulfillment of Bible prophecy. The very fact that there is a State of Israel today is a testament to the existence of the God of Abraham, Isaac, and Jacob, and further evidence that the Scriptures are inspired and that the prophecies are all true. What's more, we see the Lord strengthening His remnant of believers around the world, amidst persecution and suffering, and we know the Lord Jesus is coming back soon, and thus we can endure whatever the world throws at us.

Yes, most Israelis, and Jews around the world, have not personally and carefully studied the Word of God. But Prime Minister Netanyahu is studying the Bible on Shabbat with his son, having occasional Bible studies in his official residence, citing the Scriptures in his speeches, and is increasingly interested in the role of Bible prophecy in our current times. Indeed, more and more Jews are interested in reading the Scriptures. We are even seeing a fascinating movement of rabbis and Jewish scholars encouraging Jews to read the New Testament.

Yes, there is much resistance to the Gospel in Israel and throughout the epicenter. But the fact is the Lord is drawing more Jews and more Muslims to faith in Jesus Christ in the last few decades than in the last twenty centuries. Meanwhile, He is preparing the hearts of many more to come to faith in Jesus as Messiah in the years ahead. Indeed, we are steadily heading towards a Romans 11:26 world, in which "all Israel will be saved." God will do His part. We must now do ours, which is to teach and preach the Scriptures without fear or shame, and to do so based on a solid theological understanding of the people, the land and the future of Israel.

Yes, it's true that many pastors and Christian ministry leaders in the US and around the world do not understand, or have not carefully studied, God's love and plan and purpose for Israel. Indeed, tragically, some pastors and Christian leaders are speaking out against Israel. They say there is nothing special or important about Israel or the Jewish people. Some say God has rejected the Jews. Some call for boycotts against Israel, divestment from Israeli investments, and sanctions against the Jewish state (the "BDS" movement). This is as heartbreaking as it is unbiblical. Such efforts must be firmly and lovingly challenged. Nevertheless, the good news is that God is waking up a remnant here and around the globe of Christians and Messianic Jews eager to rediscover the purpose and power of Bible prophecy and all of God's Word with regards to Israel, and the nations, and many other topics.

In light of God's love and sovereignty, therefore, let us not despair. Rather, let us be encouraged about the people, the land and the future of Israel, even as we are sober-minded about the very real challenges that lie ahead. As we move deeper into the eschatological future, and nearer to the Second Coming, we know the nations of the world are going to isolate, accuse, and then turn on the Jewish people and the State of Israel. This is what prophecy teaches, and current trends are remarkably consistent with this biblical truth. That said, the Abrahamic Covenant is still true and valid. God will bless those who bless Israel, and curse those who curse Israel. So we need not fear. Rather, we must be faithful to the task that God has given us, and that includes strengthening the remnant.

The church is called to embrace the Jewish people and the whole house of Israel, to love them with unconditional love, to bless them in every possible way, and do so in the name of Jesus, even if we do not agree with every decision they make. At the same time, the church is called to embrace the Arab and Persian and Kurdish and Turkish people, and love them with unconditional love, and bless them in every possible way, and do so in the name of Jesus, even if we do not agree with all of their decisions. This is the heart of the Abrahamic covenant—to be a blessing to all the families of the earth. This is the purpose of the Great Commission—to go and make disciples of all nations. The God of the Bible is not "either/or" when it comes to loving Israel and her neighbors; He is "both/and." He has ordained some different roles and responsibilities for Israel and her neighbors, but He has called us to love them both. Thus, those who love Israel must also care deeply for the Palestinian people; and seek their blessing, and find practical ways to support and encourage them; and stand for both justice and mercy; and especially to love and encourage Palestinians who love Christ and have been called to know and serve Him. Likewise, those who start with a deep love for the Palestinians must also care deeply for the Israeli people; and seek their blessing, and find practical ways to support and encourage them; and stand for both justice and mercy; and especially to love and encourage Messianic believers who love Yeshua and have been called to know and serve Him. This is how the lost world will know we are His disciples, when we show love for one another.

Not every pastor and theologian and lay person understands this, but we must not lose heart. Indeed, let us be filled with hope, knowing the Lord is coming to save His people and establish His kingdom. This is the blessed hope of Israel, and it shall come to pass. Let us teach the Word in the power of the Holy Spirit and with authority. Let us preach the Gospel without fear or shame. Let us live the Gospel by living lives of great love and compassion. Let us do so with patience and humility and gentleness. And let us not grow weary in well-doing, for in due time, by the grace of God, we will reap a great harvest. Again, the Word is clear: We are heading towards a Romans 11:26 world. We are heading towards a time in which all Israel will be saved. Let us be faithful in doing our part, that in the end we will all hear from our Savior's lips, "Well done, My good and faithful servant. You were faithful in a few things; I will put you in charge of many things. Enter into the joy of your Master."

Conference Video

chosenpeople.com/rosenberg

Interview with Joel Rosenberg

chosenpeople.com/rosenberg-interview

INTRODUCTION

DR. MITCH GLASER

The tiny nation of Israel continues to be a political and spiritual football tossed about by the nations of the world.

In the heat of the current conflict, deep questions that require answers linger in the hearts and minds of concerned Christians and even within the Jewish community. Some Christians feel the need to take sides in the midst of the Middle East crisis! Is it possible to believe the Jewish people have a divine right to the land of Israel and yet care deeply about Palestinians and their concerns? Christians moved by social justice issues wonder whether Israel should have the right to dwell in the land only if Palestinians are treated according to a certain code of ethics.

These are all-important questions that will never be satisfied by answers found in political theory or in the analyses of experts on the history of the region. We believe the only place we will find answers to the profound questions that will ultimately shape how we view the Middle East—especially the conflict between Israel and the Palestinians—is in the Bible, the Word of God.

This is why Chosen People Ministries, Joel C. Rosenberg, and the leaders of the historic Calvary Baptist Church in Manhattan convened a conference to tackle these difficult biblical issues. Our hope was to provide Bible believers with the opportunity to build a firm foundation allowing for a more informed response to the raging political questions of our day.

I am grateful for the wisdom and guidance of my prolific coeditor, Dr. Darrell Bock, Director of Cultural Engagement and Senior Research Professor of New Testament Studies at Dallas Theological Seminary, as well as for Pastor David Epstein and the staff and family at Calvary Baptist Church in Manhattan who co-sponsored this conference.

Chosen People Ministries has a multi-generational relationship with Calvary Baptist Church. Over the decades, we have sponsored similar conferences at Calvary during the years of the Holocaust and immediately after the establishment of modern Israel. In light of this long-term relationship and since New York City is the Jewish capital of the United States, it seemed only reasonable that a conference of this nature and magnitude take place at Calvary Baptist Church.

I am also grateful for the hard work of the Chosen People Ministries Church Ministries and Conferences department in planning and coordinating the logistics of the conference. They worked tirelessly before the event preparing for the conference.

I am also thankful for the partnership of Joel C. Rosenberg. Joel is one of the most knowledgeable evangelicals about the Middle East, having worked with various Israeli leaders and having spent many months living in Israel and Arab countries. Joel is a leading voice in support of Israel and is passionate beyond most for the cause of bringing the Good News to both Jews and Arabs in the Holy Land. We are honored that Joel would speak at the conference and write the foreword for this book.

A special thank-you to Chosen People Ministries staff members Scott Nassau and Alan Shore, for their help in editing and in writing the introduction sections for each of the chapters.

The Importance of the Book and the Conference

We may ask the question, why is this book necessary and why was the conference significant? I alluded to the answer in my opening comments. Because of the volatile and charged atmosphere for these discussions, both among politicians and evangelicals, the conveners and contributors believed that a very significant element of the discussion was lacking and a new approach to finding solutions for our questions was needed.

The new approach, in fact, was an old approach that had been lost in the midst of many heated debates and discussions on the issues that surround Israel's land claim. We believed that the answers to the Middle East crisis, like other important questions in life, were to be found in the Bible. In other words, discussions regarding the modern Middle East crisis needed to be better informed and molded by Scripture.

Additionally, many of the fine scholars who contributed to this book believe a biblical theology of Israel and the Jewish people is sorely needed. There are Bible-believing Christians who think that in one way or another, the Church has replaced Israel. This view has become more popular even among many Christians who previously believed the land of Israel was promised to the Jewish people.

22

In recent years, there has been a marked increase in books, blogs, and films such as *O Little Town of Bethlehem* that present a more sympathetic view of the Palestinian political cause. What is evidently lacking in them, however, is a clear look at what the Bible says about the land of Israel and the role of the Jewish people in the plan of God.

Most of the responses to these weighty biblical questions have been answered with politically and historically based responses and not primarily founded upon Scripture. But, it is with the Bible that we need to begin to answer all of our deeper questions.

This is really the genesis of the conference and this book. It is our hope that Christians will view the Jewish people, the Land and the future of Israel through the lens of the Scripture. We seek to offer a biblical theology that asserts that God has a plan today and tomorrow for the Jewish people—and that this plan includes the land of Israel.

The Heart and Tone of the Book

In tone, this book reflects the loving heart of the participants for all people, including Jewish people, Arabs, Palestinians, Muslims, and groups within the Middle East who are struggling and whose only hope is found in the presence and power of Jesus the Messiah. He is the Prince of Peace and we believe He is coming soon to reign as King—and then peace will flood the hearts and souls of all those who live in the Middle East and beyond!

The Use of the Book

This book should be studied rather than read. There are introductory videos that may be watched, study questions at the end of each chapter, and a video of the chapter in sermon form given at the Calvary Baptist conference. This will enable the book to be used for Sunday schools, Shabbat schools in Messianic congregations, small groups, and even special evening services dedicated to studying these issues.

We also hope that this volume will be used as a textbook for college and seminary courses. It is written in a way that both trained scholars and average members of congregations will appreciate and understand.

We hope that you will make good use of the multimedia platform and enter into the full experience of this book in sight, sound, and word.

—Dr. Mitch Glaser
New York City
March 2014

Invitation to the Conference

chosenpeople.com/intro

Michael Zinn's Testimony

chosenpeople.com/zinn

Hormoz Shariat's Testimony

chosenpeople.com/shariat

Panel Discussion

chosenpeople.com/panel

HEBREW SCRIPTURES

ISRAEL ACCORDING TO THE TORAH

Dr. Eugene H. Merrill

Merrill, in his chapter titled *Israel according to the Torah,* provides an overview of the creation of the nation of Israel and charts God's course for the nation through a discussion of the covenants made with His chosen people. He shows why Israel's national identity is important to the plan of God beginning with the call of Abraham to leave his home and journey to a new land to become a mighty nation (Gen. 12:1–3). He also points the reader to the ultimate impact Israel and the Jewish people will have upon the nations of the world.

Merrill concludes that God will remain faithful to His unconditional covenant with Israel, by redeeming the nation and returning them to the land to "carry out successfully the mission to which God had called them" until the great day when Jesus returns to establish His Kingdom.

Introduction

The Hebrew term usually translated "people" (*'am*), though employed hundreds of times with reference to Israel, is virtually generic for humankind and lacks the specificity that is intended when Israel as a chosen people is in view. Ironically, for that denotation the word "nation" (*gôy*) is found (ca. 35x with reference to Israel out of 556 occurrences in all).[1] Thus, Israel is not an amorphous people among the peoples but a nation among the nations with all that entails.[2] This is important to keep in mind for the eschatological gathering of Israel will not be as a people alone but as a clearly recognized nation.

The Promise of a People

The first attestation of Israel as a nation (*gôy*) is in connection with the Abrahamic Covenant as articulated in Genesis 12:1–3. Speaking to Abram, Yahweh says, "I will make you to be a great nation and I will bless you and make your name great and you will become a blessing" (v. 2). The full implication of this will be developed at a later place in the chapter. For now it is sufficient to note the use of *gôy* rather than *'am*, the latter of which never occurs with reference to the Abrahamic Covenant (cf. 17:20; 18:18; 35:11; 46:3).

Part 1: The Lineage of the People
Abraham to Eber (Gen. 11:14–26; cf. 10:21–31; 1 Chron. 1:24–27)

Before any single generation of a people could be fully identified and credentialed in the ancient Near East, it was important that its antecedent lineage be established. Where did they come from? Of what people groups do they consist? What has been their history of sedentariness and migration? What is their eponymy? The linear genealogy of this passage provides a clear answer to at least the last question. Abraham was the last of seven generations in a linear genealogy commencing with Eber, he and Eber included (Gen. 11:14–26). The consonants of Eber (*'br*) are exactly the same as those in the word "Hebrew" except for the vocalic gentilic ' at the end of "Hebrew" indicating ethnicity or nationality (*'br'*). Spelled with vowels, the two words are respectively *'ēber* and *'ibr'*. Thus, Abraham was an Eberite or, in time and in line with the ancient versions, a Hebrew.[3]

As to other characteristics of nationhood, none applies in the case of Abraham's predecessors except for consanguinity and possibly common language.[4] One should therefore refer to the Eberites (=Hebrews) as a landless, disparate, and scattered people who may or may not have had any sense of calling or purpose.

Eber to Shem (Gen. 11:10–16; cf. 10:21–24; 1 Chron. 1:17–23)

The ancestry of Abraham is further defined as being transmitted via Shem, one of three sons of Noah. Only four generations are recorded between Shem and Eber; thus, Abraham was eleven generations from Shem. The name "Shem" (*šēm*) means "name," to be understood perhaps as *the* name, the one paramount in the illustrious patrimony of Abraham. Abraham and his descendants would therefore be known as Shemites (or Semites) since they descended from Noah through Shem. "Semite" (or "Semitic") is equally applicable to peoples other than the Hebrews, the most famous being the Arabic line of Abraham's son Ishmael (Gen. 16:7–14; 25:12–18; 28:9). The familial structure of Abraham's can be described as follows: Abraham was a Semite, one among one third of the world's population, but, more narrowly, he was also a Hebrew, one line among the only two known lines descendant from Eber, namely, that of Peleg (Gen. 11:16; cf. 10:25–31).

Shem to Seth/Adam (Gen. 5:1–32; cf. 1 Chron. 1:1–4)

Of the three sons of Noah, Shem was designated to be the bearer of the so-called Noachic Covenant (Gen. 9:8–17), a fact only intimated from the beginning but made clear as the descendants of the three sons of Noah at last centered on Abraham through Shem.[5] After Cain slew Abel, Seth became the son of Adam designated to form the ancestral line that would pass through Noah, Abraham, and David to Jesus Christ. Ten generations are recorded in the narrative, including Adam and Noah (Gen. 5:3–29), but special attention must be paid to three explanatory notes that underscore the nobility of humankind and the need for its restoration to glory. In the first place, the writer notes that God created humankind "in the likeness of God" and then called them "Adam" (or "mankind").[6] Second, Adam's son Seth is said to be in Adam's likeness (děmût) and image (ṣelem). The same two terms are found in the creation story of Genesis 1 but in reverse order. The point is that despite the sin and fall of Adam and Eve, the image of God in mankind, though marred and distorted, still exists and is worth restoring. The third noteworthy statement comes in the naming of Noah at his birth (Gen. 5:29).[7] After the historical plight of humankind since the Fall and the impending judgment of the Flood, Lamech prophetically sees the day when his son Noah would become the means of bringing comfort and rest to the human race. Little could he know of the great plan God had for a line of Noah's descendants that would culminate in a Deliverer who would usher in everlasting rest and peace.

Noah, the prototype of the Deliverer *par excellence*, is implicitly compared to Adam in that he would "bring us comfort[8] from our work" and "from the toil[9] of our hands" (Gen. 5:29). The latter term is found in the curse of the ground brought about by Adam's sin: "in toil shall you eat [of the ground]" (Gen. 3:17). The comparison with Adam is more explicit in the passage that introduces the Noachic covenant in which Noah is commanded to "Be fruitful and multiply and fill the earth" (Gen. 9:1). The identical words are found in the creation mandate to Adam, the implications of which will be treated later. For now it is sufficient to see that Abraham issued from Adam (the human race) via Seth, Noah (the "second Adam"), Shem (the ethnic people), and Eber (the patronym). The creation of a nation awaits a time future to the Patriarchs.

Part 2: The Descendancy of the People
(Gen. 21:1–7; cf. Josh. 24:2–4)
Abraham to Judah (1 Chron. 1:28, 34; 2:1–2; Matt. 1:2; Luke 3:33–34)
The line from Abraham to Judah is uncomplicated to say the least. Abraham, in fact, was the great-grandfather of Judah, the son of Jacob (or Israel).[10] Both Isaac and Jacob had become custodians of the Abrahamic Covenant (Gen. 17:19; 21:12; 26:3–4; and 27:27–29; 28:3, 13–15 respectively). The people of Abraham were in process of becoming a nation through the tribal stage represented by Judah. To him the covenant promise was bequeathed and through him would come the Messianic figure who would rule over all and, in a sense yet to be revealed, who would atone for the sins of the world.

From the time of his naming (yĕhûdâ, "let him praise"; cf. Gen. 29:35) and thereafter it was clear that Judah, despite his failings, was the chosen vessel by which the redemptive purposes of God would be accomplished. The clearest indication of this sovereign selection is articulated in the blessing by Jacob of his twelve sons (Gen. 49:8–12).[11] His brothers will praise him (a play on his name) and he will be the one who takes up the scepter and staff, signs of his royal status.[12] This rule will be temporary, however, for it will be surrendered at last to the "one to whom it belongs" v. 10).[13] King David certainly qualifies on the historical plane as the Old Testament makes crystal clear, but beyond him exists one who is even greater as he himself testifies. A full discussion of this important truth must be delayed for now.

Judah to David (Ruth 4:18–22; 1 Chron. 2:3–17)

This section will be treated only lightly, since other chapters will address post-Pentateuch times and texts in detail. The justification for its inclusion here is to demonstrate how the seed-bed of Old Testament thought and theology was not stifled or truncated at the end of Torah but, to the contrary, blossomed and came to fruition in the remainder of the canon.

The first canonical reference to the ancestry of David is the epilogue to Ruth, included there perhaps to demonstrate the inclusion of Gentiles like Ruth herself in the circle of God's saving grace. Beyond that, the genealogy identifies her as David's great-grandmother, surely an even more powerful sign of the grafting of those outside the Abraham-Isaac line into the "wild olive tree" (Rom. 11:17). As for David, he was born in Bethlehem of Judah and thus as a Judahite fulfilled the ancient promise to Judah that it would be the tribe from whence the Royal One would emerge. That Jesus was born in Bethlehem is self-evidently a claim to Davidic descent and to royal prerogatives.

The Chronicler devotes more space to the genealogies of Judah and then those of David than to any other tribe (Judah: 2 Chron. 2:3–55; 4:1–23; David: 3:1–24), ninety-nine verses in all! He clearly understood the messianic nature and separation of the tribe of Judah and of David, its most prominent figure. Beyond that, he is the central figure of the lengthy history of Israel and Judah compiled by the Chronicler (1 Chron. 11–29), eighteen chapters out of sixty-four in 1 and 2 Chronicles, or twenty-eight percent. The focus narrows from Adam>Seth>Noah>Shem>Eber>Abraham>Jacob>Judah>David.

David to Jehoiachin (1 Chron. 3:1–16; Matt. 1:6–11)

The descent from David to Jehoiachin consists of 14 generations and a period of about four hundred years, David and Jehoiachin included. For reasons of symmetry (14, 14, 14 generations; Matt. 1:17), Matthew omits the names Joash, Amaziah, Jehoiakim, and Zedekiah; however, the lineage from David to Jehoiachin is not rendered incomprehensibly incomplete to the last of the Davidic monarchy before the Babylonian exile.[14] Jehoichin's release from house arrest by

Evil-Merodach in 562 BC reignited hope in the exile community that the house of David would continue on to its goal of ensuring return, redemption, and restoration of God's chosen people.[15]

Jehoiachin to Jesus (Matt. 1:12–16)

In summary, two brief observations must suffice about this post-Torah record: (1) Neither the Old Testament nor any other extant literature records the genealogy preserved by Matthew. His sources are completely unknown but his fidelity to the traditions of the preceding parts of the genealogy leaves no room for doubt as to his accuracy. (2) The genealogy of Luke's Gospel supplies Mary's ancestral heritage which, like Matthew's, also links David to Jesus but through David's son Nathan rather than through Solomon (Luke 3:23–31). Thus, both Joseph and Mary were of the house of David but through parallel lines of succession (Luke 1:27; 2:4; cf. Matt. 1:20).

Part 3: The Creation Covenant

Its Nature

Though many scholars question the notion of a creation covenant, a case can be made for it but time and space limitations preclude making it here and now.[16] What is lacking is the complete formal structure of a covenant document but elements remain as follows: (1) Two parties are involved, namely, God and humankind (Gen. 1:1, 27); (2) "witnesses" are present in the form of all other created things (1:6–25); (3) there is a set of stipulations—fill the earth and have dominion over it (1:28); and (4) blessings (1:29–31; 2:15–16; 2:22–23) and curses (2:17; 3:14, 16, 17–1) accrue depending on covenant loyalty or disloyalty. Though lacking all the elements that normally indicate covenant genre, clearly in the nature of the case the creation mandate is not between parties equal in stature; hence it is of a so-called "sovereign-vassal" type. God dictates its terms and humankind, as the inferior party, has no choice but to comply if it wants to enjoy the blessings of the relationship and avoid its negative consequences.

Its Purpose

The purpose of the mandate is crystal clear: Man, as the image of God, is to exercise dominion over all other created things as God's earthly surrogate. He is not just *in* the image of God—he *is* the image of God and therefore represents God. In a sense, man is of royal stock, a king over whatever realm God places him. Thus the notion of human kingship finds its roots.

Its Failure

The use of the term "failure" must first of all be clarified. Whatever God creates or initiates cannot fail so any breakdown of the covenant relationship that might take place is the fault of man and man alone. Humankind was created with the ability to choose, as the text clearly attests (Gen. 2:16–17), so his fatal choice to disobey his God brought upon his own head the judgment about which God had already warned—he surely died (2:17; 3:19).[17] But even this seeming irreversible rupture of relationship could and would be overcome by the Creator. What he had created he would re-create. This brings into play the scheme of redemption and reconciliation that occupies virtually all the rest of sacred Scripture. Its implementation would come about through a series of covenants God would offer to fallen humanity which, if entered into and kept with loyal compliance, would grant new life and new hope. In fact it would eventuate in a "new heavens and a new earth where righteousness dwells" (2 Peter 3:13).

Part 4: Subsequent and Necessary Covenants of Redemption

The Noachic Covenant: Reinstitution of the Nations (Gen. 9:1–17)

The covenant text proper isolated here is embedded in a larger context in which God's promises (8:22–24) and Noah's prophetic outcomes to his sons (9:20–29) appear. The proposition that covenant is the instrument of reconciliation between God and humankind following the Flood is clear from the fact that the technical term *bĕr't* ("covenant") occurs in this passage seven times in the span of seventeen verses, a density of usage unparalleled elsewhere in the Old Testament. The larger context may be analyzed as follows:

God's promise never again to curse the ground (*'ădāmâ*) as he had by sending the great flood (8:22–24).[18]

The original creation mandate reiterated to Noah (9:1–2, 7), with an additional expansion concerning what could and could not be eaten (vv. 3–4); man's original vegetarian diet (Gen. 2:9, 16) now augmented by the consumption of animal meat, clearly a concession to creation's fallen nature.

Blood prohibited for consumption because it symbolized life and therefore could be "eaten" only by God in sacrificial ritual (v. 4; cf. Ex. 30:10; Deut. 12:27; etc.).

Concept of the sanctity of blood leads to the matter of murder by which a man's blood is shed (v. 6). Since man is the image of God, the penalty for murder must be *lex talionis*, that is, life for life, but only as administered by government. Thus, humanity in general must be governed by law and must in turn exercise authority as an agent of God (Rom. 13:1: "The [powers] that be are ordained by God").

All of these principles and statutes are formalized and activated by the ceremony of covenant (vv. 8–7). Twice God says he is establishing his covenant with humanity (vv. 9, 11). The verb translated "establish" (*qûm*, here the hiphil participle *mēqî'm*), bears the nuance of keeping, as in keeping one's word (HALOT, 1088). God, the one who cannot lie, pledges here to keep the covenant, no matter what (cf. Gen. 6:18; 17:7, 19, 21; Ex. 6:4; Deut. 8:18; Ezek. 16:60, 62). In the immediate situation, the Lord promises never again to destroy the earth by flood and as a sign of his solemn commitment he places a rainbow in the clouds. This he does, he says—and in highly anthropopathic language—so that he will never forget what he has promised (vv. 12–16). It is a "string around the finger" (Heb *'ōt*).[19]

Following a drunken stupor, Noah adds to the covenant document prophetic destinies for his three sons (Gen 9:25–27): (1) Canaan, son of Ham, will be cursed, principally by his becoming a slave people;[20] (2) Yahweh, God of Shem, will be blessed; and (3) Japheth will not only subdue Canaan but will find refuge in Shem. As to (1), no case can be made for African slavery, though Hamites did indeed settle in Africa. The text could not be clearer: It is the Canaanites who will be held in bondage. This began with the slave labor of the Canaanite Gibeonites who had tricked Joshua into making a covenant with them (Josh. 9:3–27) and continued intermittently until no Canaanites survived. The blessing of Yahweh (2) was in effect a blessing of Shem because it suggests that God would be with Shem in a special way, one we have traced earlier and found to center in Shem's role of covenant bearer of salvation.[21] Japheth (3) would be both large and small. It represents the Gentile nations that cover the earth but find their refuge and redemption in the tents of Shem, that is, in the line of Shem from which would come salvation.

In conclusion, the Noachic Covenant reinstates the notion of divine authority mediated through humankind, even in its fallenness. Noah was, in effect, a second Adam from whom the nations would descend and through whom the original covenant mandate could be carried out.

The Abrahamic Covenant: Establishment of a Redemptive People (Gen. 12:1–3; 13:14–17; 15:1–21; 17:1–21; 22:17–18; 26:3–4; 27:27–29; 28:13–17; 35:9–13; 46:1–4)

The Abrahamic Covenant is a (if not the) central theological rubric of the Old Testament because (1) it encapsulates in one man God's plan for the rehabilitation and restoration of his original, pre-Fall creation; (2) it engenders a fountain-head of blessing through a people who will both fill the earth and become narrowed to one descendant who will bring atonement and new life; and (3) it contains within it the promise of a people, land, and law that will form on earth a nation that, ideally at least, foreshadows the Kingdom of God in the new heavens and new earth.

The matters of its literary form and conditionality or non-conditionality, though important, cannot be discussed fully in this brief treatment.[22] However, the premise of this chapter is that God made to Abraham an unconditional grant of land (Gen. 12:1; 13:15; 15:18), nationhood (Gen. 12:2; 17:4), and blessing (Gen. 12:2; 22:17; 26:3), with the ancillary privilege of being a means of blessing the nations (Gen. 12:3; 27:29; Isa. 19:24; Zech. 8:13).[23] Moreover, this grant will never be rescinded because it is based on the sworn oath of a God who cannot lie (Gen. 22:16–17; 26:3; 50:24; Ex. 13:11; 33:1; Deut. 4:31; 6:18; 31:20; Ezek. 36:7–15).

If taken literally—and no good literary, hermeneutical, and theological reason exists not to—one should note that all three elements were fulfilled in biblical times. Israel occupied the land of Canaan under Joshua, David and Solomon greatly added to it territorially, and it was maintained all through the period of the Divided Monarchy until the Assyrian deportation of 722 BC and the Babylonian exile of 586 BC. Even after that, the state of Yehud was formed after the exile and an "Israel" was recognized in some form or other until the Romans put an end to it early in the second century AD.

The promise of nationhood was slower in coming and was not a functional reality until the beginning of the United Monarchy under Saul (ca. 1050 BC). The elements of the promise were there much earlier (ca. 1350 BC) in the tribal affiliations, but not in the structural sense that marked the transition from "people" to "nation."

Abraham's seed was blessed in numerous ways throughout the ancient historical period, and they became a blessing to others also in those times. This was evident as early as the exodus event as seen in the "mixed multitude" that accompanied them in their escape from Egypt. These proselytes were clearly impacted by Israel's God and thus blessed in unimaginable ways considering the utter depravity of Egyptian paganism from which they were converted. Examples of individuals are Rahab the Canaanite prostitute and Ruth the Moabite, both of whom were grafted into the messianic ancestral tree (Matt. 1:5 and Ruth 4:17–22 respectively), to say nothing of the much later Naaman, the Syrian soldier, who confessed that Israel's God was the only true god (2 Kings 5:15).

Even these manifestations of the efficacy of the Abrahamic Covenant are eclipsed by the eschatological revelations of a future Israel with a future land, nation, and blessing. Glimpses of these things may already be seen in the modern immigration of the Jewish people into their ancient homeland, their formation into a nation among the nations of the world, and their blessing the nations through medical, scientific, and cultural enterprise. These foretastes set the stage for what yet lies ahead. The making of *aliya* will far transcend any historical examples; the nation will no longer fear their hostile neighbors but will far outshine them; and the greatest contribution of all—their recognition, confession, and proclamation of their Messiah to the world—will transform the world as the nations also embrace the living God of Israel.

The Mosaic Covenant (Ex. 19:5–6; 24:8; 34:10, 27–28; Deut. 4:13, 23; 5:3; 9:9; 29:1, 12; 31:16, 20)

The term "Mosaic" is preferable to "Sinaitic" or the like because it suits both the Sinai and Moab versions and settings of the revelation of the covenant, that is, the ones found in Exodus and Deuteronomy respectively. The major question to be asked of the Mosaic Covenant is: What is its relationship to the Abrahamic Covenant and, later, to the Davidic? These two questions demand separate answers.

The Mosaic Covenant vis-à-vis the Abrahamic Covenant

Unlike some systems that view the covenants of the Old and New Testaments as sequential and on the same plane, this chapter argues that in both form and substance the Mosaic stands as an adjunct to the Abrahamic, in service to it, as it were. That is, the Mosaic draws out the theological implications of the Abrahamic as they pertain to the identity and role of the special nation implicitly in mind there. The narratives of Genesis and Exodus leave no question as to these matters: The nation in mind is Israel, the seed of Abraham that would be a blessing to those peoples and nations that blessed it.

One might designate the Abrahamic Covenant as an ontological or existential entity that consists of the desire of a gracious God to bring the fallen world back into fellowship with himself without explicitly saying how. The Mosaic Covenant, on the other hand, is a functional or utilitarian covenant that names the instrument that will effect this divine plan and instructs that instrument as to its several responsibilities in such an enormous enterprise. The secret lies in Israel's being a chosen vessel that will, by strict obedience to Torah, model to the rest of the world what the Kingdom should be like. At the same time, it will be custodian of the message of redemption and the "missionary" responsible for its proclamation.

Failure to do this adequately will not ultimately frustrate the plan of God, for as Paul states so eloquently, "Because of [Israel's] transgression, salvation has come to the Gentiles" (Rom. 11:11). On the other hand, "Israel has experienced a hardening in part until the full numbers of the Gentiles has come in. And so all Israel will be saved" (v. 25). The Mosaic Covenant may be broken by Israel (and was), but just as a natural olive tree may lose its branches and have wild olive branches grafted on to it, so it may also have its natural branches re-grafted in due time (Rom. 11:17–24). To this, the Old Testament also testifies in multiple passages (e.g., Lev. 26:40–45; Deut. 7:12; Isa. 10:21–22; 51:11; 55:3; Jer. 31:8, 16, 31, 34; 32:40; 44:28; Ezek. 16:60, 62; 37:26; Hos. 2:18; 3:5; Zech. 10:9).

The Davidic and New Covenants lie outside the parameters of this chapter but will receive adequate treatment by other participants in this colloquium.

Conclusion

In one sentence, Torah teaching on the land and the people may be summarized as follows: God created all things for his glory, including humankind, his own image, designed to co-reign over all else; but man's sin and fall broke the connection, a rupture that could be mended only by an unconditional covenant pledge of restoration on God's part, the agent of which was the chosen people Israel who, for a time, were set aside because of their covenant disloyalty, but who will be redeemed and returned to the land to carry out successfully the mission to which God had called them until Jesus comes to install the everlasting Kingdom.

Study Questions

1. To whom did God reveal his plan for a special people through whom the whole earth would be blessed?

2. What term in Hebrew is usually employed to describe it as a chosen people?

3. What is Israel's primary purpose in the world?

4. From what name does the term "Hebrew" derive?

5. What is the earliest book to contain the genealogy of David?

6. What is the major difference between the Sabbath command in Exodus 20 and that in Deuteronomy?

7. What is the origin of the term "Semite"?

8. From what tribal descent was Jesus the Messiah?

9. Why was humankind created in the first place?

10. Which two Gospels contain genealogies of Jesus?

Conference Video

chosenpeople.com/merrill

Interview with Dr. Eugene Merrill

chosenpeople.com/merrill-interview

ISRAEL ACCORDING TO THE WRITINGS

Dr. Walter C. Kaiser Jr.

Kaiser, in his chapter *Israel according to the Writings,* continues Merrill's trajectory established in the five books of Moses by turning to the portion of Scripture known as the "Writings." This refers to the third division of the Hebrew Bible; the Torah, the Prophets (*Nebi'im*) and the Writings (*Kethubim*). The "Writings" applies to thirteen books in the Hebrew Bible.

According to Kaiser, God's redemptive story in the Writings begins with a Moabite woman, Ruth, setting the stage for the creation of a Davidic dynasty described in 2 Samuel 7:8–17. The Psalms reflect and comment on the Davidic covenant (Psalm 89) and the future glories of the Davidic ruler. The story of Esther is the story of God's preservation of His people. While the book does not mention God, His providential hand is evident throughout the narrative.

Kaiser concludes his overview with a summary of Chronicles, detailing David's lineage and progeny and then focusing on both his human frailty and love for God. Kaiser then moves us from the historical books to the message of the prophets by showing that Chronicles in the Hebrew Bible concludes with a call to repentance so that the Jewish people might enjoy the blessing of the covenants (2 Chron. 7:14).

The "Writings," or as they are known in the Hebrew canon of the Old Testament as the "Kethubim" (cf. the Hebrew verbal root *katab*, "to write"), form the third traditional division of the Hebrew Bible, following the five books of the Torah ("Law") and the eight books of the Nebi'im ("prophets") to make the complete Tanak, or as it was later referred to: "the Old Testament." The "Writings" consist of the following thirteen books: the three poets: Psalms, Job, Proverbs; the five Megilloth: Ruth, Song of Songs, Ecclesiastes, Lamentations, Esther; and the histories: Daniel, Ezra–Nehemiah, and 1 and 2 Chronicles.

The Writings share in telling the story of the people of Israel, the land, and the nation's future as that story is continued in the book of Ruth. The narrative was initiated in the promise to Eve in Genesis 3:15, was advanced in the promise made to Shem in Genesis 9:27, and then was extended to Abraham, Isaac, and Jacob, beginning in Genesis 12:1–3. This same narrative is now the bases for what we find as we pick up the story again in the book of Ruth.

The Book of Ruth

Thus, the best place to start the story of the people of Israel, their land and their future, in the section of the Bible known as "the Writings," is in the book of Ruth. Even though this book only has four chapters and eighty-five verses, it is enormously significant in that it provides us with a direct link to the genealogy of David (Ruth 4:18–22). Here then, is the critical connection in the Messianic promise of the coming occupant who would sit on the throne of David and be the one who would point the way to the coming Messiah.

The narrative of the book of Ruth is cast mainly (more than fifty percent) in the form of a dialogue, which traces the steps of a Judean couple named Elimelech and Naomi, along with their two sons, Mahlon and Kilion, all of which left the town of Bethlehem during a famine in Israel, to travel to the adjoining country of Moab. While they sojourned in Moab, Naomi lost her husband Elimelech, and her two sons, in three deaths for unnamed causes. Naomi's sons, in the meantime, had married two Moabite women: Ruth and Orpah.

When the good news came from Israel, after a number of years, that food was once again available in Israel, Naomi decided to return back home to Bethlehem. Naomi's daughter-in-law, Ruth, was determined to return with Naomi to Bethlehem. At first, both Ruth and Orpah were going to return to Israel with Naomi, but Orpah decided to remain in Moab. So after a sad parting, Naomi and Ruth went on without Orpah and arrived in Bethlehem just as the barley harvest was beginning. Once in Bethlehem, Ruth began to glean in the fields that belonged to Boaz, who in God's gracious provision turned out to be a close relative—but Ruth was not at all aware of such a relationship. Boaz, however, upon learning who this stranger in his fields was, prayed that Ruth might be rewarded for her faithfulness in gleaning every day, by finding refuge under the "wings" (Hebrew *kenapim*) of Yahweh (Ruth 2:12), which was the same word later used for the "shirt," or "corner [of the garment]" that Ruth would ask Boaz to spread over her (Ruth 3:9) as a symbol of his acceptance of her in marriage.

Later on, Boaz did marry Ruth and the grandchild of Naomi born to Ruth became the "father" of Jesse. Jesse, in turn, became the father of David (Ruth 4:22), who in turn became the King of Israel. The blessing of God, therefore, is seen in: (1) God's kindness and grace to those who had suffered such great personal losses, (2) the inclusion of a Gentile, such as Ruth, not only in the Gospel message, but also in (3) the development of the promised line of David as the first in the genealogy of the One who would be king over Israel when the Messiah returned the second time.

The book of Ruth, therefore, is God working out his promise-plan through Ruth, which led to her being in the line of the great-grandson of King David. But this also leads to the book of 2 Samuel (a book that is part of the "Earlier Prophets"), where we are treated to one of the most brilliant moments in the history of redemption, both for that historical epoch of Biblical history in Samuel's day, but also for the entire plan of God's redemption of mankind. This is found in the text of 2 Samuel 7, which is matched in its importance and prestige only by: (1) the promise made to Eve in Genesis 3:15, (2) the promise made to Abraham in Genesis 12:2–3, and (3) the promise made later to all Israel and to all the nations in Jeremiah 31:31–34, through the "New Covenant." Second Samuel 7 is known as the "Davidic Covenant," which is repeated in 1 Chronicles 17 and used extensively in Psalm 89.

The Davidic Covenant: 2 Samuel 7; 1 Chronicles 17; Psalm 89

Moses had predicted there would be the gift of a king in Israel as far back as Genesis 17:6, 16; 35:11; and in Deuteronomy 17:14–15, but the people got ahead of the Lord and instead wanted to have a king they desired, simply so they could be "like the other nations" (1 Sam. 8:5): that is how Saul became the first king. But God subsequently rejected Saul as king, for the Lord continued to search for "a man after his own heart" (1 Sam. 13:14); accordingly, David was anointed as king by the prophet Samuel (1 Sam. 16:13) after forty years of Saul's reign.

The classical Old Testament passage dealing with this new addition about the Davidic dynasty, and the coming Messianic kingdom, rule, and reign of Christ as the final One in the line of David, in the ever-expanding promise-plan of God was laid out most fully, as already noted, in 2 Samuel 7, with its duplicate in 1 Chronicles 17, and its commentary in Psalm 89. The setting for this magnificent divine announcement to David was the dedication ceremony for the new cedar palace that David had just completed. When the prophet Nathan congratulated David on the completion of this new palace, David expressed his desire to build a "house" for God, for the tabernacle had remained in curtains ever since its construction some four hundred years earlier.

Nathan, hearing of David's desire to build the temple of God, enthusiastically encouraged him to go ahead with building this house of God as his next project. However, that night the Lord announced to Nathan that David was not to build this temple, but his son was to carry out this task (2 Sam. 7:4–16). What was more, rather than David making a "house" for the Lord, the Lord would instead make a "house/ dynasty" out of David (2 Sam. 7:13a)—a fact repeated eight times in 2 Samuel 7 (vv 11, 13, 16, 19, 25, 26, 27, 29)! In fact, God would see to it that David's dynasty, his kingdom, and his throne would last forever (2 Sam. 7:16). Moreover, the "house of David" would involve a line of descendants who would continue in perpetuity (vv 12, 16, 19, 26, 29) until Messiah came to complete that line. Here was one of the most momentous announcements in the promise-plan of God!

Even more startling, if that is at all possible, was the dramatic realization that suddenly came over David as he began to process all that he had just been told by the prophet Nathan. It began as the king went into the Tabernacle and cried out to God: "Who am I, Adonai Yahweh, and what is my family, that you have brought me this far? And as if this were not enough in your sight, O Adonai Yahweh, you have spoken about the future of the house of your servant" (2 Sam. 7:18–19b). The fact that David used this distinctive name for God in this case, "Adonai Yahweh," must not be passed over quickly, for it rarely appears in the Tanak, but it did show up significantly in the Abrahamic Covenant (Gen. 15:2, 8). It would appear, then, that in so doing, David had purposely thereby linked the two covenants as being parts of the same plan of God: the Abrahamic and the Davidic Covenants.

But David was not finished with his prayer as yet, for he went on to make an even more startling declaration, which is so important that almost every English translation has failed to grasp the proper rendering of the Hebrew text. David continued: "And [all of] this is the charter/ law/ teaching for all humanity!" (7:19c).

David suddenly realized that what was now being promised to and through him was nothing less than the Good News that had previously been given through Abraham, Isaac, and Jacob earlier in Genesis! This was God's charter for all humanity!

No wonder Psalm 89:26–27 addressed the coming Davidite as God's "son," his "Firstborn," even his "Highest" ("Most High"). Indeed, David's throne, by a figure of speech called metonymy, was called "Elohim" in Psalm 45. Accordingly, what God stood for in heaven, David was appointed to be as a symbol and pledge of God's kingdom on earth. It would appear that human language was on the brink of bursting all boundaries as it described such a filial relationship between a man and God.

The most detailed commentary on 2 Samuel 7 was found in Psalm 89. In that Psalm, Ethan the Ezrahite began by commenting at length on the Davidic Covenant in vv 3–4 and 19–37. But then, in vv 38–51, he lamented the downfall of the monarchy as he plead with God to be faithful in the promise he had made to David. There could be no doubt that David was the important link in the line of that promised "Seed" announced to Eve, Abraham, Isaac, Jacob, and David. In like manner, Psalm 101 prayed for similar guidance for God's chosen ruler.

The Davidic Kingdom and the Royal Psalms

Ever since the beginning of the twentieth Christian century, it has become traditional to speak of the "Royal Psalms" or the "Psalms of Zion." They depict our Lord as the Sovereign Ruler over the nation of Israel, and the nations of the world, as he rules from Jerusalem/Zion (Pss. 46–48, 65, 93, 96–100). But just as significant for the promise-plan of God concerning his coming royal person, are those Psalms that view David as God's son, who carries out the Lord's authority over all the nations of the world (Pss. 2, 45, 72). Thus, Psalm 2 speaks of the inauguration of the "anointed one," while Psalm 62 speaks of his majesty and glory, and Psalm 72 describes the scope of God's ultimate world-wide reign.

These Royal Psalms are steeped in the ideology of the Davidic dynasty, which is derived from the promise and oath made to King David. For example, Psalm 2 contrasted the hostility of the nations to the Lord, which was directed both to God the Father and to his Messiah. But God's answer to such hostility was given in the form of the investiture of his son, the (final) Davidic king:

> I have installed my king
> On Zion, my holy hill.
> I will proclaim the decree of the LORD;
> He said to me, "You are my son!
> Today I have become your Father.
> Ask of me,
> And I will make the nations your inheritance
> And the ends of the earth your possession (Ps. 2:6–8).

By these words, God acknowledges David as one who belonged most intimately to Him. His words, "I have begotten you" are stronger than the simple statement that "You are my son," for they describe how the Messianic king has received a higher life from God above: there was a special dignity that had been conferred upon David and it was linked to a special point in time; a "today." Some think that "day" was when David entered his office as king, but later on the Apostle

Paul marked that "day" as the day of the resurrection (Acts 13:30–33; Rom. 1:3–4). In fact, David had been taught about the resurrection of the Messianic person, for as a prophet of God, he knew this coming anointed one as his *"Hasid"*, i.e., as his "Holy One," in Psalm 16:10. This "Holy One" would not see decay, nor would he be abandoned and left in the grave. The Apostle Peter taught this same truth on the day of Pentecost, for he argued:

> Brothers, I can tell you confidently that the patriarch David died and was buried, and his tomb is here to this day. But he was a prophet and knew that God had promised him on oath that he would place one of his descendants on his throne. Seeing what was ahead, he [David] spoke of the resurrection of the Christ, that he was not abandoned to the grave, nor did his body see decay. God raised this Jesus to life, and we are all witnesses of the fact (Acts 2:29–33).

What could be stated more clearly than what Psalm 16 taught and what Peter explained from this Psalm? David was informed by God that God himself would raise that anticipated final One in his line from death and the grave itself in a resurrection! That would be an extraordinary act of God, but after all, this was the promise-plan of God.

In a beautiful combination of the Sinaitic theophany (Ps. 18:7–15) and an invincible David (31–46), Psalm 18, and its parallel in 2 Samuel 22, picture the victory and triumph of David, which results in God's name being lauded before the nations and his covenant being kept forever (Ps. 18:47–50).

> He is the God who avenges me,
> who subdues nations under me....
> Therefore I will praise you among the nations, O LORD;
> I will sing praises to your name.
> He gives His king great victories;
> He shows unfailing kindness to His anointed,
> To David and his descendants forever.

In a similar manner, Psalms 20 and 21 appear to be paired together as Psalm 20:4 petitions God for victory and it is answered in Psalm 21 as that victory is celebrated with great joy and thanksgiving for all of God's blessings. The enemy was so soundly defeated. In fact, this victory outstripped the power of the king and called more for the appearance of Messiah to explain what had happened there (Ps. 21:9–12). Marvelous were the acts of God in sustaining his man David and his works of victory.

The Book of Daniel

The book of Daniel is likewise listed among the "Writings" of the Tanak. Daniel was born some time just prior of King Josiah's reformation, after the book of the Law had been discovered in 621/622 BC, which times on other terms, turned out to be troublous times indeed. Daniel came from an unidentified family of nobility in Judah, yet he, and his three friends, Hananiah, Mishael and Azariah, were nevertheless carted off into captivity by the Babylonian conqueror Nebuchadnezzar in the third year of King Jehoiakim (Dan. 1:1, 3). Daniel and his friends were placed in a three-year course in Babylon in preparation for some type of royal service (Dan. 1:4–5). This too was all in the gracious plan of God, for all four men were examples of the sovereign work of God.

The theology of the book of Daniel sets forth in its description of the kingdom of God the very antithesis of that which the successive kingdoms of the world were experiencing at that time. According to the revelation God had given to Daniel, the kingdom of God would triumph over all the kingdoms and empires of this world. Despite the fact that Daniel was part of the exile that now lived beyond the catastrophe of the collapse of Jerusalem, the destruction of its temple as the house of God, and what appeared to be the end of the Davidic line with its promised kingdom and throne; nevertheless, God's promise of an enduring kingdom that would not fail was still in effect as an abiding promise that would triumph over all the presently observed obstacles.

It was the dream of Nebuchadnezzar in Daniel 2 that set the stage for the enduring manifestation of the kingdom of God. In this dream, Nebuchadnezzar one night wrestled in his sleep over his deep concerns for the longevity of his kingdom. God sent to him a dream about a colossal image, composed of four decreasingly valuable metals (gold, silver, bronze, iron, and clay). Moreover, this image was characterized by increasing division and weakness as one proceeded from the head to the feet and toes of this image.

It was Daniel who was able to supply the king with the description of the contents of the dream along with its interpretation, whereas the other wise men of the Babylonian ruler were at a loss to comply with such an unprecedented vigorous royal demand. The image depicted the sequence of human empires which would succeed one another: a Babylonian kingdom would be followed by a Medo-Persian empire, then a Greek empire would come along only to be divided into four parts by its four sparring generals, ending in what many believe would be a Roman/Western empire in the end of the days.

But the real shocker was not in the prediction of the sequence of empires; instead it was to be found in "the rock/stone cut out of the mountain: (Dan. 2:45), but "not by human hands," which stone "will crush all those kingdoms and bring them to an end, but it will itself endure forever" (Dan. 2:44b). While the metals of the colossal statue that Nebuchadnezzar saw in his dream were clearly identified as four successive empires in the coming days of humanity, all of these would be crushed by the Stone that would suddenly fall on the statue seen in the dream. The meaning of the dream was crystal clear, for in the future God would set up a kingdom that would never be destroyed, but it would endure forever and ever.

A parallel vision to Nebuchadnezzar's dream was given to Daniel in chapter 7. However, instead of using four major metals to describe the four successive empires, God instead gave Daniel a vision of what looked like a "lion" with "the wings of an eagle" (7:4), followed by what appeared as a "bear" "raised up on one of its sides" (7:5), with yet another that appeared as a "leopard" with "four wings like those of a bird" "on its back" (7:6), and finally a fourth beast that was "terrifying, and frightening, and very powerful" (7:7). All four beasts rose up out of a churning sea stirred up by the "winds of heaven" (7:2).

But in contrast to the beastly nature of these same four human empires that had appeared in Nebuchadnezzar's dream, this time a human Mediator came with the clouds of heaven to the Most High God (7:13–14). This was no other than the true Son of God, for his coming "with the clouds of heaven" (7:13) made his divine origins even more explicit than the "falling stone" cut out the mountain without human hands (2:34). Moreover, his divinity was underscored by the abiding and indestructible kingdom that was given to him, for that dominion would never pass away, nor would it ever be destroyed (7:14).

Each of these successive world powers were governed by a mixture of savage, sensuous, self-serving impulsive world leaders, who were depicted as being exceedingly grim with such distorted features as horns, iron teeth, and carnivorous appetites, but who would now be confronted by God's judgment as the "Ancient of Days" would take his seat in the heavenly court (7:9). God's judgment would be based on what was written in the books recorded of what they had done in their lives (7:10) as his final judgment throne was set up on earth. The Ancient of Days' was accompanied by an enormous retinue, for it included "ten thousand times ten thousand" (7:10), who stood ready to serve the Judge of the whole earth (cf. Zech. 14:5).

The people of God, on the other hand, were called "the saints of the Most High" (7:18), to whom the kingdom and dominion were given after the judgment of the nations. These were in the same line of descent as the "holy nation" (Ex. 19:6), or the "holy people" (Deut. 7:6; 26:19) mentioned in the Mosaic era, and as the "seed" promised to Eve, the patriarchs, and to Israel (Num. 24:7; Isa. 60:12; Mic. 4:8). They would be part of the kingdom that would ultimately be ruled over by the coming and final Davidic king. These "saints" formed a part of the remnant that would remain even after the peoples of the earth had faced repeated destructions.

Over against God's holy remnant, there would arise in the final day "another horn," "a little one" (7:8), a "ruler/prince" (9:26), i.e., a king who will "do as he pleases," while "magnify[ing] himself above every god" and "say[ing] unheard of things against the God of gods" (11:36). These words at one and the same time described Antiochus Epiphanes (IV), who desecrated the temple of God by sacrificing a sow on its altar in 168 BC, while at the same time these same words hyperbolically referred to the final Antichrist, who was also known as the "beast" (Rev. 13), the "man of sin" (2 Thess. 2), as well as the "little horn," or "prince" in Daniel. This mode of interpretation came from the fifth Christian century interpreters centered at Antioch, Asia Minor, which method of interpretation was known as "theoria," which meant what was "seen." In this view, the prophet was given a vision to see the future in which God revealed to him not only the final fulfillment of the word he had uttered, but at the same time the prophet often spoke of one or more currently intervening *means* and connecting personages or events that were so in tune with what would happen in the final fulfillment that the near fulfillment became one sense or one in meaning, in many respects, with the distant and final fulfillment. That is what we would expect, for would not the Apostle John later on specifically teach that "The antichrist is coming, [but] even now many antichrists have come" (1 John 2:18). This same person, who already had reeked so much havoc on the people of God, shared a corporate solidarity with the one yet to come, i.e., in a linking up of the "now/ already" and the "not yet." This same linkage can be seen in the history of the prediction of the "Seed" of Eve, that begins in Genesis 3:15, but is one with Christ who would climax that seed line, who would finally come in the ultimate "Seed", or in another illustration, with the "the Serpent" that has his first appearance in that same context with Satan who emerged in Romans 16:20 and Revelation 12:9. Oftentimes, these persons or events were but an earnest or mere harbingers of what would appear in the final day, usually signaled in the Biblical text by the use of hyperbolic language.

The future of the city of Jerusalem and the nation of Israel was set forth in the famous "Seventy Weeks" of Daniel 9:24–27. Daniel had understood from his reading of the "Scriptures" (which in this case Daniel was reading from the fairly recently completed scroll by the prophet Jeremiah 25:14–15; 29:10), that the city of Jerusalem would remain desolate for "seventy years," which time was nearly over. As Daniel prayed about his own sin and that of his people, God outlined for him the future of Israel in "seventy sevens" or "weeks" arranged in three groups: (1) the first set of sevens was to "rebuild the streets and a trench" (9:25), (2) another set of sixty-two sevens would follow, *after* which "the Anointed One would be cut off" and "a ruler who will come and destroy the city, and (3) one final seven would arrive in which this coming ruler/prince would break his covenant with Israel in the middle of that final seven year period as he set up the "abomination that causes desolation" in the temple (9:27). But this prince does not stand a chance against the Lord of the universe: the Lord will triumph.

Finally, Daniel spoke of a coming time when everyone whose name was written in the book of life would be delivered after "a time of distress, such as has not happened from the beginning of nations until then" (Dan. 12:1). But then, "Multitudes who sleep in the dust of the earth will awake: some to everlasting life, others to shame and everlasting contempt" (12:2). Job had likewise been assured of the same prospect: just as some trees will often sprout new branches after they have been cut down, so a person would sprout (live again) after he had died (Job 14:7, 14). No wonder Job affirmed so strongly that he knew his Redeemer lived and thus he would look upon his Redeemer with his own eyeballs even after the worms had destroyed his body (Job 19:25–27).

God's kingdom would irrupt and simultaneously smash the various colossuses that mortal governments had built to tyrannize the peoples of the earth. But to the final One in the line of David, the Messiah would belong all power, might, and authority as evil received its conclusive response once and for all.

The Book of Esther

The book of Esther narrates the life of a Jewish orphan, Esther, who was raised by her older cousin, Mordecai, during the days of the Persian empire and the reign of Ahasuerus, also known as Xerxes (485–465 BC). Esther became queen of the Persian empire and was able to save the Jewish people in the empire from possible annihilation at the hands of Haman, the Agagite. Thus, in a story filled with sudden and unexpected reversals of circumstances, the providential hand of God was once again most evident in preserving the Jewish people.

There is no doubt, however, that the hand of God was working in all the events that led up to what later became known as the Feast of Purim. Esther's story began with king Ahasuerus (also known as Xerxes) giving a banquet for his military leaders, nobles, and officials for 180 days, to which he summoned his Queen Vashti to appear. She, however, refused to appear before the king and his guests, which so infuriated the king that some action had to be taken. Therefore, on the advice of his nobles, he ordered that Queen Vashti was never to appear before the king and a search was to be made for a "beautiful young virgin" to replace her. As a result, Esther won the contest, but on instruction from her cousin Mordecai, she never revealed her ethnic origins or her race.

Meanwhile, Mordecai took up a vigil at the king's gate, where he overheard a plot to assassinate King Xerxes, which he reported to the new Queen Esther, who saw that this information reached the king. Meanwhile there was another subplot brewing, for the king in the interim had elevated Haman, the Agagite, to a seat higher than the other nobles of the land. Accordingly, whenever Haman passed through the king's gate, everyone bowed down to him, except a Jewish man named Mordecai. This irked Haman to no end, therefore he looked for an opportunity to teach Mordecai a lesson for his lack of respect.

But the king, as events would turn out, had failed to reward Mordecai for his discovery of the plot to assassinate him. However, at the very moment that Haman had decided to act by building a seventy-five-foot-high gallows on which he prepared to hang Mordecai, and to ask the king for permission to proceed with his plan, providentially the king had on that very morning decided to reward Mordecai for his loyalty in revealing the plot against his life.

Prior to these events, Haman had learned that Mordecai's people were the Jewish people, therefore Haman had looked for a way to kill not only Mordecai, but to liquidate all the Jewish people in the whole kingdom of Persia. He asked the king to allow the day selected by lot (called using the "pur," "lot;" Est. 3:7) to be the day when these Jewish people could be slaughtered everywhere in the empire (Est. 3: 8–10). The king foolishly agreed with Haman's plan.

On hearing this royal decree, Mordecai plead with Esther to appeal to King Xerxes for her own people even though she must now disclose her own race and risk appearing before the king without an invitation. This Esther did as she prepared two days of dinners for the king and Haman as her guests. But as Haman appeared for what he thought would be the top of his game as an official in the Persia empire, King Xerxes asked him how he would honor the man the king wanted to show his favor. Haman, thinking he was that man, discovered to his horror that it was the man he was about to ask the king to hang on his specially prepared gallows. After Haman led Mordecai through the streets with his own specially created speech of "This is what is done for the man whom the king delights to honor" (Est. 6:9c), which he had thought would be offered on behalf of himself. The banquet that followed this parade through the streets did not go any better for him, for there Esther sought the king for her own life (Est. 7:3) in the face of Haman's plan to eradicate all the Jews in the kingdom. When Xerxes inquired who was it that had devised this scheme, Esther pointed to Haman. The final result was that Haman was hung on the gallows he had prepared for Mordecai. The Jewish people, however, were allowed to defend themselves on the day set for their extermination, which they did successfully.

This text identifies Haman as an Agagite (Est. 3:1), which is almost certainly a reference to Agag, king of the Amalekites (1 Sam. 15:20), the very king and people for whom King Saul had been ordered by God's command to blot out their memory among the living. However, Saul failed to do so, for 1 Chronicles 4:42–43 said that Saul lied about completing this mission. This not only brought about Saul's own downfall, but it left a number of Amalekites who would now come back to haunt Israel, just as Haman did as one who was in that line of descent.

Can anyone doubt the providential hand of God at a number of points in the narrative of Esther? Can anyone argue that this book of Esther depicts the people, who were delivered by God at so many points in the narrative, were faithful believers who faithfully obeyed from their hearts the Law of Moses? Are these events not further evidences of the grace of God and extensions of his mercy even though it is undeserved? Even though the king of Persia thought he was in charge, was it not clear that God was the One who was ruling and reigning from behind the scenes even at this time in history?

The Book of Chronicles

The most likely author of the books of Chronicles is the scribe Ezra. Ezra had returned to Jerusalem in 457 BC, but it seems that despite the fact that the temple (later known as the second temple) had been rebuilt already in 520–516 BC, moral and religious laxity had set in among the returned exiles in the land of Judah. The times appear to be sometime around 445–400 BC.

Consequently, there were two driving purposes in these books of Chronicles: (1) to trace the line of David all the way back to Adam with a focus on his victories as military commander and his concern for the worship of Yahweh, and (2) to call for a revival in the land as set forth in the programmatic statement in 2 Chronicles 7:14 and illustrated in Chronicles 7:14, these words provided the incentive for repentance and a change in the lives of those in the nation:

"Humble [yourselves]	2 Chron. 11–12	King Rehoboam
"Seek my face"	2 Chron. 14–16	King Asa
"Pray"	2 Chron. 17–20	King Jehoshaphat
"Turn from your wicked ways"	2 Chron. 29–32	King Hezekiah
"Humble [yourselves]	2 Chron. 34–36	King Josiah

Both of these purposes were carried out in this book.

Conclusion

The words and events that were used from the Davidic rule and reign projected an image of an eschatological consummation of the promise-plan that God had inaugurated with Adam and Eve (Gen. 3:15) and had carried on to Shem (Gen. 9:27), to Abraham (Gen. 12:2–3) and handed over to David (2 Sam. 7:1–19; 1 Chron. 17). The chronicler had a vision of a reunited Israel with a capital in Jerusalem. In fact, the expression "all Israel" appears some forty-one times in Chronicles along with such additional phrases as "all the house of Israel" or "all the tribes of Israel." The hope was that the people of promise would one day see the divided kingdom reunited into one kingdom and that the people would worship the Lord with a "whole [or perfect] heart," an expression that occurs nine times in Chronicles as part of the thirty times the word "heart" appears in the earlier testament.

The divine promise given to David was repeated in 1 Chronicles 17:14—"I will set him over my house and my kingdom forever." Thus, the image of the kingdom of the Lord was indissolubly linked with King David as were the people of the promise and the land of promise as well.

Study Questions

1. What Old Testament books are included in what is known as "The Writings? Can you name their three major divisions of these Writings?

2. What important link in Scripture does the book of Ruth supply? What is the significance of including Ruth as a Gentile in the royal line of David?

3. When God told the prophet Nathan that David would not be allowed to build a "house" for God, what did the Lord offer to David as a sort of consolation prize? How important was that gift to all of us who believe in Messiah today?

4. What startling revelation came to David in 2 Samuel 7:19 as he went into the house of God to pray after he was given the news that his son would build the temple rather than him? How important is that for us in our day?

5. What view of David in his person and work as well as the future plan of God do the Royal Psalms depict for us? Can you name some of these Psalms?

6. Was David aware of the future resurrection of the Messiah? How can you prove this assertion from Scripture? Name the Psalm and/or the New Testament passage that teaches this truth. What role does the name "Hasid/Holy One" play in this disclosure from God?

7. How is the kingdom of God distinguished from the empires or kingdoms of this world in Daniel 2? Why was Daniel able to interpret the dream when his classmates of magicians were at a total loss to do so?

8. What metaphor is used for the coming Messiah in Daniel 2:45 and how is this picture of the coming Messiah strengthened in Daniel 7:13 by a parallel description?

9. What role does Scripture depict for the little horn," the "ruler/prince" who will "do as he pleases"? Does this refer to a ruler who has already appeared in history, or to one who is yet to come, or to both? Explain how your answer could be correct.

10. How does Haman and his background in the book of Esther depict some unfinished business in past history? Can you name some of the ways how God providentially overruled events in the book of Esther to work out his own plans?

ISRAEL ACCORDING TO THE PROPHETS

Dr. Robert B. Chisholm Jr.

Chisholm, in his chapter *Israel according to the Prophets*, focuses on Israel's future depicted by the "Prophets" as it relates to the land. Chisholm distinguishes between the "Latter" and "Former" Prophets. The "Latter" details the vision for Israel's future restoration as a united nation under the Davidic King, while the "Former" points to the historical accounts of how the nation gained and lost the land.

Chisholm divides his chapter into two sections. The first section looks at the vision of Israel's future. The second section examines the rocky pathway towards making this prophetic vision a reality in the life of the Jewish people, including both dispersions for disobedience, a prophetic call to repentance, covenantal fidelity, and shalom in the Promised Land.

Introduction

The portion of the Hebrew Bible known as the Nebi'im (Prophets) reveals much about Israel's future. The Latter Prophets (Isaiah, Jeremiah, Ezekiel, and the Twelve) tell how the Lord will bring his exiled people back to the Promised Land, unite them under a Davidic king who rules from Zion, and establish them as a covenant-keeping nation that enjoys his blessings. To top it off, the nations will worship Israel's God as the one true God.

The Former Prophets (Joshua, Judges, 1–2 Samuel, 1–2 Kings), which are primarily historical, have less to say about this future hope. They tell how Israel gained and eventually lost the Promised Land. In a key discourse early in the history, Joshua warns of this (Josh. 23:16). Yet the history is not simply an apology for divine judgment; it is also designed to engender hope and motivate repentance. Two key discourses in the Former Prophets support this optimism. The Lord revealed to David that he would establish Israel securely in its land and grant David a permanent dynasty (2 Sam. 7:10). In Solomon's prayer at the temple dedication, the themes of Joshua 23 and 2 Samuel 7 are merged. He anticipates Israel's defeat and exile, but he also appeals to God to listen to the people's confession of sin, grant forgiveness, and restore them to the land (2 Kings 8:34; see vv. 46–51).

This study examines the theme of Israel's future as it relates to the land. Part one surveys the Latter Prophets' vision of Israel's future. The vision prompts us to ask questions pertaining to the nature of its fulfillment. Some aspects of the vision have been fulfilled, at least in part. Others have not been fulfilled; some would even seem incapable of being fulfilled, given certain historical developments and realities. Part two examines different explanations of this "failure" of the prophetic vision. I will reject the higher critical, hyper-literal, and re-signification models and argue for essential fulfillment of the vision that allows for human freedom. To understand how the prophetic vision will be fulfilled, it is also important to recognize how the principles of contextualization, archetypal language, corporate thinking, and progressive realization work.

Part One: The Prophetic Vision of Israel's Future Restoration

Five themes highlight the prophetic vision of Israel's future restoration:

1. Return from exile

The theme of return from exile permeates the literature. Isaiah describes the exiles of the northern (Israel) and southern (Judah) kingdoms returning to the land from the "four corners of the earth" (Isa. 11:12; see 66:20). He depicts the return from Egypt and Mesopotamia as a second Exodus (Isa. 11:15) and speaks of a highway leading home from Assyria. The servant of the Lord, cast in the role of a new Moses, leads the exiles home from Babylon (Isa. 49:5–12). Jeremiah alludes to the Exodus as he describes the return of Israel's exiles from the land of the north and other regions (Jer. 16:14–15; see 23:3, 7). He anticipates a return of both northern and southern exiles (Jer. 31:2–26). Several other prophets predict this return.[1] The postexilic prophet Zechariah, long after Assyria's demise, keeps the vision alive as he describes Judah and Joseph returning from exile in Egypt and Assyria (Zech. 10:6–12).

2. Reunification of north and south under a new David

A closely related theme is the reunification of the northern and southern exiles into one nation, ruled by a Davidic king. Once the exiles have returned, Ephraim and Judah unify under a new David, called the "root of Jesse" (Isa. 11:1, 10). Judah and Israel walk together as they return from exile (Jer. 3:18). They are reunited under David (Jer. 30:8–11) as the new covenant people of God (Jer. 31:27–40; see 32:37). Jeremiah relates this reunification to God's ancient promise to David, which in turn is linked with his promise to the patriarchs (Jer. 33:14–26). This promise is like the fixed laws that God established to govern the heavens and earth (Jer. 33:23–25). Ezekiel's famous vision of the dry bones coming to life again pictures Israel and Judah being joined together under the authority of one shepherd, the Lord's servant David (Ezek. 37:1–28). Ezekiel even describes a future land allotment, which includes all twelve tribes (Ezek. 47:13–48:35).

As for the Twelve, Hosea envisions the reunification of Israel and Judah under one leader (Hos. 1:11), "David their king" (Hos. 3:5). He anticipates the fulfillment of God's ancient promise to give Abraham offspring as numerous as the sand on the seashore (Hos. 1:10). Micah too predicts a return from exile (Mic. 7:12) and the reunification of north and south (Mic. 5:3) under a mighty warrior king who is described as the second coming of David (Mic. 5:2). He too sees God's loyalty to the patriarchs as the basis for the restoration (Mic. 7:20).

Some prophets picture the reunified nation conquering the surrounding nations. Isaiah says that Judah and Ephraim will defeat the neighboring nations to the west and east (Isa. 11:14). Amos looks forward to a revived Davidic empire in which Edom is subdued (Amos 9:11–12). Obadiah also depicts the conquest of Edom (Obad. 1:17–20). According to Micah, the new David will turn the tables on the Assyrians when they seek to invade the land (Mic. 5:5–6).

3. Repentance, forgiveness, new covenant, and the gift of the Spirit

The highlight of Israel's restoration as a nation is the implementation of a new covenant. The catalyst for this will be the repentance of the people. Indeed, Isaiah offers the people the opportunity to renew their relationship with the Lord through an "eternal covenant" (Isa. 55:3), comparable to and perhaps an extension of the Lord's covenant with David (vv. 4–5). But there is a condition: Israel must turn to the Lord while he makes himself available (v. 6) and abandon their sin (v. 7a). If they repent, he will extend his mercy to them and forgive their sin (v. 7b).[2] This promise is certain of fulfillment because God's Word and plans are reliable (vv. 8–11; see Isa. 40:6–8). Yet the fact that repentance is a prerequisite to realization of the promise does introduce a conditional element, at least as far as timing is concerned. Jeremiah also pictures repentance as the prelude to covenantal renewal. He sees the Israelite exiles "shedding tears of contrition" (Jer. 31:9) and acknowledging their former rebellion (vv. 18–19) as a prelude to the implementation of the new covenant (vv. 31–34; see 32:37–44).

In conjunction with the restoration from exile and the inauguration of this new covenant, the Lord cleanses his people from their sins (Ezek. 36:25; see Zech. 13:1; Mal. 3:2–3), forgives them (Mic. 7:18), and imparts the gift of his Spirit (Isa. 59:21; Ezek. 36:27; Joel 2:28–29). The Spirit gives the people the willingness and capacity to obey God (Ezek. 36:25), something the prior covenantal arrangement was incapable of doing (Jer. 31:31–34).

4. Restoration of Zion and the temple

The renewal of Zion is especially prominent in Isaiah, where the city becomes the capital of God's worldwide kingdom (Isa. 2:2–4; 24:23). The theme is central to Isaiah 40–66, where the Lord returns to the city carrying his exiled people like a shepherd does his sheep (Isa. 40:1–11). Entire chapters of this section of Isaiah's prophecy focus on the restoration of the city (see Isaiah chapters 52, 54, 60, 62). Other prophets also look forward to Zion's restoration and glorification. Jeremiah speaks of the future city as a "holy mountain, the place where righteousness dwells" (Jer. 31:23). Zechariah pictures life-giving water flowing from the city (Zech. 14:8). In Ezekiel 47:1–12 this water flows from the new temple. Ezekiel also sees the glory of the Lord, which departed the city prior to its destruction by the Babylonians (Ezek. 10:18–19; 11:23), taking up residence in the new temple (Ezek. 43:1–5).

5. Worship of the nations

The prophets also envision the transformation of the nations into worshipers of the one true God. Isaiah describes a time when Egypt and Assyria, the mega-powers of his day, will join Israel in worshiping the Lord and being recipients of divine blessing (Isa. 19:23–25). The nations will come to Jerusalem to seek the Lord's moral guidance (Isa.

2:2–4), to pray in the temple (Isa. 56:7), and to swear allegiance to the Lord (Isa. 60:11). Zephaniah (Zeph. 3:9–10) and Zechariah share this vision (Zech. 14:9, 16). The nations will acknowledge the Lord's kingship and recognize his uniqueness.

Part Two: The Fulfillment of the Prophetic Vision of Israel's Future Restoration

The prophets see a glorious future for Israel in the Promised Land. But as one reflects on the details of the prophetic vision, one realizes that it was only partially fulfilled in some respects, or has not been fulfilled at all. Part two addresses the issue of the vision's fulfillment. I will first discuss and reject three models: (1) the higher-critical interpretation, which sees the vision as failed; (2) the hyper-literal approach, which expects the vision to be literally fulfilled in all of its details; and (3) the re-signification model, which understands a spiritual fulfillment of the vision in the Christian Church. Instead I propose an essential fulfillment of the vision through a literal Israel. This approach makes room for the principles of contingency and contextualization.

Inadequate Models
The Higher-Critical Approach

According to this model, the prophets made predictions that reflected their hopes. But this was simply wishful thinking. In some cases the vision was realized; there was a return from exile and a Davidic descendant became governor of the Persian province of Yehud. But for the most part the vision failed; any fulfillment was only a meager realization of what the prophets envisioned. Proponents of this model can point to apparently failed prophecies, including, among others, Micah's vision of the Davidic king's conquest of the mighty Assyrian empire and Haggai's prediction that "in just a little while" the Lord would over turn the nations and establish his worldwide rule through the Davidic descendant Zerubbabel. The prophets expected the vision to be realized within the geo-political setting of ancient Israel, not the world as we know it. But the vision did not materialize in that setting. The northern exiles did not return and the Davidic dynasty was not restored. The implications of this approach are profound, especially with respect to the nature of God and the character of his word. Many Christians, especially those who hold to an evangelical view of Scripture and an orthodox view of God's character, do not want to travel down this pathway.

The Hyper-Literal Approach

In the face of the apparent failure of prophecy, some argue that the prophecies will be fulfilled someday, right down to every literal detail.

They have not failed; on the contrary they await fulfillment. But this approach is forced to argue that God will resurrect, as it were, the entire geo-political context of ancient Israel. That means long gone nations like Edom, Ammon, Moab, Egypt of the Pharaohs, Assyria, and Babylon, among others, must return. Proponents of this approach argue that this should not seem so bizarre, since God will resurrect Israel. But there is an important difference. The prophets predict the resurrection of Israel (its return from exile), but they assume the continuation of the geo-political context of ancient Israel. Yet that context has disappeared, and before it did, the return from exile never reached the magnitude envisioned by the prophets.

In addition to these difficulties, a closer look shows that the hyper-literal hermeneutic falters when one tries to apply it consistently. An insistence upon hyper-literal fulfillment creates hopeless contradictions between prophecies. A few examples will have to suffice:

1. According to Isaiah 30:26, the sun will shine seven times brighter in the age of Israel's restoration, but Isaiah 60:19–20 says there will be no sun at that time, for the Lord will replace it. We can demand a hyper-literal fulfillment of one or (somehow) both texts, but it is better to see both texts as using hyperbole to make the same point: God's saving presence, symbolized by light, will be apparent to all when he restores his people.[3]

2. According to Isaiah 60:9–11, Jerusalem's walls will be rebuilt in the day of Israel's restoration, when nations will pay tribute to the Lord with their wealth. But Zechariah says Jerusalem will be an unwalled city in the age of Israel's restoration (2:1–5). Indeed the Lord himself will be a ring of fire around the city. We can demand a hyper-literal fulfillment of either or (somehow) both of the prophecies, but it is better to see hyperbole at work (at least in Zechariah's vision) and understand both texts as making the same point: The Lord will make restored Jerusalem secure.[4]

3. The prophets assign different roles to Assyria in their vision of Israel's future. Nahum and Zephaniah (Zeph. 2:13–15) predict its demise, which came in 612–609 BC. But Micah portrays Assyria as Israel's archenemy in the messianic age (Mic. 5:5–6), while Isaiah depicts the Assyrians as genuine worshipers of the one true God in the age of restoration (Isa. 19:23–25). We could propose the resurrection of Assyria and construct a strained chronology in which Assyria plays both the roles of enemy and worshiper, but there is a better way to handle these texts (see below).[5]

The Re-signification Approach

Some Christians, aware of problems with the hyper-literal model, go in a different direction. They do not expect the promises to be realized literally, but in a spiritual sense, through the Christian Church. Refuting this position is beyond the scope of my presentation, which is limited to the Old Testament Prophets. Suffice it to say that Romans 9–11 presents a huge interpretive obstacle for this approach, because Paul teaches that God intends to redeem Israel, which he distinguishes from the Church.

A Proposed Model for Interpreting the Prophetic Vision of Israel's Future

The hyper-literal and re-signification models try to salvage the integrity of the prophetic vision, but both lack hermeneutical and exegetical integrity. There is a better way to understand the prophetic vision's fulfillment. I propose that we see an essential fulfillment of the vision through a literal Israel, but also make room for contingency.

Some Important Interpretive Principles

1. Essential Fulfillment and Contingency

To understand how the fulfillment of prophecy works, we must move beyond the purely descriptive level of prophetic language, and consider its primary intention. When a prophecy is fulfilled essentially, the main point of the prophecy (its primary intention) is realized with a degree of literality, but some of the accompanying details may not materialize. An examination of fulfilled prophecies in 1–2 Kings suggests that Old Testament prophets understood that their predictions might be realized essentially without every detail materializing. In each case, God makes room for human freedom, which gives the prophecy a degree of contingency, or conditionality.

A classic example of essential fulfillment can be found in 1 Kings 21–22. In this case we have both the prophecy (1 Kings 21:19) and a narrative of its fulfillment (1 Kings 22:38). By comparing the two, we can gain insight into how the biblical author viewed the nature of prophetic fulfillment.[6] Elijah warned that dogs would lick up Ahab's blood in the very spot where they had licked up Naboth's shed blood. Ensuing events show that this prophecy was irrevocable. While Ahab's subsequent remorse did prompt God to alter the timing of the king's death, it did not cancel the prophecy (see 1 Kings 21:20–29). According to 1 Kings 22:38, the prophecy was fulfilled when dogs licked up Ahab's blood at a pool where his bloodstained chariot was cleaned following his death in battle. The author unreservedly states that this was "according to the word of the LORD which he spoke" (literal translation). Yet the prophecy was partially, not completely fulfilled. Dogs licked up Ahab's blood at a pool in Samaria, not in Jezreel, the site of Naboth's execution (1 Kings 21:1–14).

How do we account for this lack of precision? One could argue that the prophecy was revised but not preserved in its revised form in the canonical text, creating an apparent tension. But one wonders why an editor would allow such a discrepancy to stand.[7] Another option is to assume that the phrase "in the place where" in 1 Kings 21:19 simply means "in public." But usage suggests otherwise. The Hebrew phrase cannot be understood in such a general way. Elsewhere it refers to a specific location and often carries the nuance "in the same place as/where."[8]

Perhaps the language was more than simply informative to begin with and possessed an expressive, hyperbolic dimension. The intention of the prophecy was not simply to inform us of details surrounding Ahab's death. The language was designed to express God's sense of outrage at what had happened and his commitment to see that justice was accomplished in an appropriate manner. The real point of the prophecy is not so much its geography, but the fundamental truth it conveys: God would punish Ahab appropriately for his murderous deed. Ahab would die violently and experience the same humiliation as Naboth, the victim of the king's injustice, had experienced.

But there is another factor that comes into play. God makes room for human freedom and resulting contingencies in the outworking of his plan. God did not prevent the king's men from taking Ahab to Samaria. When they did so, they seemingly circumvented the last part of the prophecy pertaining to the dogs of Jezreel licking Ahab's blood. But God had dogs stationed in Samaria as well and the prophecy was fulfilled in its essence. Ahab died a violent and humiliating death; the punishment fit the crime. God's sovereignty and justice won out in the end. In this case, the inexact nature of the fulfillment actually highlights God's sovereignty over the affair. One cannot escape his justice. As one sees and hears the dogs of Samaria lapping up Ahab's blood, one must conclude that the prophetic word has hardly failed; it has inexorably pursued the criminal. Only the dogs of Jezreel have reason to object on grounds of a technicality!

We see from this case that God makes room for human freedom in the outworking of even irrevocable prophecy. This means that some of the details of the prophecy may not be fulfilled exactly, yet the prophecy is realized in its essence. Apparently for the biblical author, this is all that really matters, for he describes the incident in Samaria as fulfilling the earlier prophecy. This is instructive for those waiting for the fulfillment of God's irrevocable promises. There appears to be room for some flexibility in the outworking of incidental details, but only within a prescribed framework of essential fulfillment.

Huldah's prophecy about Josiah's death is another example of essential fulfillment. Having announced the downfall of Jerusalem, Huldah commended godly Josiah and assured him that he would die in peace and not have to witness the devastation of the city (2 Kings 22:15–20). However, the next chapter tells how Josiah attempted to prevent Pharaoh from marching to the aid of the Assyrians. Josiah was killed in battle (2 Kings 23:29–30), seemingly contradicting what Huldah had promised about his dying in peace.[9] After all, dying a bloody death on a battlefield can hardly be viewed as dying "in peace."[10] However, if we view the prophecy as implicitly conditional to begin with and make room for human freedom in the equation, we can conclude that Josiah's decision to become embroiled in international politics compromised God's intention for him to die in peace. Even so, the promise was fulfilled in its essence for Josiah still went to the grave without having to see Jerusalem's downfall, which was the main point made by Huldah.

Still another example occurs in Ahijah's prophecy to Solomon that the Lord would take all but one tribe from his son (1 Kings 11:13, 36). However, as the prophecy works itself out, the Davidic dynasty retains control over two tribes, Judah and Benjamin (1 Kings 12:21, 23). Perhaps we should understand the prophecy as hyperbolic or allow for contingency as Benjamin apparently decided to stick with Judah, despite what the prophet had said (2 Chron. 15:2; 17:17; 25:5; Ezra 1:5).

2. Contextualization and Archetypal Language

To understand the fulfillment of prophecy it is also important to recognize the phenomenon of contextualization. Contextualization may be defined as "speaking or acting in a way that reflects the cultural context of the addressee or observer and facilitates understanding and relationship." One of the ways in which the prophets contextualized their messages was to describe the future in terms of the past so that the prophetic vision might resonate with their audience (see, for example, Isaiah's use of the second Exodus motif to describe the return from exile). One also sees contextualization at work when the prophets describe the future as being realized in their own contemporary geo-political context. In some cases the prophets actually anticipated the fulfillment of a prophecy in their time, but the contingent nature of the prophecy resulted in its failure to materialize. In many of these cases, one need not look for a fulfillment at all. However, in other cases, even though the prophecy was not fulfilled in the prophet's geo-political context, one expects that it will materialize at some point because it coincides with God's revealed purposes for human history and his covenantal community. When fulfillment transcends the prophet's time and context, the language takes on archetypal status and one should expect essential or generic, not exact or literal, fulfillment of the prophecy.

We can illustrate these principles by examining Micah's prophecy of the Davidic king's victory over Assyria, which did not materialize in history. Yet, if the Davidic promise of worldwide dominion is irrevocable, then we expect the Davidic king to establish his kingdom at some point in the future. In describing this event, Micah chose to retain the image of Assyria as the archenemy of Israel, even though he knew that Judah would go into exile to Babylon, not Assyria (Mic. 4:10). By retaining the image of Assyria, Micah's message resonates with his audience, for they had seen Assyrian, not Babylonian, power firsthand and it was the Assyrian, not Babylonian, king to whom they had paid tribute for several years. Even though Assyria may be gone by the time the ideal king arrives on the scene, it remains a powerful image and symbol for Micah's audience of the hostile nations who sought to enslave Israel and Judah. For Micah, in other words, Assyria became an archetype of the hostile nations of the world who will be unable to enslave and oppress God's people when the ideal king arrives on the scene. For this king to be able to conquer such a powerful, Assyrian-like foe, he must be mighty indeed.[11]

Zechariah, who lived long after the fall of Assyria in 612–609 BC, also employed the image of Assyria as an archetypal symbol. He envisioned a time when exiles would return from Egypt and Assyria and the Lord would humble Egyptian and Assyrian pride (Zech. 10:10–11). Though the Assyrian empire was gone by Zechariah's time, as a traditional enemy of God's people, it became a code word or symbol for the hostile nations that oppose God and his people.[12]

3. Corporate Thinking

Sometimes a prophecy delivered to a specific individual is fulfilled through a descendant. One sees this in Genesis 28:14, where God promises Jacob numerous offspring and then says to him: "You (the verb form is masculine singular) will spread out to the west, east, north, and south." Jacob is identified with his offspring in the promise, which was obviously fulfilled through the offspring, not literally through the patriarch. One sees the corporate principle at work as well in Ahijah's prophecies to Solomon, where the Lord warns he will tear the kingdom from Solomon's hand, but then makes it clear that the prophecy will actually be fulfilled when the kingdom is taken from his son (1 Kings 11:11–13, 29–39).

4. Progressive Fulfillment

Some prophecies are fulfilled in stages, as we see in 1–2 Kings. In 1 Kings 13:1–3 an unnamed prophet from Judah delivers both a prophecy and a sign to King Jeroboam I (931–910 BC). The sign occurred immediately (1 Kings 13:5), but the prophecy was not fulfilled until about 300 years later (2 Kings 23:15–20). There is nothing in the prophecy itself to indicate the exact time frame of its fulfillment.[13] 1 Kings 14:10–16 is another prophecy that was progressively fulfilled. Just as the prophet Ahijah predicted (v. 10), all the males of Jeroboam's house were killed in the immediate future (1 Kings 15:29–30), but the prediction concerning Israel's exile (vv. 15–16) was not fulfilled until almost two hundred years later (2 Kings 17:7–23).

The Fulfillment of the Prophetic Vision of Israel's Future
Using the principles just outlined, I will now discuss the essential fulfillment of the different themes in the prophetic vision of Israel's future:

1. Return from exile

As we have noted, the return from exile failed to live up to the scope of the prophetic vision. While some exiles from the tribes of Judah, Benjamin, and Levi did return from Babylon, there was no mass exodus of Israelites from Assyria. The principle of contingency is crucial here, since the prophetic vision sees the repentance of the people as the catalyst for restoration to the land (1 Kings 8:33–34, 46–51; Jer. 31:18–21; see Deut. 30:1–5). Historically speaking, there was no mass repentance. Consequently, there was no mass return. But partial fulfillment does not mean the prophecy has failed, for we have seen that prophecy is sometimes realized progressively. In this case the historical return from exile may be viewed as foreshadowing and guaranteeing the full restoration that will take place when Israel does repent (Rom. 11:26–27).

But what about the specific prediction that Israelite exiles would return from Assyria? If we appeal to the principle of essential fulfillment, we need not be troubled by the failure of this detail to materialize. Indeed, the New Testament calls the Jewish people as constituted in the first century (including those in the Diaspora) the "twelve tribes" of Israel (Matt. 19:28; Luke 22:30; Acts 26:7; James 1:1; Rev. 21:12). When God renews his covenant with the repentant Jewish people in their Promised Land, the vision of the return from exile will be essentially realized as "the twelve tribes" unite under his authority.

2. Reunification of north and south under a new David

The reunification of north and south never happened in conjunction with the historical return from exile. Neither was the Davidic dynasty revived. But again, this need not mean that the prophecy has failed, if one allows for the principles of contingency and essential fulfillment. As just discussed above, the failure of the exiles to repent in mass prevented a mass return from exile and, in turn, the prophesied reunification. Jesus, the prophesied Davidic king, came to the Jewish people, but was rejected, just as Isaiah 53 predicts would happen. But historical failure need not mean that the vision has failed. Ironically, the rejection of the messianic servant is foundational to covenant renewal (see Isaiah 55), seeing that he bears the sins of God's wayward covenant people. When the Jewish people do eventually repent, the restoration envisioned by the prophets will be essentially fulfilled. When Jesus establishes his kingdom, the prophetic vision of the messianic era will materialize.

The Davidic king who rules over Israel in the age of restoration is described in a variety of ways. He is a descendant of David (Jer. 23:5), but is also called David (Jer. 30:9; Ezek. 34:23–24; 37:24–25; Hos. 3:5). He is depicted as a new David, descended directly from Jesse (Isa. 11:1), and as David reborn (see Mic. 5:2, which describes him as one who comes from Bethlehem and whose "goings forth" date back to ancient times). Furthermore, Jeremiah speaks of this king as the progenitor of a dynasty (Jer. 33:22).

The principles discussed above can help us make sense of this bewildering variety. Corporate thinking explains how the coming king can be both "David" and the offspring of David. Depicting the king as David, the second coming of David, and a new David is a prime example of how contextualization produces an archetype. David was the greatest king in Israel's history because he brought the nation security and prosperity. The very thought of David and the Davidic age would resonate with later generations who longed to experience a renewal of that era. So it makes perfect sense that the prophets would go back to the future in depicting the coming king, especially in light of the fact that he is the literal offspring of David. Jeremiah 33:22 takes contextualization to extremes by picturing the king establishing an enduring dynasty, just as David did. In ancient Israel's cultural context, an enduring dynasty was a sign of national stability and security. So by describing the coming king in Davidic terms, the prophets make David an archetype that materializes in his messianic descendant, and make it clear that the coming era would be one of national stability and security.

Contextualization is also at work when the prophets predict a conquest of the nations. This again takes us back to the future by picturing the future as a revival of the Davidic Empire, when the great king David brought Moab, Ammon, and Edom under his rule. As noted above, picturing the Davidic king defeating and conquering Assyria is a powerful way of emphasizing that Israel will eventually be immune from the invasion and oppression the nation experienced in Micah's time. But one need not expect these ancient nations to somehow be reconstituted. When Messiah establishes his kingdom of peace, the prophetic vision will be essentially fulfilled as the security it envisions materializes.

3. Repentance, forgiveness, new covenant, gift of the Spirit

When the Jewish people someday repent in mass, this aspect of the prophetic vision will be fulfilled as they experience forgiveness and the implementation of the new covenant, which will empower the people to obey as they receive the gift of God's Spirit. Of course, proponents of the re-signification model will point out that the new covenant has already been inaugurated with the Church and that the gift of the Spirit has already been granted to New Testament believers.[14] But this does not mean the fulfillment of the prophetic vision is exhausted in the Church. Consistent with the principle that prophecy is sometimes fulfilled progressively, we can and should, on the basis of Romans 11, see an already/not yet dimension to the prophecy's fulfillment. As I have said elsewhere: "The prophets were like men looking through a tunnel. In the light at the end of the tunnel, they saw God reconciling Israel to himself. But as we walk to the end of the tunnel and look outside with Paul and the author of Hebrews, we gain the advantage of peripheral vision and discover that God's new covenant involves others that the prophets could not see with their 'tunnel vision.' At the same time, the existence of peripheral participants in the lighted world should not distract us from the fact that Israel continues to stand straight ahead of us, right where the prophets saw her, awaiting the time when her people too will become participants in this new covenant."[15]

4. Restoration of Zion and the temple

The fulfillment of this element in the prophetic vision was only partial. Full realization, which Haggai expected to come in the immediate future, was postponed by the people's failure (the principle of contingency). When the prophecy was postponed, certain elements of the vision, such as the Davidic descendant Zerubbabel, became archetypal. As for Ezekiel's depiction of renewed worship in a new temple, at least some elements, such as atoning animal sacrifices, may be viewed as contextualized.[16] When the repentant Jewish people, restored to their land, celebrate the redemptive work of the suffering servant in their new temple, this aspect of the prophecy will be essentially fulfilled as it bursts out from its contextualized mold.

5. Worship of the nations

This element in the prophetic vision, like the promise of the new covenant and the gift of the Spirit, may have an initial fulfillment in the Church (the principle of progressive fulfillment may be operative here), but its full realization will come in conjunction with the restoration of the repentant Jewish people, as the prophets envisioned. When the prophets picture specific nations, such as Assyria and the Egypt of the Pharaohs (Isa. 19:23–25), worshiping the Lord, the language can be viewed as contextualized, with the nations functioning as archetypes. When the powerful, Assyrian-like nations of the world someday recognize and worship their true King, the vision will be essentially fulfilled.

Conclusion

The prophetic vision of Israel's future contains at least five main themes: (1) return from exile, (2) reunification of north and south under a new David, (3) the related themes of repentance, forgiveness, new covenant, and gift of the Spirit, (4) restoration of Zion and the temple, and (5) worship of the nations. For the most part, the prophets envision the fulfillment of this vision in their ancient geo-political context. The prophetic vision was only partially fulfilled within that setting, leading higher critics to dismiss it as wishful thinking. Believers have attempted to salvage the integrity of the vision by arguing that it will be literally fulfilled in all of its details someday or by re-signifying Israel as the Church and understanding fulfillment in a spiritual sense. But the hyper-literal model must argue that God will resurrect the ancient geo-political context, something the Old Testament does not predict, and is unable to explain adequately the contradictions between texts that the method creates. The re-signification model runs into a brick wall when it confronts Romans 9–11.

There is a better way forward that finds justification within the prophetic literature itself. The complete fulfillment of the prophetic vision was contingent upon the mass repentance of God's exiled people, something that has not happened. But human failure is not a dead end, only a detour, in God's program. While human failure does not negate God's irrevocable promises, it has pushed the time of fulfillment beyond the prophets' ancient geo-political context. The omniscient God knew this would happen, but He still contextualized the prophetic vision within the prophets' time so that it would be understandable to Israel and have integrity as a genuine incentive to the people to respond positively to God's call to repentance. Even though we are well beyond that ancient setting, we can expect the prophetic vision to materialize in its essence without expecting every literal detail to be realized. In some cases, certain elements in the vision (for example, Assyria and David) take on archetypal status.

So what will the essential fulfillment of the prophetic vision look like? Someday God will restore the Jewish people as his covenant community in the Promised Land. As a prelude to this, the Jewish people will repent in mass, experience God's forgiveness, and become God's partners through a new covenant, which will, through the gift of the Spirit, enable them to obey God's requirements (which Jesus boiled down to two in number). The contextualized elements of the vision will materialize as the essence of the prophecies is realized. The oft-divided people of Israel will reunify under Messiah, who will guarantee their security as he rules from Zion, where a new temple will remind his people that God dwells again among his people. The Gentiles, including even the powerful Assyria-like nations, will come to Zion to worship the one true God as they celebrate the sacrificial work of the suffering servant-king who made it all possible. May he receive all honor and glory and praise! Even so, come Lord Jesus!

Study Questions

1. Review the five major themes in the prophets' vision of Israel's future. Which elements of the vision were fulfilled in history? Which were not?

2. Review what the prophets say about the role of Israel's repentance in the fulfillment of the prophetic vision. Why is this so important in understanding the fulfillment (or lack of fulfillment) of the prophetic vision?

3. According to the author of this chapter, what are some problems with the so-called hyper-literal approach to the fulfillment of the prophets' vision? Do you agree with the author? Why/Why not?

4. What does the author of the chapter mean by "essential fulfillment"? What examples from 1–2 Kings does he offer to support this concept? Do you agree with his interpretation of these texts? Why/Why not?

5. Look carefully at the examples of essential fulfillment cited by the author. In each case how did the exercise of human freedom alter the fulfillment of the prophecy? In what way(s) was the prophecy essentially fulfilled?

6. What does the author mean by "contextualization" and "archetypal language"? What prophecies does he cite as examples of this? Do you agree with his interpretation of these texts? Why/Why not?

7. How does a hyper-literal model of prophetic fulfillment understand the prophecy of Israel's return from Assyrian exile? Why is this problematic? How is the return from exile understood in the essential fulfillment model?

8. How does a hyper-literal model of prophetic fulfillment understand the prophecy of the reunification of the northern and southern kingdoms? Why is this problematic? How is the prophecy of reunification understood in the essential fulfillment model?

9. In what ways do the prophets speak of the Messiah in relationship to David? How is this variety understood in the essential fulfillment model?

10. With whom does God make a new covenant? How is the prophetic vision of a new covenant with Israel to be harmonized with the New Testament's teaching that the Church is a participant in the new covenant?

Conference Video

chosenpeople.com/chisholm

Interview with Dr. Robert B. Chisholm, Jr.

chosenpeople.com/chisholm-interview

THE PEOPLE AND LAND OF ISRAEL IN JEWISH TRADITION

Dr. Michael L. Brown

Brown, in his chapter *The People and Land of Israel in Jewish Tradition*, focuses on the more traditional Jewish view of the Jewish people's relationship to the land of Israel. Although the land was "inhabited by giants" prior to Israel's conquest of Canaan, it was also "flowing with milk and honey." Brown suggests that the land is so important in Jewish tradition it is simply referred to it as "the Land."

Rashi, the great eleventh-century French rabbi, argues that the Torah begins with a description of the creation of the world to demonstrate that the Land belongs to God and He can choose to give it to whomever He wants. The Torah clearly states God chose to give it to the people of Israel.

According to the Jewish understanding of the Scriptures, "there was no concept of a blessed future for the Jewish people if they remained exiled from the Promised Land." The Jewish hope clearly taught that one day the Land of Israel would belong to the people of Israel, which is the cry at Passover, "Next year in Jerusalem." The Jewish longing for return and restoration to the land of Israel is an essential building block of Jewish life and thought, and the foundation of the Jewish national hope. Brown argues that this belief is consistent with Scripture.

Although there have been many peoples displaced from their home-lands, the relationship between the Jewish people and their ancient homeland, one from which they have often been exiled, is unique. For the Jewish people, Israel is not just a homeland but a Promised Land, promised to them by God Himself. And according to the Scriptures, it is a special land, a land "flowing with milk and honey" (e.g., Exodus 3:8). Yet Israel was a land with unique challenges, since in the years before its conquest, it was (quite ominously) inhabited by giants (e.g., Numbers 13:28). Not surprisingly, Jewish tradition enhances the descriptions of the unique elements of the land, and since Scripture speaks of the land of Israel as the Lord's special "inheritance," rabbinic literature even as-cribes supernatural elements to it. It is for good reason, then, that Jews commonly refer to Israel as "the Land," (with a capital L in English), while the return to Israel is called *aliyah* (literally, "going up," both spa-tially, because of the height of Jerusalem, and spiritually, because of the presence of God).[1]

Back to the Beginning

The foremost biblical and Talmudic commentator in Judaism is Rashi (1040–1105), and traditional Jews grow up learning to read the Torah with Rashi's commentary on the very same page to the point that they instinctively read Torah through the lens of Rashi's interpre-tations. One of his most famous comments, which are normally con-cise and occasionally cryptic, is quite expansive, found at Genesis 1:1, a text that raises unique questions for traditional Jews. For Christians, Genesis 1:1 is simply a statement of origins: The eternal God created the universe. For Jews, an immediate question comes to mind: Why start with the creation account when the purpose of the Torah is to reveal God's statues and commandments to the people of Israel?

That's the question Rashi addresses here, coming to a fascinating conclusion:

> **In the beginning:** Said Rabbi Isaac: It was not nec-essary to begin the Torah except from "This month is to you," (Ex. 12:2) which is the first commandment that the Israelites were commanded, (for the main pur-pose of the Torah is its commandments, and although several commandments are found in Genesis, e.g., cir-cumcision and the prohibition of eating the thigh sin-ew, they could have been included together with the other commandments).

Now for what reason did He commence with "In the beginning?"

Because of [the verse] "The strength of His works He related to His people, to give them the inheritance of the nations" (Ps. 111:6). For if the nations of the world should say to Israel, "You are robbers, for you conquered by force the lands of the seven nations [of Canaan]," they will reply, "The entire earth belongs to the Holy One, blessed be He; He created it (this we learn from the story of the Creation) and gave it to whomever He deemed proper When He wished, He gave it to them, and when He wished, He took it away from them and gave it to us.

How striking it is to read this in light of the ongoing debate about rightful ownership of the Land today! Do the Jewish people really have some kind of divine right to the Land, or are we mixing politics with religion even to raise this issue? The bottom line is that, from a scriptural point of view, and as emphasized here by Rashi, the land of Israel belongs to God, the Creator of the world. He apportions it to whom He will, and He has chosen to give it to the people of Israel, after whom it is named.

According to the testimony of the Tanakh:

1. The Land is God's land. Thus, in Jeremiah 16:18, God refers to it as "my land" and "my inheritance":

    "For my eyes are on all their ways. They are not hidden from me, nor is their iniquity concealed from my eyes. But first I will doubly repay their iniquity and their sin, because they have polluted my land with the carcasses of their detestable idols, and have filled my inheritance with their abominations" (Jer. 16:17–18). That's why, when His people sinned in the Land and against the Land, He took it so personally: "And I brought you into a plentiful land to enjoy its fruits and its good things. But when you came in, you defiled my land and made my heritage an abomination" (Jer. 2:7).

2. The Lord promised the Land to the patriarchs and their descendants. Although this is stated repeatedly in the Tanakh and is the basis for the exodus from Egypt (see below), Psalm 105 contains one of the clearest, most emphatic promises:

    "He remembers his covenant forever, the word that he commanded, for a thousand generations, the covenant that he made with Abraham, his sworn promise to Isaac, which he confirmed to Jacob as a statute, to Israel as an everlasting covenant, saying, 'To you I will give the land of Canaan as your portion for an inheritance'" (Ps. 105:8–11).

3. The exodus from Egypt was not only a matter of liberation from Egyptian slavery, as oppressive as that was. Rather, the exodus was a liberation *from* bondage in a foreign country *to* liberty in the Promised Land, a theme repeated often in the Torah. Thus God commissioned Moses,

    "Go and gather the elders of Israel together and say to them, 'The LORD, the God of your fathers, the God of Abraham, of Isaac, and of Jacob, has appeared to me, saying, "I have observed you and what has been done to you in Egypt, and I promise that I will bring you up out of the affliction of Egypt to the land of the Canaanites, the Hittites, the Amorites, the Perizzites, the Hivites, and the Jebusites, a land flowing with milk and honey"'" (Ex. 3:16–17).

4. Because it is God's land, set apart for His purposes, it is intrinsically holy. Sin defiles the Land (see, e.g., Numbers 35:33–34, which states that "bloodshed pollutes the land"), and if there is not true repentance, especially from certain sins, those sins brings about severe judgment to the point that the Land itself vomits out its inhabitants:

    "Do not make yourselves unclean by any of these things, for by all these the nations I am driving out before you have become unclean, and the land became unclean, so that I punished its iniquity, and the land vomited out its inhabitants. But you shall keep my statutes and my rules and do none of these abominations, either the native or the stranger who sojourns among you (for the people of the land, who were before you, did all of these abominations, so that the land became unclean), lest the land vomit you out when you make it unclean, as it vomited out the nation that was before you" (Lev 18:24–28; note also Genesis 15:13–16, where God told Abram He would not drive the Amorites out of the land until their iniquity reached its full measure).

5. Since protracted, unrepentant sin against the Land would lead to exile, the exile itself would serve to give the Land much needed rest (for example, rest from Israel's failure to observe the sabbatical year):

> "He took into exile in Babylon those who had escaped from the sword, and they became servants to him and to his sons until the establishment of the kingdom of Persia, to fulfill the word of the LORD by the mouth of Jeremiah, until the land had enjoyed its Sabbaths. All the days that it lay desolate it kept Sabbath, to fulfill seventy years" (2 Chron. 36:20–21).

6. Exile from the Land was conceived of as spiritual death, not only because of the sense of being under divine judgment, but also because the Jewish people felt separated from the unique presence of God that was in the Land, ultimately represented by the Temple in Jerusalem:

> "By the waters of Babylon, there we sat down and wept, when we remembered Zion. On the willows there we hung up our lyres. For there our captors required of us songs, and our tormentors, mirth, saying, 'Sing us one of the songs of Zion!' How shall we sing the LORD's song in a foreign land?" (Ps. 137:1–4).

7. Consequently, restoration to the Land was life and favor and one of the first matters of business was the rebuilding of the Temple:

> "When the LORD restored the fortunes of Zion, we were like those who dream. Then our mouth was filled with laughter, and our tongue with shouts of joy; then they said among the nations, 'The LORD has done great things for them.' The LORD has done great things for us; we are glad" (Ps. 126:1–3; for the priority put on rebuilding the Temple, see Ezra 3).

This is just a tiny sampling of the biblical theology of the land of Israel, but with this as the hagiographical basis of Israel's faith (in other words, the scriptural foundation, "what is written"), it's easy to see how myth and tradition could embellish this witness over the centuries, especially the longer the Jewish people languished in exile.

The Land of Israel in Rabbinic Literature

According to b. Pesachim 113a, R. Yochanan stated that, "Three inherit the world to come—one who lives in Eretz Yisrael, one who raises his children to learn Torah, and one who makes Havdalah on wine on Motza'ei Shabbos."[2] Here, simply living in Israel is as meritorious as training one's children in Torah or pronouncing the blessing over wine at the end of the Sabbath, to the point of guaranteeing one's place in the world to come.

The Talmud also states (b. Ketubot 75a), "But of Zion it shall be said: This man and that was born in her; and the Most High Himself doth establish her [Psalm 87:5]; R. Meyasha, grandson of R. Joshua b. Levi, explained: Both he who was born therein and he who looks forward to seeing it." The final comment ("and he who looks forward to seeing it") obviously had special meaning for the many generations of Jews born outside the Land but looking forward with hope to "Next year in Jerusalem."[3]

These statements, however, say nothing supernatural about the Land itself. Other Talmudic traditions make up for that lack (and note that the tradition cited here speaks of the Land at the time of the flood, long before the people of Israel lived there). As noted on the DovBear blog spot:

> There's a not-nearly-well-known-enough opinion in the Talmud [b. Zevachim 113a] that says the flood waters didn't reach Israel. Some take this to mean that the world was flooded, but an invisible wall kept the water away from the Holy Land; others see this as suggesting that Israel was the flood's southern, or western boundary, and that nothing to the south or west of Israel was flooded.
>
> A supporting opinion in the Talmud says the leaf the dove brought back came from Israel—which fits: if the world was flooded, with everything destroyed, where else might the dove have discovered vegetation? It had to have come from Israel, the only land that wasn't touched by the flood. The problem, then, is why did Noah find the leaf significant? Israel hadn't been flooded, and the leaf came from Israel so what, as they say, was the [proof] the waters had receded? They hadn't reached Israel in the first place.[4]

As for the abundant produce of the Land, the Talmud states that when the twelve tribal leaders returned from spying out Canaan, it took eight of them to carry back the cluster of grapes (b. Sotah 34b to

Numbers 13:23; the Hebrew word *môt*, commonly translated "pole" is understood by the Talmud to refer to a frame of two poles, carried by eight men).

Not surprisingly, Israel is regarded as the spiritual center of the world, with the Temple in Jerusalem serving as the epicenter:

> As the navel is set in the center of the human body, so is the Land of Israel the navel of the world... Situated in the center of the world, and Jerusalem in the center of the Land of Israel, and the Sanctuary in the center of Jerusalem, and the Holy Place in the center of the Sanctuary, and the Ark in the center of the Holy Place, and the Foundation Stone before the Holy Place, because, from it the world was founded. (Midrash Tanchuma, *Qedoshim*, ch. 10)

All that was written, however, about Jerusalem and the land of Israel in times past, times which fell far short of the glorious future promised by God. What would that future look like?

Looking Ahead to the Future

Since the Tanakh itself is rich with glorious descriptions of the final restoration of the Jewish people to the Land (and the glorious changes that would take place within the Land itself), it's easy to see how rabbinic literature would embellish these promises (see below for some of these promises). After providing a complete summary of the future expectations of the prophet Jeremiah, which were to begin with the return of the Jewish people to the Land after seventy years in exile (see Jeremiah 25:11; Daniel 9:1–2), Old Testament scholar S. R. Driver concluded,

> "It must be evident that many of these promises have not been fulfilled, and that now circumstances have so changed that they never can be fulfilled; but, like the similar pictures drawn by other prophets, they remain as inspiring ideals of the future which God would fain see realized by or for His people, and of the goal which man, with God's help, should ever strive to attain."[5]

How fascinating! From Driver's vantage point in 1906, it seemed impossible that Jeremiah's prophecies could ever be fulfilled, and so he had to attribute them to the prophet's idealism and even wishful thinking. From our vantage point—and always from the vantage point of faith—they seem eminently possible with the help of the Lord.

In practical terms, think of taking a snapshot of Palestine in 1898, just fifty years before the birth of the modern state of Israel, and then compare that snapshot to today. The changes seem almost miraculous. Now, move from that current snapshot to the picture painted by the prophets, speaking of a time when the Land will be filled with the knowledge of the glory of the Lord as the waters cover the seas, a time when there will be no more war, a time when Yeshua will be worshiped and adored by millions of Jews and when the nations will make annual pilgrimages to Jerusalem to celebrate the Feast of Tabernacles (Sukkot; see Isaiah 2:1–4; 11:1–9; Zechariah 12:10–13:1; 14:1–21). And now factor in the rise of Jewish belief in Yeshua in our day, coupled with the increasing recognition of the Jewish roots of the faith by Christian teachers and scholars,[6] coupled with the spread of the gospel worldwide in the last fifty years,[7] and it's not that great of a leap of faith to see how the biblical promises will come true.

How are these end-time promises understood in Jewish thought? According to a team of top scholars, ancient Jewish eschatological expectations (including some apocryphal and pseudepigraphical writings, along with rabbinic literature) can be summarized under ten headings: 1) The final ordeal and confusion; 2) Elijah as precursor; 3) The coming of the Messiah; 4) The last assault of the hostile powers; 5) Destruction of hostile powers; 6) The renewal of Jerusalem; 7) The gathering of the dispersed; 8) The kingdom of glory in the Holy Land; 9) The renewal of the world; 10) A general resurrection; 11) The last judgment, eternal bliss, and damnation.[8]

Focusing here on numbers 6–9, we can see that the final Messianic hope was land-centered to the point that *there was no concept of a blessed future for the Jewish people if they remained exiled from the Promised Land.* In fact, such a thought is impossible from a biblical perspective, which, as we have seen, connected divine favor with dwelling in the Land. And so, the ultimate, glorious promises to the Jewish people can only be realized in the Land. Put another way, the fate of the Land and the people are tied together, and there can be no blessed future for the *people* of Israel outside of the *land* of Israel.[9]

Regarding the return of the exiles, the Mishnah raises a question about the future hope of the Ten Lost Tribes:

> The ten tribes are not destined to return "since it is said, *And he cast them into another land, as on this day (Dt. 29:28).* Just as the day passes and does not return, so they have gone their way and will not return," the words of R. Aqiba. R. Eliezer says, "Just as this day is dark and then grows light, so the ten tribes for whom it now is dark—thus in the future it is destined to grow light for them." (m. Sanhedrin 10:3)

The full and final return of all the scattered tribes is prayed for daily in the Shemoneh Esreh (the Eighteen Benedictions, also known as the Amidah, one of the most foundational prayers in traditional Judaism):

Raise a banner to gather our dispersed, and gather us from the four ends of the earth" (10th blessing, Kibbutz Galuyot).

Return in mercy to Jerusalem Your city and dwell therein as You have promised; speedily establish therein the throne of David Your servant, and rebuild it, soon in our days, as an everlasting edifice. Blessed are You L-rd, who rebuilds Jerusalem (14th blessing, Binyan Yerushalayim).

Yet there are rabbinic texts which put restrictions on who will be able to inherit the Land. The Talmud states, "Whoever does a single commandment—they do well for him and lengthen his days. And he inherits the Land. And whoever does not do a single commandment— they do not do well for him and do not lengthen his days. And he does not inherit the Land." (m. Kiddushin 1:10). What is certain, however, is that the future of the Jewish people in the Land of Israel will be glorious.

Commenting on Isaiah 2:1–4, Rashi explains the words "and it shall be raised above the hills" to mean: "The miracle performed on it, will be greater than the miracles of Sinai, Carmel, and Tabor," while Abarbanel states, "once the nations join to acknowledge God, there will be no reason for war, since most wars are rooted in religious disputes."

As for Isaiah 11, containing the most vivid picture of the Land saturated with the presence of God, Rashi understands verses like Isaiah 11:6 (speaking of the wolf lying with lamb) allegorically, "as describing peace between different nations in Messianic times. Others, however, explain these verses literally, as describing a return to the peace which existed between the various animals in the Garden of Eden before Adam's sin (see Radak)."[10]

Isaiah 60:10, which speaks of foreigners building up the fallen walls, is explained to mean, "Those who tore the walls down will rebuild them,"[11] surely a fitting climax. As for Isaiah 62:4, which states that the Land will be espoused by the returning Jews, "the prophet compares the union between the land of Israel and the people of Israel to a marriage—specifically, the marriage of a young man to a maiden (Radak; see the next verse)." The next verse, Isaiah 62:5, states that "as a young man marries a young woman, so shall your sons marry you, and as the bridegroom rejoices over the bride, so shall your God rejoice over you." This is understood to be mean that, "Even though the land of Israel was inhabited by non-Jews while the Jews were in exile, the land is not considered 'espoused' until the Jewish people returns."[12]

Regarding some of the glorious prophecies in Ezekiel 40–48, prophecies which are taken literally by traditional Jews, since they obviously have no problem with a future Temple and future sacrifices (whereas that scenario presents issues to some believers in Yeshua),[13] rabbinic commentators explain some key words in Ezekiel 43:7 as follows: "'Throne' alludes to the heavenly Temple, 'footstool' to the earthly one (*Metzudoth*). Because the heavenly and earthly Temples are perfectly aligned with one another, they share the same physical location (Vilna Gaon)."[14] As for God's promise to dwell among the Israelites forever, this is taken to be an assurance that "the Third Temple will never be destroyed (*Metzudoth*)."[15]

Paradise Restored

Ultimately, what the prophets looked forward to, and what the New Testament affirms as well, is a kind of paradise restored. This too is enhanced by rabbinic tradition.

According to Jesus in Matthew 19:28, "In the new world, when the Son of Man will sit on his glorious throne, you who have followed me will also sit on twelve thrones, judging the twelve tribes of Israel." The Greek for "the new world" is *palengenesia*, lit., "renewal, rebirth, regeneration," and it is rendered as "the regeneration" (NKJV), "when all things are renewed" (NET; cf. NIV's "at the renewal of all things"), and "in the regenerated world" (CJB). As explained by D. A. Carson, in this verse, the term "has to do with the consummation of the kingdom," and he notes that "the idea moves strictly within Jewish teleological and apocalyptic expectation"—with the exception, of course, of the promise that the twelve apostles will judge the twelve tribes of Israel, surely not a concept found in rabbinic thought![16]

In Acts 3:19–21, Peter declares that, as a result of national Jewish repentance for the rejection of Yeshua, God will send "times of refreshing" and the return of the Messiah "whom heaven must receive until the time for restoring all the things about which God spoke by the mouth of his holy prophets long ago" (Act 3:21). The Greek term for "restoring all things" is *apokatastaseōs*, found only here in the New Testament. According to A. T. Robertson,

> Double compound (ἀπο, κατα, ἰστημι [*apo, kata, histe⁻mi*]), here only in the N.T., though common in late writers. In papyri and inscriptions for repairs to temples and this phrase occurs in Jewish apocalyptic writings, something like the new heaven and the new earth of Rev. 21:1. Paul has a mystical allusion also to the agony of nature in Rom. 8:20–22. The verb ἀποκαθιστημι [*apokathiste⁻mi*] is used by Jesus of the

spiritual and moral restoration wrought by the Baptist as Elijah (Matt. 17:11=Mark 9:12) and by the disciples to Jesus in Acts 1:6. Josephus uses the word of the return from captivity and Philo of the restitution of inheritances in the year of jubilee. As a technical medical term it means complete restoration to health. See a like idea in παλινγενεσια [*palingenesia*] (renewal, new birth) in Matt. 19:28 and Titus 3:5.[17]

Once again, as with Matthew 19:18, the New Testament anticipation of the restoration of the earth includes national repentance of the Jewish people, meaning the people of Israel turning to Yeshua as Messiah and Lord, a concept alien to traditional Jewish literature (although the theme of end-time Jewish repentance, meaning the people of Israel turning to God in Torah observance, is absolutely prevalent).[18] But the concept of an earthly "paradise restored," a glorious renewal of the world, is certainly found in rabbinic literature. To understand what that actually means, however, it's important to understand how the ancient rabbis conceived of the world before Adam's sin.[19]

Rabbinic literature pictured Adam as able to stride the entire earth with a few steps before he sinned, after which he was shrunk in size to 150 feet tall![20] According to the *Jewish Encyclopedia*:

> Adam in paradise had angels to wait upon and dance before him (Sanh. 59*b*, B. B. 75*a*, Pirk̇e R. El. xii.). He ate "angel's bread" (compare Ps. lxxiii. 26; Yoma, 75*b*; Vita Adæ et Evæ, § 4). All creation bowed before him in awe. He was the light of the world (Yer. Shab. ii. 5*b*); but sin deprived him of all glory. The earth and the heavenly bodies lost their brightness, which will come back only in the Messianic time (Gen. R. xii.; Vita Adæ et Evæ, § 21; Philo, "Creation of the World," p. 60; Zohar, iii. 83*b*).[21]

So, if *that* is what the earth looked like before the Fall, what will it look like in Messianic times? And since God's glory will be concentrated in Israel and in Jerusalem in particular, what will the Land look like? The words of Amos, beautiful in their simplicity, paint a vivid and wonderful picture:

> A time is coming—declares the LORD—
> When the plowman shall meet the reaper,
> And the treader of grapes Him who holds the bag of seed;
> When the mountains shall drip wine

And all the hills shall wave with grain.
I will restore My people Israel.
They shall rebuild ruined cities and inhabit them;
They shall plant vineyards and drink their wine;
They shall till gardens and eat their fruits.
And I will plant them upon their soil,
Nevermore to be uprooted
From the soil I have given them—said the LORD your
God. (Amos 9:13–15; New Jewish Version)

It would not be overstating things to say that, in the midst of this glorious imagery, the words that stand out most powerfully to many Jewish readers are these four: "Nevermore to be uprooted." Indeed, dwelling in the Land, in the presence of God, is the ultimate expression of the Jewish future hope until the time of the final resurrection. As noted by some rabbinic commentators, "Just as a tree takes root in the ground, the Jewish people will remain affixed in their land forever, never to be exiled again (*Metzzudoth*, Malbim)."[22]

We need only supplement that with the understanding that this includes the recognition of Jesus as the Messiah of our people, which brings with it an even more profound understanding of God's work of redemption and forgiveness. And since Israel's salvation will mean "life from the dead" for the world (see Romans 11:11–15), the hope expressed in verse by the nineteenth-century Scottish Presbyterian leader Andrew Bonar is right on target:

Crowned with her fairest hope, the Church
Shall triumph with her Lord,
And earth her jubilee shall keep,
When Israel is restored.[23]
May the Lord hasten that day!

Study Questions

1. In what sense is the relationship between the Jewish people and the land of Israel unique?

2. What is the spiritual and spatial meaning of *aliyah*?

3. How is Rashi's famous commentary to Genesis 1:1 strangely relevant to our day?

4. According to the Scriptures, what part of the earth is the Lord's own inheritance?

5. Is it possible for the Jewish people to experience the fullness of God's blessings while exiled from the land of Israel?

6. What are some examples of rabbinic literature attributing supernatural dimensions to the Land itself?

7. Why was Old Testament scholar S. R. Driver (writing in 1906) pessimistic about a future national restoration of Israel? How different do things look today?

8. How does the future Messianic hope tie in with the Land of Israel?

9. Give one example of a rabbinic interpretation of Scripture pointing to a glorious future for the Jewish people in the land of Israel.

10. What are some rabbinic descriptions of the original Paradise in the Garden of Eden, and how will Paradise one day be restored?

Conference Video

chosenpeople.com/brown

Interview with Dr. Michael L. Brown

chosenpeople.com/brown-interview

NEW TESTAMENT

ISRAEL ACCORDING TO THE GOSPELS

Dr. Michael J. Wilkins

Wilkins, in his chapter *Israel according to the Gospels*, pays special attention to the gospel of Matthew and its presentation of the Jewish people. Wilkins suggests two unique attributes that especially add to the discussion about the future of Israel. First, Matthew emphasizes both the particular and universal fulfillment of prophecy. Secondly, Matthew's gospel is a challenge, as it seems to be both positive and negative towards the Jewish people. Only Matthew records Jesus' instructions to the disciples to go only to the "lost sheep of Israel" (Matt. 10:6), but he also is the only one to record the infamous statement by the Jewish crowd, "may his blood be upon on us and our children."

Further, Matthew shows how the disciples, at least in part, are the fulfillment of God's promises to Israel, particularly in the "spiritual aspects of the Messianic Kingdom." Yet, Wilkins demonstrates that the Church did not replace Israel and that God will be faithful to His covenants as described in the former chapters of our current volume.

When we consider the people, the land, and the future of Israel, the gospels offer an invaluable perspective. In the gospels we can hear the words of Jesus and see his activities with respect to Israel, but also see and hear the perspective of the evangelists who were members of the early church. In this chapter, we will focus primarily on the perspective of Matthew's gospel, because Matthew has special interest in Israel in the ministry of Jesus.[1] To get us started, some important expressions help clarify Matthew's perspective.

The Bridge between Old and New Testaments

Matthew's gospel has been a pivotal book throughout church history to help the church understand the relationship between the Old and New Testaments, and in that sense, to help us understand the relationship between Israel and the Church. Placed first as it was in some of the earliest collections of the NT canon, Matthew's gospel is a natural bridge between the Old and New Testaments. Matthew demonstrates repeatedly that OT hopes, prophecies, and promises have been fulfilled in the person and ministry of Jesus. Matthew begins with the "fulfillment" of the messianic genealogy in the birth of Jesus (1:1–17), and then goes on to demonstrate the fulfillment of various OT prophecies and themes (e.g., 1:22–23; 2:4–5, 15, 17, 23, etc.) the fulfillment of the OT Law (5:17–48), and the initiation of the New Covenant (26:26–29) in Jesus' life, ministry, and death.

"Particularism" and "Universalism"

We also see that the gospel of Matthew emphasizes both "particularism" and "universalism." These terms indicate that Matthew's gospel places striking emphasis upon both the fulfillment of the promises of salvation to a particular people, Israel, and also includes the fulfillment of the universal promise of salvation to all the peoples of the earth. The Church, made up of every nationality, has cherished this gospel because Matthew aims to record the continuation of the history of salvation to all of the nations. Matthew's introductory statement—that Jesus Christ is both the "son of David" and the "son of Abraham" (1:1)—is the preliminary indication that salvation promises made both through David to God's chosen people, Israel (e.g., 2 Samuel 7:8–17), and through Abraham to all peoples (Gen. 12:1–3; 22:18), have been fulfilled through the life and ministry of Jesus Christ, the promised Savior of Israel and all nations.

Matthew's gospel alone points explicitly to Jesus' intention to go first to the lost sheep of the house of Israel (10:5–6; 15:24), showing historically how God's promise of salvation to Israel was indeed fulfilled. And yet the promises made to Abraham that he would be a blessing to all the nations are also fulfilled as Jesus extends salvation to the Gentiles (cf. 21:44; 28:19). The Church throughout the ages has found assurance in Matthew's gospel that God truly keeps his promises to his people.

Positive and Negative Views of Israel in Matthew's Gospel

Matthew's gospel has been called the most positive toward Israel of all the Gospels, but has also been called the most negative toward Israel of all the Gospels.

On the one hand, Jesus' instructions to his disciples when he sent them out on a mission tour provides an example from the "positive" perspective: "These twelve Jesus sent out, instructing them, 'Go nowhere among the Gentiles and enter no town of the Samaritans, but go rather to the lost sheep of the house of Israel'" (10:5–6).[2] Matthew is the only Gospel to record this statement.

Another example of Matthew's positive depiction of Israel in God's plan of salvation-history occurs in Jesus' interaction with a Gentile woman: "A Canaanite woman from that region came out and was crying, 'Have mercy on me, O Lord, Son of David; my daughter is severely oppressed by a demon.'...He answered, 'I was sent only to the lost sheep of the house of Israel'" (15:22–24).

On the other hand, passages in Matthew seem to present a "negative" perspective of Israel's place in salvation-history. For example, Jesus has harsh words in his statement to the Jewish religious leaders during his passion week, which Matthew alone records: "the kingdom of God will be taken away from you and given to a people producing its fruits" (21:43).

Another of the most prominent "negative" perspectives about Israel recorded in the Gospels, occurs in Matthew's narrative of Jesus' trial. When the crowd demands from the Roman governor, Pontius Pilate, that he release Barabbas and crucify Jesus, Matthew records solemnly the response of the people after Pilate washes his hands of responsibility, "And all the people answered, "His blood be on us and on our children!'" (27:25).

The relationship of Israel and the Church in Matthew's Gospel

The differing perspectives in Matthew's gospel toward Israel and the nations have caused diverse interpretations. We won't be able to resolve the larger issues here, but a survey of Matthew's treatment of Israel may help move us closer to understanding these thorny interpretative issues.[3]

Replacement

The negative statements about Israel in Matthew's gospel have been used to support a "replacement" perspective toward Israel. With the introductory and concluding emphases upon the nations, some scholars contend that Matthew intends his readers to see that the promises to Israel are now fulfilled through Jesus' mission, and the Church replaces Israel in God's economy. This is viewed variously as "replacement theology" or "supersessionism" or "successionist theology" in relation to Israel and the Church; that is, the Church has succeeded Israel as God's people, taking the place of ethnic Israel in the future plan of God.[4] This has been a dominant position in interpreting Matthew's gospel, and likewise characterizes many who interpret the gospel of John.[5]

Two Peoples of God

On the other extreme, some contend that the positive perspective toward Israel in Matthew's gospel leads to seeing the continuation of Israel and the Church side-by-side as different peoples of God. This has taken a variety of forms, but in its most general sense is widely held as a reaction against replacement and a rejection of anti-Semitism and the horrors of the Holocaust.[6] This is becoming a dominant view among a wide group of scholars who are trying to acknowledge a place for Israel's uniqueness. But this view has inherent dangers of minimizing the uniqueness of Jesus' saving work for both Jew and Gentile.[7]

Differing Instruments of the Kingdom

A mediating position that avoids these extremes recognizes that Israel and the Church are seen in Matthew's gospel as instruments used by God in bearing witness to the kingdom of heaven, but at differing times in salvation-history. Matthew points to a spiritual oneness of Gentile and Jew in Christ that is permanent. However, Matthew points to functional distinctions for the nation of Israel and the Church in the plan and purpose of God. As we go through Matthew's narrative and record of Jesus' teachings, we will see that Israel and the Church will be used at differing times as the instruments God will use to proclaim and further the impact of the kingdom of heaven on earth.[8]

The People of Israel in Matthew's Gospel

In the positive and negative statements regarding Israel we surveyed above, we saw hints of Jesus' intentions for the people of Israel, the land, and their future. A brief survey of Matthew's gospel will display significant points that help us to understand more clearly God's plans for Israel, and its relationship to the Church.

Jesus comes as Messiah, son of David and son of Abraham, king of the Jews, who will be the ruler who shepherds God's people, Israel (1:1, 17–18; 2:2, 6).

Matthew begins his Gospel by stating that this is "the book of the genealogy of Jesus Christ, the son of David, the son of Abraham" (1:1). Matthew immediately captures his readers' attention by emphasizing that as the "son of David" Jesus is the fulfillment of Israel's hope for the Messiah. Jesus' arrival fulfills the prophecy that one of David's descendants would sit on his throne forever (2 Sam 7:11b–16). Yet, Jesus is also "the son of Abraham," indicating that in his arrival Jesus fulfills the covenant God made with Abraham, which included the promise that his line would be a blessing not just to Israel, but to all the nations (Gen. 12:1–3; 22:18).[9]

In the subsequent infancy narrative, the magi arrive looking for the one born "king of the Jews" (2:2) and Matthew further records that the birthplace of Jesus carries great significance for Israel: "And you, O Bethlehem, in the land of Judah, are by no means least among the rulers of Judah; for from you shall come a ruler who will shepherd my people Israel" (2:6; cf. Micah 5:2).

In Galilee of the Gentiles, Jesus announces the kingdom of heaven to the people of Israel and calls them to repentance (4:12–17).
Non-Jewish populations surrounded the tribes of Israel in the north on three sides, so the region was described as "Galilee of the Gentiles" (Matt. 4:15–17; cf. Isa. 9:1–2). The inhabitants are called "the people sitting in darkness" (4:16), a description of Jews who await deliverance while living among the hopelessness of the Gentiles. The term "people" (*laos*) in Matthew regularly refers to Israel (cf. 1:21; 27:24–25). Here, where the darkness is most dense and so far-removed from the center of Jewish religious life in Jerusalem, these Jews are the first to see the great light of God's deliverance in Jesus. It will bring hope to those who understand most clearly the hopelessness of death. This light presages the universal message of hope, because from this same region of "Galilee of the Gentiles," Jesus will send the disciples to carry out the commission to make disciples of all the Gentiles (28:18).[10] The message that begins to unfold is of messianic grace, for it comes first to those who were least expecting it.

Jesus calls twelve disciples/apostles to advance his ministry to his people Israel (4:18–22; 9:36–38; 10:1–2).
Matthew narrates that as Jesus saw the crowds around him, he had compassion for them, because they were harassed and helpless, "...like sheep without a shepherd" (Matt. 10:36). The metaphor of sheep and shepherd was well-known in Israel's history, ranging from the relationship that God as shepherd has with Israel his sheep (Isa. 40:10–11) to the Davidic Messiah who will establish the everlasting covenant with Israel as shepherd (Ezek. 37:24).

The leaders of Israel in Jesus' day had not fulfilled their responsibility to guide and protect the people, and therefore the people were harassed and helpless. So Jesus calls twelve disciples (10:1)/apostles (10:2) to go to Israel with the gospel message. The number "twelve" has obvious salvation-historical significance. The number corresponds to the twelve patriarchs of Israel, the sons of Jacob, from whom the tribes of Israel descended. The twelve disciples/apostles symbolize the continuity of salvation-history in God's program, as Jesus sends them out to proclaim to the lost sheep of the house of Israel that the kingdom of heaven has arrived (cf. 10:5–6).[11] But there is a form of discontinuity as well, because the Twelve will sit on twelve thrones judging the house of Israel (cf. 19:28).[12] The twelve disciples/apostles have continuity with the twelve tribes of Israel, yet they do not replace Israel. But they will form the foundation of a new community of faith, the church that Jesus will build (16:16–20; cf. Eph. 2:19–21).

Jesus came as a Jew to the Jewish people to fulfill the salvation-historical promises to the nation Israel (10:5–6; 15:24).
Jesus begins his mission discourse with a surprising prohibition: "These twelve Jesus sent out, instructing them, "Go nowhere among the Gentiles and enter no town of the Samaritans, but go rather to the lost sheep of the house of Israel" (10:5–6). Jesus' historical ministry is intended to fulfill the promises of salvation coming first to Israel. The expression "lost sheep of the house of Israel" does not mean one separate part of Israel that is lost, but rather that the whole of Israel is lost and is being called to make a decision about the gospel of the kingdom. This is a special mission of Jesus' disciples during his historical ministry to the crowds of Israel. Jesus goes first to Israel (cf. 15:21–28) to fulfill the salvation-historical order that God established with Israel being the tool that God will use to bring blessing to the world (e.g., Gen. 12:2–3; 22:18). Then he will charge the Eleven to continue the historical outworking by going to the nations (Matt. 28:19–20). The Twelve symbolize the continuity and theological salvation-history priority of Israel in God's program.[13] Jesus' singular attention to Israel underscores God's faithfulness to his covenant promises, the continuity of his purposes and that his plan for Israel is still unfinished. Jesus dispels any doubt that his disciples or any in the audience might have as to whether he is truly the Messiah coming in fulfillment of the promises given to Israel.

Believing Israel is joined by believing Gentiles in the eschatological banquet (8:10–13).
In the interaction between Jesus and a Gentile centurion who asks Jesus to heal his servant, Matthew presents a radical example of faith. "Truly, I tell you, with no one in Israel have I found such faith. I tell you, many will come from east and west and recline at table with Abraham, Isaac, and Jacob in the kingdom of heaven, while the sons of the kingdom will be thrown into the outer darkness. In that place there will be weeping and gnashing of teeth" (8:10–12).

We find in this narrative a staggering reversal of ethnic and religious expectations. Here at this very early stage of Jesus' ministry and Matthew's narrative, a Gentile is healed, a promise of Gentile inclusion to the kingdom of heaven is revealed, and the people of Israel are warned of exclusion from God's program of redemption if they do not repent. This certainly must have shocked Jesus' audience, and is a stark reminder to Matthew's readers of the nature of salvation and discipleship to Jesus.

Jesus will continue to appeal to Israel to repent and enter the kingdom of heaven. This fulfills the covenantal promises to Israel made through Abraham, Isaac, and Jacob, which will include attendance at the eschatological banquet. And attendance at the banquet requires one primary requirement for all of God's children, regardless of ethnic identity—faith in Jesus as Messiah. Gentiles who believe will join Jews who believe.[14] Those who do not turn to him in faith as the Messianic deliverer will receive their just punishment, whether they are Jew or Gentile. The Gentile mission has not yet been declared, but Jesus' reply to the centurion indicates that the door to the kingdom is open to whomever believes.[15]

Israel, including both the leaders and a majority of the people, reject both Jesus and his message about the kingdom (12:25–32, 38–39; 13:10–17; 27:25).

At a crucial turning point in Matthew's narration of Jesus' ministry, we come to the parables of the mysteries of the kingdom of heaven, in which are found a rebuke of the leaders and people of Israel for unbelief (13:10–12). The parables are given after the increasing rejection and opposition to Jesus by the leaders and a majority of the people of Israel. The person within Israel who has responded positively to Jesus' message of the gospel of the kingdom believes and becomes his disciple. But God does not force anyone to accept the message of the kingdom, so the crowd's negative response to the parables is dictated by the nature of their heart. If a person in the crowd has no spiritual ears, his or her heart will be increasingly hardened and will turn away from Jesus and the healing that comes with the kingdom of heaven (3:15).[16]

The Jews of Galilee have been privileged to hear and see first Jesus' message and miracles that authenticated his announcement of the arrival of the kingdom of heaven (4:12–17), but their lack of repentance is their condemnation (11:20–24). The religious leaders have committed the unpardonable sin by rejecting the Spirit's testimony of Jesus' identity as their Messiah (12:25–32, 38–39). The rejection of his ministry by his hometown people of Nazareth (13:53–58), the arrest and execution of John the Baptist and his own threatened public peril from Herod Antipas (14:1–2) combine to signal the end of the Galilean ministry, so Jesus "withdraws" (see

4:17; 14:13). He and his disciples, Jews who have believed in him as Messiah, proceed to Gentile regions, and then finally he will set his sights on Judea and the final destination, Jerusalem.

However, a substantial group in Israel did respond in faith and enter the kingdom of heaven (5:1–16, 20).
"Seeing the crowds, he went up on the mountain, and when he sat down, his disciples came to him. And he opened his mouth and taught them, saying: "Blessed are the poor in spirit, for theirs is the kingdom of heaven" (5:1–3). These disciples have come out of the crowd; they are Jewish people who have believed in Jesus' message of the gospel of the kingdom of heaven; they are now the heirs to the promises made to the people of Israel. Those who responded positively to his offer of the kingdom became his disciples. Discipleship entailed unreserved commitment to him, which meant that a new disciple entered the kingdom of heaven in the presence of the person of Jesus (5:2–16, 20).

Jesus' historical ministry fulfills the promises of salvation coming first to Israel; now he is turning to the Gentiles (15:24–28).
In the Gentile region of Tyre and Sidon, Jesus maintains his commitment to fulfill the mission for which he was sent as he says, "I was sent only to the lost sheep of Israel" (15:24). But this very perceptive woman, who confessed Jesus as the messianic son of David, presses Jesus by calling upon the extended blessings promised to the Gentiles through the Abrahamic covenant (Gen. 12:3; Matt. 1:1; 8:5–13).[17] The woman draws upon that promise to seek the aid of Jesus Messiah. Although Jesus' ministry was particularistic in its attention to Israel, it responded to the faith of Gentiles and held promise of a future universal outreach.

Even though God has a program, he responds to true faith in any case.[18] The privileged people of Nazareth did not respond in faith and so could not receive Jesus' healing ministry (see on 13:58). But this Gentile woman had an openness to Jesus that allowed his healing ministry to operate. Here we understand that faith is essentially accepting the revelation and will of God as one's own reality and purpose for life. The "greatness" of faith points to the fact that in such an unlikely person—a Gentile woman living outside of Israel—this mother demonstrates one of the clearest understandings of God's salvation-historical program and Jesus' participation in it.

The kingdom is presently taken away from Israel as the agent of Jesus' messianic kingdom (21:42–43).
Jesus climaxes his indictment of the religious leadership of Israel with a stinging pronouncement: "Therefore I tell you, the kingdom of God will be taken away from you and given to a people produc-

ing its fruits (21:43). This unique Matthean statement gives Jesus' unambiguous conclusion to the preceding parable. The leaders had not fulfilled the obligations to God for which they were responsible, neither in their lives nor in leading the nation of Israel. They had not repented at the arrival of the kingdom of God, but instead rejected the very Son who had announced its arrival. Jesus declares that the kingdom of God is being taken away from Israel at this time as the ones to proclaim the arrival and presence of the gospel of the kingdom (21:43). But who will be the current agents of the kingdom? Jesus now declares their identity.

As the recipients of his messianic salvation, Jesus' disciples become his new nation of witnesses to the reality of the kingdom, producing the fruit of the kingdom, enabling them to be the agents of the kingdom (21:43).

Jesus' disciples are now his agents of the kingdom: "Therefore I tell you, the kingdom of God will be...given to a people producing its fruits" (21:43). The identity of this "people" (*ethnei*) is found in the description: a people producing the fruits of the kingdom. John the Baptist had earlier warned the religious leaders and the crowds who wanted to be baptized by him to produce fruit in keeping with repentance (cf. 3:7–10; cf. Luke 3:3–8). The manifestation of that fruit—at the very least repentance, belief, and the fruit of the indwelling Spirit of God—is the product of being in the kingdom of God, which is the characteristic of Jesus' disciples. Jesus' disciples are the people of God who are producing the fruit of the kingdom of God.

"People" is the singular *ethnei*, which prepares for the time when the church, a nation of gathered people, will include both Jew and Gentile in the outworking of God's kingdom in the present age. All those who become individual disciples out of the plural "nations" (28:19; *ethne*), will be brought together as one new "nation." Peter will later also use the singular *ethnos* in the context of the "stone" passage to refer to the church (1 Peter 2:9). This will not abolish the promises made to Israel nationally (cf. Rom. 11:25–33), but it does point to the transition of leadership and prominence that will be given to the Church in the outworking of God's kingdom program in the present age.[19]

The kingdom of God will produce its fruit in this new nation of Jesus' disciples, which points ahead to the work of the Holy Spirit in the establishment of the new covenant. The fruit produced is God's presence reigning in his regenerated people who demonstrate the power of God through lives that are distinguished by the fruit of righteousness (Matt. 5:20) and good works (Col. 1:5–10), the fruit of Spirit-produced transformation of character (Gal. 5:21–24), and the fruit of new generations of disciples (Matt. 28:18–20; cf. John 15:16) that will bear witness to the reality of the kingdom on earth.

The leadership of Israel in the first century is culpable with Rome for the death of Jesus (27:24–25).
"So when Pilate saw that he was gaining nothing, but rather that a riot was beginning, he took water and washed his hands before the crowd, saying, 'I am innocent of this man's blood; see to it yourselves.' And all the people answered, 'His blood be on us and on our children!'" (27:25).

This is one of the most difficult passages in all of Scripture. The term "crowd" (*ochlos*) has been the normal word Matthew uses to designate the masses of people who have been witnessing the trial and who have asked for Jesus' crucifixion (27:20–24), and they are persuaded by the religious leaders to ask for Barabbas and shout for Jesus to be crucified (27:15, 20–24).

As Matthew switches to a different word, "people" (*laos*), in the expression "All the people answered" (27:25) he emphasizes that the crowd and the religious leaders have had their opportunity—now they must bear responsibility for not repenting, and for asking for Jesus' death. "People" (*laos*) is the word that Matthew normally uses to designate Israel (e.g., 1:21; 2:6; 4:16; 15:8). Used here, the implications are ominous for the nation. The Jewish leaders and the crowds whom they have manipulated claim responsibility for Jesus' death as they declare boldly, "Let his blood be on us and on our children!" Blood on a person (or "on the head") is a common idiom to indicate responsibility for someone's death (e.g., Lev. 20:9; Josh. 2:19; 2 Sam. 1:16; Ezek. 18:13; Acts 5:28; 18:6); "on our children" indicates the familial solidarity of generations within Israel (e.g., Gen. 31:16). They are so convinced that Jesus deserves death that they brashly proclaim their responsibility for his death and extend that responsibility to their descendants.

This statement by the people has been called "the darkest and hardest verse in this gospel,"[20] because Matthew puts the responsibility for Jesus' crucifixion directly on the Jewish people. The Jewish people of that day share responsibility with the Romans for the death of Jesus. Pilate tried to escape the responsibility, but he cannot wash his hands of the matter. By not finding any guilt and still ordering Jesus to be executed, Pilate was just as guilty as they. The people of that day, as in any day, are responsible for their actions. But even though they ignorantly crucified their own Messiah, God takes their grievous deed and provides salvation for them and for the world (Acts 3:17–19). The apostle Peter in his first public sermon at Pentecost indicts the religious leaders, the Jewish crowds, and the Romans for Jesus' death (cf. Acts 2:23, 36; 3:17). But to those who acknowledge their guilt he also extends an offer of forgiveness of sins and salvation (2:37–41; 3:19–4:4). Thousands of Jewish people, including many priests, received that offer in the first days after Pentecost (2:41; 4:4; 6:7). Everyone is responsible for his or her own actions, but God's forgiveness awaits any who repent.

Jesus' disciples are the remnant of believing Israel and first citizens of Jesus' messianic kingdom (27:55–61; 28:1–16).
Individual persons in Israel, men and women who have believed on Jesus as Messiah and have become his disciples, are the believing remnant of Israel, and the first citizens of Jesus' messianic kingdom. They are the ones who came out from among the crowds, denied the warnings of the religious leaders, and became Jesus' disciples. These include at the end, Mary Magdalene and the other women disciples (27:56), Joseph of Arimathea (27:57), the eleven disciples (28:16), and more than five hundred brothers (28:10; 1 Cor. 15:6). These are the ones who are now the agents or instruments of the kingdom. Eventually, the privilege of kingdom citizenship would be extended to other believers, including those who respond to the gospel preaching in the early church, both Jew and Gentile. They are the ones who have the privilege and responsibility as agents of the kingdom of God in this age.

The Land and Future of Israel in Matthew's Gospel

There is no mistaking the prominent place that the people of Israel play in Matthew's gospel, but there is also striking emphasis upon the land and future of Israel. Several points stand out.

There is a continuing mission to Israel in the land during this age until the coming of the Son of Man (10:23).
In the middle of the missionary discourse, Jesus speaks of mission during the time of the twelve, and then of an ongoing mission throughout the ages. Prior to the coming of the Son of Man there will still be a mission to Israel in the land. With the mention of the end (10:22), Jesus culminates the prophetic aspect of the commissioning with a remarkable statement: "I tell you the truth, you will not finish going through the cities of Israel before the Son of Man comes" (10:23). This has been described as one of the most difficult verses in the Bible to interpret. The difficulty comes especially in trying to understand the temporal context. Some suggest that Jesus was promising the disciples that they would witness the eschatological coming of the Son of Man while they were on their first Palestinian mission, or at his resurrection, or at Pentecost, or at the destruction of Jerusalem in AD 70.[21] Others contend that this is to be associated with the coming of the Son of Man at the end of the age.

The latter appears to fit the larger context here. While the Jews have priority of salvation (10:6) and of judgment (10:15), their judgment does not permanently exclude them from God's eschatological promises. The ongoing mission to the nations continues to include both Jew and Gentile (see on 28:18–20). As Jesus offers comfort to the mission-disciples about their ultimate salvation unto the end (10:22), he warns them not to abandon Israel. There will be a continuing mission to Israel alongside of the mission to the Gentiles until the Parousia.[22]

And the mission to Israel will be conducted in the cities of the land of Israel. For hundreds of years, Israel as a nation was not in the land. But in the return to the land in the twentieth century, this saying of Jesus acknowledges the blessed place Israel has in God's providence. In spite of Israel's hardheartedness, God will remain faithful to his covenant promises to her. This is a powerful apologetic to the Jews in both Jesus' ministry and to those within hearing of Matthew's gospel in the first century and today; God has not abandoned his covenantal promises to Israel in the land. It is a challenging and sober call to mission-disciples to endure to the end with the message of the gospel to all peoples—both Jew and Gentile.

Israel will be in the land of Jerusalem until they bless the Coming One (23:37–39).
During Jesus' final week he rebuked the leadership in the Temple. His tone combines the denunciation of the religious leaders with a compassionate lament—"O Jerusalem, Jerusalem"—and concludes his address to the people of Israel—which in this context in the temple has included the crowds and the religious leaders—with a dramatic prophecy. "For I tell you, you will not see me again, until you say, 'Blessed is he who comes in the name of the Lord'" (Matt. 23:39 ESV). This is the last time that Jesus will address the crowds, who have had their opportunity for repentance. As Jesus cites Psalm 118:26, he identifies himself with God's Messiah, Israel's Savior, the "Coming One," who will once again come to his people after a time of great judgment. Israel will be in the land, in the city of Jerusalem, when Messiah returns. Israel will receive the eschatological blessings that they had previously rejected.[23]

The imperative of the Great Commission to "make disciples of all the nations" includes a continuing mission to Israel (28:19–20).
The object of the imperative "make disciples" is "all the nations" (*panta ta ethnē*). All people of every nation are to receive the opportunity to become Jesus' disciples. Jesus' ministry in Israel was to be the beginning point of what would be later a universal offer of salvation to all the peoples of the earth. Some suggest that "all the nations" means only "Gentiles," not the "Jews," since Matthew normally refers to Gentiles by this title.[24] However, most scholars recognize that Jesus' overall intention is to include Jews in his commission, and Matthew intends his readers to understand their inclusion (cf. 24:9, 14; 25:32).[25] God continues to love the whole world, for whom Christ died, which includes Jews (cf. John 3:16; Rom. 5:8). The rest of the NT clearly has in view the evangelism of Jews as a part of missionary strategies (e.g., Acts 2:22; 13:38–39; Rom. 1:16; Eph. 2:11–16). Although Israel is not at present functionally the instrument and witness of the outworking

of the kingdom of God (see on 21:43), individual Jews are still invited to participate in the salvation brought by Jesus with the arrival of the kingdom and become included in the Church.

A future desolation of sacrilege in the Holy Place, and emphasis upon the land of Judea, indicates a future role of Israel in the land (24:14–16).
Some contend that at this point Jesus focuses exclusively on the destruction of the Temple in AD 70,[26] while a wide spectrum of scholars contend that these events also presage a future time of eschatological defilement and destruction of a future Temple.[27] The latter view is preferred here, especially when it is compared with Paul's prediction of the eschatological man of lawlessness (2 Thess. 2:1–12), and the Apocalypse's vision of the eschatological beast (Rev. 13:11–18), which are remarkably similar to Jesus' prophecy. If one only looks at the account in Luke (21:20–24), the focus is apparently on the fall of Jerusalem in AD 70. But when we look at the Matthean (24:15–22) and Markan (13:14–20) accounts—with the mention of "the abomination that causes desolation" (notice that Luke only speaks of the desolation of Jerusalem)—we can see that the focus shifts to something which did not occur at the destruction of Jerusalem in AD 70. The reference to the abomination shifts the focus to activities at the end of the age. Jesus, therefore, is giving a mixture of prophetic elements that speak both to his present generation and to the future. Jesus' prophecy includes both the destruction of Jerusalem and the Temple in AD 70, but he looks beyond to a future time when another abomination that causes desolation will arise in Jerusalem to lead astray God's people and bring destruction upon those who resist him.

When these signs of the end of the age appear, those waiting for the arrival of the Son of Man are to recognize that their redemption is drawing near (Luke 21:28). This refers both to repentant Israel and to unrepentant wicked people. But it also refers to believers who are alive at that time who see these things occurring; they will be the generation of Jesus' disciples that will see their Lord appear. Therefore, the saying is a word of warning to those of the generation with Jesus and those in the future who had not yet repented that the arrival of the Son of Man will bring judgment.

The twelve apostles will sit on twelve thrones, "judging" the twelve tribes of Israel (19:28).
Jesus here refers to the future eschatological time of renewal, a hope that is basic to Jewish expectation of Israel's future national restoration.[28] Although "judging" can indicate condemnation of Israel for rejecting Jesus as national Messiah,[29] the idea of Jesus as the Son of Man and the Twelve ruling or governing is paramount (cf. Rev. 3:21; 20:6). Condemning Israel would bring no great pleasure to the disci-

ples, but reward would, which was the point of Peter's request (Matt. 19:27). Jesus indicates a future time of renewal when the Twelve will participate in the final establishment of the kingdom of God on the earth, when Israel will be restored to the land, and the Twelve will rule with Jesus Messiah over the renewal of all things.[30]

Conclusion

Jesus' disciples are the Church that is the fulfillment in part of the promises to Israel, especially the spiritual aspects of that messianic kingdom, including the blessings of the New Covenant: e.g., regeneration, the indwelling Spirit, forgiveness of sins. Jesus' disciples, whether Jew or Gentile, experience the blessings of the New Covenant, are born-again, are in-dwelt by the Spirit, and are the ones who can claim God's forgiveness of sins. That is the sign of the kingdom on earth today.

Jesus' disciples as the Church currently produce the fruit of the kingdom of God and bear the responsibility of the role of carrying the message of the Gospel of the kingdom (21:43; 28:18–20). We bear the fruit of the Kingdom of God, which is righteousness and good works. Jesus' disciples as the Church now functionally perform the role of being used as the agents or instruments of the kingdom, especially in announcing the presence and means of entrance to the kingdom, and demonstrating the fruit of the presence of the Kingdom. But Jesus' disciples as the Church do not replace Israel or become Israel.

The role of carrying out God's purposes through the Kingdom of God has been given to the Church in the present age. But Israel is still kept in view as receiving in the future the eschatological fulfillment of the promises of the Kingdom, including both the mediation of the Kingdom and the land of the Kingdom (10:23; 23:37–39; cf. Rom. 11:25-32; 15:7–13; Rev. 7:1–8).

Study Questions

1. Early in church history the Gospel of Matthew was placed first in the New Testament canon. How does it function as a "bridge" between the Old Testament and New Testament?

2. What do the words "particularism" and "universalism" indicate with reference to Matthew's gospel? How do they help in understanding Matthew's purposes for writing his gospel?

3. What are some contrasting positive and negative perspectives on Israel in Matthew's gospel? What accounts for those contrasting views?

4. The author discusses three variant views of the relationship

of Israel and the Church in Matthew's gospel. What are those three views, and which of those do you presently adopt? Why?

5. Why does Jesus call twelve disciples/apostles to advance his ministry to his people Israel? What is the significance of the number "twelve" for their relationship to Israel and to the Church?

6. Why did Jesus give the directive to the twelve apostles, "Go nowhere among the Gentiles and enter no town of the Samaritans, but go rather to the lost sheep of the house of Israel" (Matt. 10:5-6). Would he say the same thing to you today? Why or why not?

7. What is Jesus' purpose for speaking to the crowds in parables (see Matt. 13:10–17)? What does this reveal about Jesus' developing relationship to the people of Israel?

8. In Jesus' interaction with the Canaanite woman he exclaimed, "O woman, great is your faith!" (Matt. 15:28). What accounts for the greatness of her faith? How could you exhibit the same kind of greatness of faith?

9. In Matthew 21:43, Jesus gives one of the harshest statements to the leadership and the majority of the people of Israel: "Therefore I tell you, the kingdom of God will be taken away from you and given to a people producing its fruits" (21:43). What does that mean for Israel in the first century, and Israel and the Church today?

10. In that quote in Matthew 21:43, Jesus says that the kingdom of God will be given to a "people producing its fruits." Who are those "people" and what are "its fruits"? How does that relate to you?

11. Matthew records that at the trial of Jesus, the crowds call for Barabbas to be released, and for Jesus to be crucified. Then the dramatic words are recorded, "and all the people answered, 'His blood be on us and on our children!'" (Matt. 27:25). Who are those "people," and how does this affect our relationships with Jews today? How have those words wrongly been used to support anti-Semitism or anti-Judaism? How should that be rectified?

12. How do Matthew 10:23; 19:28; 23:37–39; 24:14–16; and 28:19–20 hold out hope for the people of Israel in the future, and instructions for the Church today and in the future?

Conference Video

chosenpeople.com/wilkins

Interview with Dr. Michael J. Wilkins

chosenpeople.com/wilkins-interview

ISRAEL IN LUKE–ACTS

Dr. Darrell L. Bock

Bock, in his chapter *The People, the Land and the Future of Israel in Luke–Acts*, illustrates how Luke gives Israel a continuing role in God's plan of redemption. The chapter examines common Christian perceptions of Israel, specifically the belief that the Church is the New Israel. Bock presents compelling evidence to show that Luke's writings are critical in forming a Christian view of Israel. Luke originally penned his works to "legitimize the inclusion of Gentiles in an originally Jewish movement as part of God's plan." The arrival of God's Spirit initiates a new era, but Luke's message shows how the Church is in continuity with Israel's promised hope.

As Bock reiterates, the inclusion of the Gentiles does not require the exclusion of the Jewish people. In fact, the inclusion of both has always been part of His plan.

In some circles of New Testament study, it is said that Israel has become the church. In her rejection of Jesus, Israel has lost her place as the people of God. The church is the new Israel.

A good example of this perspective is Gary Burge's book, *Jesus and the Land: The New Testament Challenge to "Holy Land" Theology*.[1] Working through the New Testament, Burge argues for a landless and nationless theology in which the equality of Jew and Gentile in Christ is the key and only ecclesiological reality. In this view, Jesus as Temple or as forming a new universal temple community becomes the locus for holy space. So Israel is absorbed into the church and hope in the land is spiritualized to refer to a restored earth.[2] There is some truth in this, even a lot of truth, but to get there Burge ignores many texts and misses completely the role of Israel in the story. By making this move, the faithfulness of God is undercut and an important aspect of God's grace goes missing, as his persistence in the midst of our unfaithfulness is lost.

This chapter seeks to redress the balance. When I speak of Israel in this essay it is the Jewish people I have in mind as opposed to *a new Israel*.[3] Since most of the texts not treated by Burge appear in Luke–Acts, we will survey these two volumes for Israel's continuing story.[4] Burge is not alone. The comprehensive work on the Kingdom and Covenant by Gentry and Wellum makes the same omission of material from Luke–Acts.[5] Such an omission is significant since Luke writes more of the New Testament than any other single writer. These two biblical books comprise almost a third of the New Testament. Is there hope for God's restoration of original Israel in these texts? What do those books add to the fulfillment the Messiah of Israel brings ot the world?

Setting the Stage: The Context of Luke-Acts

Luke–Acts was written between AD 60–80 in order to legitimate the inclusion of Gentiles in an originally Jewish movement as part of God's plan.[6] Theophilus (Luke 1:3; Acts 1:1) is a Jesus-believing Gentile who needs assurance. Luke–Acts presents Jesus as God's exalted and vindicated bearer of kingdom promise, forgiveness and life for all who believe, Jew and Gentile. The bestowal of God's Spirit marks the new era's arrival (Luke 3:16; 24:49; Acts 1:4–5; Acts 2:16–36 with Joel 2:28–32 and Psalm 110:1; Acts 11:15–17; 13:16–24). This message completes promises made to Abraham and Israel centuries ago.

Luke argues that the church roots its message in old promises, a story in continuity with Israel's promised hope found in God's covenantal promises to her. The entire saga involves Israel's restoration, now delayed by her rejection of Messiah but still to come. For all that Gentile inclusion and equality in the new community brings, we never lose sight of the fact that it is *Israel's story and Israel's hope* that brings blessing to the world, just as Genesis 12:3 promised. God keeps his promises to Israel, the seed with as many grains as the sand on the sea and as many people as stars in the sky.

Luke 1–2
Infancy Material as a Whole

Luke's infancy material tells Israel's story. Just look at all the early references associated with the Jewish nation. John the Baptist is sent to the sons of Israel (Luke 1:16). The child born to Mary is given the throne of David and will reign over the house of Jacob forever (Luke 1:31–32). God has helped his servant Israel realize promises spoken to Abraham and to his posterity forever (Luke 1:54–55). Zechariah blesses the God of Israel who has raised up a Davidic horn of salvation as the prophets foretold (Luke 1:68–70). Jesus is born in David's city because Joseph is a descendant of David (Luke 2:4). The angels hail Jesus' birth in the city of David (Luke 2:11). Simeon looks for the consolation of Israel (Luke 2:25). Jesus is a light of revelation for the Gentiles and a glory for his people Israel (Luke 2:32). Jesus causes the rise and fall of many in Israel (Luke 2:34). Anna looks for the redemption of Jerusalem (Luke 2:38). The pious in Israel are looking for the Jewish Messiah. However, Gentiles are impacted by the Jesus story, and the impact is comprehensive, we never lose Israel in the fresh mix. The themes introduced in this section point to Israel's story. This is confirmed by a closer look at a few of these texts.

Luke 1:32–33

Mary is told that the child she will bear will sit on David's throne and rule over Jacob's house (Luke 1:32–33). The Davidic throne reflects the Davidic covenant's promise of a son, a house, and an everlasting rule (2 Sam. 7:8–16, esp. vv. 13, 16; on Solomon's accession, 1 Kings 1:48; 2:24). The promise to David found its initial fulfillment in Solomon. However, the ultimate fulfillment of the everlasting character of this dynasty is realized in Jesus (Luke 1:33). The initial promise to David was reiterated throughout the Old Testament (1 Kings 2:24, where Solomon is seen as fulfilling the promise; Ps. 89:14, 19–29, 35–37 [89:15, 20–30, 36–38 MT]; 132:11–12; Isa. 9:6–7 [9:5–6 MT]; 11:1–5, 10; Jer. 23:5–6).[7] First Chronicles 29:23 tells us this throne on which Solomon now sits after his appointment as king by David is also the throne of the Lord. So the announcement in Luke 1:32–33 recalls a deeply held Old Testament hope with roots back into the rule of God over Israel.

Luke made much of Davidic descent (Luke 1:69; 2:4, 11; 3:31). Jesus' regal Davidic connection is the basic christological starting point for Luke's Jesus.[8] Luke's theology is rooted in the Davidic son's kingdom rule. The kingdom in Luke includes earthly elements that are not transformed or redefined into something else. As his two volumes will show, Luke's story involves divine history for *this* earth. Nothing in Luke's story points us to deliverance only into a new realm. All the language Luke uses when describing the Kingdom of God is about this world and its deliverance.

Luke 1:32–33 represents a continuation of Israel's story. Jesus not only has a regal position (1:32) but an everlasting reign (1:33). *Basileusei epi* means "to reign over" a people. The phrase *house of Jacob* is another way to refer to the nation of Israel (Ex. 19:3; Isa. 2:5–6; 8:17; 48:1). Some see an allusion here to Jesus gathering a "new Israel."[9] There is, however, nothing in the context to suggest this. In fact, Mary's hymn expresses purely national sentiments (1:46–55), as do Simeon's remarks (2:29, 32, 34–35). Jesus, as God's Messiah, is King of the Jews, whether or not they recognize him. The Davidic king comes to his own as well as to the world. When Gentiles are included, Israel is not excluded, as the example of Paul always starting in the synagogue in Acts shows (see also Romans 1:16–17, "to the Jew first").

Jesus rules forever. The idea of an eternal rule in the New Testament emerges from the promise of an eternal line of kings or deliverance figures (2 Sam. 7:12–16; 1 Kings 8:25; Isa. 9:6–7 [9:5–6 MT]; Ps. 110:4; 132:12; Mic. 4:7 with 5:1–4 [4:14–5:3 MT] portrays God's regal rule; esp. Dan. 7:14).[10] Second Temple Judaism also reflected this idea (Ps. Sol. 17.4; 1 Enoch 49.1; 62.14; 4Q174 [= 4QFlor] 1.11; 2 Bar. 73 [early second century]). The phrase *eis tous ainas* (into the ages; i.e., forever) parallels *ouk estai telos* (shall not be an end), emphasizing the everlasting duration of Jesus' rule. Luke–Acts makes clear that neither official Jewish rejection nor crucifixion will stop God's Davidic king. Israel's story will move on and never end.

These two core infancy account verses show how Luke roots Jesus' story in Israel's hope. There is little "Christianized" language here. Even the Greek style of the two chapters echoes the LXX to evoke the nation's story. The hope operates in continuity with God's promises.

Luke 1:68–69

Zechariah declares that the "God of Israel" has raised up a Davidic horn for his people. Zechariah's praise focuses on God's visitation in messianic redemption (Luke 1:68). This opening call to praise points to a praise psalm.[11] The language is that of Israel's national salvation, as the God of Israel is blessed in terms common in the Old Testament (Gen. 9:26; 1 Sam. 25:32; 1 Kings 1:48; Ps. 41:13 [41:14 MT]; 72:18; 89:52 [89:53 MT]; 106:48) and Second Temple Judaism (Tob. 3:11; Pss. Sol. 2.37). Such nationalistic features in Luke 1:68–69 argue against reading these verses as holding only "transferred Christian significance" for Luke. Israel is in view here, as Luke 1:71–73 confirms.

The basis of the praise (*hoti*, for) is God's visitation (Luke 1:68b), specifically God's redeeming (*lytrōsin*, setting free) his people. Ravens notes that "on the four occasions when Luke uses these words [for redemption] they always refer to 'Israel', never to Christians or Gentiles (Luke 1:68; 2:38; 24:21; Acts 7:35)."[12]

As the entire hymn will show, God's visitation comes through Messiah's visitation. Though Zechariah speaks in the past tense in part because Messiah is already conceived, his focus is on what is yet to happen through that Messiah (see the future tense verb *shall visit* in 1:78). For Luke, God's visitation means God's coming salvation in the Messiah Jesus (Luke 1:78; 7:16; 19:44; Acts 15:14).

What Messiah's visitation means for God's people is redemption, a deliverance from enemies, so that God's people are free to serve their God in righteousness and holiness. Luke 1:71 and 1:74–75 suggest a political connotation, especially since the God of Israel is addressed in terms parallel to the Psalms. This is restoration language, but is a political deliverance really in view?

Hendriksen argues that the context refers to a spiritual restoration only, citing 2:38 in support.[13] However, Luke 2 refers to Israel's consolation (2:25), to Jesus as a light to the Gentiles and a glory for his people Israel (2:32), and to Jerusalem's redemption (2:38). The latter phrase goes beyond spiritual restoration, as Luke 21:24, 28; 24:21; Acts 1:6; 3:19–26 suggest. These Lucan texts show that Jerusalem's redemption includes the Son of Man's rule and judgment on earth. The political connotation is not absent. Rather political redemption is delayed because of the nation's failure to respond (13:31–35; 19:44). Again, even though Gentiles are included in the blessing noted here, there is no indication their presence negates Israel's role in blessing. It is a complete *non sequitur* to argue that Gentile inclusion means Israel's exclusion.

Thus, redemption involves both political and spiritual elements, nationalistic themes (1:71, 74) and the offer of forgiveness (1:77–78). Zechariah praises God for the expectation of a total deliverance. Such a linkage between spiritual and political blessing is not surprising, since it parallels the blessing-and-curse sections of Deuteronomy. What is new is the division into two distinct phases tied to Jesus' two comings. Of course, Zechariah has no such twofold conception here: he simply presents the total package. Subsequent events explain the division and present a hope split into two parts due to the vindication of Israel's rejected Messiah.

Luke 2:25–34

Simeon, an old pious man, is awaiting Israel's consolation (*paraklēsin tou Israēl*; v. 25). Such consolation is a key theme in many strands of Old Testament and Second Temple Jewish eschatology that refer to Israel's deliverance (Isa. 40:1; 49:13; 51:3; 57:18; 61:2; 2 Bar. 44.7).

Echoing Isaiah 42:6, Simeon refers to Jesus as light, a revelation for the nations and glory for "your people Israel." In Luke, we do not choose between Israel and the nations. Rather, Israel's story is for the nations as well. Again, Gentile inclusion does not mean Israel's exclusion. The appearance of Jew and Gentile alongside each other is a theme of the infancy material. It is a theme one should never lose sight of in thinking about eschatology.

Luke, chapters 3–24
Luke 4:16–30
At the synagogue in Nazareth, Jesus declares that his Spirit-anointed ministry unfolded Israel's story described in Isaiah 61. Pointing to the time of Elijah and Elisha, and the healing of the widow of Zarephath and Naaman the Syrian, Jesus notes how in times past blessing bypassed Israel and went to the Gentiles. The warning to the nation is that if she rejects God's message, then blessing may not come to her but may go to Gentiles. Israel's story has an obstacle, her own rejecting heart. The question is whether that obstacle is permanent or not. Some may claim it is permanent. Israel has lost her place because she turned her back on God and the promise of Messiah. Later texts in Luke answer this question. So this result should not be assumed.

Luke 13:34–35
When substantial rejection comes out of Israel, Jesus warns the nation about the risk. In Luke 13:6–9, Jesus says that the vine that does not produce fruit will be cut down. Again the question surfaces, is this a permanent judgment against Israel?

This leads us into Luke 13:34–35, a crucial text. Luke 13 details the nature of the penalty Israel faces for "missing the time of her visitation" (Luke 19:41–44).

In Luke 13:34, Jesus speaks as a prophet of the Lord's repeated longing to gather the nation as a hen gathers her brood. The image of God as a bird is common in the Old Testament and Second Temple Jewish texts (Deut. 32:11; Ruth 2:12; Ps. 17:8; 36:7 [36:8 MT]; 57:1 [57:2 MT]; 61:4 [61:5 MT]; 63:7 [63:8 MT]; 91:4; Isa. 31:5; 2 Bar. 41.3–4; 2 Esdr. [= 4 Ezra] 1:30). The God of Israel's desire is to intimately care for, nurture and protect his people. The reference to repeated attempts to gather the nation might allude to the many prophets he sent throughout Israel's history. Only one thing stopped God from exercising his parental care: the people did not wish him to do so. As a result, the gathering and its protection could not take place. The same risk applies now to Jesus' offer.

In Luke 13:35, Jesus underscores the situation. Israel is in peril. The language of the empty, desolate house recalls Jeremiah 12:7 and 22:5 (cf. Ps. 69:25 [69:26 MT]; Ezek. 8:6; 11:23). The parallel in Matt. 23:39 mentions that the house is desolate (*ermos*), but Luke lacks this term.

The Old Testament declared the possibility of exile for the nation if it did not respond to God's call about exercising justice (Jer. 22:5–6). As such, Jesus' use of "house" (*oikos*) does not allude to the temple. Jesus is more emphatic than Jeremiah's statement of the nation's potential rejection; a time of abandoning exile has come. Rather than being gathered under God's wings, their house is empty and exposed (Luke 13:6–9). But for how long? It is important to recall that exile is not permanent. There is the hope of return and restoration, even in the midst of temporary judgment and isolation.

Jesus adds a note about the judgment's duration: Israel will not see God's messenger *until* they recognize "the one who comes in the name of the Lord" (*heōs ... eipēte eulogēmenos ho erchomenos en onomati kyriou*), from Psalm 117:26 LXX [118:26 Eng.]. Luke already made clear that the key term "one who comes" (*ho erchomenos*) means Messiah (Luke 3:15–16 and 7:19). Israel is to accept Jesus as sent from God. Until the nation accepts him, it stands alone, exposed to the world's dangers. The quotation from Ps. 118 is positive, not negative.[14] It suggests that Israel's judgment is only for a time.

Luke 21:24

This verse pictures a turnaround in Israel's fate. Near the end of the eschatological discourse, Luke describes Jerusalem being trodden down for a time and refers to this period as the "times of the Gentiles." What does this verse mean? It refers to a period of Gentile domination (Dan. 2:44; 8:13–14; 12:5–13), while alluding to a subsequent hope for Israel (Ezek. 39:24–29; Zech. 12:4–9). There are three reasons to maintain this reading.

First, the city's fall is of limited duration. Why else mention a time limit? The natural contrast to the times of the Gentiles would be a subsequent period including Israel again. This means that Luke sees a future for ethnic Israel, however he conceives of the new movement's relationship to the Jewish nation.

Second, there is a period in God's plan when Gentiles dominate, which implies that the subsequent period will be characterized by Israel's role.[15] Jesus' initial coming and his future eschatological return represent turning points in God's plan.

Third, this view of Israel's judgment now but vindication later suggests what Paul also contends in Romans 11:25–26: Israel has a future, grafted back in when the fullness of the Gentiles leads her to respond (see also Rom 11:11–12, 15, 30–32).[16] These chapters certainly have ethnic Israel in view, not any concept of a spiritual Israel. Romans 9–11 develops the temporary period of judgment noted in Luke 13:34–35.

It is crucial to understand that Romans 9–11 is about Israel, not a spiritualized Israel. The people Paul weep for in Romans 9:1–5, wishing he were cursed so they might be saved, are the same people he hopes for in "all Israel" in Romans 11. Nothing Paul says changes that audience for this hope in that section of Romans. In fact, the contrast in Romans 11 with Gentiles that leads into the *all Israel* claim makes it clear that ethnic Israel is in view in Romans 11. So Romans 11 matches the hope of Luke–Acts.

This means that the two most prolific authors of the New Testament declare a future hope for Israel.

Luke 24:21

These two passages in Luke 13:34–35 and 21:24 describe the hope that seemed to have been blocked by Jewish rejection of Jesus as Messiah. Jesus' death revived this hope as a result of resurrection, but immediately after the resurrection this was not yet clear. Luke 24:21 has one of the disciples still sorting out what the empty tomb meant. He says they had hoped Jesus would "redeem Israel" (*lytrousthai ton Israel*). This is the only time that Luke uses the verb *lytroō* (to redeem). If this hope is the same as what Zechariah expressed (1:68–79), then it included the connotation of a political release (cf. Isa. 41:14; 43:14; 44:22–24; 1 Macc. 4:11; Ps. Sol. 9.1).

Dillon's comment that Israel means broadly "the people of God" and not strictly the Jewish nation fails (1) to note the disappointment expressed here, (2) to take seriously the infancy narrative background, (3) to recall that part of the disappointment was that "our" chief priests and rulers handed Jesus over, and (4) the Jewish perspective that pervades the account.[17] The Jewish disciples in Luke 24:21 still think of Israel as a socio-political unit. They had hoped for her deliverance. Jesus' death had seemingly put an end to that hope. The prospect of the empty tomb was leaving the door open for that hope. But those speaking with Jesus on the Emmaus road had not put that puzzle together yet. This uncertainty fits the time period of the remarks, before the church operated as an autonomous unit. The focus on the nation in the early chapters of Acts adds to the weight of this interpretation.[18] Israel here means Israel. They were hoping for the nation's future.

So at the end of Luke's gospel, where are we? Israel's story remains and develops. None of the above Lucan texts we have focused on appear in Burge's *Jesus and the Land*. They represent a significant omission. To include Gentiles does not mean Israel has been excluded. Jesus comes for both groups. The judgment on Israel for rejecting her Messiah is a temporary one, like putting her in exile. That judgment does not mean the door on hope is closed for her. With a future return to faith in Messiah Jesus (calling on the name of the Lord), her place and role in blessing will be restored.

Does the book of Acts help to complete the picture?

Acts
Acts 1:4–7

On a literary level, the remark in Acts 1:4–5 points back to Luke 24:49. Jesus commands the disciples not to depart from Jerusalem but to begin the mission from there, waiting for the "promise of the Father" (*tēn epangelian tou patros*). The disciples perceive this event as an indication of the end's full arrival, which leads to their question in verse 6 about the restoration of the kingdom to Israel.

Many Jewish texts expected that Israel would be restored to a place of great blessing (Jer. 16:15; 23:8; 31:27–34 [where the new covenant is mentioned]; Ezek. 34–37; Isa. 2:2–4; 49:6; Amos 9:11–15; Sir. 48:10; Ps. Sol. 17–18; 1 En. 24–25; Tob. 13–14; Eighteen Benedictions 14).[19] The question is a natural one for Jews. Luke 1–2 expressed this hope vividly (1:69–74; 2:25, 38). What was debated in Judaism is whether the centrality of Israel would be positive or negative for Gentiles. Would it come with salvation or judgment for the nations? The disciples are not even thinking in mission terms here. Their question reflects a nationalistic concern for vindication. Nothing Jesus did or said in the forty days he was with them after his resurrection dissuaded them from this expectation. Neither does Jesus' answer. Nothing in Luke's story also should dissuade us from holding onto this hope for Israel. Gentile inclusion does not mean Israel's exclusion.

Neither does Jesus' reply in verses 7–8 reject the question's restoration premise. This reading following the Luke–Acts story line stands in contrast to interpretations such as Stott's, who sees the question as full of errors.[20] In Stott's view, the disciples should not have asked about restoration, since that implied a political kingdom; nor about Israel, since that anticipated a national kingdom; nor about "at this time," since that implied the kingdom's immediate establishment. Jesus' reply does not suggest that anything they asked was wrong except that they are excessively concerned about exactly when this will happen, something that is the Father's business.[21] The other major argument Stott makes is that there is no mention of the land in the New Testament. However, the land is not mentioned, since (1) Israel is in its land when all of the New Testament is written,[22] and (2) the rule of Jesus is anticipated to extend over the entire earth, so why focus on the land?

In fact, neither the definition of Israel nor the expectation for Israel changes. Rather, God's eschatological work is now centered in Jesus. Throughout Acts, Jesus is the blessing's mediator. Throughout Acts, Israel's role remains central to the hope of salvation, including the expectation of national restoration. Acts 10–15 works out this story as it extends the taking of the gospel into *all the* world.

Jesus does not answer the question about Israel's restoration and its timing. Nor is his response a renunciation of an imminent end.[23] It makes no commitment at all as to when the end comes. These verses show that the disciples are still thinking in terms of Israel's story. Nothing Jesus did or said in these key days altered their ultimate hope for the nation. What was changing was the scope of their assignment and concern. They were to take Messiah's message to the entire world. A global perspective was becoming more important as a part of Israel's story. God would take care of his business and promises to Israel one day. In the meantime, the disciples were and are to take the message of hope to the world.

Acts 3:18–21

In this speech Peter puts everything together and speaks of Jesus' return.[24] The "times of refreshing" (*kairoi anapsyxeōs*) refers to a future restoration.[25] *Anapsyxeōs* normally refers to a "cooling" to relieve trouble or to dry out a wound.[26] In the LXX the only use of refreshment is in Exodus 8:11 LXX (= 8:15 Eng.), where it refers to relief from the plague of frogs. The verb *anapsychō* (to refresh) is used of the Sabbath rest of slaves and animals and the soothing of Saul by David's music (Ex. 23:12; 1 Sam. 16:23). Peter prophesies a messianic refreshment, the "definitive age of salvation".[27] The idea has parallels in Second Temple Judaism (2 Esd. [4 Ezra] 7:75, 91, 95; 11:46; 13:26–29; 2 Bar. 73–74; 1 En. 45.5; 51.4; 96.3). Peter urges them to read what God has already said through the prophets. Texts such as Isaiah 65–66 are in view, where Israel is restored to fullness (also Isa. 34:4; 51:6; Jer. 15:18–19; 16:15; 23:8; 24:6; Ezek. 17:23; Amos 9:11–12). Nothing in any of this says that the story already revealed has been changed. God is faithful. He keeps his promises to Israel even as he extends himself to include the nations. Gentile inclusion does not preclude Israel's inclusion. The question is not if, but when. In the end, Israel also will be blessed.

In our narrative sequence, this is a crucial text. It tells us that what is to come was already disclosed. Whatever the expansion of the promise to Gentiles entails, it does not remove nor redefine Israel's story. When Peter says that what is to come is revealed in the "mouth of his holy prophets from of old" in Acts 3:21, he is saying God has revealed what he will do for Israel one day. You can still read about it in the Hebrew Scripture. Nothing God said there is changed by what Jesus did and does. God can add detail to his program and develop it, but that does not take place at the expense of what he has already revealed and committed himself to do for Israel.

Sometimes it is suggested this is a speech early on in Acts before Peter learned more about Gentile involvement. That point is correct. Peter did learn more about how Gentiles were included in God's program and plan as the book of Acts proceeds, but that does not mean the commitments to Israel changed. We have shown that Gentile inclusion does not mean Israel's exclusion. So as Peter learns more about Gentile blessing, that does not mean the promises and program for Israel have changed.

Summaries of Other Key Acts Texts: Acts 10–11; Acts 28:20

In the two passages involving Cornelius in Acts 10–11, the Spirit's coming shows that Gentiles are equal to Jews in blessing, so that circumcision is not required of Gentiles. The Spirit occupying uncircumcised Gentiles shows they are already cleansed and sacred.[28] The new era's sign comes to Gentiles as Gentiles. There is no need for them to become Jews. Israel's story has finally come to touch the world and bless the nations as Genesis 12:1–3 had said. God keeps his word to Gentiles as well as the Israel.

In Acts 28:20, Paul tells the Jews he is in chains for the hope of Israel. Paul is on trial for the hope of the twelve tribes (Acts 26:6–7).[29] Hope involves declaring light both to the people of Israel and Gentiles with a story from the prophets and Moses (Acts 26:22–23). Paul says that he "worships the God of the fathers, believing everything laid down by the law or written in the prophets, having a hope in God which they themselves accept that there will be a resurrection of both the just and unjust" (Acts 24:14–15). Paul tells Israel's story. Nothing suggests that the story has changed from the one told in the infancy material and the teaching of John, Jesus, and Peter. In Luke–Acts, this is one story.

Conclusion

For Luke–Acts, Israel's story has not changed and it is a story of hope for the world. Gentile inclusion does not mean Israel's exclusion. This warns us not to rewrite the story that the Torah and the Prophets give us about original Israel. We can add the nations into the promise through Christ, the ultimate seed, but we cannot lose sight of the hope in the promised one that belonged to original Israel and still exists for her.

Some contemporary readings of Paul and the New Testament suggest that we should change this story when we read those ancient texts and think of Israel in a different way that excludes or minimizes original Israel. However for Luke–Acts, Jesus' story is Israel's story, as well as a story that blesses the world. It anticipates a future time when Israel responds to Jesus and God restores the nation as the prophets promised. Israel and the nations one day will respond to God as one. This is where the hope of the land comes in, for when Jesus returns, it is to rule from Jerusalem. The times of the Gentiles will be over. Jesus, the glory of Israel, will bless the world with his presence. Israel and the world will be at peace because gentile inclusion completes Israel's inclusion as promise becomes reality for both groups. Reconciliation will be achieved, as will peace for all. In the meantime, the gospel goes out into the world for both Jew and Gentile to preview what is to come for Israel and the world.

For Further Reading

Bauckham, Richard. "The Restoration of Israel in Luke-Acts." Pages 435–87 in *Restoration: Old Testament, Jewish and Christian Perspectives*. Edited by James M. Scott. Leiden: Brill, 2001.

Bock, Darrell L. *The Real Lost Gospel: Reclaiming the Gospel as Good News*. Nashville: Broadman & Holman, 2010.

_____. "The Restoration of Israel in Luke-Acts," in *Introduction to Messianic Judaism*. edited by David Rudolph and Joel Willets. Grand Rapids: Zondervan, 2013, 168–77.

_____. *A Theology of Luke-Acts*. Grand Rapids: Zondervan, 2012.

Carras, George P. "Observant Jews in the Story of Luke and Acts." Pages 693–708 in *The Unity of Luke-Acts*. Edited by J. Verheyden. Leuven: Leuven University Press, 1999.

Fuller, Michael E. *The Restoration of Israel: Israel's Regathering and the Fate of the Nations in Early Jewish Literature and Luke-Acts*. Berlin: DeGruyter, 2006.

Hill, Craig C. "Restoring the Kingdom to Israel: Luke-Acts and Christian Supersessionism." Pages 185–200 in *Shadow of Glory: Reading the New Testament after the Holocaust*. Edited by Tod Linafelt. New York: Routledge, 2002.

Jervell, Jacob. *Luke and the People of God*. Minneapolis: Augsburg, 1972.

_____. *The Theology of the Acts of the Apostles*. Cambridge: Cambridge University Press, 1996.

LeCornu, Hilary and Joseph Shulam, *A Commentary on the Jewish Roots of Acts*. 2 vols. Jerusalem: Academon, 2003.

Ravens, David. *Luke and the Restoration of Israel*. Sheffield: Sheffield Academic Press, 1995.

Spencer, F. Scott. *The Gospel of Luke and Acts of the Apostles*. Nashville: Abingdon, 2008.

Tannehill, Robert C. *The Narrative Unity of Luke-Acts: A Literary Interpretation*. 2 vols. Minneapolis: Fortress Press, 1990.

_____. *The Shape of Luke's Story: Essays on Luke-Acts*. Eugene, OR: Cascade, 2005.

Tyson, Joseph B., ed. *Luke-Acts and the Jewish People: Eight Critical Perspectives*. Minneapolis: Augsburg, 1988.

Wendel, Susan J. *Scriptural Interpretation and Community Self-Definition in Luke-Acts and the Writings of Justin Martyr*. Leiden: Brill, 2011

Study Questions

1. What is the position that argues Israel does not have a future?

2. What books of the New Testament does this position ignore?

3. What passages in Luke 1–2 point to a concern for Israel?

4. Name the "until" texts in Luke–Acts that are relevant for thinking through a future for Israel.

5. What does Luke 13:34–35 teach?

6. What does Luke 21:21–24 teach?

7. Why would one discuss times of the Gentiles being fulfilled and what would follow it?

8. What does Acts 3:18–22 teach?

9. Which OT texts might one think Peter is alluding to in Acts 3:18–22?

10. How does Romans 9–11 fit into what Luke–Acts shows?

11. How would you explain what is at stake in the view Israel does have a future as a people?

12. Does Gentile inclusion mean Israeli exclusion? Why or why not?

Conference Video

chosenpeople.com/bock

Interview with Dr. Darrell L. Bock

chosenpeople.com/bock-interview

THE JEWISH PEOPLE ACCORDING TO THE BOOK OF ROMANS

Dr. Michael G. Vanlaningham

Vanlaningham, in his chapter *The Jewish People according to the Book of Romans*, shows why it is crucial for God to keep His promises to Israel. He argues, "if God breaks His promises to Israel then how can the Church trust God?" The chapter explores what Paul says about the future of Israel and the relationship of the Jewish people to the Land.

The bulk of the chapter addresses aspects of Romans 9–11. This section begins with Paul listing nine blessings of being part of Israel, "my kinsman" (9:3–5). Four of these privileges have implications for the land. Israel's blessing to the world looks into the future, creating a distinction between Israel and the world (11:12–15). This seems to depict God reigning over Israel in her land and allowing His blessing to flow to the world. The statement "all Israel will be saved," has led to significant discussion, particularly in reference to the identity of "Israel" (11:25–29).

Vanlaningham concludes his chapter by reminding us that the issues at stake go beyond the role of Israel and the Jewish people in the plan of God—it is not only about Israel, it is about God's character and His faithfulness to His promises.

Introduction

One of the classes I teach at the Moody Bible Institute is "The Epistle to the Romans," which I've taught more than thirty times. When I come to my introductory considerations of Romans 9, I always ask my students, "Have you ever had anyone important to you make a promise that was not kept?" I follow up with the question, "How did that make you feel?" Predictably, the answers range from "I felt betrayed" to "I felt as if I were completely unimportant" to "It was a stab to my heart I've never gotten over."

We want others to keep their promises to us, and we should keep our promises. But what if God were to break His promises to us? What if He broke His promises about working all things together for good (Rom. 8:28) or nothing separating us from God's love (Rom. 8:39)? God is faithful, and we can count on Him to keep all His promises. Or can we?

What about the promises He has made to Israel, many described in the earlier chapters of Romans? Are the Jewish people still the special people of God? What about the land promised to them? Do they have any ongoing claim to the land God promised the patriarchs, or have those promises been rescinded?

The purpose of this chapter is to explore what the apostle Paul says about the future of the Jewish people as a nation and their future relationship to the Holy Land. There are several passages in Romans that are informative about his view of this vexing question. The procedure will be to consider those passages and to provide a brief response to the scholars who claim that the apostle sees no future for Israel in its Promised Land.

Hermeneutical Groundwork

Those who believe that the Church fulfills[1] the promises to Israel, and that Israel has no claim to its land, are committed to three hermeneutical strategies.[2] First the OT must be reinterpreted in light of the NT, and the NT has pride of place in Scripture. Second, the Church must be viewed as the typological fulfillment of the people and nation of Israel. Third, the fulfillment proponents claim that many of the promises made to Israel in the OT have a spiritual fulfillment in the Church and cannot be invoked as an argument in support of a future for national Israel.

The hermeneutical differences between those who defend the fulfillment view of the Church as the New Israel, and those who argue that God will fulfill all of His national and spiritual promises for Israel, are palpable. I deny that Paul introduces a theological novelty (i.e., Israel no longer has a right to its own land) lacking continuity with the OT. I deny that he sees Israel's promises as an expired OT type fulfilled by the Church. Furthermore, I deny that Paul spiritualizes the promises God made to Israel about its national status and possession of the land. An examination of the relevant texts in Romans will attempt to demonstrate that the apostle did not allot Israel's privileges to the Church.

I. Heir of the World (Rom. 4:13)

The controversy with this verse centers on the phrase "heir of the world." Gary Burge argues that in the one place Paul explicitly connects Abraham's heirs with the possession of land, it is not the land of Israel they stand to inherit, but the entire world. On this reading, then, Paul removes the land promise from Israel and assigns to it spiritual promises directed now to the Church consisting in Jewish and Gentile believers who will possess the entire world.

Paul does universalize Israel's land promise. But Burge's claim that this removes Israel's privilege of the land is built upon some shaky logic. Several points suggest this. First, it appears logically fallacious to argue that if Abraham and his diverse family inherit the world, the land of Israel is excluded for the Jewish believers. When this time of inheritance comes, will Jewish believers have a right to New York and not Netanya? Will they possess Tokyo but not Tel Aviv? Will Jewish believers have possession of Jamaica but not Jerusalem? Even if one grants the universalizing of the land promise, this does not eliminate the possibility that Israel might still possess its Promised Land as its share in the inherited world.

Second, admittedly, the OT does not explicitly say that Israel will inherit the world. Neither is the word "land" as it relates to Israel's inheritance found in Romans 4. However, this does not mean that it has no role to play in Paul's argument.[3] Abraham's spiritual paternity involves "offspring." It is this offspring in Romans 4:13 that inherits the world. "Offspring" is used again in Romans 4:18, where "offspring" encompasses both Israel and "many nations." The Abrahamic Covenant guarantees blessings to the nations who bless Abraham and his seed (Gen. 12:2–3; 18:18; 22:16–18; 26:4). In the OT the blessings for the nations come as God restores, prospers, and multiplies Abraham's seed (specifically the Jewish people) who will then "possesses the gates of his enemies" (Gen. 22:17; similarly 24:60). It is by the inestimable seed from Abraham's own loins who spreads and possesses other lands that the blessing of the nations comes about as Genesis 22:16–18 suggests, and as found in other connections where the Abrahamic Covenant is reiterated (to Isaac in Gen. 26:4, and to Jacob in Gen. 28:14).[4]

A similar promise is found in Isaiah 54:1–3 where Israel, the barren, desolate woman without children, will become so numerous as to expand, and in the process "will possess the nations" as Israel stretches out from Zion. "Possess" could be translated "inherit," and in the LXX the verb is *klēronomeō*, a cognate of the noun *klēronomos* Paul used in Romans 4:13 translated "heir." Isaiah 60:3 says that when Israel begins to reflect God's glory nations will come to its light.[5]

But the question arises: How does this relate to Abraham's physical fatherhood of Israel and spiritual fatherhood of Gentiles in Romans 4? In the OT, the blessings God promised for the entire world appear to be mediated through blessed Israel. And these are not spiritual blessings alone. The blessings Abraham experienced for himself were multidimensional, having not only spiritual components but economic (Gen. 13:2; 24:35) and social components as well (Abraham had a good reputation among people; 2 Chron. 20:7; James 2:23). Paul asserts that these are now promised to his physical and spiritual descendants. Abraham had faith that God would fulfill what He had promised, but what Abraham was promised must not be reduced to spiritual blessings. What we have here, in Romans 4, is the end of the process of Israel's being blessed by God and that blessing being mediated through the people to the nations.

This process presupposes the presence of Israel in its own land precisely so that God can bless the Jewish people and bring about the blessing to the nations (see for example Deut. 4:5-6; 26:18–19; Ps. 67:1–2, 7; 102:13–14; Isa. 52:7–10; 55:3–5; Ezek. 36:22–36; 39:27). Israel's final preparation for such a role will come when God institutes the New Covenant blessings which will bring about a spiritual restoration that has implications for Israel's mediatorial role for the Gentile world. Ezekiel 36:25–29 is a New Covenant passage bracketed by promises of Israel restored to its own land in vv. 24 and 28, with this restoration and blessing having implications for the spiritual awakening of the nations in v. 36. Another New Covenant text, Jeremiah 31:31–37, concludes in vv. 35–37 with God's promise to institute the New Covenant with national Israel.[6] Similar concepts are found in the literature of Early Judaism that does make explicit Israel's inheriting the world (see Sir. 44:21; *1 Enoch* 5:7; *Mek. Exod.* 14:31 (40[b]); *Jub.* 22:14; 32:18–19).[7]

What these texts seem to indicate is that God, in the Abrahamic Covenant, launches a theological arrow that pierces the whole OT and the literature of Early Judaism and lands squarely at the feet of Paul which he also takes up. Because of the promises bound up in the Abrahamic Covenant, Israel *as a nation in her own land* will prosper at the hand of God, expand into the nations, and as the Gentiles see God's beneficence to the Jewish people, Israel becomes a conduit of His grace to bless them so that God is glorified. Rather than removing the privilege of the land from Israel, Paul appears to affirm it. Abraham's seed, with its constituency made up of both believing Jews and Gentiles, will inherit the entire world in this fashion.

It is possible, of course, that Paul introduces a complete doctrinal novelty at this point and disregards the OT themes explored above.[8] It is also possible that Paul sees a diffusing of the promises to Israel in the Abrahamic Covenant and the prophets to include Gentiles in the people of God so that the guarantees of Israel's land become irrelevant. But it is not necessary to ascribe this view to Paul. Inheriting the world is Paul's way of describing how Abraham's physical offspring (the Jewish people) "will possess the gates of his enemies," expand into the Gentile nations of the world, and be used by God to bless those nations. It is preferable, precisely because the OT and Early Judaism indicate that Israel will inherit the world, to place Paul in continuity with the OT teaching rather than in contrast to it.

II. Blessings for Israel (Rom. 9:3–5)

Some of the fulfillment advocates deny from these verses that Israel has any future right to the land. Stephen Sizer writes regarding Romans 9, "Significantly, Paul omits only one blessing, the land. There is no suggestion in Romans that the future salvation of the Jews is related in any way to the land."[9]

There are several points that support the view that these blessings, while the privilege of Israel as both a nation and a people in the past, continue to be the special privilege of Israel, even *unbelieving* Israel, in the present with implications regarding the land as well. Paul's anxiety relates to the unbelieving Israel in his day who stood in a position of being accursed (*anathema*, v. 3). Yet he ascribes to them nine blessings, all said to belong to "my kinsmen" in the present ("who *are* Israelites . . . .").[10] Four of these privileges have special implications for the land.

First, "the covenants" may be more-or-less synonymous with the phrase "the promises" coming later in the list. In support of this is his plural use of "covenants" with the word "promise" in Ephesians 2:12, where Paul appears to distinguish the promissory covenants (namely, the Abrahamic, the Davidic, and New Covenants) from the Law as an administrative covenant (Eph. 2:15). The use of the plural "covenants" and "promises" later suggests that it would be arbitrary to restrict the referent to just one covenant (e.g., the Abrahamic Covenant), or just one aspect of one covenant (e.g., the spiritual blessings).

Second, the word "worship" ("the temple service," NASB) in the LXX is used for observing the Passover or feast of the unleavened bread (Ex. 12:25–26; 13:5), for sacrifices (Josh. 22:27), for the general priestly work in the Temple (1 Chron. 28:13; see also Heb. 9:1, 6). These required the presence of a temple and a city in which to house it, Jerusalem.[11] Sizer surely goes too far in claiming that Paul omits all hints of the land in this list.

Third, "the promises" should not be restricted to a single referent, such as the spiritual or salvific aspects of the New Covenant. Nevertheless, Paul uses the plural of the word twice in connection with "the fathers" as he does here (in Rom. 15:8, for which see below, and in Gal. 3:16). When he does, Paul seems to have in mind especially the Abrahamic Covenant and its multidimensional features (salvation, a vast seed, blessings to the Gentiles). But in the context of Romans 9, he offers no such restrictions as to the referent of "the promises."

Fourth, "fathers" refers to Abraham, Isaac, and Jacob. "Fathers" also appears in Romans 11:29 (see the discussion on these verses below). Taken in connection with "the covenants" and "the promises," the probable sense of "the fathers" in this section is to emphasize "the covenantal promises made to the fathers." Those promises are still valid, still relevant for the people of Israel, making it difficult to believe that Paul sees no distinct future for Israel as a nation living in its own land. Even unbelieving Israel in Paul's day—and our own—continues to have these prerogatives promised by God. They imply an as-yet future fulfillment in keeping with God's faithfulness.

III. Blessings for the World (Rom. 11:12, 15)

The important observation related to Israel's possession of the land relates to the blessings that accrue to the Gentile world at the time of Israel's "fulfillment" (v. 12) and "acceptance" (v. 15). O. Palmer Robertson emphasizes the pattern which includes the rejection of the Messiah by the Jewish people, belief by Gentiles, the jealous provoking of Jews, and their resultant faith. Each of these occurrences happens during the present era, even Israel's acceptance, on the basis of what Paul says in Romans 11:30–31.[12] Palmer is correct to emphasize the realization of this cycle during the present era, including Israel's full inclusion (v. 11) and acceptance (v. 15). But Palmer flattens out precisely how it comes about. There is a more definite temporal sequence of distinct events than he sees. Specifically, in Paul's day, the majority of the Jewish people were hardened. There were a few Jews like Paul who had embraced Jesus, but Paul does not connect the riches for the Gentiles (v. 11), the reconciliation of the world nor life from the dead (v. 15) to the faith of the remnant in his day. These blessings for the world await Israel's fullness, that is, its restored "full number" (v. 11) and acceptance (v. 15).[13] Paul envisions this taking place during the present era, but in the future of it, not quite in his own day.

The precise identity of "life from the dead" in v. 15 is beyond the scope of this chapter. In light of the use of similar phrases in Romans 4:17 and 6:13, it probably refers to spiritual revivification rather than the general resurrection, so that what Paul foresees is a time when the Gentile world erupts with spiritual life following Israel's restoration. What must not be missed is the distinction between restored Israel and blessed Gentile nations in the future. What happens to Israel triggers unparalleled blessings for the Gentile world. Paul thus envisions a distinction between Israel and the world in the future that cannot be explained by an amalgamated people of God in the Church as the new Israel. His words are best accounted for if Israel is present in its own land and the blessings for the world flow from the nation under God's governance in accordance with OT expectations.

IV. All Israel Will be Saved (11:25–29)

The questions that will concern us in this passage are: "What does Paul mean when he refers to 'Israel' in this passage? Is Paul redefining the term to refer to the Church as the 'new Israel?' Is there any room here for these verses indicating a wide-spread conversion of the Jewish people *along with a restoration in their own land?*"

A. The identification of "Israel" in the phrase "All Israel"

N. T. Wright argues that "Israel" must be understood as a reference to the Church consisting in both Jewish and Gentile believers.[14] He supports this with four arguments.[15]

First, Wright argues that the reason there is no distinct future for Israel as a nation is because Israel has been fulfilled by her Messiah and His people, the Church. All of God's covenant purposes and promises for Israel have been fulfilled by the Messiah, who is the ultimate representative of the Jewish people.[16] The blessings of the Abrahamic Covenant are put into effect through Christ and are now found in connection only with Him, not Israel, and are the sole prerogative of His people attached to Him by faith, namely the Church consisting in both Jewish and Gentile believers.[17]

In response to Wright on this point, on a purely logical level there is nothing in what he maintains that rules out the possibility of a distinct future for ethnic and national Israel. Even if Christ fulfills the promises made to Israel, and those promises are fulfilled only in Him and derivatively applied to the Church during the present era, there is nothing either in Paul or in Wright that precludes God revisiting His covenant promises to Israel and fulfilling all of them. Nowhere does Paul indicate that the spiritual condition of Israel in his day was to be a permanent condition.

Second, Wright maintains that the term "Israel" loses its ethnic distinctiveness when Paul uses it especially in Romans. It takes on a more universalized, comprehensive scope than simply national or ethnic Israel. When "Israel" is employed by Paul in Romans 9:30–10:21, it has already shifted in its referent to all those who have faith in Christ so that "Israel" is a mixed group absent of any ethnic or national specificity.[18] The true family of Abraham consists in members broader than his physical descendants, and include *"all* who share the faith of Abraham" (Rom. 4:16) both Jews and Gentiles.[19]

Wright's argument contains an apparent inconsistency. In *Climax of the Covenant,* he offers no substantial exegetical warrant for asserting that "Israel" becomes universalized. But in his Romans commentary, each place *Israël* is used, he assigns to it the meaning everyone else has always assigned to it, namely "the Jewish people," not "the people of God consisting in Jewish and Gentile believers."[20] And regarding Wright's view of Romans 4 in which he proposes that Paul applies the land promises to the Church, see the discussion above on Romans 4:13.

Third, Wright argues that the meaning of "Israel" in 11:26 is different from the meaning of "Israel" in 11:25. He claims that such redefining is typical of Paul. For instance, the apostle redefines "Israel" in 9:6 to refer to the Church. When Paul says "all Israel will be saved," "all" must be understood to include Gentiles in light of the universal aspect of "all" in Romans 10:11–13 (*"all* who call upon Him will not be put to shame"; *"all* who call on the name of the Lord will be saved"). Paul reapplies "the Lord" in Romans 10:13, which cites Joel 3:5 where it refers to the LORD, to Jesus, signaling yet again his tendency to redefine terms. These considerations lend support to "all Israel" referring to the Church, and to Paul's denial of a distinct future for ethnic and national Israel.[21]

On this point, Wright refers to several wide-ranging and contextually remote points to support his contentions, and addressing many of these are beyond the scope of this chapter.[22] But Wright's claim that Paul redefines "Israel" in 11:26 can be challenged on several levels. Thomas R. Schreiner draws attention to the contextual clues:

> When salvation is promised to "all Israel" in Romans 11:26, it is difficult to believe that Israel should be defined differently in verse 26 than in verse 25. It is scarcely clear that Paul suddenly lurches to a new definition so that verse 25 refers to ethnic Israel whereas verse 26 refers to spiritual Israel. In both verses Paul refers to ethnic Israel, but verse 25 describes the hardening of most of Israel during the time when Gentiles are converted, and verse 26 promises the future salvation of ethnic Israel. Is it possible, though, that Paul suddenly shifts the definition of Israel in verse 26? Yes, it is possible, but the succeeding context reveals that it is implausible and unpersuasive. Romans 11:28–29 confirms that ethnic Israel is the subject of Romans 11:26, for they are enemies of the gospel, but they are beloved by God and the recipients of God's irrevocable promises because of God's covenantal promises to the patriarchs. Paul does not restate his argument in Romans 11:28–29 by conceiving of Israel in a spiritual sense, as if Israel comprises believing Jews and Gentiles. Rather, he emphasizes again that ethnic Israel is the object of God's saving and elect love because of God's

sovereign and effective grace. No contextual warrant appears for widening the definition of Israel. The climax of the mystery is that God will pour out his grace again on ethnic Israel, the children of Abraham, Isaac, and Jacob.[23]

In addition, Wright offers no substantial comment on the phrase "until the fullness of the Gentiles has come in." He says that the salvation of all Israel (the Church) happens continually throughout the church age.[24] But the presence of "until" undermines this point. If there is a hardening upon Israel *until* the fullness of the Gentiles arrives, then one cannot say that all Israel which is the Church is being saved throughout the present era. The future tense of "will be saved" also undermines Wright's contention.[25] Paul is not envisioning the iterative process of deliverance for the Church throughout history. He foresees a widespread conversion of ethnic Israel in the future. Wright's references to more remote contexts in Paul cannot trump the immediate context of 11:25–29.

Before leaving "all Israel" in 11:26a, four observations may be helpful. First, Paul probably draws upon the LXX for his use and understanding of "all Israel." The phrase refers to a large representation of Jewish people from most locales or tribes depending on the context. Rarely "all Israel" refers to the entirety of the twelve tribes (Ex. 18:25; 1 Chron. 12:38; 2 Chron. 30:1, 5, 6); more often to representative groups from the twelve tribes or from the northern tribes after the secession (1 Sam. 4:5; 2 Sam. 10:17; 1 Kings 8:65; 2 Chron. 31:1), and sometimes exclusively for the northern tribes (1 Sam. 18:16; 1 Kings 12:1, 16, 18, 20). In addition, "all Israel" could refer narrowly to a group of soldiers (1 Kings 11:16), to the Jewish people who buried Samuel (1 Sam. 25:1), to those who were in close proximity to Korah at his demise (Num. 16:34), and those who apostatized along with Rehoboam (2 Chron. 12:1). It always refers to a specific group as suggested by the context.[26] Not often does it refer comprehensively to every Jewish person without exception. If it is possible to propose a common denominator for the phrase "all Israel" in the LXX upon which Paul may be drawing, it might be that it means "the Jewish people," those specified in the context by the phrase "all Israel." If this is the case, then by "all Israel" Paul may mean simply "the Jewish people" without referring to every Jew universally.

Second, the phrase "all Israel," even when it is most comprehensive in its scope, is never used diachronically (throughout all time), but only synchronically (at specific points in time) in the LXX. Even when "all Israel" refers to all the Jewish people being led by the Lord in the wilderness, "all Israel" refers specifically to that group at that particular point in time. It never refers to the Jewish people throughout all of time, or throughout the entire span of the Church age. This supports the futurist view of all Israel being saved. This is "all Israel" being saved at a point in the future, not throughout church history by turning to Jesus in faith and becoming a part of the Church.

Third, it is "all Israel" that will be saved. The Jewish people in Paul's day occupied the Land though they were under the dominion of Rome. While Paul saw the salvation of a vast Jewish people in the future potentially all over the world, it seems unreasonable to argue that their future salvation would be irrelevant to their possession of their own Land. They were already there, dwelling in it. It makes little sense to argue that it would not belong to them when the Jewish people who lived there became spiritually right with God.[27] When the Jewish people turn to their Messiah, will God put up a fence around Israel with signs on it that say, "Jewish people not allowed"?

Fourth, Paul is coy about placing the salvation of all Israel within the wider eschatological landscape. Two passages are informative on this question: Matthew 23:39 and Acts 3:19–21. Both indicate that before Jesus will return to Israel, Israel must repent, and the repentance functions as a virtual prerequisite for the second coming.[28] Along with this, Paul embraces the hope of Israel being saved "now," during the current age, based on Romans 11:30–31.

B. Evidence from Isaiah 59 and 27 in Romans 8:26b–27

Consideration of these verses will focus on the question, "Does Paul's use of Isaiah 59:20–21 have any bearing on the question of whether or not Israel has a future in its own land?" Christopher R. Bruno's article is extremely helpful in this. He writes, " . . . Romans 9–11, Isaiah 59:20–21, 27:9, and 2:3 all center on similar themes: God's faithfulness to his covenant people, the inclusion of the nations, and the salvation of Israel."[29] The LORD vanquishes His enemies (Isa. 59:16–17), renews the covenant and returns to Zion (59:20–21), and blesses the nations (a point drawn from the broader context of Isaiah 56—66, and implicit in 59:19). Similarly, in Isaiah 27, the LORD returns to Zion and renews the covenant (27:6), defeats His enemies and removes sin from Israel (27:1, 9), and blesses the nations (27:12–13).[30]

In his citation of Isaiah 59:20–21, Paul appears to have in mind the blessing of the nations in the wake of Israel's restoration as well.[31] He draws heavily upon the themes of God's unilateral work to rescue Israel (Isa. 59:16–19), and the theme of Israel's sinfulness (Isa. 59:2–15) in spite of which God acts for the people. He also draws on the theme of the nations sharing Israel's wealth (see Isa. 60:5 and Rom 11:12 in which the words *ploutos*, "riches," and *ethnōn*, "nations" [or "Gentiles"] are used). The theme of God's mercy (LXX, the noun *eleon*) in Isaiah 60:10 is echoed in Romans 11:31. In both verses, God's mercy comes upon Israel after punishment by God. If the thematic connections extend from Isaiah 59 into Isaiah 60, then it is likely that Israel's restoration has a national component as well, suggested by Isaiah 60:1–4. In 60:21, the prophet states explicitly that, as part of the matrix of Israel's restoration and the blessing of the nations, the Jewish people "shall possess the land forever." Isaiah 27:9 is located in a broader context of Isaiah 24–27, a well-recognized unit called Isaiah's "Little Apocalypse." In this context, it has numerous themes in common with Isaiah 59:20–21, namely, God's personal presence to reign over Israel (24:23; 25:6–7), and cleansing the nation (26:16–19; 27:9–10). But Israel's deliverance has international implications as the Gentile nations share in Israel's blessings (24:14–16a; 25:6–10a).[32] Found among this mix of themes is the anticipation that the Lord will "increase the nation" and enlarge "all the borders of the land" (26:15; see also Isa. 27:12–13 for national implications in the immediate context).

Paul has the spiritual restoration of Israel primarily in view in Romans 11:26–27. Paul did insert from Isaiah 27:9 forgiveness of Jacob's sin, a matter not included in the longer Isaiah 59:20–21 portion of the citation. But the contexts of these verses open the door on the likelihood that Paul viewed the salvation of all Israel as having the power to bless the Gentile nations, just as Paul proposed in Romans 11:12 and 15.

C. Evidence from Romans 11:28–29

What clues are there in these two verses that shed light on the identity of "all Israel" in Romans 11:26? Several items point toward ethnic and national Israel being in view.

First, the "enemies" are contrasted with "you" (translated "your" in the phrase "for your sake" in the NASB). This makes it unlikely that "all Israel" in Romans 11:26 is the Church consisting in Jewish and Gentile believers, for that would require that the Church simultaneously be "enemies of the gospel" and "beloved because of the fathers," surely an unlikely interpretation.[33]

Second, there is an untranslated "on the one hand . . . but on the other hand" construction here that suggests the dual elements of antagonism to the gospel *and* being beloved by God existed simultaneously for the same group, unbelieving Israel, at the present time.

Third, Waymeyer draws several provocative contextual connections between Romans 11:28–29 and the wider context of Romans 11. He maintains that 11:28 describes a dual status for Israel. Israel's enmity in 11:28a is reflected previously in chapter 11 ("stumble" and "transgression," v. 11; "transgression," v. 12; "rejection," v. 15), and is also reflected in 11:28a by their animosity to the gospel. But 11:28b presents the second side of Israel's current status, utilizing two prepositional phrases: "but according to election [or "in keeping with" election] [they are] beloved" and "on account of the fathers." "Fathers" is a reference to the Jewish patriarchs as supported and nourished by the covenant promises of God (see the comments on 9:5 above). The substantiation for Israel's on-going status as "beloved" comes in 11:29. The "gifts and calling of God" refer to the covenant promises whereby God called Abraham and his offspring to be in a special loving relationship with Himself. Paul's readers can know that Israel's perpetual status as God's beloved people has not waned even though she was opposed to the gospel. Waymeyer concludes,

> On the one hand the unbelieving nation of Israel is an enemy of God, but on the other she is beloved by Him. When the partial hardening of Israel is removed at the end of the present age (Rom. 11:25), her present "transgression" will give way to her "fulfillment" (Rom. 11:12); her present "rejection" will give way to her "acceptance" (Rom. 11:15); and the natural branches will be grafted back in (Rom. 11:23–24). And in this manner, all Israel will be saved in accordance with God's covenantal love and in fulfillment of His promise (Rom. 11:26–27). God has not, and will not, forsake His chosen nation.[34]

And what are "the gifts and calling of God?" While Paul primarily has salvation in mind in Romans 4:4 and 16 (where "grace" also occurs), in 11:29, "gifts" is plural and implies that Paul is thinking multi-dimensionally about the blessings of God to the patriarchs.[35] It would be arbitrary to limit "the gifts" only to the salvific aspects of the Abrahamic Covenant.[36] These promises are "irrevocable," referring to "something one does not take back,"[37] and the initial aspects of their fulfillment will begin "now," in this era, future to Paul but before the second coming.[38]

V. Jesus Christ, Servant to Confirm the Promises (Rom. 15:8–12)

The syntax of Romans 15:8–9 is both unclear and convoluted. Mark A. Seifrid[39] presents a good case for the following understanding:

(v. 8)   Christ became a servant
    (a)   of the circumcision for the truthfulness [faithfulness] of God,
    (b)   in order to confirm the promises to the fathers

    and

(v. 9)   [Christ became a servant of the circumcision]
    (a')   for the sake of mercy with reference to the Gentiles
    (b')   in order for [Christ] to glorify God . . . .

"The Gentiles" could be the subject of v. 9, but Christ is the more likely subject since He is the one who glorifies God in 15:7 and since the OT verses following vv. 8–9 all refer to the actions of the Messiah whereby Gentiles are led to glorify God. In vv. 9b–12, it is the Messiah who is speaking as in 15:3. The citations that follow vv. 8–9 are drawn from the three divisions of the Hebrew Scriptures—the writings, Psalm 18:49 (LXX 17:50; MT 18:50) cited in 15:9b and Psalm 117:1 (LXX 116:1; MT 117:1) in 15:11, the Law (Deut. 32:43) cited in 15:10, and the prophets (Isa. 11:10) cited in 15:12, providing diverse support for what Paul says here.[40]

But the noteworthy point is that Jesus' ministry is distinct for Israel *vis-à-vis* the Gentiles. For the Jewish people, Jesus' life and death establishes the covenant promises made to the fathers. For the Gentiles, Jesus' life and death *on behalf of Israel* is with respect to the Gentiles' reception of mercy so that He might glorify God. What this means is that there is a practical distinction between the intent of Christ's death for Israel and for Gentiles, suggesting that Israel does not just get folded into the predominantly Gentile Church. They remain distinct. And the promises (note the plural) to the fathers that He establishes include the promise to possess the Land after which the Gentiles are blessed.

Seifrid notes that Paul "makes a significant theological statement— As the servant of the circumcision, the Messiah also acts with respect to the Gentiles—that is, for their benefit. Perhaps there are faint echoes here of the Isaianic Servant Songs, in which the Servant's mission to Israel becomes salvation for the nations (Isa. 42:1–4; 49:1–6; 52:13— 53:12)."[41] If this connection is correct, then, as argued above especially on 4:13; 11:26b–27, 29, salvation for the nation comes in the wake of Israel's spiritual and national deliverance. Bell writes, "the promise of the land is made more concrete through Jesus Christ. For by becoming a servant of the circumcision, he has confirmed the promises made to the patriarchs. Jesus Christ does not make the promises to Israel less concrete; he makes them more concrete."[42]

Conclusion

When I was ten, my Dad planned a father-and-son weekend fishing trip to Lake Lenice in eastern Washington. I remember how we prepared our air mattresses and sleeping bags in the back of our 1952 Plymouth station wagon, which was the size of Wyoming. And I remember how, as we snuggled together before falling to sleep, he told me how he and his Dad planned several father-son campouts when he was little, and how his Dad let other matters get in the way of their retreats. They never went. How well I remember the sadness in his voice as he told me, even maybe with a whisper of bitterness, but mainly sadness. He was so thrilled to be able to take me on this trip, and it was the first of many others. These are precious memories to me.

It's painful when someone important to us breaks his or her promises. What if God could not be counted on to keep His promises? When it is implied that God cannot be counted on to keep His promises to Israel, what makes us think He would keep His promises to us *in Christ*? Shouldn't we be able to trust in God's promises, such as, "God causes all things to work together for good," and "nothing will separate us from the love of God" at the end of Romans 8, which immediately precedes Paul's discussion about Israel's situation with God in Romans 9?

I have attempted to show the continuity between Paul and the OT. Both indicate that Israel will experience the judgment of God because of its sinfulness, deliverance by God in spite of this, the restoration of the people to their own land with inestimable blessings that are both spiritual (including salvation) and material. As God does this, He will utilize Israel to funnel His blessings to the Gentile nations, blessings that also include spiritual and material dimensions. And both indicate that this will happen in connection with the Messiah. God will keep all His promises to Israel. He will keep all His promises to believers, both Jewish and Gentile ones.

Study Questions

1. What do you consider to be the strongest argument that indicates Paul believed Israel had a right to possess the land God promised it? What do you consider to be the weakest argument?

2. How do you feel about so much of the future blessings that will come on the Gentile world being based on what God will do in and through Israel?

3. What implications do Paul's words have for Christian anti-Semitism?

4. Do you think Bible-believing Christians should be supportive of Israel? Why or why not?

5. Do you think Bible-believing Christians should be antagonistic toward Palestinians? Why or why not?

6. Fulfillment theologians decry the concept that the nation of Israel has a future in its own land. What would be gained if the Jewish people do not have a future in their own land? What would be lost?

7. Consider your own church's stance and ministry as it relates to Israel. In light of what Paul says about Israel's future, what might need to change at your church? How might these changes be brought about?

8. In Romans 4:13, Abraham's seed is "heir of the world." Does this phrase indicate Paul pictures a different future for Israel and his Gentile "spiritual children" than Abraham was told by God? Why or why not?

9. "It is arbitrary for fulfillment theologians to maintain that 'the covenants,' 'the promises,' and God's guarantees to 'the patriarchs' in Romans 9:4–5 only relate to the forgiveness of sins found in the Abrahamic and New Covenants." Do you agree or disagree with this statement? Please explain why.

10. Based on the treatment of Romans 11:12 and 15 (the future "full inclusion" and "acceptance" of the Jewish people), how likely is the position that says that in the future, restored Israel is included in the Church and is not distinct from Gentile believers?

11. Some fulfillment theologians maintain that "Israel" in Romans 11:25 and "Israel" in 11:26a have different meanings. They say in 11:25, it refers to the Jewish people, but in 11:26a it refers to the Church, consisting in believing Jews and Gentiles, as the new Israel. What evidence do you see that supports this view? What evidence is there that this view is unlikely?

12. Paul draws substantiation for his assertion that "all Israel will be saved" from Isaiah 50:29 and 27:9. What do those OT verses and their contexts contribute to Paul's understanding of the future of the Jewish people in their own land?

13. In Romans 11:28, what is the most likely referent of the word "enemies?" If "all Israel" is the Church, the new Israel, then who are the enemies? Do you see a problem with understanding "enemies" as a reference to the Church?

14. Please explain why you would agree or disagree with this statement: "The 'gifts and calling of God are irrevocable' should be understood only in reference to the spiritual and salvific benefits of the Abrahamic Covenant."

15. In Romans 15:8, Paul writes that Christ became a servant to the circumcised in part "to confirm the promises given to the patriarchs." Which promises did Paul had in mind? To help you answer this question, please review Genesis 12:1–3; 15:5–7; 17:6–8; 22:16–18.

Conference Video

chosenpeople.com/vanlaningham

Interview with Dr. Michael G. Vanlaningham

chosenpeople.com/vanlaningham-interview

ISRAEL ACCORDING TO THE BOOK OF HEBREWS AND THE GENERAL EPISTLES

DR. CRAIG A. EVANS

Evans, in his chapter *Israel according to the Book of Hebrews and the General Epistles*, seeks to show how ethnic Israel is the primary audience for both the General Epistles and the book of Hebrews. He begins his discussion with an overview of the authorship of each. While the authorship of Hebrews is uncertain, the book clearly has a Jewish author. Although scholarship debates the authorship of the other General Epistles (James, 1 and 2 Peter, and Jude), there is strong evidence for Jewish authorship and they represent "important themes in early Jewish messianic theology."

Evans concludes his study of the General Epistles by investigating how these core New Testament writings view the Land. While they do not often refer directly to the Land, they contain inferences, and to some degree, an assumption that the Land and the people are inextricably linked. In Hebrews, the Land, following Psalm 95, provides a type for rest. James does not mention the Land, but presents an ethic congruous to the way Israel was to behave in the Land. For Peter, the Land functions as a type of the inheritance in heaven.

Although the General Epistles do not focus on Israel's future, they are written from a Jewish perspective and affirm both Jewish themes and God's promises to Israel.

Nothing is more important personally for the authors of the book of Hebrews and the General Epistles than the people, the Land, and the future of Israel. Who these people are seems clear in these writings but how exactly the land of Israel itself is envisioned, either in the present or in the future, is not nearly as clear. Let me begin with a few words about the authorship of these writings.

Authorship of Hebrews and the General Epistles
Hebrews
Almost no one has disputed the Jewish authorship of the book of Hebrews. Its opening verses clearly imply that the author identified with Israel: "In many and various ways God spoke of old to our fathers by the prophets; but in these last days he has spoken to us (Heb. 1:1–2a). The "fathers" and the "prophets" mentioned in v. 1 are the patriarchs and prophets of Israel. The most natural understanding of the possessive "our" is that the author includes himself among the descendants of the patriarchs. There is no symbolism here; he speaks literally. Moreover, given the Scriptures that are cited, the manner in which they are applied, the warnings, the typologies, and the encouraging examples of the Israelite men and women of faith reviewed in chapter 11, there really is no other plausible interpretation left open. The author of the book of Hebrews was a Jew and his intended readers were Jews. They are identified as the "seed of Abraham" (2:16).

No one knows who this Jew was. It is almost universally agreed that he was not Paul. Tertullian (c. 190 CE) suggested Barnabas (*On Modesty* 20), which is not a bad suggestion. The language of the last eight verses (i.e., 13:18–25) overlaps with Pauline language, suggesting not Pauline authorship but rather connection with communities (in Antioch and Jerusalem) and individuals with whom Paul lived and ministered. Martin Luther considered Apollos.[1] The fourth-century-church historian and apologist Eusebius includes Hebrews in the list of disputed books (*antilegomena*), evidently because it is not by Paul, as some think (*Hist. Eccl.* 3.3.5; 6.13.6). The inclusion of Hebrews in the collection of Paul's letters preserved in P[46] encouraged the reading and circulation of Hebrews, which in turn increased its recognition and chances for inclusion in the Christian canon of Scripture.

Whether Barnabas, Apollos, or someone else wrote Hebrews, we shall never know, apart from an astounding discovery. What we do know is that this Jewish author was deeply committed to Jesus, the fulfiller and mediator of the promised new covenant (Heb. 7:22; 8:6–8, 13; 9:15; 12:24) and provider of Israel's salvation (Heb. 2:10; 5:9).

James
The same can be said for the author of the epistle of James. He was Jewish. Unlike the author of Hebrews, however, the author of this

writing gives us a name and a description of himself. He says he is "James, a servant of God and of the Lord Jesus Christ" (James 1:1a). Most think this James is none other than "James the Lord's brother," as Paul puts it in Galatians 1:19. The early martyrdom of James, son of Zebedee (Acts 12:2), rules out this leading figure as the James of the epistle. We know nothing of the other men named James who were linked to Jesus during his ministry. By the process of elimination we are left with James the brother of Jesus. Indeed, James the brother of Jesus is the *only* man named James in the early Jesus movement who possessed such stature in the Church that referring to himself simply as "James" would have been sufficient identification.

Some scholars think the epistle of James was not written by James but was written under his name at the end of the first century, or even sometime in the second century, as a corrective to Paul. But would such a late letter circulate widely enough and find acceptance in enough churches to gain entry into the New Testament canon? Given Paul's popularity, it seems unlikely. And in any case, the epistle of James is not much of a correction to Paul. Rightly understood, the letter challenges those whose faith never results in righteous acts towards those in need. The works of which this epistle speaks are works of compassion not the "works of law" that Paul vehemently insists cannot justify. Insistence on works of compassion is consistent with what Paul says in Ephesians 2:10, where the apostle declares that believers are God's "workmanship, created in Christ Jesus for good works, which God prepared beforehand, that we should walk in them."

It should be added that the language of the epistle of James echoes the words of James at the second Jerusalem council in Acts 15 and echoes dominical language throughout, as we might expect from a brother of Jesus.[2] All of these factors tilt slightly in favor of accepting the traditional authorship. However, a bit more needs to be said.

James lead the Church in Jerusalem after the departure of Simon Peter (Acts 12:17; 21:18) and was executed at the hands of high priest Annas, son of the high priestly patriarch Annas, whose five sons and son-in-law Caiaphas served as high priest in the final decades of the second temple (see Josephus, *Ant.* 20.199–200). James, almost grudgingly acknowledged by Paul as one of the "pillars" of the early Church (Gal. 2:9, along with Peter and John), came to be highly regarded for his piety and earned the sobriquet "Just James" (Eusebius, *Hist. Eccl.* 2.1.5; 2.23.6–7). This reputation is fully consistent with the tone and content that find in the epistle of James.

However we decide with regard to the question of authorship, the writer of the epistle of James is Jewish through and through. He addresses his epistle "To the twelve tribes in the Dispersion," that is, the Diaspora (1:1). Recent study of James has focused with greater attention on the Judaic tradition and character of the epistle.[3] Recent commentaries have underscored these important qualities.[4]

1–2 Peter

The authorship of the Petrine epistles is highly debated. Most scholars flat out reject Petrine authorship of 2 Peter, while a goodly number doubt 1 Peter. Eusebius also rejects 2 Peter, along with the *Gospel of Peter*, the *Preaching of Peter*, and the *Apocalypse of Peter*. He states: "I recognize only one (of the letters) as genuine and admitted by the presbyters of old" (Eusebius, *Hist. Eccl.* 3.3.4; cf. 3.4.2; 3.25.2). Elsewhere Eusebius claims that Papias made use of 1 Peter (2.15; 3.39.17), which is very early attestation. There appear to be allusions to 1 Peter in *1 Clement* (c. 95), which is even earlier attestation.

An objection often raised against the authenticity of 1 Peter is the assumption that a Jewish man from Galilee would not be able to write Greek, at least not the quality of Greek that we see in 1 Peter. This assumption is problematic at many levels. The evidence suggests that many Galileans knew Greek. Given Peter's leadership and itinerant ministry, including journeys to Antioch and eventually to Rome, one should assume he acquired Greek. But perhaps most pertinent of all there is no need to assume that for Peter to be the author of 1 Peter it was necessary for him to possess fluency in Greek. The Greek of 1 Peter reflects the linguistic and literary skill of the *scribe* (who may well be Silvanus, mentioned in 5:12), not that of the author/sender Peter, who in Acts is described as "unlettered" (Acts 4:13).[5] Ongoing study of papyri has shown how so many objections to authenticity of this letter or that letter, on the basis of imagined linguistic requirements, are misguided. We must become better acquainted with the actual practices of antiquity.[6] We simply cannot prove or disprove the authenticity of 1 Peter; and certainly not on the basis of the quality of its Greek. Whether or not Petrine authorship is accepted, we do have good reason to believe that the author of the letter was Jewish.

Jude

Jude begins with the words, "Jude (lit. Judas), a servant of Jesus Christ and brother of James" (v. 1a). Traditionally it has been understood that the author has identified himself as the brother of the James who is the brother of Jesus. Recall when Jesus visited Nazareth and preached in the synagogue; the names of his brothers were mentioned: "James and Joses and Judas and Simon" (Mark 6:3; cf. Matt. 13:35). Accordingly, we may have in our collection of New Testament writings two letters by brothers of Jesus, one by James and one by Jude.

Eusebius rejects Jude (*Hist. Eccl.* 2.23.24–25; 6.13.6), but he notes (in *Hist. Eccl.* 6.13.6) that it was accepted by Clement of Alexandria, who also quoted it in two of his works (*Paed.* 3.8.44–45;

Strom. 3.2.11). Tertullian apparently knew of a Latin translation of Jude (*Apparel of Women* 1.3). It is also quoted several times by Origen (*Comm. Matt.* 10.17; 17.30; *Comm. Joh.* 13.37; *Hom. Ezek.* 4.1; *First Princ.* 3.2.1) and is quoted and alluded to in some second-century writings (e.g., Polycarp, *Philippians* 3:2; 11:4; *Barnabas* 2:10).

A number of authorities were uneasy with Jude, primarily because of its allusion to the *Assumption of Moses* in v. 9 and its quotation of *1 Enoch* 1:9 in vv. 14–15, works which in the Greek-speaking Church were viewed as lacking authority and perhaps as spurious. In some Jewish circles, these works, especially *1 Enoch*, were respected. Indeed, some scholars think *1 Enoch* might have been viewed at Qumran as authoritative Scripture.[7] It is not surprising that 2 Peter, which rewrites and expands Jude, omits the apocryphal traditions. Indeed, revising Jude, regarded as an important, authoritative work, written by Jude, brother of Jesus and James, may have been a major part of the rationale for its production.

Before concluding this part of the discussion, I want to make an observation regarding our surviving New Testament papyri (see Figure 1). All of these papyri are from Egypt and about one third are from Oxyrhynchus. Matthew is represented by twenty-three papyri, of which eleven are early. John is represented by thirty papyri, of which nineteen are early. Clearly, the Gospels of Matthew and John were very popular early Christian writings in Egypt. Only two of Paul's letters stand out: Romans, which is represented by ten papyri, of which five are early, and 1 Corinthians, which is represented by eight papyri, of which three are early. The rest of Paul's writings are noticeably less well represented, typically ranging from four to two papyri (and none, in the cases of 1–2 Timothy). It will surprise some to learn that the General Epistles are rather well represented by the papyri. Hebrews is represented by eight papyri, of which four are early, James by six, of which four are early, 1 Peter by three, of which one is early, 2 Peter by two, of which one is early, and Jude by three, of which two are early.

Compared to the Pauline Epistles the General Epistles are only overshadowed by Romans and 1 Corinthians. Indeed, Hebrews and James are better represented than the remainder of Paul's epistles, while the other General Epistles hold their own. This pattern of distribution suggests that in the first two centuries of the Christian movement the General Epistles were well represented among the epistles that in time would be recognized as authoritative. The General Epistles are only overshadowed by the Gospels and Paul's two best known letters, Romans and 1 Corinthians. The evidence of distribution, for what it is worth, does not support theories to the effect that most or all of the General Epistles were late and pseudonymous. I think the evidence suggests that the General Epistles, with perhaps the exception of 2 Peter, are early and represent important themes in early Jewish messianic theology.

DISTRIBUTION OF PAPYRI WITNESSES FOR EACH NEW TESTAMENT BOOK

NT Book	Total	Early	NT Book	Total	Early
Matthew	23	11	1 Timothy	0	0
Mark	3	1	2 Timothy	0	0
Luke	10	6	Titus	2	1
John	30	19	Philemon	2	1
Acts	14	7	Hebrews	8	4
Romans	10	5	James	6	4
1 Corinthians	8	3	1 Peter	3	1
2 Corinthians	4	2	2 Peter	2	1
Galatians	2	1	1 John	2	1
Ephesians	3	3	2 John	1	0
Philippians	3	2	3 John	1	0
Colossians	2	1	Jude	3	2
1 Thessalonians	4	3	Revelation	7	4
2 Thessalonians	2	2			

FIGURE 1

The People of Israel in the General Epistles

In the General Epistles the people of Israel are identified as such, either explicitly or implicitly.

Hebrews

The author of Hebrews emphasizes Christology. He argues vigorously that the Messiah Jesus is superior to the angels, to the prophets, to Moses, and to the Aaronic priesthood and sacrificial system. In comparing Jesus with the angels the author quotes part of Psalm 8 (according to the Greek version), in which the "son of man" is said to have been made a little lower than the angels (Heb. 2:7). This reduction in glory is understood in reference to the incarnation and, especially, the passion. In the passion Jesus suffers and in suffering he is perfected and becomes the author of salvation (Heb. 2:10).

But this is where it gets interesting. Jesus is not only his people's Savior, he is their brother: "He is not ashamed to call them brothers" (Heb. 2:11, followed by quotations of Ps. 22:22; Isa. 8:17–18). In the incarnation Jesus becomes like his brothers and, likewise, the people of Israel (or "seed of Abraham") become Messiah's brothers. The people of Israel not only remain special in God's plans and purposes, those

138

who embrace God's Messiah become part of the Messiah's family. The form of his argument is innovative, to be sure, but the doctrine itself is not. Recall what Jesus said when told his mother and brothers were seeking him: "And he replied, 'Who are my mother and my brothers?' And looking around on those who sat about him, he said, 'Here are my mother and my brothers! Whoever does the will of God is my brother, and sister, and mother'" (Mark 3:33–35).

James

James addresses his readers in a very Jewish manner, stating that his epistle is "To the twelve tribes in the Dispersion," i.e., the Diaspora (1:1; see John 7:35). The word Diaspora, or Dispersion, occurs about one dozen times in the Greek version of the Old Testament. Moses warns Israel if they fail to keep the covenant they will be scattered "in all the kingdoms of the earth" (Deut. 28:25). But if the people of Israel repent, then the Lord will regather his people, even if their "dispersion be from an end of the sky to an end of the sky" (Deut. 30:4). This language is echoed in Nehemiah (at 1:9) in a post-exilic setting. Both the Psalter (at Ps. 146:2) and the prophets Isaiah and Jeremiah promise that God will gather his dispersed people (Isa. 49:6; Jer. 15:7; 41:17 [Heb. 34:17]). However, Daniel warns the wicked that they will be scattered (Dan. 12:2). Later literature recalls the Dispersion of Israel for its sin (2 Macc. 1:27; Judith 5:19; *Pss. Sol.* 8:28; 9:2).

The principal concern of James is that those who have embraced Jesus in faith live out their faith in tangible ways. Several times he exhorts, often calling them brothers. In fact, the word brother (*adelphos*) occurs some nineteen times. For James, living out a true faith means loving one's neighbor as one's self (James 2:8, where Lev. 19:18 is quoted). The neighbor James has in mind is the poor neighbor: "Listen, my beloved brethren. Has not God chosen those who are poor in the world to be rich in faith and heirs of the kingdom which he has promised to those who love him?" (James 2:5).

James exhorts his readers not to show partiality toward the rich, while despising the poor man. Instead, fulfill the "royal law," the very commandments Jesus himself espoused. When asked what the greatest commandment was, Jesus replied: "The first is, 'Hear, O Israel: The Lord our God, the Lord is one; and you shall love the Lord your God with all your heart, and with all your soul, and with all your mind, and with all your strength.' The second is this, 'You shall love your neighbor as yourself.' There is no other commandment greater than these" (Mark 12:29–31).

The whole of chap. 2 is devoted to an exposition of Jesus' famous Double Commandment, with most of the attention falling on the second commandment, the commandment to love one's neighbor. Merely affirming that God is one (the beginning of the first commandment,

Deut. 6:4–5) and wishing a cold and hungry man well (ostensibly the beginning of the second commandment, Lev. 19:18) amount to little more than lip service. If you really love God and if you really love your neighbor, you will help your neighbor in material, tangible ways, according to his needs. That is truth faith. It is a faith that works; anything less is dead.

Of course, James is not talking about "works of the law," such as circumcision, kosher food, the Sabbath, and purity. He is talking about putting one's faith into practice, especially as it relates to the "royal law," the commandment to love one's neighbor. James is not correcting Paul; he is exhorting his readers to obey the teaching of his brother Jesus.

1 Peter

Reminiscent of James, Peter addresses himself to "the exiles of the Dispersion" (1 Peter 1:1). He refers again to their "exile" in v. 17. In a variety of ways, Peter alludes to or assumes the Israelite heritage of his readers. He reminds his readers that they "were ransomed from the futile ways inherited from (their) fathers" (v. 18). These fathers are the Israelites of old. In chapter 2, Peter distinguishes his readers from Gentiles (v. 12). Alluding to Hosea he reminds his readers of their calling:

> But you are a chosen race, a royal priesthood, a holy nation, God's own people, that you may declare the wonderful deeds of him who called you out of darkness into his marvelous light. Once you were no people but now you are God's people; once you had not received mercy but now you have received mercy. (1 Peter 2:9–10)

Accordingly, Peter's readers should regard themselves as "aliens and exiles" with regard to the world and its temptations (2:11). Peter ends his letter on the same theme, with his words of farewell: "She who is at Babylon, who is likewise chosen, sends you greetings" (1 Peter 5:13).[8]

2 Peter

In the second letter attributed to Peter, the author addresses his readers in a most unusual manner: "those who have obtained a faith of equal standing with ours in the righteousness of our God and Savior Jesus Christ" (1:1). What the RSV translates as "faith of equal standing" could also be rendered "faith of equal value" (*isotimon . . . pistin*). It is an interesting expression.[9] What exactly is being said? Most commentators think the author is saying that the faith of his readers (who are not apostles) is equal in value to the faith of the author and his colleagues (who are apostles). A few commentators wonder if the author is hinting at the Jewish identity of the readers. In other words, the author (ostensibly the apostle Peter) closely identifies with the faith of his readers because the author and his readers are Jewish Christians.[10]

The author exhorts his readers: "Therefore, brethren, be the more zealous to confirm your call and election, for if you do this you will never fall; so there will be richly provided for you an entrance into the eternal kingdom of our Lord and Savior Jesus Christ" (1:10–11). The concern that his readers "confirm (their) call and election" coheres with the warning passages in Hebrews. What the RSV translates "confirm" (*bebaios*) can also be rendered "firm," "certain," or "sure." If his readers make their call and election sure they will gain "an entrance into the eternal kingdom of our Lord and Savior Jesus Christ." The language recalls the wise counsel found in the intertestamental Jewish work, also written in Greek, the Wisdom of Solomon: "The beginning of wisdom is the most sincere desire for instruction . . . giving heed to her (wisdom) is assurance (*bebaiosis*) of immortality, and immortality brings one near to God; so the desire for wisdom leads to a kingdom" (Wisdom 6:17–20).

The author of 2 Peter speaks to his readers as fellow Jews, encouraging them and exhorting them. But he also warns them: "But false prophets also arose among the people, just as there will be false teachers among you" (2:1). The warning recalls the language of Deuteronomy 13:1 "If a prophet arises among you . . . ." The balance of chapter 2 is given over to Old Testament examples of divine judgment that befell sinful humanity. At the end of the chapter, the author speaks of those who have known the way of righteousness but have abandoned it: "For it would have been better for them never to have known the way of righteousness than after knowing it to turn back from the holy commandment delivered to them" (2:21). His statement carries with it an implicit warning to his readers, that they not follow the example of the apostates. Again the language of 2 Peter is faintly reminiscent of Hebrews, in this case the warning in Hebrews 6:4–8.

Jude

Jude addresses his readers as "those who are called, beloved in God the Father" (v. 1). As in the other General Epistles Jude warns his readers by appealing to Israel's history: "Now I desire to remind you, though you were once for all fully informed, that he who saved a people out of the land of Egypt, afterward destroyed those who did not believe" (v. 5).

Near the end of his brief epistle, he exhorts his readers to have mercy on those who lack faith (v. 22) and to "save some, by snatching them out of the fire" (v. 23a). Jude's vivid language, "snatching them out of the fire," alludes to the words of the prophet Amos, who warns ancient Israel: "I overthrew some of you, as when God overthrew Sodom and Gomorrah, and you were as a brand plucked out of the burning; yet you did not return to me" (Amos 4:11).

The Land of Israel in the General Epistles

In the General Epistles, there are no explicit references to the land of Israel. However, some inferences can be detected.

Hebrews

The principal purpose of Hebrews is to encourage and warn Jewish believers not to lose heart and abandon their faith in Jesus. If they abandon their faith, they will not enter the promised rest (Heb. 3:7–4:11). The promised rest, of course, is a typology centered on the land of Israel.

The author of Hebrews develops his typology of rest by appeal to Psalm 95:7b–11 (= LXX Ps. 94:7b–11).

> Therefore, as the Holy Spirit says, "Today, when you hear his voice, do not harden your hearts as in the rebellion, on the day of testing in the wilderness, where your fathers put me to the test and saw my works for forty years. Therefore I was provoked with that generation, and said, 'They always go astray in their hearts; they have not known my ways.' As I swore in my wrath, 'They shall never enter my rest'" (Heb. 3:7–11).

Psalm 95 recalls Israel's complaining in the wilderness. The story is told in Exodus 17:1–7. On later occasions Israel was reminded of her sin and warned not to repeat it (Num. 20:13; Deut. 6:16).[11] Due to their lack of faith, the people doubted God and as a consequence the original generation was denied entry into the land promised Abraham and the patriarchs and so died in the wilderness. The failure to enter the Promised Land is what is meant by the words, "They shall never enter my rest."

The author of Psalm 95 recalls Israel's faithlessness in the wilderness long ago. If Psalm 95 was composed and used for worship in the early post-exilic community (c. 500 BC),[12] then the threat of not entering God's "rest" would have been quite relevant. Israel was beginning to return to the Promised Land. "Let there be no faithlessness this time, lest the judgment that befell the wilderness generation long ago fall upon us," was the thinking. The word "rest" may have carried with it spiritual meaning also (e.g., fellowship with God), but the primary reference was to the literal Land from which sinful Israel had been expelled some seventy years previously and to which chastened Israel was now returning.

The author of Hebrews adapts and modifies the typology of Psalm 95. He knows, of course, that behind the prophetic warning was literal history and geography. But for him the "rest" of Psalm 95 refers not to the literal land of Israel. After all, when Hebrews was written most of ethnic Israel lived in the Land. Rome and her puppet rulers may have exercised authority over this Land, but the Jewish people at least lived in it. For the author of Hebrews, entering the "rest" (Greek: *katapausis*) that God provides means receiving from the Lord all that he has promised, to enter into his fellowship and blessing. The hope of Israel was the kingdom of God. Through Messiah Jesus, this rule was now at hand. Failure to receive the Messiah would result in not entering God's rest.

Given the hardship that the Jesus movement experienced in its early years, it is not hard to imagine why some Jewish believers became discouraged. Hebrews 11 is designed to counter this discouragement by recalling the great men and women of faith in Israel's colorful history. "These all died in faith, not having received what was promised," the author of Hebrews tells his readers, "but having seen it and greeted it from afar, and having acknowledged that they were strangers and exiles on the earth. For people who speak thus make it clear that they are seeking a homeland . . . " (11:13–14a).

Here again the Promised Land is used as a symbol. People of faith, like the patriarchs of old, seek a homeland. But this homeland is not literal Israel; it is "a better country, that is, a heavenly one" (11:16), the realm in which God's rule is respected and obeyed, a realm that can be entered thanks to the saving work of God's Son. The author of Hebrews develops his typology further in the next chapter, assuring his readers: "But you have come to Mount Zion and to the city of the living God, the heavenly Jerusalem, and to innumerable angels in festal gathering, and to the assembly of the first-born who are enrolled in heaven, and to a judge who is God of all, and to the spirits of just men made perfect, and to Jesus, the mediator of a new covenant . . . " (12:22–24).

James

James seems to presuppose life in the land of Israel and in the Dispersion. He warns the rich against oppressing the poor and treating them with injustice. The rich enjoy lives of luxury and at the same time withhold wages due those who work in their fields (5:1–6). James does not tell us if he is speaking of those who live in Israel or those who live in the Dispersion, to whom his letter is addressed. The ethic with which James is concerned approximates the Mosaic ethic by which Israel in the land was expected to conduct herself. Apart from this, James tells us nothing about the land of Israel as such.

1 Peter

Peter addresses his letter to "the exiles of the Dispersion," who live in many regions of Asia Minor (today's Turkey). He does not speak of the land of Israel directly, but the land as Israel's promised "inheritance" may have provided him with a typology. He reminds his readers of their "inheritance which is imperishable, undefiled, and unfading, kept in heaven for you" (1:4). To speak of an inheritance that is in heaven seems to militate against the idea of an earth-bound inheritance, of dwelling in a literal land of Israel. I will say more about this in the final section that is concerned with the future of Israel.

After describing his readers as "a chosen race, a royal priesthood, a holy nation, God's own people" (2:9), Peter goes on to refer to them as "aliens and exiles" (2:11), living among "Gentiles" (2:12). Such language could be taken literally, in the sense that because Peter's readers live in the Dispersion, they are aliens and exiles among Gentiles, even as Israel was in the exilic period. Indeed, all believers in Jesus, whether Jewish or non-Jewish, are aliens living in the present world, awaiting God's inheritance.

The Future of Israel in the General Epistles

Eschatology is expressed in various ways in the General Epistles, but nothing directly is said about the future of the people of Israel as such. There is no equivalent of Paul's declaration that "all Israel will be saved" (Rom. 11:26). But something to this effect may be implied here and there.

Hebrews

The author of Hebrews reminds his readers that "Jesus also suffered outside the gate in order to sanctify the people through his own blood" (13:12). Therefore believers should join him "outside the camp and bear the abuse he endured" (13:13). Leaving the camp harks back to Israel's old stories of wilderness wanderings and settling into the Promised Land. Those who leave the camp are unwelcome or in some way undesirable. Jesus was thrust out; we should join him. And why not? "For here we have no lasting city, but we seek the city which is to come" (13:14). Believers in Jesus may be outside the city (and every reader would think of Jerusalem), but they "seek the city which is to come."

The future of Israel lies not with the earthly city of Jerusalem or the land of Israel; it lies in the hands of God, who is preparing a city, a new Jerusalem. This is an image depicted in great detail in the book of Revelation. It is also well attested in the Qumran scrolls.

James

The closest that James comes to eschatology is in chapter 5. There he warns the wealthy, whose expensive garments will become moth-eaten, whose gold and silver will rust, and who face judgment in the last days. His warnings are reminiscent of the Sermon on the Mount, especially Matthew 6:19–21.

James enjoins his readers to remain patient and uncomplaining in the face of injustice and suffering (James 5:7–11). His concluding admonitions are again reminiscent of dominical tradition (Matt. 5:34–

37). He emphasizes prayer, confession of sin, and outreach to those who have strayed from the faith.

1 Peter

Similar to what we have seen in Hebrews, Peter speaks of an "inheritance which is imperishable, undefiled, and unfading, kept in heaven" (1:4). God's people "by God's power are guarded through faith for a salvation ready to be revealed in the last time" (1:5). Peter envisions the salvation of those who have placed their faith in Messiah Jesus. What he envisions regarding the people of Israel in general he does not say.

2 Peter

The author of 2 Peter assures his readers that they will have "an entrance into the eternal kingdom of our Lord and Savior Jesus Christ" (1:11). This eternal kingdom is something other than this world, for "the heavens and earth that now exist have been stored up for fire, being kept until the day of judgment and destruction of ungodly men" (3:7). The old heavens and earth will be destroyed; "we wait for new heavens and a new earth in which righteousness dwells" (3:10–13).

Jude

Finally, Jude says nothing about the future of the people of Israel as a whole. He admonishes believers to build themselves up on their holy faith, to pray in the Holy Spirit, to keep themselves in the love of God, and to "wait for the mercy of our Lord Jesus Christ unto eternal life" (vv. 20–21).

Concluding Comments

There are common emphases and themes present in the General Epistles. Ethnic Israel—that is, the genetic descendants of Abraham—are the primary audience in these writings and the writings themselves are written very much from this perspective. The Jewish believers in Jesus are a scattered people and, because of persecution in some quarters and perhaps the delay in the appearance of a triumphant Messiah, they are a discouraged people. Accordingly, the authors of these writings encourage these believers with the examples of their ancestors who despite much opposition and persecution remained faithful. Their fidelity stands in sharp contrast to the faithlessness of the wilderness generation, who did not enter the Promised Land and so did not enter the rest that God had long ago promised. God has promised Israel many things; the authors of Hebrews and the General Epistles long to see Israel embrace those promises.

Study Questions

1. Why did some of the leaders in the early Church "speak against" the book of Hebrews and General Epistles?

2. How well represented among our earliest Greek New Testament manuscripts are the book of Hebrews and the General Epistles? What does the evidence suggest?

3. The book of Hebrews is anonymous. What authors have been suggested? Why do you think Paul wrote or did not write the book of Hebrews?

4. Why do you think the book of Hebrews and the General Epistles are grouped together at the end of the New Testament, if they are as old (and authoritative as) the epistles of Paul?

5. What are some of the Jewish characteristics of the book of Hebrews?

6. What are some of the Jewish characteristics of the General Epistles?

7. When James talks about the importance of works in chapter 2, does he contradict Paul, who argues that no one can be justified by works of the Law? What "works" is James talking about?

8. In what ways does the author of the book of Hebrews show that Jesus is unequaled in authority?

9. In what ways does the author of the book of Hebrews warn his Jewish readers with regard to maintaining their faith?

10. Would it have been necessary for the apostle Peter to have a command of excellent Greek to have written the letters attributed to him in the New Testament? If not, why not?

11. How do the authors of the book of Hebrews and the General Epistles speak of Israel's future and the fulfillment of the biblical promises?

Conference Video

chosenpeople.com/evans

Interview with Dr. Craig A. Evans

chosenpeople.com/evans-interview

HERMENEUTICS, THEOLOGY, AND CHURCH HISTORY

9

ISRAEL AND HERMENEUTICS

DR. CRAIG A. BLAISING

B laising, in his chapter *Israel and Hermeneutics*, describes the methods we use to interpret the Bible. He summarizes the historical difference between literal and figurative approaches to Scripture and shows how an allegorical reading of the Bible was used to minimize the role played by the Jewish people in the plan of God.

Blaising shows how typology is used today by a supersessionist approach to the Bible to reject the national and territorial promises of Israel and spiritualize them as being fulfilled in Jesus and thereby the Church.

He demonstrates the weakness of this approach and argues for a holistic reading of the Bible in which all of God's promises, including those that speak of the Jewish people and the Land of Israel, are truly fulfilled.

Evangelical theologians basically divide into two camps on the ques-tion of the future of Israel: there are those who say that the Bible teaches a future for ethnic and national Israel and those who claim that it does not. Both sides appeal to the Bible in making their cases, which could be somewhat disconcerting. One might be tempted to dismiss the difference as "just a matter of interpretation," which in modern parlance often means a subjective decision on the order of a preference. Howev-er, this would be a mistake for two reasons. First, the subject—national and ethnic Israel—is not merely theoretical but a reality that is vitally important in our world today. Secondly, the question is not peripheral but central to the story line of the Bible. How one answers this question affects how one understands the story of the Bible from its beginning to its end. So, it is "a matter of interpretation," but one of such vital impor-tance that we need to make sure we are interpreting correctly.

If this was a dispute on the football field or the basketball court, we would turn to the officials for a ruling. In the absence of officials, we would have to consult a rule book, which explains the game and how it is to be played. In our case, we are looking for "rules" of inter-pretation, and the place to find them is in the many books on herme-neutics, the disciplinary field that addresses the methods and practice of interpretation.[1] In this chapter, we will look at some of the princi-ples and guidelines for correct interpretation and see how they might resolve the dispute on how to correctly interpret what the Bible has to say about the future of Israel, its land and people.

Traditional Categories

Traditionally, the dispute has been characterized as a difference re-garding the correct practice of *literal* and *spiritual* interpretation. Super-sessionists, those who believe that the church has replaced ethnic and national Israel in the plan of God so that there is no future for the latter, argue that non-supersessionists, those who see a future for ethnic and national Israel in the divine plan, interpret parts of the Bible literal-ly that are supposed to be understood spiritually. Non-supersessionists reply that supersessionists spiritualize parts of the Bible that should be interpreted literally.[2]

The problem is often compared to the difference between *literal* and *figurative* interpretation. Most people would know that Robert Burns' famous poem, "My Love is Like a Red Red Rose," is a figurative descrip-tion of the poet's sweetheart. It would be a mistake, a misinterpretation, to think he was speaking of a bush. On the other hand, if I receive a text from my wife asking me to pick up some potatoes at the grocery store on my way home, and I interpret it figuratively as a request that I stop by the bookstore and purchase a book on hermeneutics for my light reading, that would be a mistake. Knowing when to interpret literally and when to interpret figuratively is somewhat intuitive, but mistakes

can be made, and that's when one needs to clarify the "rules" of hermeneutics. This has led to an identification of various figures of speech and
figurative genre (types of literature), their customary uses, and ways to
recognize them.

The difference between *literal* and *spiritual* biblical hermeneutics
has also been compared to the difference between *literal* and *allegorical* interpretation. Allegory is a particular kind of literary figure. It is
a story in which the literal elements of the narrative are symbolic of
philosophical, religious, or other ideas. John Bunyan's *Pilgrim's Progress*
is a good example of allegory. Its real meaning, intended by the author,
lies on the allegorical, the symbolic level. Consequently, to interpret it
correctly, one must read it *allegorically*. One would misinterpret *Pilgrim's
Progress* if one thought that it was intended to be a literal narrative history of someone named Pilgrim.

Disputes arose in ancient times on the correct reading of the Greek
epics of Homer, the *Iliad* and the *Odyssey*. These epics tell stories of the
deeds of gods and men, and many of the ancients took them literally.
However, some Greek philosophers, embarrassed by literal interpretations of Homer, suggested that the stories were to be read allegorically
as teachings of philosophical ideas.

In the early centuries of the church, the question likewise arose as to
whether the Bible should be read allegorically. On the one hand, Gnosticism taught that behind the façade of the literal narrative of Scripture
lay a completely different symbolic world, construed according to the
ideas of the particular Gnostic system. Gnosticism was clearly heretical
on a number of points of Christian doctrine and Christian churches
rejected the allegorical methods of various Gnosticisms as falsely im-
posing alien ideas upon the text. On the other hand, the church did
accept forms of allegorical interpretation within clear doctrinal boundaries. Early Christian supersessionism used allegorical methods to interpret Israel in biblical narrative and prophecy as symbolic of a spiritual
people, the church revealed in the New Testament. This way of reading
the Bible became traditional in the church, but it came to be challenged
in the last few centuries by non-supersessionists as a mistake. They
argued that supersessionists *spiritualized* or *allegorized* what should be
interpreted *literally*. The terms *spiritual* and *allegorical* were often used
interchangeably in this critique.

Contemporary Evangelical Hermeneutics

Today, there is general agreement among Evangelical theologians
and biblical scholars that *spiritual interpretation* as traditionally prac-
ticed is not acceptable. Evangelicals today are particularly sensitive to
the problem of reading ideas into Scripture rather than receiving ideas
from Scripture. One should not come to the Scripture and simply read
into it what one wants.

In modern times the art and science of interpretation has come to be studied and articulated more carefully with the result that even the categories of *literal* versus *spiritual* are not as useful as they once seemed to be. It's not so much that they are wrong as that they are not sufficiently precise. It's like attempting to do surgery with flint knives in an age of scalpels and lasers.

So, what are the categories, principles, and methods that characterize evangelical biblical interpretation today? Generally, interpretation is described as a three-way relationship between the author, the text, and the reader. The author has formed the text as a communication to the reader(s). The reader needs to come to the text with a desire to understand what the author has said. Scripture is unique in that it has a Divine author, who superintended its composition. So, we seek to interpret Scripture properly so as to understand what the Author through and together with authors has communicated in the form of its text.

In order to do that, the reader needs to read the text in a manner that accords with its reality. This is often described as a *historical, grammatical, literary* interpretation of the Bible. However, there are a number of other terms that describe the approach. Each is important in explaining an aspect or focus which interpretation needs to take into account. These terms are listed below.

The *historical* nature of interpretation recognizes that language doesn't just come out of the blue; the historical setting of the text provides its linguistic context. An author, a human author, writes within a specific historical setting and makes reference to things of that day and uses language within the vernacular of that day; we need to be aware of the historical situation of the text as we attempt to interpret it.

Interpretation is *lexical*, that is, it considers the definitions of words. The interpreter needs to be aware of all possible definitions, but the precise definition will be clear only in context. Consideration of context takes us first to the *grammatical* level where words are nuanced by grammar to combine in larger syntactical structures. Interpretation is then *syntactical*, recognizing that sentences and paragraphs are the primary level of meaning.

Interpretation must also take into account the *literary/formal* level of word and sentence combinations. At the literary level, we see how language is structured not just into sentences but into literature. Here one finds various *conventions* of word usage, such as various kinds of metaphor. But also, one notes the larger structural conventions that mark out different literary *genre*—the larger literary forms of poetry and prose. Most people recognize that a poem is a different kind of literature than a report, a letter, a narrative, or a chronicle. Larger works of literature often combine not just multiple words and sentences but multiple genre and multiple conventions. Interpretation of a text requires an understanding of the kind of literature in which a passage is located and the literary relationship it has to its surrounding context.

Interpretation needs to recognize the *performative* function of literary units—words, sentences, and genre. This is an aspect of interpretation that has come under discussion only in the past few decades. Performative studies reveal that words and sentences not only describe things, they also do things.

Thematic is an aspect of contextual interpretation that recognizes that themes weave their way through larger literary structures. Thematic connection in a larger literary work is a context just as important as, and maybe more than verbal proximity. In the Bible, this includes themes such as the "Kingdom of God" or the "Day of the Lord." How a theme develops through the canon of Scripture will be important to interpreting its appearance at various places in the text.

That brings us to the *canonical* level of interpretation. The canonical level, the whole canon of Scripture is the ultimate context for anything within it. The canon is a collection of writings that demonstrate not only thematic but inter-textual literary connections. We see this when biblical authors reuse words and phrases from other biblical writings intending to evoke within the reader's mind those earlier contexts and associated patterns of meaning. This is similar to what sometimes happens when someone today quotes popular phrases from a movie or song. More may be intended than the mere repetition of a phrase. The quote may be intended to evoke images, ideas, or emotions associated with the original context of the quotation. We have come to see that connections like this occur in Scripture at the canonical level.

Finally, as we speak of the canonical level of interpretation, we need to note that such interpretation must be canonically *narratological*. Narrative is a literary genre. But we need to note that at the canonical level—a level that contains multiple genres: legal literature, poetry, hymns, historical accounts, and several of other types of literature—the whole Scripture also presents a story. To interpret it correctly requires one to grasp the whole and discern the movement from beginning to end that connects and relates all the parts.

This list of categories, methods, and practices would generally be accepted by most evangelical biblical scholars, including supersessionists and non-supersessionists alike.

Evangelical Supersessionist Hermeneutics

The difference between evangelical supersessionists and nonsupersessionists is seen primarily at the canonical narratological level of interpretation. Supersessionists believe that a *reality shift* takes place in the overall story of the Bible when one moves from *promise* in the Old Testament to *fulfillment* in the New. In the Old Testament the story of the Bible unfolds with promises regarding Israel, the land, the people, and the nation. But as the story moves to the New Testament, fulfillment takes place in an alternate reality—a different kind of Israel, one that transcends the land, the people, and the nation. This reality shift is from the material, the earthly, the ethnic, to a heavenly, a spiritual, a non-ethnic reality. It moves from a political, national reality to a non-political, universal reality. It changes from a focus on the particular to a universal focus. When supersessionists say that the promises to Israel are fulfilled in Christ, the church, or the new creation, this kind of reality shift informs their view.

A clear example of this kind of interpretation can be found in W. D. Davies' book, *The Gospel and the Land*.[3] Davies acknowledges that the Old Testament covenant promise of land to Israel is clear and explicit. However, he argues that the New Testament shifts the substance of the promise from land to Christ. The territorial promise to Israel becomes "Christified" in its fulfillment.[4] More recent scholars such as N. T. Wright, Collin Chapman, Gary Burge, and Peter Walker have adopted Davies' view.[5] The reality shift from a particular territory to a universal new creation, from a particular ethnic people to a new universal people, takes place in Christ in whose person the promises are singularly realized and fulfilled.

This kind of reality shift in canonical narrative is promoted in Reformed biblical theology, as seen, for example, in the works of Geerhardus Vos and Palmer Robertson.[6] The influential writings of scholars mostly associated with Moore Theological College, such as those by Graeme Goldsworthy, William Dumbrell, and T. Desmond Alexander, feature this same supersessionism in their presentations of the story of the Bible.[7]

These evangelical supersessionists generally argue that their perception of a reality shift in the canonical narrative is not due to any allegorization they have performed on the text. They do not claim to have read into the text meaning that is alien to it. Rather, they argue that this reality shift in the nature and substance of Old Testament promise is explicitly taught by the New Testament. It is not a matter of the interpreter allegorizing the text, they say, but a matter of the interpreter recognizing a typology embedded in the text.[8] This typology is a literary convention by which symbolism is recast. The text of the New Testament clarifies the working of this typology by explicitly recasting the symbolism of the Old Testament. The duty of the interpreter is to recognize this typology and incorporate it in the interpretation of the overall canonical narrative.

Let's look more closely at typology and how supersessionists see it functioning in the Bible. Types are essentially patterns that are repeated in the canonical narrative. Noticing these patterns in the canonical narrative may create something like a déjà vu experience in the reader. For example, after crossing the Red Sea, Israel comes up out of the water onto dry land (Ex. 14). But this pattern can be seen in Genesis 1, where God causes the land itself to come up out of the water. It can be seen in the flood narrative, where once again God causes the land to emerge from the water and brings Noah and his family onto the dry land. It can be seen in the Gospels where Jesus comes up out of the water in his baptism. And the pattern is seen in various psalms. This is a repetitive pattern, a narrative type.

The New Testament occasionally uses the word "type" in referring to this kind of pattern. Israel was *baptized* in both the cloud and in the sea and these served as types and examples to us (1 Cor. 10:6). Adam is a type of Christ (Rom. 5:14). The flood is a type of baptism (1 Peter 3:21). But supersessionists see this typology as more than narrative patterns. They cite these passages to argue for a progression in the narrative away from earthly to heavenly realities.

Matthew's use of the word "fulfillment" is cited as evidence for this. For example in Hosea 11:1, the Lord says, "When Israel was a child, I loved him, and out of Egypt I called my son." Matthew applies the verse to the infant Jesus being taken to Egypt to escape Herod and then returning after Herod's death. Matthew says, "Thus it was *fulfilled*, "Out of Egypt I called my Son" (Matt. 2:15). In supersessionist thought, "fulfillment" brings about a shift in the reality of the referent of Hosea's language. It has shifted in a spiritual and Christological direction away from Israel to Christ.

The references to "shadows" in the book of Hebrews are thought to indicate this same typological progression. Hebrews says that the tabernacle was built according to a pattern, or type, from heaven (Heb. 8:5; cf 9:23–24). Moses was shown this pattern on the mountain, and he built the tabernacle according to that pattern. As a type, the tabernacle is also seen as a "shadow" because the heavenly is fixed, whereas the earthly, like a "shadow" passes away (Heb. 8:3–13; cf. 10:1). Hebrews is written in anticipation of the destruction of the Temple, and it speaks of the passing away of the things that were made. It is talking particularly about the things made with hands, as opposed to that which is heavenly (cf. Heb. 9:11). However, supersessionists often overlook the fact that Hebrews is not speaking simply of a vertical dualism between earthly and heavenly realities since the writer expects that those heavenly realities are coming here in the future (Heb. 2:5; 13:14). This future coming in Hebrews is consistent with eschatological expectation elsewhere in the New Testament of a future renewal of all things.

The fourth gospel is also cited as evidence of the typological progression. In John 4:21–24, Jesus tells the Samaritan woman that the time is coming "when neither on this mountain nor in Jerusalem will you worship" but "true worshipers will worship the Father in spirit and truth." Jesus also speaks of himself as the true bread come down from heaven in contrast to the manna that the fathers ate in the wilderness (John 6:31–58). This way of speaking and other imagery in John's Gospel is thought to show a progression from earthly, particularly Israelitish realities to a heavenly, spiritual reality in Christ.

Evaluating Evangelical Supersessionist Hermeneutics

How does one evaluate supersessionist interpretation? If it were a matter of an individual passage of Scripture, the task would be relatively straightforward. One would offer an alternative interpretation of that passage taking into account the words, grammar, syntax, and conventions found there in conjunction with its larger literary context, giving attention to genre, thematic issues, and broader narratological concerns. However, supersessionism is primarily a conviction held at the canonical narratological level which then construes numerous passages of Scripture in light of its overall reading of the Scripture story. How does one evaluate a comprehensive system of interpretation like this?

In his book, *Epistemology: The Justification of Belief,* David Wolf offers four criteria for evaluating broad interpretive systems. These criteria are that a system of belief (or interpretation) must be *comprehensive, congruent, consistent, and coherent.*[9] An interpretive system is strong to the extent that it meets these criteria. It is weak to the extent that it fails to do so. *Comprehensive* means that the interpretive system must cover all the data to be interpreted. In this case, it must cover all Scripture. To the extent that it does not cover portions of Scripture, it is weak at best. *Congruent* means that it must also *fit* the text. If it does not actually fit, if it does not accord with, or is not correct with the text, then again it is weak at best. *Consistent* means that the interpretations produced by this overall reading are not in conflict with one another; they do not contradict one another. Finally, the system must be *coherent,* which is to say that it makes sense.

I believe that supersessionism, as a system of biblical interpretation, is not comprehensive, congruent, consistent, or coherent. The following will briefly illustrate why.

Not Comprehensive

This criterion may seem idealistic. Is it really possible to cover all the data? Can an interpretative system actually address every passage, every verse in Scripture? Well, no, we don't really expect that any published work offering an interpretation of the whole story of the Bible will actually cite every passage of Scripture. But that is not what this criterion is saying. Comprehensiveness means that the interpretation does not leave out crucial data in the formulation of its interpretative system. By covering all crucial, or all relevant data, the system may plausibly be said to cover all data, since there would be nothing *left out* that could actually change or alter the interpretative system. Sometimes, however, supersessionist publications omit key texts that arguably challenge their system.

Consider for example, G. K. Beale's recently published *A New Testament Biblical Theology: The Unfolding of the Old Testament in the New.*[10] The book attempts to explain the theological teaching of the New Testament as the fulfillment of the Old Testament. Many passages of Scripture are addressed in his attempt to give an account of the overall biblical story line (the Scripture index alone is thirty-four pages with references in small font size). However, when he comes to Romans 11:25–26, he gives one paragraph complaining that "the passage is too problematic and controverted to receive adequate discussion within the limited space of this book."[11] The book is 1,047 pages long, plus twenty-four pages of front matter! One would think that *this passage* especially would require treatment in an overall interpretation that sees no future for Israel nationally or politically.

Another example can be seen in Michael E. Fuller's *The Restoration of Israel: Israel's Re-gathering and the Fate of the Nations in Early Jewish Literature and Luke-Acts.*[12] The book focuses especially on Luke's narrative concerning the restoration of Israel in both the Gospel and in Acts, examining passage after passage. However, he completely ignores Acts 3:17–26, a passage in which the word *restoration* appears linked to prophesy and covenant promise!

These examples, of course, could be dismissed as the oversights (although major ones) of individual publications. But they illustrate the point that any attempt to offer an overall interpretation of the story of the Bible must take into account crucial texts that speak to the fulfillment of the promises of God to Israel. Failure to address these texts is itself indication that the interpretation may be weak. When it is shown that these very texts refute a central conviction of supersessionist interpretation, that interpretation is seen not only to be weak but wrong.

Not Congruent

The "fit" or lack thereof of an interpretative system to individual texts can only be shown text by text. Evaluating a large comprehensive system of interpretation will necessarily entail the hermeneutical examination of many passages. However, one needs to note that with respect to a system of interpretation, each text does not have equal force. The system may be compared to a spider web, where the cross points of the web represent the interpretations of individual texts.[13] Showing that the system is not congruent to a particular text may be seen as cutting the web at that juncture. What will happen? It depends on where the web is cut. Some points can be cut with little damage to the web overall. Other points are crucial to the integrity of the web. They are deeply ingressed into the structure and if rendered unstable, the stability of the whole web is put in jeopardy. In the book you are reading, several chapters address passages of Scripture with respect to the theme of Israel, the land and the nation, and criticisms of supersessionist interpretation are offered therein. But here, I would like to note three problems that challenge the web of supersessionist interpretation at a deep structural level. The first two have to do with the *performative force* of key texts. The third has to do with a central assumption of the supersessionist notion of typological progression. Each problem entails multiple texts that the system must *fit* in order to be considered plausible.

Speech-Act Implications of Divine Promise

Performative language, or speech-act analysis is a relatively recent hermeneutical tool. The philosophers J. L. Austin and John Searle were the formative thinkers whose publications first appeared in the 1960s.[14] Since then, many have utilized and developed the insights both for hermeneutics and for language theory.[15] The key insight of speech-act analysis is that language has a performative force. By language, people not only refer to things, they also do things. And, the paradigmatic example of a speech-act, which Austin himself cited, is a promise.

A promise entails an obligation. When somebody makes a promise, they're not just stating something, they are doing something. They are forming a relationship and creating an expectation that carries moral obligation. Failure to complete a promise is a violation of one's word. It is a serious matter. Certainly, we can make promises with conditions. The language of promise will make that clear. But once the promise is made, a relationship has been enacted and an expectation has been grounded in personal integrity.

In Scripture, we see that God has made key promises to Abraham and Abraham's descendants. Not only have promises been made, but conventions are followed in order to reinforce the point. A speech-act occurs in God's communication to Abraham in Genesis 12—a promise concerning a land, a people, a nation, and blessing to all nations. In Genesis 15, Abraham questions God about the fulfillment of this promise of a land to his descendants, asking, "How shall I know that I will inherit it?" (Gen. 15:8). So God enacts a covenant with a ceremony, a very ancient ceremony, where God alone passes through the covenant pieces of the sacrifice and takes an obligation on Himself alone. This was so that Abraham would know that his descendants would inherit the Promised Land.

Compare this, for example, to the performative language of a wedding ceremony. As Richard Briggs has noted, when one says in a wedding ceremony "I do," there is no convention by which one can turn around an hour later and say "well, really, I didn't."[16] To say "I do" in the wedding ceremony is to accept formally the marriage relationship. By those words one forms a relationship with another person which has expectations and obligations. Similarly, when God takes the covenant upon Himself in Genesis 15, a relationship of expectation is grounded in the integrity of God Himself. Divine intention and resolve could not be more clear. Later, God adds to the ceremonially established promissory word the further convention of a solemn oath (Gen. 22:15–18). God swears that He will accomplish that which he promised. The writer to Hebrews, whose language of "shadows" and "types" (Heb. 8:5; 10:1) supersessionists like to quote, also says that "when God desired to show more convincingly to the heirs of the promise the unchangeable character of his purpose, he guaranteed it with an oath" (Heb. 6:17). The promise and the oath are referred to as "two unchangeable things" (Heb. 6:18). To the recipients, these speech acts function as "a sure and steadfast anchor of the soul" (Heb. 6:19). God's word is certain, which means His people can confidently rely on what He promises.

God's promise, covenant, and oath to Abraham is not a peripheral element in the story of the Bible. It is a key structural component in the central plot line. It is repeated to the line of patriarchs and is the ground and basis for the covenant at Sinai and the promise and covenant made to David and his house. To postulate a "fulfillment" of these covenant promises by means of a reality shift in the thing promised overlooks the performative nature of the word of promise, violates the legitimate expectations of the recipients, and brings the integrity of God into question. Such an interpretation is not congruent to the textual string of divine promises, covenants, and oaths—a string of texts that lie at the heart of the canonical narrative.

Performative Force of Prophetic Reaffirmation

The second problem for supersessionist interpretation also has reference to performative language, namely the performative force of prophetic reaffirmation of these covenanted promises to Israel. Not only are the promises made early in the canonical narrative, but in the later narrative they are reinforced by prophetic speech acts of swearing, reaffirming, and emphatically restating God's resolve to fulfill them as promised. The resolve is further underscored in several texts by sweeping rhetorical features like posing impossible odds, unsurmountable obstacles only to dismiss them as trifles to the powerful Creator of all things, and by dramatic scenes, such as the anguish and sorrow of adultery or the pain of parental rejection which in spite of punishment, hurt, and suffering is nevertheless overcome by an unquenchable, triumphant love. The supersessionist reading of the canonical narrative in which Israel is replaced and God's promises are "Christified," spiritualized, or otherwise substantively changed is not congruent with this line of prophetic reaffirmation and restated divine resolve.

Particularism and Universalism in the Old Testament and New Testament
The third problem has to do with the way supersessionist interpretation typically construes the progression of the canonical narrative from particularism to universalism. In this view, the Old Testament tells a story about God's plan for and blessings to one particular people, whereas the New Testament expands the plan and blessing to include all peoples. There is a progression from the particular to the universal, from an ethnic political Israel among the nations to a multi-ethnic, universal Israel inclusive of all nations!

Certainly, much of the Old Testament is taken up with God' promises to and dealings with the particular ethnic people and nation of Israel. And, certainly, we see in the New Testament a mission to the nations and the establishment of the church inclusive of peoples of all nations through faith in Christ. However, reading the canonical narrative as a progression from particularism to universalism is not congruent with either the Old or New Testaments. From the beginning of God's promise to Abraham, both the particular and the universal are present: "I will bless you . . . I will bless all peoples through you" (Gen. 12:2–3). God's promise to the David house was not just rulership over a particular nation. Rather, the Davidic king is invited in Psalm 2:8, "Ask of me, and I will give the nations as your inheritance." Many Psalms speak of blessing coming upon the nations as do the prophets. The dominion of the coming kingdom of God was predicted to be worldwide (Dan. 2:35), with all nations in their places and in peace (2 Sam. 7:10–11; Ezek. 37:26–28; Isa. 2:1–4). Isaiah foresaw the extension of the favored term "my people" to Gentile nations *in addition to not in substitution of or through redefinition of* Israel (Isa. 19:24–25). This is certainly compatible with John's vision in Revelation 21:3, where many manuscripts read, "Behold, the dwelling place of God is with man. He will dwell with them, and they will be *his peoples.*" Similarly, John foresees *"nations* . . . and kings of the earth" in the new creation walking by the light of the Jerusalem come down from heaven (Rev. 21:24). God's plan for Israel and the nations are not mutually exclusive or successive programs but complementary throughout the entire canonical narrative. It is not necessary to eliminate the particular in order to institute the universal nor is it necessary to expand the particular to become the universal, rather, the particular is both the means to the blessing of the universal as well as a central constitutive part of it. How the overall canonical narrative is read needs to be congruent with these and many other texts.

Not Consistent or Coherent
For brevity sake, these two criteria will be treated together. Consistency means freedom from contradiction, and coherence means that the assertions of the system make sense. Many interpretative systems

seem to make sense. Usually the problems have to do with how they relate to the data they are interpreting. However, even apart from an examination of the facts, a sign of weakness in an interpretative system is a lack of internal consistency or coherence. Supersessionism is often thought to be a tight consistent, coherent reading of Scripture. However, the four matters cited below are just some examples that reveal internal problems with this viewpoint.

New Creation Eschatology

In the past couple of decades, many theologians, including some prominent evangelical supersessionists, have come to embrace what I call *new creation eschatology*.[17] New Creation Eschatology believes that the eternal state is not a heavenly, timeless, non-material reality but a new heavens and new earth. That's what Scripture says in passages like Isaiah 65, 2 Peter 3:13, and Revelation 21 and 22. The dwelling place of the redeemed in that new creation is not in heaven but on the new earth. Again, that is consistent with prophecies in Isaiah and Revelation. This new earth, like the old earth, has geographical particularity, which also fits with prophecies in Isaiah and Revelation as well as a number of other texts in Scripture. In fact, the imagery of refinement extending from Isaiah to 2 Peter is a basis for believing that the new earth is not an utterly new creation from nothing but a refinement and renovation of the present earth.[18] God's plan for his creation is not to destroy it and start over from nothing but to redeem, cleanse, and renew it. In light of this, it is clear that new creation eschatology envisions not a non-material eternity, but a redeemed earth and redeemed heavens fit for an everlasting (durative rather than static) glorious manifestation of the presence of God.

Now, given that the new earth has geographical particularity and that it is essentially this earth redeemed for an everlasting glory, is it not important to ask about the territorial promises to Israel? The land and nation promises to Israel were repeatedly stated to be everlasting. In Isaiah, the promise of the new earth is linked to the promise of a restored Jerusalem (Isaiah 65:18–25), the chief part of the land of promise. The blessings of the new earth parallel the promised blessings of the land of Israel in many texts so that the land becomes an example of what is intended for the whole earth.

Many supersessionist theologians have embraced new creation eschatology. N. T. Wright has celebrated his personal discovery of it and the change that has brought to his thinking.[19] The material particularity of new creationism is especially appealing in addressing environmental and creation-care concerns. However, Wright still finds no place in his eschatology for national and territorial Israel. For him, as for many others, the nation and the land become entirely "Christified."[20] Are these views consistent or coherent? So, let's just imagine traversing the new earth, crossing its various and particular geographical features, and coming to the Middle East. What do we find there? A void? A spatial anomaly? But then, where would the New Jerusalem be? In Ohio? Maintaining new creation eschatology while arguing that the territory of Israel has been spiritualized or "Christified" is not a consistent or coherent view.

Interconnection of Covenant Promises

Supersessionists typically affirm the progression argued in the book of Hebrews from the Old Covenant to the New Covenant. But they read this progression as an abandonment of God's particular national and territorial promises to Israel. However, Hebrews explicitly quotes the Jeremiah 31 prophecy of the new covenant as a covenant that the Lord "will establish . . . with the house of Israel and with the house of Judah" (Heb. 8:8). The implication of the last declaration quoted in Hebrews 8:12: "I will forgive *their* [Israel and Judah in context] iniquity and remember *their* sin no more" is explained in Jeremiah 31:35–37: Israel will be a nation forever before the Lord! It is not consistent or coherent to affirm the fulfillment of new covenant promises while denying a national future for Israel. The national and territorial promise to Israel is a constituent feature of covenant promise from Abraham to the new covenant prophesied by Jeremiah. There is no reason to exclude it from "the world to come" expected by the writer of Hebrews (Heb. 2:5). To include it would be the most consistent and coherent reading of that book together with the rest of the canon of Scripture.

False Hermeneutical Dichotomy

As noted earlier, a key assumption of many supersessionist readings of Scripture is a dichotomy between the particular and universal in the plan of God. The universal must replace the particular. Really? Is a whole a *replacement* of a part—such that the part disappears and its place is taken by a whole? Is that coherent? What is a whole if it is not the total collection of parts? The part *must* be present and remain for a whole to be complete. The universal does not replace the particular in the story of the Bible. Rather the story of the Bible encompasses an interaction among parts, individuals and nations, until a whole with all its constitutive parts is completed. This is why Romans 11 is so important for understanding the main story line of the canonical narrative.

Theological Consistency and Coherence

Briefly, let us return to an implication of the discussion of performative language above. By virtue of the performative nature of a promise (not to mention the additional conventions which underscore its resolve), to argue that the Lord "Christifies," spiritualizes, or revises *so as to essentially discard* the national and territorial promises to Israel in the fulfillment of the plot line of Scripture is to call into question the integrity of God. It is particularly inconsistent for Evangelical theologians, who affirm the inerrancy of Scripture, to make such claims. Typically, the doctrine of inerrancy is rooted in the integrity of God which extends to the integrity of His Word. How can His word in general be considered trustworthy if in its most paradigmatic trust-engendering form it is found untrustworthy? But even more, failure here extends to the very being of God as revealed by His Name. Ezekiel 37:26–28 and 39:25–29 speak of the resolution of the theological problem of Israel's exile from the land, a problem repeatedly voiced in Ezekiel. God's Name, God's very character as God, is tied to the fulfillment of His covenant promises to Israel. The constitution of Israel as a nation among the nations in the eschatological kingdom is coordinate with true theology (*"they will know* that I Am the Lord," Ezek. 39:28). To factor national and territorial Israel out will not produce a coherent theology—certainly not the theology that was prophesied in Scripture.

Hermeneutical Importance of a Holistic Eschatology

In conclusion, how one perceives the end of a story will affect one's estimate of the story as a whole—the significance of its various parts and their relevance in the story line. Supersessionism, the belief that Israel has been replaced, or redefined, in the story line of the Bible, is first of all an eschatological view—one in which there is no place for *Israel* as it was created, defined, and made the object of everlasting promises in Scripture. This necessarily impacts how one estimates various elements of the biblical story line not just as narrative but in terms of their ultimate theological importance. I do not think that it is a coincidence that the excision (considered by some to be a *revision*) of Israel from eschatological fulfillment is often coordinate with a reduction of theological concern regarding earthly, material realities. But it also impacts many areas of theology, such as Christology, ecclesiology, anthropology, even theology proper.[21] In contrast to supersessionism, I would recommend a *holistic eschatology* in which "all the promises of God find their Yes in Christ" (2 Cor 1:20). This includes promises regarding Israel. And, it extends to promises regarding the nations. It includes God's plans and purpose for the earth as well as the heavens. It envisions human beings not only as individuals but in their various corporate connections from their ethnic identities to their political and social organizations. In a holistic eschatology, the kingdom of God is a robust rather than thin concept. And, the person of Christ, rather than being a mystical reductive principle, as in notions of "Christification," is seen instead in the full reality of his holistic kingdom, bringing to completion the rich fullness of an inheritance that has been planned, promised, and proclaimed throughout the amazing story of Scripture.

Study Questions

1. How can we know when to interpret a text literally or figuratively?

2. Give some examples of misinterpretation from everyday life. Can you identify the problem in each example?

3. When is allegory a legitimate—or an illegitimate—method of interpretation?

4. List the categories, principles, and methods that characterize evangelical biblical interpretation today. Can you detect a movement from individual words to larger levels of context in these methods?

5. How do supersessionists read the movement from promise to fulfillment in the biblical story?

6. Explain briefly the four criteria for evaluating broad interpretative systems.

7. What must an interpretative system do to claim to be comprehensive? What are some texts that should not be ignored in considering how God's promises to Israel will be fulfilled?

8. How does performative language, or speech-act analysis help to evaluate the congruence of supersessionist and non-supersessionist approaches to Scripture?

9. What is a common mistake in reading the relation between God's purpose for Israel and God's purpose for all people in the movement from Old Testament to New Testament? How should that mistake be corrected?

10. What are some problems of consistency and coherence with supersessionist readings of Scripture? How does a holistic reading of Scripture answer these problems?

Conference Video

chosenpeople.com/blaising

Interview with Dr. Craig A. Blaising

chosenpeople.com/blaising-interview

10

ISRAEL AS A NECESSARY THEME IN BIBLICAL THEOLOGY

Dr. Mark R. Saucy

Saucy, in his chapter *Israel as a Necessary Theme in Biblical Theology*, begins by stating, "salvation is from the Jews" (John 4:22).

His chapter describes the seven major acts in the biblical story, which focus on key threshold moments from Genesis to the Book of Revelation. Saucy's overview illustrates how Israel is a crucial part of the entire biblical story and weaves the story of God's plan for the Jewish people, the land of Israel, and the future of Israel together with His heart for the nations of the world. Once again, and within the context of creating a biblical theology of Israel and the Jewish people, Saucy emphasizes the role of the Jewish people as God's prophetic and Messianic light to sinful humanity.

De-emphasizing the role of Israel and the Jewish people as God's means of reaching the nations takes away from the power and comprehensiveness of the biblical story of redemption that "blesses" the world.

"...for salvation is from the Jews."
—Jesus to the woman at Jacob's well in Samaria"

The words of the Savior to the Samaritan woman frame the two-fold task of this chapter. First is the task of telling Scripture's story of salvation. Among the academic disciplines, biblical theology is best poised for this task in its commission to investigate Scripture's diverse themes to "get to the theological heart of the Bible," as Elmer Martens has put it.[1] Unfortunately, and to some extent ironically, the early practice of biblical theology was dominated by study of the thematic elements of Scripture with presuppositions antithetical to the possibility of a unified whole. For many in the field, Scripture's diversity ended up as evidence against the possibility of a coherent whole.[2] Still, the Church that biblical theology ideally must serve needs its story too, and numerous recent works have attempted to bring the themes of Scripture to service of the whole.[3]

To this lively chorus this essay takes its place, but in distinction to the other accounts recently offered—and this is now to the second task of this chapter—I will highlight the necessary place of the Land and People of Israel to the Bible's story. Of course the notion of "necessary" for any topic entails a bold claim, but as I hope to show, it is a claim warranted for Israel as the story of Scripture is told. Without the Land and People of Israel that prepares us for Christ or the *nationed* people that Christ will one day rule with all nations, one struggles with a reduced view of salvation that would be unrecognizable to the Jew who uttered those words and the Samaritan woman who heard them that day at the well of Jacob.

The story that follows will come in a series of acts, like the true drama that it is. The different acts offered indeed paint with a broad brush in the face of Scripture's rich, multi-textured story, but the brevity demanded of us will serve to encourage focus upon threshold moments of the story's development. This can also be an asset. The first act from the book of beginnings, Genesis, will get us started.

Act I: Genesis

As the original audience of Genesis, Israel has a connection to the Bible's story that begins in Genesis chapter one. According to recent observation, literary conventions of Israel's Ancient Near Eastern (ANE) context not only fund the *way* Genesis narrates the world's beginning; they also find concrete parallel in the nation God formed at the Exodus. For examples, the Garden of Eden as conveying the essence of ANE temples with Adam, the human, as a priest figure strikes clear chord with Israel's own internal temple-cult and her larger function as a "kingdom of priests" to the world.[4] Likewise, the Sabbath-rest that crowns the world's narrative in Genesis finds practical and concrete expression in the Sabbath and Jubilee rhythms of Israelite society. The result for this is that rightly seen by Okoye: Israel's history is the world's history *en breve*.[5]

The Israel-formed telling of the world's story leads us in other directions for Genesis as well. Three themes in particular bear noting not only as to how they frame the beginnings of the story, but how they are perfected in Israel's story.

1. A Divine Story

"In the beginning God..."—these words open the Bible's story and immediately address the Who-question so important to ancient Israel's context.[6] Who is the God that created the world? What is he like? And, most importantly, how does he relate to his world? All are questions central to the developing fabric of Scripture story. When the story ends in Revelation, knowledge of this creating God will be face-to-face knowledge (Rev. 22:4). Along the way, however, this triune God's identity and presence with this creation is revealed in important dimensions in the story of Israel's Land and People. Some of this story the world has already seen and some it still needs to.

2. A Kingdom Story

Jesus of Nazareth, the central figure in Scripture's story, was a proclaimer of the reign of God. His practice in this must not be seen as bound only to his first century Judean environs. Rather, as Paul's Second Adam-doctrine shows us (Rom. 5 and 1 Cor. 15), the God-man who proclaimed and performed the kingdom punctuates a storyline that long-preceded him. Indeed, the Psalter, which is Israel's commentary to the Torah, reveals the royal identity of the God who created the world (Ps. 95:1–3). Moreover this Creator-King crowned his creation with an image of himself commissioned to "be fruitful, multiply, fill, *subdue* and *rule*" the earth as his vice regent (Gen. 1:28).[7] The movements of the Bible's unfolding story are the movements of a King's story with his kingdom.[8] That kingdom is *material*; it *subdues its adversaries*; and it *orders every aspect of its subjects' existence*—as the People and Land of Israel must show the world.

3. A Human Story

The human role naturally enters through the kingdom dimensions of the story. At the outset it is a contentious role as the Creator-King-God calls his creation to be the means of overcoming the Adversary—the Antagonist of the story. Whether already in the background in the context of Genesis 1:2,[9] or soon to come on stage (Gen. 3:1ff.), this Evil One is destined to be finally subdued by human beings (Gen. 1:28; 2:15).[10] Of course, the Bible's script will show in the next ACT the failure of the First Adam in this calling, but shadows of a Second Adam who will crush the Antagonist soon appear (Gen.

3:15). Human subduing of sin, not mere annihilation of it, is the end to which the plot points for history. The Land and People of Israel will enrich the world in fulfillment of this human role.

Act II: Fall

The story of God, humanity, and the kingdom takes a tragic turn in Genesis 3 with the Fall of Adam into sin. Curse now enters the created order that originally had been made for blessing in its Sabbath goal (Gen. 2:4). Instead of ruling and subduing evil, God's vice regents now became its slaves, and every dimension of human and non-human creation is compromised. Human identity before God and God's Adversary, relationships with people, institutions and structures of society, and the creation itself all now require restoration. Like the pristine order that preceded it, the Fall provides a signpost—an *anti*-signpost—for Scripture's story. Evil must be overcome *within history* and it must be overcome by means of a restored human vice regency (Heb. 2:8–9; Ps. 8).[11]

Act III: Abraham

The entrance of Abram, the Chaldean, to history's stage in Genesis 12 marks the next major phase of the Bible's restoration story. Much has transpired up to this point in the story, but most significant for our purpose is to highlight two themes from the covenant with God and Abraham. First is that Abraham demonstrates the fundamental covenanted-nature of the biblical story. Since the first articulation of "covenant" with Noah (Gen. 6:18), and likely earlier with Adam and Eve,[12] covenant arrangements between God and humanity have been inherent to the kingdom program.[13] Moreover the covenant that bears Abraham's name provides the redemptive framework for all subsequent covenant moves Scripture makes including covenants made with Moses, David, and the so-called new covenant inaugurated with Christ's blood. Here with Abraham is the bud from which redemption's flower of blessing will grow.

The second theme of this act is important to us in how the Abrahamic covenant in all of its different iterations foretells the salvation of God framed in a nation, specifically the Land and People of Israel. The point is significant not only for Abraham's place in the unfolding narrative of Genesis, but also for when the nation of Israel enters in the next act as we will see. Immediately preceding Abraham's appearance humanity's nationed identity has been introduced in Genesis 10 and 11. Abram's appearance in chapter 12 stands in stark contrast to the organization and humanist spirit (11:1–8) of the nations. With Abraham, for the first time God's own nation will be introduced, and it will be the means of blessing all others.[14]

The backstory to all of this concern for human life and identity at the nation-level is Scripture's intrinsic *theological* worldview. Against modern secularism that poaches spiritual beings like God, angels and demons from the consciousness, Scripture understands no aspect of human life as separated from them. At the nation-level the tripartite covenant of deity-people-land marches without interruption throughout all of Scripture's record.[15] So the promise of a nation through Abraham marks a new advance in the spiritual dimension of the kingdom story. Specifically, the constitution of Israel *as a nation* marks a new beachhead for salvation against the *gods of the nations* as we shall see in the following act.

Act IV: Israel

The theological reality of human national life forms the backdrop for the formation of Israel from Egypt. For the Exodus was not merely the deliverance of a people from oppression—it was the formation of a nation and the presentation of that nation's God on the world's stage as supreme over all gods of the other nations.[16] The "theo-political act" that Martin Buber sees in the Exodus is aimed at the prophetic refrain for Israel's purpose to make God's name great among the nations (Mal. 1:11).[17] It also funds the intriguing thesis of David Torrance that modern Israel today, even in unbelief, continues to confront the gods of the nations, in particular Allah.[18]

However, the greatness of Israel's God was not only in display of raw power over other gods. Israel's constitution as a "kingdom of priests, a holy nation" (Ex. 19:6) highlights another aspect of God the nation would reveal to the world. Specifically, as God's confrontation with Egypt's gods meant salvation for Israel, so confrontation of the nations' gods is meant for their salvation, too. And this salvation was not intended as some autonomous freedom, but Israel's constitution teaches the world that life consists of experiential knowledge of the Living God. It was a note unheard of in the ancient pantheons where a deity desired the love of his people over their servile fear, and that he desired communion with them over transcendent distance.[19] Service to Israel's God was a heart religion (Deut. 30). It was a religion of clinging faith that infused all dimensions of human life—faith for everything from daily bread to political expedience and military security. Fullness of human life is presented to the world in this nation as William Dumbrell has well noted: "Probably...we are here...thinking of Israel as offering in her constitution a societary model for the world. She will provide, under the direct divine rule which the covenant contemplates, the paradigm for the theocratic rule which is to be the biblical aim for the whole world."[20] Spiritually, socially, and individually, Israel under God's *Torah* is "tutored" to Christ (Gal. 3:24) and also the foretaste of full-bodied salvation to which Jesus led the Samaritan woman and the rest of the world (John 4:24).

Act V (Prelude): New Covenantalism of the Prophets

Israel's calling to reveal the living God to the nations takes a darker turn when we now consider the prophetic preparation for the coming of Christ. As the prophets make clear, even in her apostasy Israel will make God's name great to the nations. They will see him as holy and abhorring before the treachery of a faithless people (Ezek. 39:26–39). But as the Ezekiel 39 text iterates, the nations will also see God's name great in the *restoration* of his people to their Land. And as we have seen in the story since Act I where the world's story has connection to Israel's story, in Israel's restoration there is salvation for the nations and the created order itself.

We call this wider hope of Israel's prophets as a prelude to the next act when Christ first comes. This is because the new covenant prophecies provide us with the scripting for the "what" and "how" of the story all the way to its end. This script also includes elements that have been passed over to this point, such as the David-centered contours of Israel's life and hope,[21] but they too find their level within the larger prophetic account of the new covenant. As we shall see, failure to pay attention to the prophets in all of these matters sets a trajectory alien to the biblical story as we enter the New Testament, not just for the Land and People of Israel, but also for the larger biblical themes of God, humanity, and the kingdom. We turn now to the new covenant's hope and the new covenant's way.

1. The New Covenant Hope

It is one of the stunning ironies of academic biblical theology that the entity for which the New Testament corpus is named receives so little attention in understanding the New Testament's theology. However, the new covenant hope, *new covenantalism* in this essay, needs to be given the place in the Bible's story that Marshall sees: "The old covenant-new covenant distinction is not at all that prominent on the surface of the New Testament, but it seems to underlie Christian thinking on the understanding of the progress of salvation history."[22] The new covenant is the sum of God's story to its end, including the destinies of Israel, the nations, and even the cosmos itself.[23]

The *locus classicus* for the prophets' new covenantalism is Jeremiah 31:31–34. This text beginning in verse 33 highlights the *individual* dimension of the message in terms familiar to us as: a new heart—the Law written on the heart instead of on tablets of stone, a new depth in relationship with God—"they will know Me" that is no longer mediated by a temple cult—"they will no longer say to one another 'know the Lord' which was the priests' job,[24] and finally the basis for this all in the forgiveness of sins—"for I will remember their sin no more," v. 34, which the prophet Isaiah describes so elegantly in the work of the Suffering Servant in Isaiah 53.

Other texts like Ezekiel 36:24–27 offer concrete examples of the power source and broader scope of the new covenant. The Lord putting His Spirit within his people, v. 27, identifies what the prophets saw as the driving force for all of the new covenant era. This is why Walther Eichrodt rightly calls the Holy Spirit's advent "the central miracle" of the new covenant.[25] Further, the *human social* aspects of the hope are again reiterated in v. 24 when as in chapter 39 noted earlier, God aims to "take you from the nations and gather you from all the countries; then I will bring you to your land." The People of Israel replanted in their Land will appear again on history's stage to model the fullness of the Lord's salvation in a return of blessing to every dimension of human life by the removal of all that has cursed it. Their restoration precipitates the nations' conversion from false gods to the living God (e.g., Isa. 43:10; 55:3–5) in a final summation of the human-kingdom story to reign over evil in a newly ordered world.[26]

2. The New Covenant Way

The prophets not only sketched the essential features of the new covenant era, they also revealed important aspects of the manner in which it would come about. While they didn't realize the twofold coming of the Priest-King to deliver Israel and the world, they do provide the roadmap of what's ahead. This is critical to note because it here that other versions of the Bible's story begin imputing to the NT authors notions of "re-interpreting," clever "new twists," "redefining," and "new visions" to subsume the prophetic vision of Israel into the NT Church. Such invention is indeed needless if we attend to how the prophets themselves understood the manner the story should unfold. Four dimensions of the prophets' new covenantalism are particularly important to set the stage for the subsequent story for the Land and People of Israel. We note these dimensions here and the points of theological revisionism they address.

a. People and Land

In the view of the prophets there would be a literal, physical re-gathering of the Jewish exiles under a new movement of the Holy Spirit. The process ends in Israel's spiritual, as well as physical, restoration to their Land in a kingdom-state like other kingdoms and nations (Dan. 2:44; Isa. 49:6). In revisionist readings, Israel is replaced by a "New Israel" (Church), "exile" ends in Christ who is the "new Moses" and himself "Israel," and God gets glory in the typological "restoration" of some other "Israel." So also the Land promises are fulfilled in the Gospel outreach that is going throughout the whole world.[27]

b. Temple cult

The prophets foresaw the obsolescence of the mediated approach to God narrated in Israel's Temple cult (Jer. 31:33). This means they foresaw a redefinition of what Temple will mean to God's people in the coming acts of God's story. This is a significant point because when the NT writers follow the prophets' script and reveal the new institution of atonement in Christ, this is often taken by revisionists as a novel move that justifies similar moves toward the Land and People.[28] The difference is that in the case of the Temple, the prophets sanction such a move; while for the Land and People they clearly do not. The NT writers follow the prophets' lead precisely.

c. Messiah and the Nation of Israel

The new covenant script understood the presence of an anointed Individual and the restored Land and People in history *together* at some point. The Servants to the world are two: Nation and Messiah (Isa. 40–66). The advent of the Messiah does not mean he becomes the "nation" so that all of its functions to the world are fulfilled in him. Nor is his glory eclipsed by the presence of a restored Land and People of Israel as revisionists fear.[29] The prophets of the new covenant had no such concern.

d. Israel and the Nations

Against a re-visioned story in which the Gentile nations convert to the living God as a spiritual, "New Israel," the prophets saw a restored Israelite nation *and* Gentiles together as the people of God without redefinition or "new vision" for either.[30] Isaiah is clear—Gentiles join God's people *as Gentiles*, not Israel: "In that day Israel will be the third member of the group along with Egypt and Assyria. 'Blessed be my people Egypt, and the work of my hands Assyria, and my special possession Israel'" (Isa. 19:24–25).

Following these cues will be important as we move into the NT account of the new covenantal script. As we shall see, beginning with the mission of Jesus himself, the phases of the drama the NT writers sketch stay to the prophetic script without wavering and without redefinition.

Act V: New Covenantalism in Jesus Christ (Phase 1)

The grand biblical narrative for God, humanity, and kingdom finds its climax in the appearance of the God-man, Jesus. The record of his person and ministry in the Gospels together with the Spirit-inspired interpretation offered by his apostles show the prophets' new covenantal vision had indeed entered the world's story. As we saw in the Prelude to this act above, the prophets detailed the content and manner the fulfillment should have. Both issues come into focus as we consider the future of the Land and People of Israel in this work of Jesus Christ.

Jesus, Kingdom and New Covenant

In the Gospel record, Jesus, John before him, and Jesus' disciples are heralds of the kingdom of God (Matt. 4:17; 3:2; 10:7). The kingdom is near, at hand, or even breaking in through the personal ministry of Jesus. As fully human, Jesus takes up the mantle of the human calling in his confrontation of the spiritual forces that bind humanity and all creation alike.[31] Most significantly, Jesus interprets everything about his person and mission in terms of the prophets' new covenant. At the Last Supper he raises the cup of the Seder and proclaims it as "the blood of the new covenant which is poured out for many for the forgiveness of sins" (Matt. 26:28). Kingdom, God, humanity, and salvation all coalesce in Jesus' fulfillment of the new covenant hope.

The NT writers continue the new covenantalism of Jesus, although it is now clear to them that the new covenant's fulfillment would be divided into two phases.[32] Associated with the first phase, the cross provides the necessary final resolution of the sin problem upon which all of the new covenant blessings rested (Jer. 31:34; Heb. 8–10). Also, the new covenant Spirit has come through the one who himself lived the Spirit-filled life and poured the Spirit on all flesh after his ascension (Acts 2:38). All as the prophets announced. Further, Jesus provides a new knowledge of God as the 'Abba'-Father of his people.[33] Lastly, Israel's Temple cult is rendered obsolete by the ministry of the better High Priest with a better sacrifice and a better covenant (Mark 15:38; Heb. 8–10).[34] Again, all as the prophets had foreseen, exactly and literally. As to content and manner of fulfillment the NT so far the authors appear to be following the way of the prophets blamelessly.

Jesus, the Land and the People of Israel

But what about the Land and People of Israel? The physical restoration of the nation of Israel for the benefit of the world is a clear feature of the prophets' new covenant hope. Did Jesus and the apostles subtly and cleverly begin the replacement-process of creating a New Israel? Aside from the complete anomaly—such a move would be compared to their treatment of other new covenant expectations—which have been closely, even literally, followed, two important observations are in order. First, in their account of the prophetic script there is *nothing explicit* in anything the NT writers describe of the present age that should require a deviation from the prophets. In other words, there is nothing explicit in their writings calling for revising: (1) A literal restoration of the Land and People of Israel at some point; (2) Messiah's historical presence together with a restored nation; (3) the Gentiles as joining God's people along side, but not replacing, Israel; or (4) that the universal scope of the covenant flows from the restored nation of Israel without obliterating it. "New Israel" is never a term for the people of God in the present age. Neither is the language of being "replanted in the Land" ever taken up for the Church in the NT.[35]

The second observation: When the NT writers do explicitly take up the present condition and mission of the Church, it is clear that the present time is not yet the age the prophets spoke about concerning the Land and People of Israel. The present period is but the first fruits of that blessed kingdom age that is coming for both Gentile and Jew (Rom. 11:12, 15). Three areas of comparison highlight the false equation of the Church age and the one the prophets foresaw for a restored Israel.[36]

1. Manifestation of God's Kingdom

The prophets foresaw a literal, restored nation in its Land. The Church, however, is not a nation; she has no political status in the present age as a theocratic nation among other nations; she does not preside over political institutions, wielding coercive consequences from legislation in the achievement of political ends.[37] The Church will never demonstrate before the world's nations a military or political structure that is ordered by the living God.

2. Experience in Mission

The prophets' new covenantalism featured the nation of Israel with a mission as a light to the nations to bring them deliverance (Isa. 49:6). Under the patronage of Messiah, Israel would fulfill this mission from a position of cultural supremacy. Like Israel, the Church also has a mission to the nations (Luke 24:46–68), but the posture from which its mission is conducted is very different from Israel's. First, the Church's mission is now conducted in the *absence* of her Messiah (Luke 19:11–27). Second, far from being socially on top, the Church now exists as aliens, strangers, even as this world's dirt and scum (1 Cor. 4:13). Witness for the Church in the present age is just as it was for her Lord, namely by means of *suffering*, not by commanding domination (cf. 2 Cor. 12:9; Col. 1:24; 1 Peter 2:21–25).

3. Result of Mission

Israel's fulfillment of her mission leads to worldwide peace as the nations come under Messiah's rule (Isa. 49:6; cf. also chapters 2 and 11). For the Church, the NT writers entertain no such glorious end in this age. With the way of rejection broad (Matt. 7:13), under the deceiving power of the "ruler of this age" (John 16:11), the nations hurtle headlong in blind allegiance to Antichrist and the spiritual forces empowering him (Rev. 13). Meanwhile persecutions of the righteous continue to the end (Rev. 9:6).

The first coming of Christ represents the inauguration of the new covenant contours of the Bible's story. Aspects of the story's end are already on the stage of world history. Final installation of those promises awaits the next act when salvation is fully known and completed, when human vocation to subdue evil is realized, and when God is glorified in mercy and holiness.

Act VI: New Covenantalism in Jesus Christ (Phase 2)

Somewhere between the first coming of Christ and his glorious second coming, the Church now waits. This means that all the remaining acts of Scripture's drama lie in the future. As we have already seen, Israel's prophets' saw all the way to end of this salvation, which means they still stand as our guides today. The other essays in this volume make it clear that this new covenant hope still includes a future for the People and Land of Israel to be God's channel of blessing and the fullness of salvation to the nations of the world. Jesus (Matt. 19:28; 23:37–39), Peter (Acts 3:18–21), Paul (Rom. 9–11; 15:8–12; 1 Cor. 15:24–28), and the writer of Hebrews (2:5–9) all see a future reign of God's people on earth.

The last major contributor to the NT record, the apostle John, also clearly shows us he stands in the full new covenant vision in the prophecy of his apocalypse, the book of Revelation. As is well known, the clearest millennial text in the Bible comes from his hand (Rev. 20:1–10). But it would be a distortion of John's message to merely recite this text, note its place in the sequence of events in Revelation 19–20 *before* the new heavens and new earth,[38] note its parallel in all contemporary extant literature,[39] and move on. For such a move would fail to show how the entire fabric of Revelation is laden with the new covenant hope of the prophets. In actuality, the thousand-year reign of Revelation 20 following the return of Christ is but the final celebration in history of a redemptive story that has always been aimed at every tribe, tongue, people, and nation.

The role of Psalm 2 in the background of Revelation is well established.[40] The nations rage and devise rebellious plots (2:1); the kings of the earth conspire and stand against the Lord's anointed (2:2); yet the Lord's king will smash them and take them back as his inheritance and rule over them (2:8–9). In Revelation, this basic plot famously establishes Christ's royal majesty as "ruler of the kings of the earth" (1:5) and his coming conquest and rule of the nations with the rod of iron (Rev. 12:5; 19:15). But Revelation also uses Psalm 2 to locate this rule of the nations in the *future*. The believers at Thyatira (Rev. 2:26–27), if they remain faithful, are given the same promise as the Lord's anointed king out of Psalm 2—authority over the nations and to shepherd them with the rod of iron.[41] But when is this authority exercised?

In Revelation, the rule of the nations naturally falls in the millennium of chapter 20 right where the prophets placed it in Psalm 2 and the other OT texts that undergird Revelation, like Zechariah 12–14.[42] It is not a spiritualized, heavenly "rule" going on in the present age, because like the rest of the NT, Revelation describes the condition of the Church as one of suffering, persecution, and even personal lapse (Rev. 2–3). The cry of the martyrs for their vengeance in chapter 6 (v. 9–11) haunts the bloody trail beneath the entire book until vindication comes at last in the rule of Rev. 20:4–6. McNichol rightly catches the significance:

Revelation 20.4–6 is a victory celebration. A straightforward reading would indicate that integral to the victory celebration of those who refused to bear the mark of the beast is their assumption of power over the nations. Psalm 2, a paradigmatic text for the Apocalypse, is now fulfilled (1.5–6; 2.26–27; 3.21; 5:10; 12.5 and 19.18). The Lamb (God's son) is now the evident ruler over the kings of the earth. The martyrs (6.9–11) now have the answer to their prayers.[43]

So, again, in Revelation the prophetic word is made more firm. And not only the prophetic word—indeed, the goal of gaining the fallen world by human domination of the evil that has been God's aim from the beginning (Gen. 3:15) is accomplished. Revelation's account of salvation is now fully human and now covers every aspect of human life, fulfilling completely the human vocation. The final act is ready to come.

Act VII: God All in All

Paul writes to the Corinthian church that when Christ has completed his part in the Kingdom story, he gives the kingdom up to the Father, "so that God may be all in all" (1 Cor. 15:28). And there can be no better place to conclude this account, too, than God all in all. The work of salvation is completed and full; evil is vanquished; the vocation of human beings is fulfilled in putting down all that is hostile to it and the world; and the Living God is revealed in unveiled glory. The eschatological joy permeates the cosmos and the eternal feast of light and life ensues (Rev. 21 and 22).

Conclusion

We began our account of the People and Land of Israel in the Bible's story with the words of Jesus to the Samaritan woman that "salvation is from the Jews." Having now traced Scripture's story to its *summum*, we have a fuller glimpse of the meaning behind Jesus' words. We see a fullness that eclipses the retooled, individualistic, dehumanized and merely spiritualized versions of salvation that are all too common in the affluent western world. We see here in Scripture, the story of all stories; the one story for which human life was made from the beginning and is returned to in the end. And as the Divine, Human, and Kingdom dimensions of the story trace through to an unending, eternal resolution, the Land and People of Israel also shine indeed as the Lord's servant of that goal. In Israel, God is offering the nations his divine object lesson, both negative and positive. The glory of his faithful mercy and zealous holiness both are told through this nation. Israel is a *national* exemplar of a salvation that doesn't just free its victim. Rather it frees them to rule and subdue the oppressor according to their original calling. Thus Israel's story is the world's story *en breve*. It is a story that is yet unfinished, but not unknown. Blessed be the God of Israel and the Savior of the world.

Study Questions

1. Describe the task of biblical theology.

2. What do we mean by saying the world's story, even from the creation in Genesis, is told in Scripture in an "Israel-formed" way? What is the justification for such a claim?

3. Explain the essence of Divine, Kingdom, and human themes of the Bible's story. How do they each begin in Genesis and end in Revelation?

4. What do you make of the claim that God has always intended to subdue and rule evil through human beings? What does this suggest about Jesus the God-man's activities against Satan in his first coming?

5. What is the significance of Abraham (Act III) to the Bible's story?

6. Identify and describe what Israel (Act IV) contributes to the Divine, Kingdom, and Human themes of the Bible's story.

7. What is gained from the Bible's story specifically from Israel's status as a nation?

8. What do we mean by new covenantalism from the prophets, and what is the relationship of the prophets' new covenant hope to the New Testament documents?

9. Why was it considered as unwarranted revisionism of the OT to consider the Church as the replacement of Israel?

10. In what ways does the present age of the Church differ from the age the prophets saw for a restored People and Land of Israel? What is the implication of the difference for the claim that the Church is a "New Israel"?

11. Describe the role of the millennium in Revelation 20:1–10 to the whole book of Revelation.

12. What contribution does the nation of Israel make to the meaning of salvation in Scripture?

Conference Video

chosenpeople.com/saucy

Interview with Dr. Mark Saucy

chosenpeople.com/saucy-interview

ISRAEL IN THE LAND AS AN ESCHATOLOGICAL NECESSITY?

Dr. John S. Feinberg

Feinberg, in his chapter *Israel in the Land as an Eschatological Necessity?*, demonstrates why national Israel is important in God's future plans. He argues, "Israel not only *will* possess the land, but biblically speaking, she *must* possess it." He believes the various end-times prophecies cannot occur until "Israel is in the land with both political and religious control over her own destiny." His chapter explores three significant end time prophecies.

First, he looks at the *seventy weeks* in Daniel 9:24–27 with verse 27 as its crux. Second, he examines Zechariah 12. Third, Feinberg addresses Isaiah 19:16–25, where Isaiah describes three countries: Egypt, Israel, and Assyria, although he focuses on the first two. This prophecy must look forward to the literal kingdom, because both Egypt and Assyria fear the Lord.

Feinberg argues that these three prophecies cannot occur unless Israel returns to the land and establishes political, military, and religious control over it.

For much of their history, the people of Israel have been scattered throughout the world and there has been no Israeli national state in the land promised to Abraham and his descendants.

According to some evangelicals, it is sad that Israel as a nation disobeyed God in many ways, culminating in the rejection of her Messiah, but they see Israel's loss of the land as part of God's just judgment on the nation. Even more, these same evangelicals believe that Israel's loss of the land (and all other blessings promised to Abraham) is irreversible, and any claim that Israel had to the land has been forfeited forever. Of course, the remnant of Jews throughout history who have embraced Jesus as Messiah will partake in the blessings of a literal physical kingdom when the Lord establishes it upon his return, but there will be no special "Jewish flavor" to the millennial kingdom, and most Jews who have ever lived will not be included in the reign of their Messiah and King Jesus.

In this book, there are various chapters whose intent is to reassert that despite Israel's rejection of her Messiah and despite God's judgment of the nation, some day the nation of Israel as a whole will turn back to God and embrace her Messiah. Then all the promises made to Abraham and the other patriarchs will be fulfilled after all. There are, of course, various biblical passages which directly and unconditionally promise to the people of Israel the blessings of the patriarchs, including the possession of all the land promised.

My chapter employs a different kind of argument to support the belief that Israel, despite everything that has happened, will in fact in the end times and through the kingdom possess the land. In fact, I believe that Israel not only *will* possess the land, but biblically speaking, she *must* possess it. My point, however, is not that she *must* possess it because clear biblical passages promise the land to her. Rather, it is that various end-time prophecies cannot be fulfilled unless Israel is in the land with both political and religious control over her own destiny. What is especially interesting is that none of the prophecies I shall discuss are *per se* predictions that Israel must return to the land and possess it as a national entity. Instead, they are about other end-time events which involve Israel, but those events cannot happen unless Israel is a national entity in the land of Palestine with political, military, and religious control over her own people and anyone else living in the land during the end-time.[1]

While there are many end-time prophecies I might invoke, I have chosen only three OT passages. The first is Daniel 9:24–27, the vision of the seventy weeks. My concern is especially with verse 27, but to understand it we must also focus on verse 26. As Daniel 9 begins, we learn that Daniel realized that Jeremiah had predicted that Judah would be in Babylonian captivity for seventy years. Daniel knew that the seventy years had passed and yet his people were still in Babylon. So, Daniel writes that he began to pray about this and to beseech the Lord to act on behalf of his people. In answer to Daniel's prayer, the Lord sent the angel Gabriel to Daniel. Gabriel's response was not what Daniel expected. In essence, Gabriel told Daniel that though Daniel was concerned about the prediction of 70 years of captivity, God wanted Daniel to know God's plans for Israel that span not seventy years, but seventy times seven years, i.e., 490 years![2]

According to this passage, seventy weeks were decreed for Daniel's people and his holy city (v. 24), which people and city would be the Jews and Jerusalem. Conservative Bible scholars generally agree that these are not literal weeks (490 literal weeks would be roughly nine and a half years), but weeks of years. That is, each day of a literal week stands for one literal year. Hence, seven of these days would stand for seven years. Since the prophecy is about seventy of these groups of seven years, seventy times seven is 490 years.

It would have been natural for Daniel (and anyone else familiar with this prophecy) to think the 490 years would be consecutive years; that is, the 490 years would occur one right after the other. However, verses 24–25 take us through the first sixty-nine weeks, but then verse 26 speaks of things that happen after the sixty-ninth week. It would seem, then, that verse 26 should speak about the seventieth week, but verse 27 suggests otherwise. Verse 27 speaks of another week, so if verse 26 is about the seventieth week, then this must be a prophecy of seventy-one weeks! No Bible scholar would say this vision is about seventy-one weeks, and probably Daniel understood that our verse 26 would occur after the first sixty-nine weeks but before the seventieth week. Thus, the seventy weeks are not evidently consecutive weeks, happening one after another.

Verse 25 predicts that by the end of the sixty-ninth week Messiah would come. Verse 26 says that after the sixty-ninth week (but before the seventieth) Messiah would die ("Be cut off and have nothing"). In addition, after the sixty-ninth week, Jerusalem and the temple would be destroyed by an invading people. We know that this part of the prophecy was fulfilled when the Roman Emperor Titus invaded Jerusalem, and destroyed much of the city and the temple in AD 70. The temple has not been in use ever since, though from time to time one hears of supposed "plans" to rebuild the temple and reinstate temple worship.

Verse 26 predicted that the capture of Jerusalem and destruction of the temple would be at the hands of "the people of the prince who is to come." We know that the *people* who did come were the Romans. Since the whole prediction in verse 26 was of a time future to Daniel, it would be understandable to think that the "prince who is to come" would come when his people would come. If so, then the prophecy of the "prince" should have been fulfilled by Rome's Emperor Titus. But, verse 27 begins by saying "and he will make a firm covenant." Who is this "he"? Surely, Daniel would think that the referent of "he" is "the prince" mentioned in verse 26. The only other possible referent for "he" in verse 26 is the Messiah, but verse 26 predicted that Messiah would die, and what verse 27 predicts would never be something the Messiah would do to his people and their city of Jerusalem.

So, "he" in verse 27 must refer to "the prince" of verse 26, but Emperor Titus never did what verse 27 predicted that prince would do. Why would Titus make a covenant (presumably) of peace with a people he had just destroyed? And why would he stop sacrifices in their temple three and a half years later ("in the middle of the week"—v. 27) when he had destroyed the temple and made sacrifices impossible three and a half years before the middle of this seventieth week? Clearly, Titus capturing Jerusalem and destroying it and the temple in AD 70 cannot be the fulfillment of verse 27.

Returning to verse 26, I note a certain ambiguity in the phrase "the people of the prince who is to come." Upon first reading, one would assume that the prince would come when his people come, i.e., he would lead the Roman armies that invaded and sacked Jerusalem. But since "the prince" is the subject of verse 27 (Daniel's seventieth week), and verse 27 was not fulfilled in AD 70 or shortly thereafter, it begins to become clear that the prince who would come (v. 26) would not necessarily come when his people would come.

From our vantage point, we can see that the prince of verse 27 has not yet come and done the things that verse predicts. Hence, many students of Scripture and of end-time prophecy, including myself, believe that verse 27 is about the end-time and that Daniel's seventieth week is what Scripture elsewhere calls the tribulation, a time at the very end of the age before Jesus returns to set up his literal, physical kingdom on earth.

So, Daniel 9:27 is an end-time prophecy, but what does it say and how is it relevant to our topic? The verse predicts that this prince will do several things. At the outset of the seven years, he will make a peace treaty (a covenant—surely this must be some kind of treaty of peace) with the many that is to last seven years. In the middle of that seventieth week, i.e., three and one-half years later, he will stop sacrifice and grain offerings. Where? Once it was built the only place to make any sacrifice in Israel was and still is the temple. This means that either prior to the tribulation, or very early in it, the temple in Jerusalem must be rebuilt and a system of temple sacrifices must be reinstated. We know that between AD 70 and now none of this has happened.

Verse 27 says that this prince will also do abominable things that make desolate. In the Olivet Discourse Jesus offers more details when he says in Matthew 24:15, "when you see the abomination of desolation which was spoken of through Daniel the prophet, standing in the holy place (let the reader understand). . . ." In Jesus' thinking, it is most likely that "the holy place" is the temple.

Putting Daniel 9:27 and Matthew 24:15 together, it becomes evident that the prince of Daniel 9:27 will do something that desolates the temple. Exactly what he will do is not stated in these verses, but for our purposes, identifying the abomination of desolation is not crucial.[3] No wonder that the sacrifices will be stopped! Jesus' words in Matthew 24:15 confirm not only that Daniel 9:27 will be fulfilled, but in effect also that the whole prophecy of the seventy-weeks will be fulfilled. That is, all of Daniel 9:24–26 is preparatory to what happens in verse 27. Therefore, if the events predicted in those verses don't occur, there is no reason to think the predicted events in verse 27 will come to pass. However, Jesus affirms that Daniel 9:27 will be fulfilled. So, given its connection to verses 24–26, it only stands to reason that those verses would need to be fulfilled. In fact, by the time Jesus uttered Matthew 24:15, Dan. 9:24–26a had already been fulfilled, so it would be absurd for him to think the rest of verse 26 would go unfulfilled. And if most of Daniel 9:24–26 had been fulfilled, there was no reason for Jesus to think verse 27 wouldn't be fulfilled! In Matthew 24:15 Jesus affirms the fulfillment of Daniel 9:27!

Thankfully, Daniel 9:27 does not end with the abomination of desolation, but also predicts that desolation and destruction will be poured out on the prince. Presumably, his destruction happens at the end of the tribulation when the Lord returns to destroy his enemies and set up his kingdom!

Whether or not you agree with this interpretation of Daniel 9:26–27, you may be wondering how it is relevant to Israel possessing the Holy Land. The answer is that it is quite relevant in several respects. The seventieth week begins with the prince (many would call him the Antichrist, the political leader of the tribulation, the first beast of Revelation 13) making a peace treaty with the many. In the context of Daniel 9, this can only refer to the people of Israel. But how can you make a treaty of peace with a nation that does not exist and with a people who are scattered all over the world, with only a small number of Jews in the Holy Land, which is itself a non-Jewish, non-Israeli nation? In order for this part of the prophecy to be fulfilled, Jews must inhabit the land, but more than that. There must be a nation of Israel with political and military control over its own destiny. The Antichrist cannot make a peace treaty with a non-existent people and nation!

But, there is more. In order for the Antichrist to stop sacrifices in the temple and set up the abomination of desolation, there must be a fully functioning temple in Jerusalem which is used for daily sacrifices. That is not so now, so sometime before the tribulation begins (or right at its outset) the temple must be rebuilt and sacrifices reinstated. Who would do such a thing? Christians wouldn't be interested, nor would Muslims. Who but Jews wanting to practice their faith would do this? But how could they rebuild the temple and perform daily sacrifices (sacrifices the Antichrist will stop) if they don't possess the land and have enough political control over Jerusalem (and really, over all of Israel) to allow them to order such a "rebuilding project" and to restart sacrifices? Without being in the land as a national political and religious entity, it seems impossible to fulfill this prophecy. So Israel possessing the land as a national political entity is an absolute necessity for these predictions to be fulfilled![4]

A second passage for consideration is Zechariah 12. Zechariah 14 deals with the same time period and the same basic events, but our specific focus is two things in chapter 12. Zechariah was written after the return of Judah from Babylonian captivity. Thus, when Zechariah speaks of an upcoming attack on Jerusalem and its deliverance by God, he cannot be predicting anything related to the Babylonian Captivity, because it was already over when Zechariah wrote.

Zechariah predicts that a day will come when Jerusalem is surrounded and all of Judah will be under attack (12:2). Lest we think this refers only to nations immediately surrounding Israel in the middle east, verse 3 clarifies that all the nations of the world will be gathered against it. Zechariah 14:2 also speaks of this same attack, but this verse teaches something that we learn nowhere else in Scripture. Zechariah 14:2 tells us that at the outset of this climactic battle, Israel will be losing very badly.[5]

Both Zechariah 12 and 14 predict that in that day the Lord will intervene to fight for his people. Chapter 12 tells us that God will empower the people of Israel to fight as never before (vv. 5–6, 8). In addition, God will himself overpower Israel's enemies by sending confusion upon them (12:4; 14:12–13, 15).

When are these prophecies about a worldwide military alliance against Israel and Jerusalem to be fulfilled? To date none of this has happened. It is hard to see these passages fulfilled until the end-time. In fact, what we see in Zechariah 12 and 14 is a battle that the NT identifies for us as the battle of Armageddon. We read of this battle in Revelation 16:12–21; verse 16 tells us that the battle will happen at a place called (in Hebrew) *Har-Magedon*. I also believe that Revelation 14:14–20 describes the extent of the destruction of God's and Israel's enemies, though Armageddon is not specifically named as the place where this happens. Revelation 19:17–21 also speaks of these events, and though it does not name the battle Armageddon, clearly, these events occur when the Lord rides out of heaven with his armies to do battle (19:11–16).

Zechariah 12 and 14 say that on that day the Lord will go forth to do battle for his people Israel. Revelation 19 shows that God literally will go forth to fight; this is not just a metaphorical way of saying that God will help his people to win the battle, but will do so as he watches from heaven. Momentarily, we shall also see that both Zechariah 12 and 14 literally require the Lord to return to earth to fight for his people. Given the parallel descriptions in Zechariah and the chapters mentioned in Revelation, it is hard to imagine that we are looking at separate climactic battles, especially when you read in both books that what ensues after the Lord destroys his enemies is the Kingdom. It makes most sense to understand both Zechariah and Revelation as predicting the climactic battle of the tribulation, the battle of Armageddon.

Perhaps you agree but wonder what this has to do with Israel and the land. Actually, it fits precisely the case I am making that there are end-time prophecies which don't predict Israel's return to the land and possession of it as a nation, but they do require it. Put simply, why would all the nations of the world gather armies around Jerusalem and attack it and the rest of the country if no Jews or few Jews live there? If there is no state of Israel possessed by the Jewish nation, why would the nations attack if their intent is to destroy the Jewish nation? Moreover, if there is no Jewish state in the land, how could the Jewish nation muster an army to fight the enemy? If Jews are scattered all over the world, why would they travel to Israel, form an army and get ready to be attacked while they defend Jerusalem and the rest of the land? If some Gentile peoples possess the land as their own country, why would Jews come back to the land to defend this Gentile nation? And, perhaps, most important, how could the Lord's going forth to do battle on that day be an act of defending his people Israel (as Zechariah 12 and 14 demand), if Israel is a Gentile nation that happens to possess the land at that time? That would not fulfill the promise that God will defend his people Israel on that day!

Clearly, the only way that any of these prophecies (recorded in Zechariah 12 and 14 and Revelation 14, 16 and 19) make sense is if Jews in numbers and power sufficient to control the land of Israel as a nation and have a military that can defend it upon attack are in the land and possess it as a national entity. So, Israel in the end times must be present in and possess the land.

We are not done just yet, however, with Zechariah 12 and 14. Previously, I noted that when the events predicted in these chapters occur, God will literally return to earth to fight for his people. How can we know that will happen? Actually, both chapters 12 and 14 show us things that clarify that the Lord will return. Chapter 14 verse 3 says that the Lord will go forth to fight against the nations attacking Israel, and then verse 4 shows that it is not a figurative "going forth," because it says that "in that day his feet will stand on the Mount of Olives, which is in front of Jerusalem on the east; and the Mount of Olives will be split in its middle from east to west by a very large valley, so that half of the mountain will move toward the north and the other half toward the south."

Just before the Lord's feet stand on the Mount of Olives, he will come from heaven into the air. Chapter 12 also says the Lord will go forth to do battle for his people. That this is a literal return to the earth is confirmed by Zechariah 12:10. The verse reads: "And I will pour out on the house of David and on the inhabitants of Jerusalem, the Spirit of grace and of supplications, so that they will look on Me whom they have pierced; and they will mourn for Him, as one mourns for an only son, and they will weep bitterly over Him, like the bitter weeping over a first-born."

The key is the phrase "they will look on Me whom they have pierced." How could this happen if the Lord does not literally, physically return? Even more, who could this possibly be? Who would have come to the people of Israel at one time and was rejected and pierced? Moreover, who could later return to rescue them and when they see him they will recognize him as the one they had pierced? This could be none other than Jesus their Messiah!

Put simply, Zechariah predicts the salvation of the nation of Israel living at the time of Jesus' return. As they look on him and repent, Zechariah 14 shows that he will come physically to earth and the Mount of Olives will be divided in two.

Jesus himself in the Olivet Discourse speaks of this same event. He tells us that immediately after the tribulation, the sign of the Son of Man will appear in the sky, and then all the tribes of the earth will mourn. They will see the Son of Man coming on the clouds of the sky with power and great glory (Matt. 24:29–30). Commentators of various stripes agree that the tribes of the earth mourning is a reference to Zechariah 12:10. For any who have ever wondered how Paul's prediction in Romans 11:25–27 of the salvation of Israel as a whole could ever take place, Zechariah 12 gives you the answer (and Jesus confirms that it will happen)!

No doubt, some may respond that Israel as a nation could be saved even if they don't possess the land and are scattered around the world. Christ's return will likely be so spectacular (see Matt. 24:29ff) that no one could miss it. Perhaps this is so, but if it is a Gentile nation in control politically and militarily of Israel, as already noted, it is hard to see this event as a return of the Lord to deliver that Gentile nation from this worldwide confederacy. Moreover, if Jews are merely scattered all over the world (but not in the land), they might find the Lord's return perplexing, but since he would not apparently be coming to deliver their nation from extermination, who knows what his return would mean about the Jews' long-awaited Messiah?

Further confirmation that the Jews involved will be in the land as part of a nation under attack comes from Zechariah 12. The picture in Zechariah 12 is that those who do the mourning will be in the midst of the battle, losing at first (Zech. 14:2) and desperately in need of deliverance.

Though Jesus in Matthew 24:30 does not talk about a military battle, his reference to the "tribes mourning" links Matthew 24:30 with Zechariah 12:10, and we know that Zechariah 12:10 happens in the midst of the climactic battle of Armageddon. So, Matthew 24:29–30 must also happen at Armageddon. Zechariah 12:10ff predicts that the whole nation will get involved in repenting for their sin of rejecting the one whom they have pierced. This makes most sense if Israel is a nation in the land with political, military and religious control of her own destiny.

The spiritual salvation of Israel as a nation amidst the situation described in Zechariah 12 and 14 makes the most sense if Israel possesses the land, has its own government and military, and comes to the battle of Armageddon primarily disbelieving in Jesus as their Messiah. There will be a tribulation, and there will be a battle of Armageddon where the nations seek once and for all to destroy Israel. The Lord will return and the nation of Israel as a whole alive at that time will be saved. Scripture predicts these things, so they must happen. But they cannot happen without Israel possessing the land, and in control of her political, military, and religious destiny.

A third passage, Isaiah 19:16–25, takes us beyond the tribulation to the kingdom. It speaks of three different countries, Egypt, Israel, and Assyria, though most of it is about the former two. Assyria consisted of parts of modern day Iran, Iraq, and Syria. What this passage predicts about Egypt has never been the case. In fact, it is hard to see this prophecy being fulfilled at any time before the millennial kingdom. Specifically, the passage teaches that several things will happen. First, the people and land of Egypt will fear both the God of Israel and Israel itself (vv. 16–17). When Moses told Pharaoh that God wanted him to let the people of Israel go, Pharaoh was unmoved. Why should he pay any attention to a God who had left his people in bondage to Egypt for more than four hundred years? As the centuries of world history passed, Egypt continued to worship a variety of gods, none of them the God of the Bible. For much of the last two thousand years, Egyptians and their Arab neighbors have embraced Islam. However, Isaiah predicts that there will be a day when Egypt fears the Lord because of judgments he brings upon them and more that he threatens (vv. 16–17).

In addition, Isaiah clearly states in verse 17 that Egypt will fear Israel because of "the purpose of the Lord of hosts which he is purposing against them." In other words, Egypt, already dealing with God's judgment, will fear Israel because it will see that God is planning to use Israel as an instrument of more judgment upon Egypt.

It goes without saying, but I'll say it anyway—how can the land of Judah become a terror to Egypt if there is no Jewish political and military entity? Are we to believe that Judah will be occupied and ruled by Gentiles and that they will be a threat to Egypt? That hardly fits the rest of Isaiah 19:16–25, let alone what we have already seen about

Israel's presence in and possession of the land, beginning from at least the start of the tribulation.

Isaiah says that Egypt will not just fear God. Verse 18 says that the land of Egypt will swear allegiance to the Lord of hosts. Even more, Egypt will build a pillar to the Lord near its border (v. 19). This will show to anyone who comes to Egypt that this is a country that is loyal to the God of Israel and of Scripture. There will also be an altar in Egypt for worshiping the Lord, and Egypt will worship Him. Verse 21 says this and adds that Egypt will make promises to the Lord and fulfill them.

As mind boggling as these predictions are, Isaiah predicts even more fantastic things to come. In verse 23, he writes that there will be a highway built that will go from Egypt to Assyria. Even a brief glance at a map will show that such a highway will most likely go through the land of Israel. Notice, however, that this will not be a highway used for military ventures. Rather, the Assyrians will use it to come into Egypt, and the Egyptians will use it to travel to Assyria for the purpose of worshiping together (v. 23). "Of course," some will say—"they are all Muslims and so they will worship Allah together." But, that cannot be so because the verses just before verse 23 say that Egypt will worship the Lord, and verse 24 shows that Israel will be a partner with Egypt and Assyria in worship. Jews have never worshiped Allah, and there is no biblical evidence that they ever will. It is hard to see Jews worshiping Allah except by force, but force is foreign to the state of affairs between Israel, Egypt, and Assyria as portrayed in this passage!

Notice as well how Isaiah 19 ends. It ends with a blessing of the Lord upon all three. Surely, this would not happen if they were worshiping some other god than the God of Israel. And, look at the blessing God gives to each. God will say, "Blessed is Egypt my people"—*ami*, a term typically reserved for Israel. God will add a blessing upon Assyria whom he will call "the work of my hands," another phrase usually used to refer to God's relation to Israel. And blessing will also be upon Israel whom God calls "my inheritance." Applying these titles usually reserved for Israel to Egypt and Assyria does not show that Israel has lost God's blessing! Rather it shows the wideness in God's mercy to welcome, pardon, and bless all three of these nations!

How does this relate to Israel and possession of the land? Again, the point should be clear. The highway built from Egypt to Assyria can be of little use to Israel in partnering with Egypt and Assyria in worshiping the Lord if there is no land of Israel or if the Jewish people are not in the land. But we have already seen in Zechariah 12 that there will be a day when the nation of Israel will turn back to God and claim Jesus as her Messiah (as Matt. 24:29–30 and Rom. 11:25–27 confirm). And we saw that those prophecies cannot be fulfilled without Israel in the land as a national entity. Moreover, the return of the Lord and the salvation of Israel is a prelude to the kingdom and the events of Isaiah 19:16–25.

In sum, we have looked at three OT passages that predict a number of end-time events involving Israel. Many of those events are confirmed by NT passages, so evidently Israel's rejection of her Messiah did not cancel these prophecies. None of these OT prophecies *per se*, however, predicts that Israel will return to the land and set up a political, military, and religious state. They are all about other end-time events. But, none of them can be fulfilled if Israel is not in the land as a national political, military, and religious entity. So, we must answer affirmatively the question posed in the title of this chapter. It isn't just wishful thinking that Israel will possess the land as a nation. It is nothing less than an eschatological necessity that she will. God knows this, the biblical writers who wrote these portions of Scripture surely understood this, and we should know it too!

Study Questions

1. What does it mean to say that the argument in this chapter is an indirect argument, not a direct one?

2. Do any of the passages discussed in this chapter (Dan. 9:24–27; Zech. 12, and Isa. 19:18–25) predict that Israel will some day return to the land of Palestine as a distinct Jewish nation with control over its political, military, and religious affairs? If so, which verses explicitly say that? If not, why are these passages at all relevant to the topic of this book?

3. In Daniel 9:26–27 who is "the prince who will come" and what is his relation to "the people of the prince" in verse 26?

4. According to Daniel 9:27, what will the prince do that will outrage and afflict the people of Israel and when will he do these things?

5. Why must Israel be a national, political entity in the land in order for Daniel 9:27 to be fulfilled?

6. What events does Zechariah 12 predict, and when will they most likely be fulfilled?

7. Why couldn't the events of Zechariah 12 still happen if there is no nation of Israel, but only Jews living in various countries around the world?

8. What does Jesus say in the Olivet Discourse (Matthew 24–25) that confirms that Daniel 9:27 and Zechariah 12:10 are in

fact going to be fulfilled? Similarly, does what Paul says in Romans 11:25–27 confirm either of these OT prophecies, and if so, how does it do that?

9. What nations are the subject of the prophecy in Isaiah 19:18–25, and how do we know that this prophecy has not already been fulfilled?

10. What changes will happen to the nations mentioned in Isaiah 19:18–25, and when will these predictions most likely be fulfilled?

11. Why can't Isaiah 19:18–25 be fulfilled if there is no Jewish nation of Israel and Jews are merely living in nations scattered around the world?

Conference Video

chosenpeople.com/feinberg

Interview with Dr. John S. Feinberg

chosenpeople.com/feinberg-interview

12

ISRAEL IN CHURCH HISTORY

Dr. Michael J. Vlach

D r. Vlach, in his chapter *Israel in Church History*, presents a historical overview of "how the Christian church has viewed Israel and Israel's land." Sometimes the church affirmed the continuing significance of Israel, but at other times it believed the church replaced the promises God gave to Israel.

He begins by presenting the two broader paradigms regarding Israel. The first being the *replacement* position which believes the church has replaced Israel as the "people of God." The second being the *restoration* model which recognizes God is "not finished with the nation of Israel."

Vlach devotes the largest part of his chapter to his survey of the development of these two views, which exist throughout church history.

The Middle Ages (450–1517), almost invariably, continued to promote replacement theology, with few glimpses of hope for Israel's restoration. The Reformation (1517–1650) initially rejected any hope for Israel, but later generations began to recognize ethnic Israel's significance. The nineteenth and twentieth centuries, led by Spurgeon and the rise of Dispensationalism, have witnessed a resurgence in the belief that "God has not rejected His people Israel and that Israel will experience a salvation and restoration."

Israel and the land are important biblical and theological issues for Christians. But how the church has understood these issues historically is also worthy of study. The purpose of this chapter is to survey the history of how the Christian church has viewed Israel and Israel's land. When it comes to Israel and the land, the church's testimony is mixed. At times the church has affirmed the continuing significance of Israel and the land, but at other times it has denied these truths, opting for a replacement position in which the church is viewed as taking over Israel's promises.

Replacement or Restoration?

To start this discussion, it is necessary to point out two broad paradigms or models that the church has often adopted in regard to how it views and relates to Israel. There can be variations within these paradigms, but they serve as helpful models, nonetheless. The first is a *replacement* view. The second is a *restoration* perspective. Christians who have offered their ideas on Israel throughout church history usually can be identified with one or the other.

The replacement view holds that the New Testament church has replaced or superseded the nation Israel as the people of God.[1] Whether through God's displeasure with the nation or His intent to transition to a purely spiritual community once Jesus arrived, the replacement view asserts that the church is now the new or true Israel. And with this understanding, there is no longer significance for Israel as a nation in God's plans. Some hold that God may save a large number of Jews in the end times, but He is no longer working with Israel as a national entity. He has transitioned to the church which is the true Israel. Thus, with the replacement view there is no remaining theological importance for the nation Israel or the land of Israel.

On the other hand, the restoration view asserts that God is not finished with the nation of Israel. Even though Israel is experiencing judgment for rejecting her Messiah, God has kept a remnant of believing Jews, and this remnant is evidence of what is to come for the nation as a whole. The current partial and temporary hardening of Israel will give way to national salvation and restoration. When Jesus the Messiah comes to rule the nations, Israel will exist as a nation that offers leadership and service to the rest of the nations, under the leadership of Jesus. The restoration view acknowledges the great importance of the church and its mission of gospel proclamation in this present age, yet it does not view this present age as the final stage of what God is doing. A day is coming when the nations as national entities will worship and serve Jesus the Messiah in an earthly kingdom, and Israel will have a function of leadership to them during this time. Thus, with the restoration view, there is theological significance for the nation Israel and the land of Israel.

Both the replacement and restoration views have been held throughout church history, sometimes simultaneously. And there have been times when one perspective is dominant. Conflicting statements can even be found within certain writers themselves. In the Patristic Era or era of the church fathers (AD 100–450), both the replacement and restoration views were held. During the Middle Ages (450–1517) the replacement view, with rare exception, was heavily dominant. The era of the Reformation (1517–1650) was mixed in that the first generation of Reformers held a replacement view while the second generation of the Reformation was more open to the significance of Israel and the land. The post-Reformation era has witnessed a great renewal of the restoration view, which is where we stand today.

Restorationism in the New Testament

The era of Jesus and the apostles (first-century AD) affirmed the Old Testament expectation of a restoration of the nation Israel. The angel Gabriel told Mary, "The Lord God will give Him [Jesus] the throne of His father David; and He will reign over the house of Jacob forever, and His kingdom will have no end" (Luke 1:32–33). This is an explicit statement that Jesus will rule over Israel. When the disciples asked Jesus about rewards for following Him, Jesus said that when He sits on "His glorious throne," the twelve apostles will "sit upon twelve thrones, judging the twelve tribes of Israel" (Matt. 19:28). This reaffirms the future significance of Israel and its twelve tribes. On the day of His ascension into heaven, the apostles asked Jesus, "Lord, is it at this time that you are restoring the kingdom to Israel?" (Acts 1:6). Jesus does not correct their understanding of a restoration of the kingdom to Israel, but He tells them that only the Father knows the timing of this event (see Acts 1:7). So after forty days of kingdom instruction from the risen Jesus (see Acts 1:3), the apostles expected a future kingdom to include a restored Israel. In addition, Paul affirmed that the promises and covenants of the Old Testament still belonged to Israel even after the church began and with Israel in a current state of unbelief (see Rom. 9:4–5).[2] He declared that the salvation of all Israel would occur with the second coming of Jesus (Rom. 11:26). Also, like Jesus, the apostle John mentioned a future for the twelve tribes of Israel (see Rev. 7:4–8). So not only does the Old Testament teach a future for national Israel (see Deut. 30:1–10; Jer. 31–33; Ezek. 36–37), the New Testament writers affirm a future for Israel as well.

Patristic Era (AD 100–450)
The Rise of Replacement Theology

In spite of the testimony of both the Old and New Testaments, the mostly Gentile church started to gravitate toward the view that God rejected Israel and replaced Israel with the church as the people of God.

Paul addressed this error in his letter to the Romans: "I say then, God has not rejected His people, has He? May it never be!" (Rom. 11:1a). That Paul made such a statement reveals that some in the church were viewing Israel as permanently rejected by God. This was something that he had to emphatically address in Romans 11.

Around AD 160, Justin Martyr became the first to explicitly identify the church as "Israel."[3] He still affirmed a future salvation of Israel and a coming earthly kingdom in Jerusalem, but he did hold that the church was now Israel. And it would not be long before belief that the church was the true Israel would be widely held. There are three main reasons for this shift toward a replacement view. First, as Gentile membership in the church increased and Jewish membership decreased, the increasingly Gentile church viewed itself as taking over the title and blessings of Israel. According to Jeffrey Siker, Jewish Christians "were eventually absorbed into an overwhelmingly Gentile Christianity."[4] As a result, the church increasingly became the *ecclesia ex gentibus* ("church of the Gentiles"). This growing Gentile presence in the church led to "theological questions regarding the status of the Jews before God."[5]

Second, the destructions of Jerusalem in AD 70 and 135 stimulated many Christians to conclude that God permanently rejected Israel. The result was, as Lee Martin McDonald notes, "The church fathers concluded from God's evident rejection of the Jews, demonstrated by the destruction of their Temple, and their displacement from Jerusalem, that the Christians themselves constituted the 'new Israel.'"[6]

And third, the rise of allegorical interpretation led many to take physical and national promises to Israel to mean spiritual blessings for the church. Tertullian (160–220), for example, allegorically interpreted Genesis 25:21–23 and its statement that "the older will serve the younger." For him, this was evidence that national Israel would become subservient to the church:

> Accordingly, since the people or nation of the Jews is anterior in time, and "greater" through the grace of primary favor in the Law, whereas ours is understood to be "less" in the age of times, as having in the last era of the world attained the knowledge of divine mercy: beyond doubt, through the edict of divine utterance, the prior and "greater" people—that is, the Jewish— must necessarily serve the "less" and the "less" people—that is, the Christian—overcome the "greater."[7]

The adoption of allegorical interpretation did much harm to the claims of the Bible concerning Israel and the land since it offered opportunity to deny the straightforward statements of Scripture on these matters and make them something else. It became easier to make the church Israel and to transfer physical and national blessings to spiritual blessings for the church. Together, these three factors were the ingredients that led to an entrenched Replacement Theology that would, for some, leave little room for the nation Israel in God's plans.

The conversion and reign of the Roman Emperor, Constantine, (272–337) in the early fourth century, was also significant for the developing replacement view. Constantine converted to Christianity and created a strong merger between the Christian church and state. With this came the belief that the church was the kingdom of God on earth. Constantine's historian, Eusebius (270–340), even viewed Constantine's reign as the messianic banquet, a far cry from what the Bible indicated was the true messianic banquet (see Isa. 25:6–8; Matt. 8:11).

Thus, several statements espousing a replacement view were found in the early church. Clement of Alexandria (c. 195) claimed that Israel "denied the Lord" and thus "forfeited the place of the true Israel."[8] Tertullian (c. 197) declared, "Israel has been divorced."[9] Cyprian (c. 250), too, promoted a supersessionist approach when he wrote:

> I have endeavoured to show that the Jews, according to what had before been foretold, had departed from God, and had lost God's favour, which had been given them in past time, and had been promised them for the future; while the Christians had succeeded to their place, deserving well of the Lord by faith, and coming out of all nations and from the whole world.[10]

In his summary of the early church fathers, Carl Ehle stated, "The church fathers from the second century on did not encourage any notion of a revival of national Israel."[11] As we will see below, this is somewhat of an overstatement, but it does reflect the trend for some in the early church toward downplaying Israel's significance in God's plans.

Hope for Israel in the Early Church

As mentioned earlier, the early church offered conflicting statements concerning Israel's place in God's plans. The early church was trending toward the replacement view which would bloom in full flower in the Middle Ages. But there were statements from the fathers regarding a future for Israel. For example, Justin Martyr stated:

> I and others, who are right-minded Christians on all points, are assured that there will be a resurrection of the dead, and a thousand years in Jerusalem, which will then be built, adorned, and enlarged, the prophets Ezekiel and Isaiah and others declare.[12]

Several points are noteworthy here. In addition to affirming a coming resurrection and kingdom of one thousand years, Justin mentions the physical city of "Jerusalem" as the site of the kingdom. He also states that the city will be built in the way that the prophets Ezekiel and Isaiah discussed, thus expecting a literal fulfillment of what these prophets predicted. Justin was not alone in this understanding, pointing out that these were also held by other "right-minded Christians." Tertullian also expected a future restoration of Israel:

> "[F]or it will be fitting for the Christian to rejoice, and not to grieve, at the restoration of Israel, if it be true, (as it is), that the whole of our hope is intimately united with the remaining expectation of Israel."[13]

The influential theologian Origen also made some declarations concerning a future for Israel. For example, in his comments on the *Song of Songs*, Origen mentioned "two callings of Israel." In between these two callings is God's call of the church. But after the call of the church Israel will experience salvation:

> For the church was called between the two callings of Israel; that is to say, first Israel was called, and afterwards when Israel had stumbled and fallen, the church of the Gentiles was called. "But when the fullness of the Gentiles has come in, then will all Israel, having been called again, be saved."[14]

According to Cohen, "Origen does appear to assume that the Jewish people as a whole will regain their status as a community of God's faithful, that all Jews will ultimately be saved."[15] This is true even though Israel, for a time, has rejected Christ. "Despite the Jews' rejection of Jesus and his apostles, the potential for restoration and renewal remains inherent within them."[16] What it surprising about Origen's statements is that he is known as the main promoter of allegorization in the early church which led many away from more literal understandings of God's purposes for Israel and Israel's land. Yet he did make some statements concerning a restoration of Israel.

Jerome (347–420) used exodus terminology for a coming salvation of Israel: "[W]hen the Jews receive the faith at the end of the world, they will find themselves in dazzling light, as if Our Lord were returning to them from Egypt."[17] Also, Augustine, in his *City of God*, linked the salvation of the Jews with the coming of Elijah:

> It is a familiar theme in the conversation and heart of the faithful, that in the last days before the judgment the

Jews shall believe in the true Christ, that is, our Christ, by means of this great and admirable prophet Elias who shall expound the law to them. . . . When, therefore, he is come, he shall give a spiritual explanation of the law which the Jews at present understand carnally, and shall thus "turn the heart of the father to the son," that is, the heart of the fathers to the children.[18]

Significantly, Augustine mentions that his view concerning the salvation of the Jews was "familiar" to believers of his day. Thus, his belief in the salvation of the Jews went beyond just his own personal view. This perspective was common for those of his generation.

In sum, the early church's views on Israel and the land are mixed. Both restoration and replacement views are espoused, sometimes even by the same writers.

The Early Church and the Land

What about the land of Israel? Some of the early church fathers affirmed a future significance of Jerusalem, but as a whole the early church did not express much interest in the land of Israel. Initially, pilgrimages were not encouraged or viewed as having any benefit, but that soon changed. Constantine and Helena took great interested in finding the holy sites and encouraged Christians to visit the holy land. Jerome also viewed pilgrimages to Israel as beneficial saying, "so we also understand the Scriptures better when we have seen Judea with our own eyes."[19] But not all viewed such pilgrimages as beneficial. Augustine (354–430), John Chrysostom (344–407) and especially Gregory of Nyssa (335–94) discouraged Christians from visiting Israel.

Middle Ages (450–1517)

The early church evidenced mixed views on Israel and its future. The Middle Ages, though, almost exclusively went the way of a strong replacement theology that left little place for a future restoration of Israel. Hood observes that "the supersession theory" was one of the primary "givens" among Christian theologians of this time.[20] The church fully adopted amillennial theology which relegated Jesus' kingdom to a spiritual kingdom that was occurring now through the established church. Allegory was a common method of interpretation and very few theologians held positive views of the Jews or Israel. This often coincided with anti-Jewish sentiments during this period. A solid replacement approach would remain for nearly a thousand years until the era of the Protestant Reformation.

However, there were a few bright spots concerning a hope for Israel during this time. Thomas Aquinas (1124–74) expected a future salvation of the Jews:

It is possible to designate a terminus, because it seems that the blindness of the Jews will endure until all the pagans chosen for salvation have accepted the faith. And this is in accord with what Paul says below about the salvation of the Jews, namely, that after the conversion of the pagans, all Israel will be saved.[21]

One person during this period who affirmed a restoration of Israel was John of Rupescissa (1310–66). Summarizing his views, Lerner says: "For him [John] the converted Jews would become God's new imperial nation and Jerusalem would be completely rebuilt to become the center of the purified faith."[22] Another, Gerard of Borgo San Donnino (c. 1255), "taught that some Jews would be blessed as Jews in the end time and would return to their ancient homeland."[23] So while the overwhelming view of the church of the Middle Ages was that of replacement theology and no hope for national Israel, John is evidence that not all went with the consensus replacement view.

The period of the Middle Ages experienced interest in the holy land, although the reason was less than sound. This was largely due to the desire to wrest the holy land from Muslim control and not from the belief that the Bible predicted a future restoration of Israel to the land. The Crusades began in 1095 as a way to reclaim the Holy Land from the Muslims. Pope Urban II, who launched the Crusades, viewed the Crusades as a way of renewing the church and leading to pilgrimages to Israel that could usher in the return of Christ.

Reformation (1517–1650)

The Protestant Reformation of the sixteenth century was a reformation in several areas. Not only did it bring needed reform in the areas of salvation and the church, it also unleashed a reformation concerning how Israel and the Old Testament should be understood. Regina Sharif points out that, "Prior to the Reformation, traditional Catholic thought had no place for the possibility of a Jewish return to Palestine nor any such concept as the existence of a Jewish nation."[24] But the Reformation changed this perception, not initially, but eventually with the second generation of reformers.

Sadly, the originator of the Protestant Reformation, Martin Luther, promoted a harsh replacement position. The early Luther actually expected and welcomed a salvation of many Jews, but the later Luther espoused a strong replacement theology approach in which God angrily rejected the Jews. For him, the destruction of Jerusalem was proof of God's permanent rejection of Israel:

> Listen, Jew, are you aware that Jerusalem and your sovereignty, together with your temple and priesthood,

have been destroyed for over 1,460 years?". . . For such ruthless wrath of God is sufficient evidence that they assuredly have erred and gone astray. . . . Therefore this work of wrath is proof that the Jews, surely rejected by God, are no longer his people, and neither is he any longer their God.[25]

Luther also stated, "Therefore the Jews have lost this promise, no matter how much they boast of their father Abraham. . . . They are no longer the people of God." He would also make vicious anti-Jewish statements that would not only contribute to replacement theology but serve as fuel for later attacks on the Jewish people.[26]

John Calvin's views on Israel are harder to discern. According to Willem VanGemeren, "Some have seen the utter rejection of Israel in Calvin's writing, whereas others have also viewed the hope for national Israel."[27] Williamson, for example, believes there is a tension in Calvin's writings on this issue when he states, "On the one hand, Calvin strongly insisted that God's promise to and covenant with the people Israel was unconditional, unbreakable, and gracious. . . . On the other hand, Calvin often makes statements exactly opposing the above."[28] For example, in his commentary on Isaiah 59:20, Calvin stated:

Paul quotes this passage, (Rom. xi. 26,) in order to shew that there is still some remaining hope among the Jews; although from their unconquerable obstinacy it might be inferred that they were altogether cast off and doomed to eternal death. But because God is continually mindful of his covenant, and "his gifts and calling are without repentance" (Rom. xi. 29), Paul justly concludes that it is impossible that there shall not at length be some remnant that come to Christ, and obtain that salvation which he has procured. Thus the Jews must at length be collected along with the Gentiles that out of both "there may be one fold" under Christ. (John x. 16). . . . Hence we have said that Paul infers that he [Christ] could not be the redeemer of the world, without belonging to some Jews, whose fathers he had chosen, and to whom this promise was directly addressed.[29]

With the second generation of the Reformation, more positive views of Israel began to develop. In their comment on Romans 11:26, the editors of the *Geneva Bible* (1581) stated, "He [Paul] sheweth that the time shall come that the whole nation of the Jewes, though not every one particularly, shall be joyned to the Church of Christ."[30] This is an explicit statement concerning a future for the Jewish people.

The seventeenth century experienced an explosion of interest in the future of the Jews and Israel. This occurred as more people gained access to the Bible and interest in the Old Testament and the Hebrew language increased. In his study of the Puritans of the seventeenth century, Iain Murray notes that "belief in a future conversion of the Jews became commonplace among the English Puritans."[31] Thomas Brightman (1552–1607), an English clergyman who wrote a commentary on the Book of Revelation, argued that the Jews would return to the Holy Land in fulfillment of the Scriptures: "Shall they return to Jerusalem again? There is nothing more certain: the prophets do everywhere confirm it and beat upon it."[32] Sir Henry Finch, an English lawyer and politician, also promoted a restoration of Israel. In 1621 he published *The World's Great Restauration, or Calling of the Jews, and with them of all Nations and Kingdoms of the Earth to the Faith of Christ.* He declared, "Where Israel, Judah, Zion and Jerusalem are named [in the Bible] the Holy Ghost meant not the spiritual Israel, or the church of God collected of the Gentiles or of the Jews and Gentiles both. . . . But Israel properly descended out of Jacob's loynes."[33] William Perkins (1558–1602), an English cleric and theologian, also predicted a future for the nation Israel: "The Lord saith, All the nations shall be blessed in Abraham: Hence I gather that the nation of the Jews shall be called, and converted to the participation of this blessing: when, and how, God knows: but that it shall be done before the end of the world we know."[34]

So belief in a restoration of Israel was common among the Puritans. As Smolinski summarizes, "In fact, Puritan millennialists strongly asserted that the restoration and national conversion of the Jews was a *prerequisite* to the Second Coming. Christ's Second Advent was indefinitely postponed until such time as Israel's 'dry bones' were enlivened and restored to their ancient position of prominence."[35] Yet English Puritans were not the only ones affirming a coming restoration of Israel. Wilhelmus à Brakel (1635–1711), a Dutch Reformed minister in Rotterdam, Holland, predicted this as well:

> One more question remains to be answered: Will the Jewish nation be gathered together again from all the regions of the world and from all the nations of the earth among which they have been dispersed? Will they come to dwell in Canaan and all the lands promised to Abraham, and will Jerusalem be rebuilt?" We believe that these events will transpire. . . . They will be an independent republic,

governed by a very wise, good-natured, and superb government. Furthermore, Canaan will be extraordinarily fruitful, the inhabitants will be eminently godly, and they will constitute a segment of the glorious state of the church during the thousand years prophesied in Revelation 20."[36]

A Brakel's statement goes beyond just a salvation of Jews to national restoration. He discusses the "Jewish nation" being "gathered" to "dwell in Canaan" with a rebuilt Jerusalem. Petrus Serrarius (1600–1699) of Amsterdam also expressed belief in both a conversion of the Jews and a restoration of Israel when he said, "The time of the Conversion of the Jews and the restoring of the Kingdom of Israel (of which the Prophets are full) . . . is at hand."[37]

In eighteenth-century America, optimism concerning Israel also existed. Jonathan Edwards (1703–58) argued that the stubbornness of ancient Israel will give way to a national conversion:

However obstinate [the Jews] have been now for above seventeen hundred years in their rejection of Christ, and however rare have been the instances on individual conversions, ever since the destruction of Jerusalem. . . . Yet, when this day comes, the thick veil that blinds their eyes shall be removed. 2 Cor iii.16. And divine grace shall melt and renew their hard hearts. . . . And then shall the house of Israel be saved: the Jews in all their dispersions shall cast away their old infidelity, and shall have their hearts wonderfully changed, and abhor themselves for their past unbelief and obstinacy. . . . Nothing is more certainly foretold than this national conversion of the Jews in Romans 11.2.[38]

Nineteenth and Twentieth Centuries

The nineteenth century witnessed great interest in Israel's future and the land. The Calvinist theologian, Charles Haddon Spurgeon (1834–92), taught a restoration of Israel to the land: "It is also certain that the Jews, as a people, will yet own Jesus of Nazareth, the Son of David, as their King, and that they will return to their own land."[39] This is in connection with a coming earthly millennial reign. Jesus "will reign amongst his ancients gloriously, and . . . there will be a thousand years of joy and peace such as were never known on this earth before."[40] Spurgeon's explicit belief in a national restoration of Israel as a governmental entity to her land is seen in his 1864 sermon, "The Restoration and Conversion of the Jews":

There will be a native government again; there will again be the form of a body politic; a state shall be incorporated, and a king shall reign. Israel has now become alienated from her own land. . . . If there be anything clear and plain, the literal sense and meaning of this passage [Ezekiel 37:1–10]—a meaning not to be spirited or spiritualized away—must be evident that both the two and the ten tribes of Israel are to be restored to their own land, and that a king is to rule over them.[41]

In his extensive study of Spurgeon's eschatology, Dennis Swanson notes nine "key points" regarding Spurgeon's views on Israel and the land:

• Israel as a nation will come to faith in Christ.
• Israel will have a national or geo-political identity.
• The political system will be a monarchy, "a king shall reign."
• Israel will be in the Promised Land.
• The borders will correspond to the promises given to Abraham and David.
• Israel will hold a special place among the nations in the millennial kingdom.
• However, Israel remains spiritually part of the church.
• There will be a national prosperity that will be the admiration of the world.
• That the prophecies of the Old Testament should not be handled in a non-literal fashion.[42]

The rise of Dispensationalism in the mid-nineteenth century did not begin but continued the trend of expecting a future for the nation Israel. Dispensationalism and its leaders affirmed a distinction between Israel and the church and asserted that a future salvation and restoration of Israel would occur, including a return of Israel to the land and a place of prominence for Israel among the nations. Dispensationalism's influence in the United States was accelerated through the Bible conference movement, books, schools, and the popular Scofield Reference Bible.

Between 1800 and 1875, around two-thousand authors wrote about the Holy Land. Yet as significant as this century was, the twentieth century was even greater. Perceptions concerning Israel were impacted greatly by two twentieth-century developments—the Holocaust and the establishment of the modern state of Israel. These events pushed questions and issues concerning Israel and the church to the forefront of Christian theology. Ronald Diprose notes, "Since the tragic events of the *Shoah* [Holocaust] and the birth of the modern State of Israel on May 14, 1948, the interest shown in God's ancient people has been widespread and sustained."[43] As a result, several denominations and Christian groups have renounced replacement theology. "Over the last two decades, denominational assemblies have mostly done away with the traditional doctrine that Israel's election has been transferred to the church."[44]

The twentieth century was a strong century for reasserting the theological significance of Israel and Israel's land. With the beginning of the twenty-first century, this trend continues. The replacement view is still well represented and a strong challenge to the restoration view exists. Many, though, affirm that God has not rejected His people Israel and that Israel will experience a salvation and restoration, including a restoration to the land. It is unlikely that the replacement view will become dominant again, at least in the near future.

Conclusion

A survey of church history reveals mixed and conflicting views toward Israel and the land. Jesus and the apostles taught a salvation and restoration of Israel. The early church of the Patristic Era was mixed on this issue at times promoting both future significance for Israel and a replacement view in which the church took over Israel's place. The Middle Ages was dominated by a strong replacement view. The Reformation initially affirmed replacement theology but the second generation swung the door wide open to belief in significance for the nation Israel. The nineteenth and twentieth centuries witnessed widespread belief in a future restoration of Israel—a belief that continues today.

Study Questions

1. What are the two main models or paradigms concerning the church's views on Israel in church history?

2. How would you summarize the early church's views on Israel and the land?

3. What are the three main reasons the early church started to drift toward a replacement view in regard to Israel and the church?

4. How would you view the church's view of Israel and the land in the Middle Ages?

5. Were there any people who held positive views of Israel in the Middle Ages? If yes, who?

6. How would you compare Luther's views on Israel compared to the second generation of Reformers?

7. How would you summarize the Puritans' views on Israel and the land?

8. What was Charles Spurgeon's views on Israel's restoration?

9. What two twentieth-century events dramatically impacted how Christians and churches viewed Israel?

10. How would you summarize the entire history of the church's views on Israel?

Conference Video

chosenpeople.com/vlach

Interview with Dr. Michael J. Vlach

chosenpeople.com/vlach-interview

13

ISRAEL IN LIGHT OF THE HOLOCAUST

Dr. Barry R. Leventhal

L eventhal writes about the long journey home for the Jewish people, *from Hitler's Death Camps to Israel's Homeland.*

According to Dr. Leventhal, the Holocaust continues to present difficulties for both Jewish and non-Jewish scholars. "This horrific 'final solution' was carried out by the most advanced country in all of Europe: Germany, the most intellectual, scientific, theological, and even the most artistic nation of the day! It remains a significant 'stumbling block' to faith in God."

The Holocaust continues to cast "its spell over the Jewish people's entire framework of thinking: their past, their present, their future." It challenges the Jewish people to never allow such a horrific event to happen again.

The rebirth of Israel looks forward to the rebirth of the Jewish people in the land, following the biblical pattern of "Trespass-Exile-Return." Israel experiences this pattern on three occasions. The first exile and return occurred in Egypt. The second exile and return happened under the conquest by the Babylonians and Assyrians. The final exile began with the Roman destruction of Jerusalem, with a two-phased final return. This began when Israel arose out of the ashes of the Holocaust. Israel continues to hope for the final restoration of the Jewish people in the Land.

From Hitler's Death Camps to Israel's Homeland (The Long Journey Home)

In May 1961, on the eve of Israel's thirteenth Anniversary of Independence, the boat carrying Rachmiel Frydland pulled into the port city of Haifa. Rachmiel's long journey home had finally ended. Rachmiel's eyes filled with tears as he looked out upon his traveling companions: Jewish emigrants from Poland, Morocco, Rumania, Russia, and many other parts of the world. They all had finally come home, home to the Land of Israel. But on that same day, tears fell from heaven as well. For six million Jews, including a million Jewish children, never made it home. They perished in the Nazi death camps.

For Rachmiel Frydland, however, it had been a long horrific journey, a journey through the valley of the shadow of death. This Holocaust shadow would cast its spell over him for the rest of his life. Rachmiel Frydland's journey is recounted in his autobiography, *When Being Jewish Was a Crime.*[1]

Rachmiel's journey actually began when he was born, according to his father's recollection, sometime "before Passover in 1919." He was born in the small Jewish village of Lesniczowka (meaning "the little forest village"), situated about nine miles west of the river Bug and four miles southeast of Chelm in the Lublin district of Poland.[2] Within a short twenty-six years, Rachmiel Frydland, his family, and friends would be cast into the Holocaust Kingdom. Most of them never made it out.

One of Rachmiel's closest friends described this Holocaust journey in graphic words:

> The worst place a man could be in World War II was in central Europe, and the worst country in Europe was Poland; the worst religion a man could have was Judaism, and perhaps the worst form of Judaism— Hebrew Christianity. Rachmiel Frydland was almost a man alone against World War II. He wandered for years through burning Poland, dazed, bewildered, but always spared. He infiltrated *into* the Warsaw ghetto at a time when Jewish people were trying to tunnel their way out. He challenged the Gestapo face to face. He ran through hails of bullets.[3]

But in the truest sense, however, Rachmiel's horrific journey back to the Land of Israel began when he came to faith in Yeshua [Jesus] as his personal Messiah, Lord, and Savior. The year was 1937. Rachmiel had just turned eighteen. He was baptized almost immediately.[4] For the next seven years, death journeyed with Rachmiel as his constant companion, a companion he learned not to fear. During these seven years, Rachmiel's life hung on the brink for six reasons: (1) He was a Jew. (2) He had escaped the authorities. (3) He was away from his place of residence. (4) He refused to wear the yellow Jewish armband (embroidered with the Star of David). (5) He boarded a public train, forbidden to Jews since 1930. And (6) he carried no personal documents.[5] But during this same period, God also journeyed with Rachmiel, the divine hand sustaining him as his constant traveling companion. "Thus I became used to living daily by miracles."[6] Rachmiel fled from the Nazis as well as the bounty-hunting Polish peasants. The Gentile churches turned him out. His unbelieving Jewish kinsmen rejected him.

But it was the Lord Yeshua who had planted the Land of Israel as a dream in Rachmiel's heart, a living dream that sustained him through his journey into the darkness of the Holocaust kingdom. Through the agony and suffering of the Holocaust, Rachmiel's dream became a vision, the vision became a journey, and finally, after twenty-four years, in 1961, the journey became a reality. Rachmiel was home in the Land of Israel. He was forty-two years old.

As Rachmiel Frydland journeyed from Hitler's death camps to Israel's homeland, he experienced the horror of the Holocaust in a most personal way.

The Horror of the Holocaust

"The Holocaust," "The *Sho'ah*" or The *Churban*, The "Catastrophe," "Genocide," "Mass Murder," "Auschwitz." Like a child's first attempts at speech, we have the echoes of humanity's struggling attempts to describe the horror of the Holocaust! But in reality, how can one truly describe the annihilation of six million Jews? What does the number six million really mean? How can one actually wrap his or her mind around the number six million? Let's try this: The figure of six million Jews being exterminated means that during the twelve year period from 1933 to 1945, the Nazis slaughtered almost 1,400 Jews, on average, each and every day! And not just slaughtered, but butchered in ways beyond human imagination. And this horrific "final solution" was carried out by the most advanced country in all of Europe: Germany, the most intellectual, scientific, theological, and even the most artistic nation of the day!

Jewish scholars and non-Jewish scholars alike are still grappling with the relationship between the Holocaust and "the best and brightest" of Germany, no one more than Holocaust survivor and storyteller Elie Wiesel:

> If the Holocaust proved anything, it is that it is possible for a person both to love poems and kill children; many Germans cried when listening to Mozart, when playing Haydn, when quoting Goethe and Schiller— but remained quite unemotional and casual when tor-

turing and shooting children. Their act had no effect on their spirit; the idea had no bearing on the course of inspiration. Heidegger served as Chancellor of the Freiburg University under the Nazis. Karl Orff, the composer, was Goebbel's favorite musician. As for Von Karajan, he did not lose his talent when conducting in Berlin and elsewhere, wearing a Nazi uniform.

Something then must be wrong not only with their concept of evil, but with man's as well.[7]

Again, Wiesel remarked:

How is it possible that the same civilization that produced Goethe, Bach, Voltaire, and Rousseau could also have produced such dehumanization of man? Something must be wrong with man himself and with man's vision of himself, and something must be wrong with culture if Germans could quote Schiller and Fichte at the same time they were killing Jews. Something must be wrong with books and language if people who write so impressively and who play music so artistically could become allies of non-human death. And something must be wrong with us if during those years of the Third Reich all movements of the spirit failed. Communism failed. Rationalism failed. And religion failed. Evil's conquest was easy, too easy.[8]

Jewish Holocaust scholar Michael Berenbaum also lamented the same terrible, but true, fact concerning Germany's pre-World War II so-called cultural sophistication:

Why is the Holocaust an unrelenting event? The Holocaust, by its scope, nature, and magnitude transforms our understanding of human culture and human existence. An unspoken premise of the advocates of culture and learning somehow make us into better people and intensify our moral worth. Yet the Holocaust was perpetrated not by the least cultured and least sophisticated of nations but by the most cultured and most advanced of societies. Furthermore, the elements within that society that proved capable of perpetrating the evils were not the least cultured, but came from all spectrums of society including philosophers and scientists, musicians and engineers, lawyers and ministers, artists and intellectuals. No segment of German society proved immune. . . . We see that people could love good music and kill young children. They could be admirable husbands and concerned fathers yet spend their days in constant contact with death and destruction. Human society can be organized and given meaning in such a way that the enterprise of death becomes triumphant. All this is possible in the twentieth century with technology facilitating the process.[9]

Not only are older commentators struck by Germany's pre-World War II treacherous relationship between the political beast and cultural beauty, but so are some of our brightest contemporary journalists, like Charles Krauthammer in his new book *Things That Matter*:

Politics, the crooked timber of our communal lives, dominates everything because, in the end, everything—high and low and, most especially, high—lives or dies by politics. You can have the most advanced and efflorescent of cultures. Get your politics wrong, however, and everything stands to be swept away. This is not ancient history. This is Germany 1933. . . .

Politics is the moat, the walls, beyond which lie the barbarians. Fail to keep them at bay, and everything burns. The entire 20th century with its mass political enthusiasms is a lesson in the supreme power of politics to produce ever-expanding circles of ruin. . . . [Various 20th century tyrants and revolutionaries] tried to atomize society so thoroughly—to war against the mediating structures that stand between the individual and the state—that the most basic bonds of family, faith, fellowship and conscience came to near dissolution. Of course, the greatest demonstration of the finality of politics is the Holocaust, which in less than a decade destroyed a millennium-old civilization, sweeping away not only 6 million souls but the institutions, the cultures, the very tongue of the now-vanished world of European Jewry.[10]

For Rachmiel Frydland and the Jews of Eastern Europe, the Holocaust descended upon them like an unending, bloody nightmare. Abba Eban, the late Israeli Deputy Prime Minister and Minister of Foreign Affairs, graphically described this Holocaust nightmare, "At the end of the Second War the curtain went up on the burned and mangled bodies of six million Jews, including a million children. The Jewish people had fallen victim to the most fearful agony which had ever beset any nation or group of people. A whole continent was saturated with its blood and haunted by its unexpiated sacrifice."[11]

As one can imagine, for many, this Holocaust nightmare has become a major stumbling block to faith in God.[12] And this stumbling block, which has been for the most part ignored by the Christian world, remains the foremost barrier between contemporary Jews and God. Seymour Cain addressed this matter:

> Auschwitz, or "the Holocaust," looms as the stumbling block of contemporary Jewish theology. Whatever may be the case with Christian theologians, for whom it seems to play no significant generative or transformative role, the Jewish religious thinker is forced to confront fullface that horror, the uttermost of evil in Jewish history.[13]

In many different ways, the Holocaust has proven to be unique. Rabbi H. J. Zimmels pointed to a uniqueness specifically related to the historical return to the Land of Israel in 1948:

> Another great tragedy which makes the Nazi holocaust distinguishable from all the other persecutions and expulsions was the fact that the Jews in countries under the Nazi heel, had great difficulties in finding places to which they could emigrate. Only a small portion of Jews were successful. . . . In the Nazi era no country opened its gates freely to anyone. For that reason emigration became deportation, leading to extermination. Had the gates of Palestine been opened, six million Jews might not have perished.[14]

But the gates of Palestine were not open. Therefore, Rachmiel Frydland's horrifying journey into the Holocaust, raises two basic questions: First, how did the Holocaust pave the way for the establishment of the modern State of Israel in 1948 (the historic return)? In other words, what was the causal relationship between the Holocaust and the rebirth of the modern State of Israel? And second, how did the establishment of the Nation of Israel in 1948 foreshadow Israel's glorious future (the prophetic return)? In other words, how are human history and divine prophecy wedded together in the Nation of Israel?

So first then, how did the Holocaust in some sense pave the way for the reestablishment of the modern State of Israel in 1948 (the historic return)?

Israel's Historic Return in 1948

Christians are fond of calling Israel "The Holy Land." But what does the phrase "The Holy Land" actually mean? Robert L. Wilkin, Professor of the History of Christianity at the University of Virginia, addressed this unfortunate ignorance among so many Christian people:

> For many Christians the term *Holy Land* conjures up images of shepherds and olive trees, of dusty hills and donkeys, of Jerusalem as it existed in the age of King David or Bethlehem at the time of Jesus. It is a land without history, its people and places frozen in a biblical time frame. . . .
>
> The very notion of the Holy Land as a historical land, not a mawkish apparition of the past, a land whose history is continuous with the biblical story yet not limited to it, a country whose people have displayed Christian wisdom, piety, and architecture in distinctive ways— this idea of the Holy Land is foreign to Christians, particularly those in the West. Even today few Christian pilgrims to the Holy Land venture beyond the familiar holy places associated with the Bible, returning to their homes unaware that Christian history in the land did not end with the age of the apostles.[15]

In light of Wilkins' accurate estimation, it is not surprising then that so many people who have fallen into this blind spot of the centuries, also have such a minimal knowledge concerning the Jewish people and their relationship to the Land of Promise, especially in regard to Israel's return to the Land both in history and in prophecy. The Christian public in particular, as Wilkins pointed out, is like a blind man walking in the darkness without a dog or even a cane.[16] It's time to turn on the light! So let's begin with the Jewish people's historic return to the Land of Israel in 1948.

The Jewish people's historic return to their eternally Promised Land in 1948 was nothing short of miraculous. "There is no witness more perplexing to the unbelieving, skeptical world than the miracle of the Jewish people."[17] Prophetic scholar Randall Price also highlighted the modern miracle of the return of Jewish people to the Promised Land:

> The modern return of the Jewish people to the Land of Israel has been called the "Miracle of the Mediterranean." Such a return by a group of people that had been scattered among the nations is unprecedented in history. Indeed, the Jewish people are the only exiled people

to remain a distinct people despite being dispersed to more than 70 different countries for more than 20 centuries. The mighty empires of Egypt, Assyria, Babylon, Persia, Greece, and Rome all ravaged their land, took their captive, and scattered them throughout the earth. Even after this, they suffered persecution, pogrom, and Holocaust in the lands to which they were exiled. Yet, all of these ancient kingdoms have turned into dust and their former glories remain only as museum relics and many of the nations that opposed the Jews have suffered economic, political, or religious decline. But the Jewish people whom they enslaved and tried to eradicate live free and have again become a strong nation.[18]

Biblical scholar Stanley A. Ellisen drew the connection between 2,000 years of Jewish suffering, culminating in Hitler's gas chambers, and Israel's national rebirth in 1948:

Few races of people have suffered as much as the Jews. Before the coming of Christ they were constantly between the hammer and anvil of Gentile powers. Their location made them the brunt of international intrigue. That bitter role of scapegoat tended to intensify if anything, driving many to ghettos for sheer survival. The sordid "final solution" pursued by Hitler only epitomized the plaintive plight of the wandering Jews.

A new day dawned in 1948 and they now have a homeland of their own. Though jubilant and euphoric at times, they have had little time to savor victory or gloat. Rather they have united to wielded trowel and sword in an effort to carve out what they see as their messianic future. Hard work and sheer doggedness have paid off. Their massive feat of rebuilding Palestine from a barren, malaria-ridden land into a thriving garden and industrial beehive is almost without parallel. In half a century they have planted an oasis of democracy in the Middle East, hoping to fulfill their age-old dreams in a modern world.[19]

Likewise, historian J. Rufus Fears described Israel's momentous return in 1948:

Of all the nations that have passed through the Middle East—the Achaeans [the Greeks], the Sumerians, the

Hittites, the Egyptians—Israel remains an enduring part of our world.

Did you ever ponder that? How many people speak ancient Egyptian today? How many people speak Lydian or Hittite? No one does. How many people worship Anubis, the god of the ancient Egyptians? How many worship the Baal of the ancient Canaanites and Phoenicians? But Hebrew is a living language, and the Old Testament is still read all over the world every day by millions of people. The Old Testament is the chronicle of the rise and fall of Israel. . . Israel speaks to us today, both in terms of history and of our own legacy.[20]

No other country in the history of the world has seen so many wars as has this land bridge nation. Why is this so? Military historians and strategists Chaim Herzog and Mordechai Gichon answered this question directly: Israel's geopolitical properties, her strategic position in terms of both the military as well as politics:

Eretz Israel—the land which according to biblical tradition has been promised by God to Abraham as the permanent and particular home of the Jewish people—has been one of the main military thoroughfares as far back as written annals record. . . .

The first and foremost of the geopolitical properties that have always governed the fate of the Holy Land is Palestine's position. The country is the sole land-bridge that connects Eurasia with Africa. There is no detour between the sea and the desert and there is no alternative but to pass along the Palestinian roads either west or east of the Jordan River. Consequently, the powers of the day usually did not refrain even from armed conflict to seize hold of this strategic area, which has proved itself absolutely indispensable both for the flow of commerce in peacetime and the movement of armies in war. Nor did the rulers of adjacent lands willingly abandon their goal of incorporating this important crossroad into their territories. Any nation aspiring to establish an independent national state on the Palestinian land-bridge has thus to accept a primary fact of life: it was destined to live under nearly constant concentric pressure from near and far, and only constant military preparedness could guarantee its survival.

It is probably no coincidence that the only people to create a national commonwealth on the Palestinian land-bridge that lasted (with only short interruptions) for an appreciable period (twelve centuries from the twelfth century BC onwards) is the Jewish people. During this long period, the Jews were more often than not forced to make up by spirit and devotion for their numerical inferiority, which was another factor in the geopolitical character of Palestine. The very smallness of the country set definite limits on its population. . . .

[I]t must be stressed that only a people imbued with religious zeal, a steadfast belief in its right to the county as its Promised Land by divine decree, and with religious tenets which make the exercise of its cult within the confines of this country one of its paramount duties, could develop the necessary moral and spiritual endurance to forge a state out of Palestine and sustain the pressure and hardship involved in its preservation.[21]

Likewise, military historians Monroe Rosenthal and Isaac Mozeson argued the same point:

Peaceful caravans and hostile armies were inevitably drawn to this land bridge country. The land of Israel has seen 145 major wars. Sixty-five of these were begun by countries to the north, fifty by armies striking from the south, and thirty were between rival nations in and round the region itself. Israel has seen a war per generation since ancient times, the last century not helping the average at all. Independence is a difficult commodity in a crossroads country like Israel. Even partial autonomy would require the temporary weakness of neighboring giants or the benevolence of a reigning empire.[22]

And again, it was Jewish theologian and philosopher Abraham Joshua Heschel who so vividly depicted the divine hand behind Israel's continual presence in the land, as well as the return to the land in 1948:

Any attempt to impair the vital link between Israel the people and Israel the land is an affront to biblical faith. . . .

What we have witnessed in our own days is a reminder of the power of God's mysterious promise to Abraham [Genesis 12:1–3; etc.] and a testimony to the fact that the people kept its pledge, "If I forget you, O Jerusalem, let my right hand wither" (Psalm 137:5). The Jew in whose heart the love of Zion dies is doomed to lose his faith in the God of Abraham, who gave the land as an earnest of the redemption of all men.

We have never abandoned the land, and it is as if the land has never abandoned the Jewish people. Attempts to establish other civilizations in the land ended in failure. Numerous conquerors invaded the land; Romans, Byzantines, Arabs, Kurds, Mongols, Mamelukes, Tartars, and Turks. But what did these people make of the land? No one built the state or shaped a nation.

The land did not respond.[23]

Many able scholars have argued for a continuous Jewish presence in the Land of Israel, in spite of the Holocaust. For example, in responding to the question, "Has there been a continuous presence of Jews in the land of Israel for the last two thousand years?" messianic scholar Michael L. Brown answers:

. . . With rare exception, there has been a continuous presence of Jews in the land of Israel for the last two thousand years. And when we speak of the nation as a whole, dating back to the time of Moses, there has been a virtually unbroken Jewish-Israelite presence in the land for almost 3,400 years, and this despite much suffering and forced dispersion through the centuries.

. . . [A]nd that is why the Jewish Passover Seder every year includes the words "Next year in Jerusalem!" That has been the hope and passion of religious Jews through the ages, and for that reason, there has been a virtually continuous presence of Jewish people in Israel despite the collapse of a national state for almost 1,900 years. Living in the post-Holocaust era, a national Jewish slogan has been "Never again!"—meaning, there can never be and will never be another Holocaust for our people—and it is understood that a national homeland is the only way to ensure this.[24]

And in another place, speaking of the messianic suffering Servant of the LORD in the Book of Isaiah, Brown drew a unique relationship between the Holocaust and the Servant when he said:

The horrors of the Holocaust should draw us *to* the side of the suffering Servant rather than drive us *away* from him. He can identify with us in our pain. And out of death (the Holocaust and the cross) came resurrection—the State of Israel and the raising up of the Messiah. There are some similarities.

Yet we must recognize that there are some profound differences as well in these two experiences of suffering—the suffering of the Jewish people and the suffering of Yeshua—since by recognizing these differences, the work of our Messiah becomes all the more important, essential, and even appealing to us.

During the Holocaust, as Jews we suffered unwillingly. If we could have stopped the atrocities, we would have. But Jesus suffering willingly, telling his disciples not to fight on his behalf, since he came to die. He came to give his life as a ransom for us all [Matthew 26:53–54; Mark 10:45].[25]

And even before the Nazi Holocaust and the establishment of the State of Israel in 1948, the founder of the modern Zionist movement, Theodor Herzl, asserted that "The Jews who wish for a State shall have it, and they will deserve to have it. . . . Palestine is our ever-memorable historic home."[26]

According to historian Michael B. Oren, this all-controlling idea, "Zionism, the Jewish people's movement to build an independent polity in their historical homeland,"[27] struck a deep chord in the hearts of Jewish people worldwide, and not just in the hearts of the Jewish people:

What began as a mere idea in the mid-nineteenth century had, by the beginning of the twentieth, motivated thousands of European and Middle Eastern Jews to leave their homes and settle in unthinkably distant Palestine. The secret of Zionism lay in its wedding of modern nationalist notions to the Jewish people's mystical, millennial attachment to the Land of Israel (*Eretz Yisrael*). That power sustained the *Yishuv*, or Jewish community, in Palestine throughout the depredations of Ottoman rule and during World War I, when many Jewish leaders were expelled as enemy (mostly Russian) aliens. By war's end, the British had supplanted the Turks in Palestine and, under the Balfour Declaration, pledged to build a Jewish national home in the country. . . . Though the British had steadily abandoned their support for a Jewish national home, that home was already a fact: an inchoate, burgeoning state. . . . [When Lyndon Johnson received Levi Eshkol at the White House in June 1964, becoming the first Israeli prime minister to be so received], Eshkol replied to Johnson, "We cannot afford to lose. This may be our last stand in history. The Jewish people have something to give to the world. I believe that if you look at our history and at all the difficulties we have survived, it means that history wants us to continue. We cannot survive if we experience again what happened to us under Hitler . . . I believe that you should understand us."[28]

Hebrew Christian theologian, Jakob Jocz, also connected the agony of Auschwitz with the sovereignty of Israel:

Auschwitz is a landmark ranking high in the scale of tragic events in the history of the Jewish people, equal to, if not surpassing, the tragedy of the Fall of Jerusalem in AD 70. But Auschwitz is not only a tragedy for Jews; it is a tragedy for mankind. . . .

In the annals of Jewish history the date May 14, 1948, is of momentous significance: Israel became a sovereign nation. Though the struggle for survival is far from over, the cry *"Yisrael hai!"* ("Israel lives") has brought new hope and a new dignity to millions of Jews the world over.[29]

In conclusion then, in both prose and poetry, the Jewish longing for the return to their ancient, promised homeland reverberated down through the centuries; first then, the prose of historian Martin Gilbert:

Since the destruction of the Second Temple by the Romans in AD 70, the Jews, who were dispersed all over the Roman Empire, had prayed for a return to Zion. "Next year in Jerusalem" was—and remains—the hope expressed at the end of every Passover meal commemorating the ancient exodus from Egypt. For two millennia the dream of such a return seemed a fantasy. Everywhere Jews learned to adapt to the nations within whose borders they lived. Frequent expulsion to other lands made a new adaptation necessary, and this was done. But Zion, which had been under Muslim rule almost without interruption since the seventh century, and under the rule of the Ottoman Turks since the early sixteenth century, was possible only for a few. . . .

[Until Max Nordau, a supporter of Theodor Herzl] who stressed the material and moral misery of the Jews in the Diaspora. In eastern Europe, North Africa and Asia, where as many as nine-tenths of world Jewry were living, "the misery of the Jews is to be understood literally. It is a daily distress of the body, anxious for every day that follows, a tortured fight for bare existence." . . .

[And then] at five o'clock on the afternoon of 14 May 1948, in the main hall of the Tel Aviv Museum, a ceremony took place that inaugurated the State of Israel.[30]

And, second, the poetry of Samuel Cohen. A Roumanian-Jewish poet, Naphtali Herz Imber, wrote a poem, *Hatikvah* ("The Hope") in the late 1800s, which was to become the Zionist hymn, and later the State of Israel's national anthem. Imber read the poem to the farmers of Rishon le-Zion. Samuel Cohen was in the audience that night. He had emigrated from Moldavia four years earlier. When he heard Imber read his poem *Hatikvah*, he was so moved, he set it to music. The poem read:

> As long as deep in the heart
> The soul of a Jew yearns,
> And towards the East
> An eye looks to Zion
> Our hope is not yet lost
> The age-old hope,
> To return to the land of our fathers
> To the city where David dwelt.

Within a few years, Cohen changed the second verse to the version now in use:

> Our hope is not yet lost
> The hope of two thousand years,
> To be a free people in our land
> The land of Zion and Jerusalem.[31]

In summary then, the establishment of the State of Israel in 1948 forged a new identity for the worldwide Jewish community. Out of the fires of the Holocaust, where the Jews were seen, even by themselves in many cases, as helpless victims, emerged the Nation of Israel, now seen as triumphant overcomers.[32]

Therefore, in discussing how the Holocaust paved the way for the establishment of the modern State of Israel in 1948, we will need to address two factors: (1) the Holocaust as the cause that led to the establishment of the State of Israel, and (2) another set of causative factors that led to the establishment of the State of Israel.

The Holocaust as the Cause That Led to the Establishment of the State of Israel in 1948

When discussing on the Holocaust as the cause that led to the establishment of the State of Israel, we need to realize that not all Jewish theologians, philosophers, and historians agree that the Holocaust was, in some sense, the causative factor that led to the establishment of the State of Israel. For some Jewish scholars the rebirth of the State of Israel was a redemptive moment. But for others the idea that God used the death of six million Jews, a million children, as "the price of redemption," to bring about the rebirth of the State of Israel, is an unacceptable premise.

First then, there are some Jewish Holocaust scholars who saw the rebirth of the State of Israel as a redemptive moment. Orthodox Holocaust scholar Irving Greenberg put forth a positive perspective in regard to the Holocaust and the rebirth of the State of Israel:

> The reborn State of Israel is this fundamental act of life and meaning of the Jewish people after Auschwitz. To fail to grasp that inextricable connection and response is to utterly fail to comprehend the theological significance of Israel. The most bitterly secular atheist involved in Israel's upbuilding is the front line of the Messianic life-force struggling to give renewed testimony to the Exodus as ultimate reality. Israel was built by rehabilitating a half-million survivors of the Holocaust. Each one of those lives had to be rebuilt, given opportunity for trust restored. . . . The real point is that after Auschwitz, the existence of the Jew is a great affirmation and an act of faith. The recreation of the body of the people, Israel, is renewed testimony to Exodus as ultimate reality, to God's continuing presence in history proven by the fact that his people, despite the attempt to annihilate them, still exist. . . . The re-creation of the state is the strongest suggestion that God's promises are still valid and reliable.[33]

Abraham Besdin also affirmed that the rebirth of the State of Israel reverberates with transcendental overtones, "Matching the holocaust in power and mystery is the reconstitution of the State of Israel in May of 1948. Only a dogmatic agnostic would fail to see the transcendental overtones of this sudden transformation of Jewish dignity and hope."[34]

Orthodox rabbi Nachum L. Rabinovitch further affirmed that whatever one saw as a causative factor to the rebirth of the State of Israel, one thing is obvious to all, "There is one simple fact which is there for all the world to see. It is so utterly simple and so totally obvious that thousands of millions of people all over the globe know it and see it. Israel *is*, and it bears God's Name, and it has restored God's crown!"[35]

Marc Samuels asserted that the rebirth of the State of Israel has resurrected Jewish history as well as the God of Jewish history:

> The Holocaust has, indeed, made it very difficult to believe in a God of love, a God of justice and goodness. It has also made it difficult to believe sincerely in a God of history. Until 1948, history, and especially Jewish history, became practically meaningless to many Jews, but the establishment of the State of Israel in that year, and the splendid and almost supernatural victory of Israel in June, 1967 [the recapture of the city of Jerusalem], have helped to make Jewish history perhaps a little more meaningful now.[36]

Eliezer Berkovits also asserted that without the return to Israel after the Holocaust, Jewish history becomes meaningless—the return was "a messianic moment":

> Without the return to Zion, Judaism and Jewish history become meaningless. The return is the counterpart in history to the resolution in faith that this world is to be established as the Kingdom of God. The thought has its roots in the very foundations of Judaism, but might have been mere wishful thinking had it not been supported by the reality of Israel, its existence, its survival, its return to Zion. . . . Is this the Messiah already? It is enough to look out of the window to realize that nothing could be further removed from the truth (unless he, too, came unexpectedly "like a thief"). But it is a messianic moment, in which the unexpected fruits of human endeavor reveal themselves as the mysterious manifestations of divine guidance of whose coming the heart was forever sure.[37]

Berkovits further belabored this so-called messianic fulfillment in the rebirth of the State of Israel, when he said:

> The assurance of the messianic fulfillment of history is beyond doubt. The most convincing indication of its coming is the survival of Israel. The survival of Judaism and of the Jewish people in all ages, in conditions of utter political and material weakness, in spite of continuous discrimination and persecution, and in defiance of an endless series of the most barbarous and sadistic attempts at their extermination, baffles all explanation. It is the mystery of all ages. The return of Israel to its ancient homeland in our days, as Israel maintained for numberless generations that it would do, is the incomparable historic event of all times.

Not only did Berkovits maintain that this return to Zion was a messianic moment, but he also declared that divine providence had no other choice—the redemption of Israel's nationhood, after so radical an annihilation as the Holocaust, had to take place:

> In our times, when the phase of the Exile has to be recognized as total crisis, the radically new event which with the total threat, has entered Jewish history has been— what is usually referred to as—the *Shoa*, the Holocaust. It is probably not the right term. . . . The proper name for it is not *Shoa*, but *Hurban*, the annihilation. For the first time in our history the Exile itself was destroyed. . . . The rise of the State of Israel after two millennia of such Exile and at the moment when it occurred, the event itself has become the reviving force, calling back to life the "dry bones" of the shattered *Galut* [Exile]. Divine providence had no other choice but to grant us a measure of national redemption to meet the national *Hurban*.[38]

Jacob Neusner maintained that the emotional tie between the Holocaust and the rebirth of the modern State of Israel is probably stronger than the theological tie; in other words, the heart speaks louder than the head:

> [T]he events of Europe from 1933 to 1945 and of the Middle East from 1948 to 1967 (and beyond) are interrelated and meaningful in a more than commonplace way. It is not just the killing of millions of people that

happened in Europe, not merely the creation of another state in the Middle East. It was a holocaust and a rebirth, the fulfillment of prophecy, interpreted by prophetic teachings about dry bones [Ezekiel 37], the suffering servant [Isaiah 53], and the return to Zion [Ezekiel 36].

And, as we saw, these same supposedly secular people see *themselves* as having been asphyxiated at Auschwitz and reborn in the state of Israel. They understood their group life in the most recent times as conforming to the paradigm of ancient prophecy. The state is not merely another nation, but the state of Israel. Events of the day remain highly charged, full of meaning. . . .

Let me confess at the end that I have never read the vision of the valley of the dry bones without tears. We Jews were the dry bones in 1945, without hope. We Jews were given sinews, flesh, the breath of life in 1948 and afterward—until, in 1967, we returned to the old Temple wall. And all of this bore immense meaning not only for the religious sector within Jewry, but for the millions of secular, assimilated individuals who long had supposed they were part of no particular group, least of all the Jewish one into which they were born.[39]

But second, while there are some Jewish Holocaust scholars who saw the rebirth of the State of Israel as a redemptive moment, there are other Jewish scholars who saw the rebirth of the State of Israel as anything but a redemptive moment. For them, the Holocaust and the rebirth of the State of Israel are not a portrayal of a messianic dream, but rather a Nazi nightmare from which they can never awaken. Once again, it was Eliezer Berkovits who admitted that while we cannot exonerate God for His responsibility in all the suffering of history, one can nevertheless rest in His recompense beyond history:

The sorrow will stay, but it will become blessed with the promise of another day for Israel to continue on its eternal course with a new dignity and a new self-assurance. Thus, perhaps in the awful misery of man will be revealed to us the awesome mystery of God. . . .

Yet all this does not exonerate God for all the suffering of the innocent in history. God is responsible for having created a world in which man is free to make history. There must be a dimension beyond history in which all suffering finds its redemption through God. This is essential to the faith of the Jew. The Jew does not doubt God's presence, though he is unable to set limits to the duration and intensity of his absence. There is no justification for the ways of providence, but its acceptance. It is not a willingness to forgive the unheard cries of millions, but a trust that in God the tragedy of man may find its transformation. Within time and history that cry is unforgivable.[40]

Jacob Talmon, professor of history at the Hebrew University in Jerusalem, totally rejected the "metaphysical and theological" perspective that sees the rebirth of the State of Israel as a redemptive moment:

Some people profess to see the Holocaust as an ineluctable [inescapable] stage in Jewish history—the labour pains of national rebirth, so to speak, or the price of redemption. One hears this kind of interpretation from extreme nationalists as well as from certain extremely religious Jews.

This I shall never be able to understand. I shall never be able to believe in a Guardian of Israel who claims the lives of a million children as the price of national revival. One must not confuse metaphysical and theological questions with historical and empirical statements about the role of Jewish despair after Auschwitz, the guilt feelings of the Christian world, and the fluid situation at the end of the war aiding the restoration of Jewish statehood in modern Israel. There is, of course, unparalleled grandeur in the explosion of Jewish energies and the display of an inconquerable will to live on the morrow of the most horrible bloodletting and deepest degradation and wretchedness that any people has ever experienced—in the struggle for independent Jewish nationhood.[41]

Irving Greenberg, while maintaining that the rebirth of the State of Israel may have been a redeeming act of God (perhaps *the* redeeming act of modern Judaism), one would be better served by holding to some kind of modern dialectic:

But if Israel is so redeeming, why then must faith be "moment faith," and why should the experience of nothingness ever dominate?

The answer is that faith is living in the presence of the Redeemer, and in the moment of utter chaos, of genocide, one does not live in His presence. One must be faithful to the reality of the nothingness. Faith is a moment truth, but there are moments when it is not true. This is certainly demonstrable in dialectic truths, when invoking the truth at the wrong moment is a lie. To let Auschwitz overwhelm Jerusalem is to lie (i.e., to speak a truth out of its appropriate moment); and to let Jerusalem deny Auschwitz is to lie for the same reason.[42]

Jacob Agus maintained that the rebirth of the State of Israel out of the ashes of Auschwitz was an unjust scale of justice: "We cannot be content with the old clichés, rehearsing the 'sins' of our people and reveling in visions of Israel as the counterweight to the tragedy of the Six Million. The scales do not balance, however much you try."[43]

Elie Wiesel, the great Holocaust storyteller, also reaffirmed that no modern comparison between the destruction of the six million and the reestablishment of the State of Israel should ever be made:

To me, the Holocaust teaches nothing. I object to Israeli politicians when they claim that "Israel is the answer to the Holocaust." It is not. It has no right to be. Sometimes I feel it is a disgrace to link these two events and thus diminish them both. They are two mysteries, both historic and Messianic. I refuse to give children in tomorrow's Israel such a burden, such guilt. I do not want them to think: If we were free and independent, it is because of the Holocaust. This would mean being, in a way, responsible for the past.[44]

Emil Fackenheim, Jewish philosopher and theologian, likewise rejected the modern paradigm of Jerusalem as an answer to Auschwitz:

Jerusalem, while no "answer" to the Holocaust, is a response; and every Israeli lives that response. Israel is collectively what every survivor is individually: a No to the demons of Auschwitz, a Yes to Jewish survival and security—and thus a testimony to life against death *on behalf of all mankind*. The juxtaposition of Auschwitz and Jerusalem recalls nothing so vividly as Ezekiel's vision of the dead bones and the resurrection of the household of Israel [Ezekiel 37:1–14]. Every Israeli—man, woman or child—stakes his life on the truth of that vision.[45]

Once again, in more detail, Fackenheim further maintained that the Holocaust survivor is gradually becoming the paradigm for the entire Jewish people, especially with the rebirth of the State of Israel:

> Nowhere is this truth [i.e., the Holocaust survivor as a paradigm for the entire Jewish people] as unmistakable as in the State of Israel. The State of Israel is collectively what the survivor is individually—testimony on behalf of all mankind to life against death, to sanity against madness, to Jewish self-affirmation against every form of flight from it, and (although this is visible only to those who break through the narrow theological categories) to the God of the ancient covenant against all lapses into paganism. . . . [T]he truth is obvious: the State of Israel is a collective testimony against the groundless hate which has erupted in this century in the heart of Europe. Its watchword is *Am Yisrael Chi*—the people of Israel lives." Without this watchword the State of Israel could not have survived for a generation. It is a watchword of defiance, hope and faith. It is a testimony to all men everywhere that man shall be, and be human—even if it should be necessary to cast Truth to the ground.[46]

In fact, Fackenheim went on to assert that the authentic Jew of today is forbidden to hand Hitler yet another posthumous victory, which Fackenheim called "a 614th commandment," that is, *Am Yisrael Chai*: "The People of Israel Lives!" (i.e., the Jewish people are commanded to survive as Jews, lest the Jewish people perish).[47]

In conclusion, in light of this modern Jewish struggle on whether or not the Holocaust played any kind of causative role in the reestablishment of the State of Israel in 1948, it is not surprising that the modern State of Israel survives in a kind of time warp, expressing itself as a siege or ghetto mentality. The Holocaust is an ever-present and foreboding shadow that casts its spell over the Jewish people's entire framework of thinking: their past, their present, their future. With every breath a Jew draws, a vow of allegiance echoes into every corner of the Earth where our people have been scattered: "Never again! Never again! Never again!"[48]

However, there is a more comprehensive way at looking at this causative role in the reestablishment of the State of Israel in 1948, (i.e., the causal relationship between the rebirth of the State of Israel and the Holocaust). This way of looking at causation goes back to the classical Greek philosopher Aristotle, and has been employed by both philosophers and theologians down through the centuries.[49] As Aristotle grappled with how and why things change, he detailed at least four different but related causes. These four causes (and I will add one more) are still as relevant as when Aristotle first described them. No philosophical system has ever proven these causes false. And for our purposes, Aristotle's take on causation will prove helpful in seeing the multiple causes behind the Holocaust and the reestablishment of the State of Israel in 1948.

Another Set of Causative Factors That Led to the Establishment of the State of Israel in 1948

So what are these four Aristotelian causes (plus one more) and how will they help us to understand the multiple causes behind the Holocaust and the reestablishment of the State of Israel in 1948 (i.e., the causal relationship between the rebirth of the State of Israel and the Holocaust)?

First, by way of introduction, we need to define what we mean by "causation" (or cause) and, even more to the point, what we mean by "change." By the term "change" we mean the transformation between two or more things. Certainly the relationship between the rebirth of the State of Israel and the Holocaust can be defined as a transformative change.[50] And what do we mean by "causation" or "cause"? By the term "causation" or "cause" we mean that which brings about an effect. Again, as with the above definition of "change," the relationship between the rebirth of the State of Israel and the Holocaust can be defined as a causal transformation (i.e., the effect).[51]

And second, let's look at the four Aristotelian causes (plus one more) behind every form of change and see how these causes relate to the rebirth of the State of Israel in light of the Holocaust. We will first define each cause, then illustrate each cause (by the making of a table), and then finally we will apply each cause to the rebirth of the State of Israel and the causal relationship of the Holocaust. By investigating these five causal relationships, we should be able to better understand the Holocaust and its causative relation to the reestablishment of the State of Israel in 1948.

1. The first cause is called "the Efficient Cause," that is, Who made the table? (i.e., by whom: the carpenter).

   "The Efficient Cause" of the Rebirth of the State Israel out of the Holocaust was: the Lord God, the Lord Yeshua the Messiah, and the Spirit of God.

2. The second cause is called "the Material Cause," that is, What is the table going to be made of? (i.e., of what: the wood).

   "The Material Cause" of the Rebirth of the State Israel out of the Holocaust was: the Jewish people coming out of the Holocaust (i.e., the Holocaust survivors).

3. The third cause is called "the Formal Cause," that is, What is being made? (i.e., to what: the table).

"The Formal Cause" of the Rebirth of the State Israel out of the Holocaust was: the nation of Israel itself, reborn in 1948.

4. The fourth cause is called "the Final Cause [the *Telos* Cause]," that is, What is the table being made for? (i.e., for what: the dinner).

"The Final Cause" of the Rebirth of the State Israel out of the Holocaust was and is: the glory of God (i.e., when the Formal Cause is actualized).

5. The fifth cause is called "the Instrumental Cause," that is, What was used to make the table? (i.e., by what? the carpenter's assistants, a hammer, nails, a saw, etc.).[52]

"The Instrumental Cause" of the Rebirth of the State Israel out of the Holocaust was: the twentieth-century worldwide political powers: the UN affirmative nations, Harry Truman, Winston Churchill,[53] plus the herculean efforts of men and women like Theodor Herzl, Chaim Weizmann, Golda Meir, David Ben Gurion, etc.

In summary, as one can see, the relationship between the Holocaust and the reestablishment of the State of Israel in 1948 was multifaceted. Having looked at the five different causative factors in this regard, one can now see the different causes that God used in founding the modern State of Israel.

So, having seen the two causative approaches that have shed light on the relationship between the Holocaust and the reestablishment of the State of Israel in 1948, we now need to see how that historic event of the rebirth of the State of Israel points forward as a foreshadowing of the final and greater prophetic return to the land: the glorious messianic kingdom in the Promised Land of Israel. And finally, it must be remembered that while divine mysteries do abound in these matters, we dare not fall short of the divine revelation on these issues (cf. Deut. 29:29; etc.).

Israel's Prophetic Return in the Future

Israel's final prophetic return to her promised homeland forms one of the major events of biblical prophecy, as was pointed out by prophetic scholar John F. Walvoord:

Of the many peculiar phenomena which characterize the present generation, few events can claim equal significance as far as Biblical prophecy is concerned with that of the return of Israel to their land. It constitutes a preparation for the end of the age, the setting for the coming of the Lord for His church, and the fulfillment of Israel's prophetic destiny.[54]

In discussing Israel's final and glorious prophetic return to the Promised Land and how it was foreshadowed in the rebirth of the Nation of Israel in 1948, we will need to survey two matters: (1) Israel's biblical pattern of Trespass-Exile-Return, and (2) Israel's biblical progress of Three Exiles and Three Returns.

First then, in regard to Israel's prophetic return, what is Israel's biblical pattern of Trespass-Exile-Return (T-E-R)?[55] When God cut an unconditional, unilateral, and therefore eternal covenant with Abraham,[56] He would later establish another covenant with Moses, a covenant that laid out a definite pattern in His temporal relationship with Israel. It has been called the Deuteronomistic or Deuteronomic Pattern of temporal blessings and temporal curses detailed by Moses in the Mosaic Covenant or Law (Deut. 28–30ff.; cf. Lev. 26; etc.).[57] In other words, the Book of Deuteronomy recorded a series of closing sermons that Moses proclaimed to the new generation of Israelites, the generation that came through the wilderness wanderings and that would follow Joshua in the Conquest of the Promised Land of Canaan.[58] So, in essence, the Book of Deuteronomy is a summary of the Mosaic or Sinaitic Covenant (or the Mosaic Law), in which God laid down several divine stipulations that if obeyed would lead to temporal blessings (i.e., private and public victories), but if disobeyed, would lead to temporal curses (i.e., private and public defeats).[59]

In principle (in the patriarchal historical narratives), this Trespass-Exile-Return Pattern had been the divine pattern with Israel since the call of Abraham (cf. Gen. 15:13–21; etc.). However, in practice (in the Mosaic legal literature), it was definitively expressed through the Sinaitic Covenant/Law with its *temporal* blessings and its *temporal* curses in regard to Israel as God's theocratic nation (cf. Amos 3:1–2ff.; etc.). In other words, the *temporal* blessings were the rewards [gifts] from God for Israel's obedience to the Mosaic Covenant, while the *temporal* curses were the judgments [disciplines] from God for Israel's disobedience to the Mosaic Covenant.[60]

The final "time of Jacob's trouble" (i.e., the Tribulation) in "the latter/last days,"[61] will be the last and worst expression of God's *temporal* curses [judgments] on the nation Israel (cf. Jeremiah 30:7; Daniel 12:1ff.; Joel 2:1–32, esp. 2; Zechariah 12:1–14:21; Matthew 24:1–25:46, esp. 24:21; Revelation 6–19; etc.). This final "time of Jacob's trouble" will be the culminating expression of the Trespass-Exile-Return [T-E-R] Pattern.

Now second, in regard to Israel's prophetic return, what is Israel's biblical progress of Three Exiles and Three Returns? The Word of God makes it critically clear that Israel will only experience three exiles and three returns. The first two of these exiles and returns have already occurred historically, in Israel's past. The remaining exile and return will occur prophetically, in Israel's future. In one sense, the Holocaust was the precipitating factor leading up to "the beginning of the end," culminating in the return of the Lord Yeshua and the establishment of His messianic kingdom. So what are these three exiles and three returns?

The First Exile[62] and the First Return occurred in the following ways:

1. *The First Exile* took place in the time of Joseph, Jacob, and Jacob's twelve sons and one daughter, when God took them into Egypt [c. 1875 BC] (prophesied to Abraham in Genesis 15:13; and executed in Genesis 37:1–36; 39:1–50:26; Exodus 1:1–22ff.; etc.).

2. *The First Return* took place at the time of the Exodus [c. 1440 BC], when God brought the Jews out of Egypt and back into the Promised Land, using Moses as His Great Deliverer and Law-Giver (again prophesied in Genesis 15:14, 16; and executed in Exodus 2:1–18:27; also 19:1–40:38; Leviticus 1:1–27:34; Deuteronomy 1:1–34:12; etc.).

Likewise, the Second Exile and the Second Return occurred in the following ways:

1. *The Second Exile* took place in two phases, *the initial phase* in the time of the ten tribes of the Northern Kingdom of Israel (in 722 BC) into the Assyrian Empire (prophesied by Jonah and Amos, plus Hosea later; and executed in 2 Kings 1:1–17:41; etc.); then *the final phase* in the time of the remaining two tribes of the Southern Kingdom of Judah (in 606/605 BC, 597 BC, & 586 BC when the Solomonic Temple was destroyed) into the Babylonian Empire and then into the Medo-Persian Empire (prophesied by Isaiah, Jeremiah, and Ezekiel, plus see Daniel later; and executed in 2 Kings 18:1——25:30; 2 Chronicles 10:1–36:21; etc.).

2. *The Second Return* took place at the end of the seventy-year captivity [c. 538–400 BC], with Cyrus the Persian king, in the hands

of God, acting as the Servant of God (again prophesied by Isaiah, Jeremiah, Ezekiel, and Daniel; and executed under Ezra, Nehemiah, Zerubbabel, Haggai, Zechariah, and Malachi, with the believing remnant), from the two southern tribes, 50,000 in numbers, Ezra 2:64f.; Nehemiah 6:66f., from Persia and even some from the ten northern tribes, to rebuild the city of Jerusalem and the Solomon Temple; see also 2 Chronicles 36:22–23; etc.).

In his usual artistic prose, Abraham Joshua Heschel described Israel's first and second courageous exiles and returns:

From the time of Joshua to this day, for a period of more than 3,300 years, Jews have lived in the land of Israel in unbroken sequence. After the destruction of Jerusalem by the Babylonians in the year 586 BCE, and again after the destruction of the Second Commonwealth by the Romans, in the year 70, Jews continued to live in the land.

Though the major part of the nation was forced into exile, there has always remained a Jewish settlement in Palestine. It fortunes varied from generation to generation, but its continuity was never broken. However terrible the oppression, the Jews never abandoned their native land. Nor did they merge into any of the numerous racial and religious communities which held sway in Palestine in subsequent centuries. They remained a distinctive national-religious entity, temporarily subjugated, but never doubtful of their ultimate restoration.

They clung to their native soil with fierce tenacity, as evidenced by the literature and the historical monuments of their conquerors. They never resigned themselves to their exile, as did so many other conquered nations of antiquity. When they were released from the Babylonian captivity, it was Jewish noblemen and high officials in the Persian service who headed the returning exiles. They fought with unparalleled courage and resource against the imperial power of Rome. The last phase of the second Jewish state was an almost uninterrupted series of revolts against the Roman provincial governors. The final revolt, known as the Judean War, was, according to Roman records, one of the fiercest national struggles which the Roman legions ever had to face. Even after the conquest of Jerusalem and the destruction of their national sanctuary, they did not give up the struggle for their independence.

Fifty years later they rose again in a great national insurrection and for many months defied the Roman forces until at last they were crushed. It was as the result of that devastating defeat that the Jewish political power in Palestine was finally destroyed. Yet for centuries after that destruction the Jews continued to cling stubbornly to the country, and it was only the policy of extermination and expropriation pursued by the Romans and the Byzantines which in the end drove the bulk of the Jewish people out of Palestine.[63]

And finally, the Third (and Last) Exile and the Third (and Last) Return will occur in the following ways:

1. *The Third and Final Exile* in the Bible took place in the time of the Lord Yeshua, His Apostles, and the Early Believers, in the First Jewish Revolt, when the Temple was destroyed and thousands of Jews were taken into the Roman Empire [AD 70] (prophesied by the Lord Yeshua in Luke 21:20–24; plus Matthew 23:37–24:3ff.; Mark 13:1–4ff.; etc.; and executed by the Roman Legionnaires in the writings of Josephus, *The Jewish Wars*; etc.).

2. *The Third and Final Return* in the Bible will also take place in two phases,[64] *the initial phase* when the Jewish Nation returns in unbelief in preparation for "the Time of Jacob's Trouble" [the Second Half of the Tribulation, three and a half years: the Temporal Curses], with the Antichrist [the Beast], in the hands of Satan, acting as the so-called Protector of the Jewish people (again prophesied in Isaiah 11:11–12; Jeremiah 30:1–24; Ezekiel 20:33–38; 22:17–22; 36:22–24; 38:1–39:29; Daniel 2; 7; 9 [24–27]; Zephaniah 2:1–2; Zechariah 12:1–13:9; Matthew 23:37–39ff.; Luke 21:20–24; Romans 11:11–32; 1 Thessalonians 5:1–11; 2 Thessalonians 2:1–17; Revelation 6–19; etc.); then *the final phase* when the final Jewish Remnant returns in belief [faith] in preparation for the Messianic Kingdom [the Millennial Reign of the Lord Yeshua: the Temporal Blessings], with our Lord Yeshua, in the hands of God, acting as the Messianic Warrior Hero for the final Believing Remnant of Israel and for the whole world of His Believing People (and prophesied in Ezekiel 40–48; Daniel 9:24–27; Psalms 83; 105; Zechariah 8–14; Romans 11:25–29; Revelation 6–22; etc.).[65]

The late messianic scholar, Louis Goldberg, summarized the frightful loss of life in both the Holocaust and especially in the final exile and return:

> The Holocaust of Hitler's Third Reich was and is still horrible to contemplate. How does one comprehend the loss of six million people simply because they were Jewish? The figure included the death of one million children, the future generation that would have provided continuity to the Jewish community in the future. The several thousand who were able to survive the concentration camps still carry within themselves in both body and spirit the scars from their horrible experiences of suffering and deprivation.[66] But as we view the darkness in Israel yet to come, it is with a wrench in one's heart concerning what is yet to happen in the land. . . .

The prophet Zechariah described the [future] holocaust in the land of Israel:

> "And it will come about in all the land,"
>   Declares the LORD,
>   "That two parts in it [the land] will be cut off and perish;
>   But the third will be left in it.
> And I will bring the third part through the fire,
> Refine them as silver is refined,
> And test them as gold is tested"
>   (Zechariah 13:8–9a).

The dire proclamation is that two-thirds of the land's population will perish. This means that of the three-million population today in Israel, should this horrible event take place now, two million will die because of the political antichrist's fury against Israel, in exact accordance with Satan's desires [cf. Matt. 24; 2 Thess. 2; Rev. 12–13; etc.]. It will be a day when Israel will have few friends, and those who would wish to help will be unable to come to her aid. A people who have suffered so much in the past will again have their backs to the wall as they never have had before [cf. Zech. 12–14; etc.]. This is not a situation where only one nation like Rome tried to subdue Israel because of sheer military might, but instead, all the power blocs will be involved in attempting to snuff out Israel's life. . . . Israel has had many attempts against her to harm her, first in one country in Europe, and then in another country, but this [final] attack is a holocaust in the land itself. It is terrible to contemplate![67]

These three returns are also described in the Bible as three different, but related, Exoduses. Thus, Israel's prophets look forward to a future Exodus:

- The motif of the exodus (as distinct from the book of Exodus) is one of the unifying images of the Bible. . . .
- No other OT motif is as crucial to understand. No other event is so basic to the fabric of both Testaments. . . .
- The central meaning of the exodus is deliverance or salvation. . . . The exodus motif was used by prophets and poetic writers to transfer the significance of the original exodus to new situations requiring deliverance, obedience, identity or belief. . . .
- The prophets transform the original exodus into a new exodus. In the same way that God delivered Israel from Egypt in the past, he will deliver Israel in the future from bondage in the exile.[68]

Only following the miraculous nature of the original Creation (everything out of nothing by the word of God: the making of the whole universe), does the miraculous mature of the Exodus become the historical memory of the Nation Israel (something out of something by the word of God: the parting of the Red Sea). God will then forge the Exodus into His primary motivating factor in Israel's history and prophecy. This is the Exodus that God uses to return His people back into the Land under the leadership of Moses. It is recorded both historically (Ex. 14) and poetically (Ex. 15).

This First Exodus then became the miraculous event and motif that God used for pointing forward toward both the Second Exodus/Return and the Third and Final Exodus/Return.[69]

The Second Exodus/Return is laid out in the following prophetic passages: Isaiah 40:26–31; 42:5–9; 44:24–28; 51:9–16; cf. Jeremiah 25:10–11; 29:10–14; Daniel 9:1–2, 24–25ff.; etc.

The Third and Final Exodus/Return is likewise laid out in the following prophetic passages (some of these prophetic passages also include pilgrimage and festival): Isaiah 11:11–16; 14:1; 19:23–25; 25:6–10; 27:9–13; 35:1, 8–10; 41:17–20; 42:14–17; 43:1–7, 13, 19; 49:20–22; 51:3, 9–11; 52:7–12; 54:17; 56:6–8; 59:20–21; 60:4–7; 62:4–7; 66:18–23; Jeremiah 3:11–20; 12:14–17; 16:10–18; 23:1–8; 24:1–10; 29:1–14; 30:1–3, 10–11; 31:2–14, 15–20, 27, 33–36; 32:1–44; 50:17–20; plus indirectly, 30:18–22; 31:23–25; 33:1–18; Ezekiel 11:14–21; 20:33–44; 34:1–16; 35:1–36:15; 36:16–38; 37:1–14; 39:21–29; plus indirectly 28:20–26; 34:17–3; Hosea 2:14–23; 3:5; Amos 9:11–15; Micah 4:1–8; 7:12–13, 17–20; Zephaniah 3:9–10, 15–20; Haggai 1:7–8; 2:6–9; Zechariah 1:16–17; 2:8–13; 8:1–8, 19–23; 10:1–12ff.; 12:1–14; 13:1–9; 14:1–14ff.; etc.

And, of course, it must be remembered that these end-time prophetic promises of Israel's final return to the Land are based on the unconditional, eternal Abrahamic Covenant (Gen. 12; 15; 17; 22; Deut. 30; Ps. 105; etc.).

In conclusion, like ocean waves cascading in and then receding out again, so Israel's exiles and returns move Israel ever closer to the end. For the rebirth of the Nation of Israel, arising out of the ashes of Auschwitz, was "the beginning of the End"![70] The impact of the rebirth of the modern State of Israel has challenged Christian theology in a significant way, as is acknowledged by H. N. Ridderbos:

> The existence of Israel once again becomes a bone of contention, this time in a theoretical and theological sense. Do the misery and suffering of Israel in the past and in the present prove that God's doom has rested and will rest upon her, as has been alleged time and again in so-called Christian theology? Or is Israel's lasting existence and, in a way, her invincibility, God's finger in history, that Israel is the object of His special providence (*providential specialissima*) and the proof of her glorious future, the future that has been beheld and foretold by Israel's own seers and prophets.[71]

Not only has the rebirth of the Nation of Israel challenged Christian theology, but it has also reaffirmed the Jewish "master story" which points forward to God's ultimate plan for the world, which will occur only after God brings Israel back into her promised homeland. Jocelyn Hellig states this most graphically:

> What happens to Jews is intimately bound up with what will ultimately happen to the entire world, which since God is good, will eventually be redeemed. First, the Jewish people will be returned to their homeland. Thereafter, a global transformation will take place. . . .

> The Jews' mythical dimension, or master story, is the Exodus from Egypt, in which God chose a small band of slaves as his "treasured possession" (Exodus 19:5), delivered from bondage and called upon them to live by his commandments. The Jews' story is, however, linked to a larger world-encompassing one in that it promises to bring about a transformation of the entire world. All the world's people will be brought into the service of the one God when he establishes his Kingdom on earth. The whole Jewish history—and indeed

world history, from the Jewish perspective—pivots around this central event.[72]

And finally, Abraham Joshua Heschel reminds us that the eternal hope and dream of the Jewish people for their return to the Land of Israel is just that, an eternal hope and dream:

> Return to Zion is more than a phenomenon of our time. As a hope, a dream, as an article of faith, it lived in the hearts of Jews of all ages. Indeed, there never was a time in which the Holy Land was not an object of attraction and deep longing for the pious Jew, even though he was not always able to gratify his longing. There was an awareness in many minds that life was incomplete, that one's service was deficient, unless one lived in the Holy Land.[73]

Conclusion

So, God has planted a Zionist component into the Jewish DNA (i.e., an embedded desire to go home, back to Israel). In other words, God has so worked in the collective soul of the Jewish people that we experience moments of recall built into the psychic memory of the nation Israel. These echoing memories are fortified by such collective reminders as:

- During the Passover Seder, we echo the command of Moses and Aaron: "Let my people go!"
- At the close of the Passover Seder, we affirm together, "*Leshana haba'ah b'Yerushalayim*, "Next year in Jerusalem!"
- Our national anthem is *Hatikva*, "The Hope."

Even into the lengths, depths, and breadths of the Diaspora, we offer up to God this prayer:

> [5] If I forget you, O Jerusalem, may my right hand forget her skill.
> [6] May my tongue cling to the roof of my mouth if I do not remember you,
> if I do not exalt Jerusalem above my chief joy (Psalm 137:5–6, NASB).

> [5] If I ever forget you, Jerusalem, let my fingers wither and fall off like leaves.
> [6] Let my tongue swell and turn black if I fail to remember you,
> if I fail, O dear Jerusalem, to honor you as my greatest (Psalm 137:5–6, *The Message*).

God fortified Rachmiel Frydland's long, painful journey through the Holocaust kingdom by a biblical dream, the dream of the Rebirth of the State of Israel in 1948. God had promised it. It must come true. And it did. Not only had God fortified Rachmiel by this biblical dream, but through the Rebirth of the State of Israel in 1948, He also foreshadowed the final Regathering of Israel's glorious messianic kingdom. God has promised it. It must come true. And it will.

> [1] When the LORD brought back the captive
> ones to Zion,
> we were like those who dream.
> [2] Then our mouth was filled with laughter
> and our tongue with joyful shouting;
> then they said among the nations,
> "The LORD has done great things for them."
> [3] The LORD has done great things for us;
> we are glad.
> [4] Restore our captivity, O LORD,
> as the streams in the South.
> [5] Those who sow in tears
> shall reap with joyful shouting.
> [6] He who goes to and fro weeping, carrying his
> bag of seed,
> shall indeed come again with a shout of joy,
> bringing his sheaves with him
> (Psalm 126:1–6, NASB).

> [1] It seemed like a dream, too good to be true,
> when God returned Zion's exiles.
> [2] We laughed, we sang,
> we couldn't believe our good fortune.
> and our tongue with joyful shouting;
> we were the talk of the nations—
> "God was wonderful to them!"
> [3] God was wonderful to us;
> we are one happy people.
> [4] And now, God, do it again—
> bring rains to our drought-stricken lives
> [5] so those who panted their crops in despair
> will shout hurrahs at the harvest,
> [6] so those who went off with heavy hearts
> will come home laughing, with armloads
> of blessings
> (Psalm 126:1–6, *The Message*).

Yes, it had been a long, horrific journey for Rachmiel Frydland, a journey through the valley of the shadow of death. But like so many hundreds of other Messianic Jews who also arose out of the ashes of Auschwitz, he completed his journey and returned to his home, at the rebirth of the Nation of Israel. For he realized that the Nazi Holocaust, which gave way to the rebirth of the State of Israel, also prepared Israel for her most glorious, prophetic future.

But Rachmiel's story bears the painful scars of the Holocaust: both of his parents, his grandmother, his four sisters, and his new bride, along with several thousand other Jewish believers, including numerous other relatives, all perished in the gas chambers and ovens of the Holocaust. Even though Rachmiel had become a believer, he was nonetheless on the run from the Nazis, the unbelieving Jews, the churches, and the Polish peasants in the forests where he tried to hide. Rachmiel was truly "a man on the run"! However, he and so many others survived because of "The Hope": The Rebirth of the State of Israel.

On January 12, 1985, Rachmiel departed this world (of cancer) to be with His Lord Yeshua who he had faithfully served for 66 years. He also rejoined his beloved parents, his four sisters, and his first wife, along with all those thousands of faithful messianic believers who perished in the Holocaust, "those of whom the world was not worthy" (Heb. 11:38).

You see, when Rachmiel finally returned the Land of Israel in 1961, he wasn't alone. The Lord was with him. Other Jewish survivors were with him, some believers and many not. His beloved family and friends who perished were also with him, safely carried in his heart. He promised them he would make the return for them as well, which he did. His return was also their return. The day is coming when all of us who are believers will also return, this time with the Lord Yeshua when He returns the second time (Rev. 19) and with Him in His messianic kingdom (Rev. 20). Not only that, but we will spend eternity in the New Jerusalem, the Lord's capital city of the New Heaven and the New Earth (Rev. 21–22). For Jerusalem, mentioned some 808 times in the Holy Bible, is built into the eternal plan of God—a divine plan that bonds together the Jerusalem of the past, the Jerusalem of the present, and the Jerusalem of the future (Rev. 21:1–22:5).

Randall Price reminds us of Jerusalem's glorious, *eternal* future:

> By the end times, Jerusalem will have had a long history of sin, scandal, deception, and destruction. Worn by the ravages of wars and stained by struggles over sovereignty, it awaits a new day when its faded past will greet a glorious future. It alone of all cities on earth

has a promise of eternally abiding. For when time ends and eternity begins, Jerusalem will still be standing, the city and home of God's people forever![74]

The New Jerusalem is a real city, with twelve gates, with the names of "the twelve tribes of the sons of Israel," the believing remnant of Israel (Rev. 21:12–13); and also with twelve foundation stones, with "the twelve names of the twelve apostles of the Lamb," the believing members of the Body of Christ, the Messianic Body of our Lord Yeshua (Rev. 21:14–15).

Rachmiel came to faith in 1938 (at the age of nineteen) and was baptized almost immediately; on January 15, 1945, at twenty-five years of age, he celebrated the seventh anniversary of his original baptism—now as a free man on his journey to the reborn State of Israel!

Rachmiel reminds all of us that during the worst of times—during the Holocaust—the Jewish believers lifted their hearts to God in song with the words of this hymn:

> Let your hearts always be joyful. Praise and thank Him without fears.
> For our Father in the Heavens,
> On His arm His children bears.
> Joyful, joyful, always joyful,
> Day by day His sun doth shine;
> Full of beauty is the road to Heaven,
> God and Christ are always mine.[75]

Rachmiel closes *When Being Jewish Was a Crime* with these words:

> My story is at an end now. It was written for the purpose of honoring and giving some account of the large group of Jewish believers in Europe, and especially in Poland, who perished. God would want their names to be remembered. Among them were giants of Jewish learning, like Yosele Sommer; giants of preaching, like Joseph Walfin; giants in piety and dedication to God, like the Soffer family; and so many more.

It is also a tribute to those brethren who ricked their lives to attempt to save a Jewish man, woman, or child. They did it altruistically because they loved their Lord Jesus better than their own lives. Only Jesus could inspire people to do it, so He must be the Messiah, Savior, Son of God. He was Jewish. . . .

Let us search our ways and investigate our direction, and let us return to the Lord. There is no way of salvation without Him.

What a wonderful future there is to look forward to! I am confident that all the horrors that befell the Jews was simply the night before the Light will break for Israel and through her to the whole world.

For his anger endureth but a moment; in his favor is life: weeping may endure for a night, but joy cometh in the morning (Ps. 30:5).[76]

So, the Apostle Paul finally completed his Jewish apologetic for God's saving acts in the past, present, and future of Israel and the Jewish people (Rom. 9–11), a glorious future when "all Israel will be saved" in our Lord's messianic kingdom (Rom. 11:26). And then he lifted up his praise and worship to God:

> [33] Oh, the depth of the riches both of the wisdom and knowledge of God! How unsearchable are His judgments and unfathomable His ways!
> [34] For who has known the mind of the LORD, or who became His counselor?
> [35] Or who has first given to Him that it might be paid back to Him again?
> [36] For from Him and through Him and to Him are all things. To Him be the glory forever. Amen
> (Romans 11:33–36, NASB).

Along with the Apostle Paul and with Rachmiel Frydland, may we also lift up this praise and worship to God!

Study Questions

1. What does the term "The Holocaust" mean?

2. What are Israel's two returns to the Land of Promise?

3. What are the various relationships between the Holocaust and the Rebirth of the State of Israel in 1948?

4. What is meant by T-E-R?

5. What are Israel's three exiles from the land and her three returns back to the land?

6. How does the rebirth of the State of Israel in 1948 foreshadow Israel's final, glorious return to the Land of Promise?

7. What is the Abrahamic Covenant and how does it guarantee Israel's final, glorious return to the Land of Promise?

8. What is the biblical basis for Israel's final, glorious return to the Land of Promise?

9. What are God's plans for Jerusalem's glorious future, especially the New Jerusalem (Rev. 21–22)?

10. In light of Israel's prophetic future, how should we be praying for the Jewish people (Rom. 10:1; Ps. 122:6–9; etc.), and what difference should it make in our own lives?

Conference Video

chosenpeople.com/leventhal

Interview with Dr. Barry R. Leventhal

chosenpeople.com/leventhal-interview

PRACTICAL THEOLOGY

THE JEWISH PEOPLE: EVIDENCE FOR THE TRUTH OF SCRIPTURE

Dr. Michael Rydelnik

Rydelnik, in his chapter *The Jewish People: Evidence for the Truth of Scripture*, shows how the "only possible way to discover the reason for the Jewish people's continued existence and influence is by examining the Scriptures." The historian Arnold Toynbee called the Jewish people "fossils of history," while Mark Twain marveled at their immortality. They recognized the mysterious nature of the Jewish people. Only Scripture gives rationale for Jewish survival. Their existence testifies to the truth of Scripture.

Dr. Rydelnik provides three critical reasons why Israel is a witness to the truth of Scripture and the power of God. He concludes that the restoration of the people of Israel to the land of Israel is a tangible witness to the power and faithfulness of God and a harbinger of what is to come when Messiah returns to establish His kingdom.

Fossils of history! In the 1930s, historian Arnold Toynbee maintained that Jewish people did not fit into any definition of nation, race, or religion. According to Toynbee, Jewish people are not a nation because they have lived for centuries without a land, scattered throughout the world. Moreover, the historian asserted that Jewish people could not be categorized as a race because they have accepted and continue to accept proselytes. Additionally, Toynbee argued that Jewish people do not constitute a religion because there are Jews who do not even believe in God. However, given the Jewish presence in world history for more than 3000 years, Toynbee classified the Jewish people as "fossils" of history.[1] Although Toynbee's characterization was unfair, his assessment does highlight the mysterious aspect of the Jewish people.

Like Toynbee, Mark Twain also sensed the enigmatic nature of the Jewish people when he wrote:

> If the statistics are right, the Jews constitute but one percent of the human race . . . Properly the Jew ought hardly to be heard of, but he is heard of, has always been heard of. He is as prominent on the planet as any other people, and his commercial importance is extravagantly out of proportion to the smallness of his bulk. His contributions to the world's list of great names in literature, science, art, music, finance, medicine, and abstruse learning are also away out of proportion to the weakness of his numbers. He has made a marvelous fight in the world, in all the ages; and has done it with his hands tied behind him . . . The Egyptian, the Babylonian, and the Persian rose, filled the planet with sound and splendor, then faded to dreamstuff and passed away; the Greek and the Roman followed, and made a vast noise, and they are gone; other peoples have sprung up and held their torch high for a time, but it burned out, and they sit in twilight now, or have vanished. The Jew saw them all, beat them all, and is now what he always was . . . All things are mortal but the Jew; all other forces pass, but he remains. What is the secret of his immortality?[2]

Twain was an agnostic and a skeptic. Although, he could recognize the amazing, seemingly miraculous, nature of the Jewish people's preservation and influence, but he could not answer his own question. He had no explanation for "the secret of his (the Jew's) immortality" because the answer is related to God and His Word, the Bible. The only possible way to discover the reason for the Jewish people's continued existence and influence is by examining the

Scriptures. And when that is done, it becomes clear that the Jewish people themselves, their land and their future, all constitute remarkable evidence for the truth of Scripture.

The Preservation of the People of Israel

The first way the Jewish people constitute an evidence of the truth of Scripture is through their preservation throughout history. When speaking of the Jewish people, the Bible promises that God would always preserve His people. Beginning with Genesis, in one of the narratives of God's covenant with Abraham, God promises the patriarch, "I will keep My covenant between Me and you, and your offspring after you throughout their generations, as **an everlasting covenant** to be your God and the God of your offspring after you" (Gen. 17:7). This verse identifies the Abrahamic covenant as eternal. One way the passage does this is by repeating the word "everlasting."[3] Further, this eternal covenant was not made just with Abraham, Isaac, and Jacob, but with all their descendants afterwards. As such, it marks the Jewish people as forever distinctively related to God. According to G. J. Wenham, this is "the heart of the covenant, that God has chosen Abraham and his descendants, so that they are in a unique relationship: he is their God and they are his people."[4] As a corollary of this covenant, therefore, God is guaranteeing that the descendants of Abraham (through Isaac and Jacob) would be preserved as His everlasting people. In a sense, these are the words of the Everlasting God, making an everlasting covenant, with His everlasting people.

Nearly one thousand years after the writing of the Pentateuch, the prophet Jeremiah also promised the preservation of the Jewish people. This was especially significant because Jeremiah had predicted God's judgment of Israel through the Babylonians, foreseeing the desolation of Judah (Jer. 25:8–14).[5] Israel needed to be assured that defeat and exile would not mean destruction. So, in chapter 30, Jeremiah predicted events that would take place in the far distant future, at the end of days.[6] The prophet, while anticipating the Lord's eschatological restoration of Israel to their promised land, includes the Lord's promise to Israel, "For I will be with you—this is the LORD's declaration—to save you! I will bring destruction on all the nations where I have scattered you; however, I will not bring destruction on you. I will discipline you justly, but I will by no means leave you unpunished" (Jer. 30:10). The verse reminds Israel of God's presence with the nation and thereby provides assurance to the people. First, God's presence guarantees Israel's salvation at the end of days. Second, the Lord promises to vindicate Israel, bringing judgment on all the nations among whom Israel had been scattered. Third, the Lord's association with Israel insures that He will discipline His people for their sins (as will happen in the time of Jacob's trouble). Fourth, and most significant to this discussion, although the people of Israel will be disciplined, they will not be destroyed. Despite the expectation that God will apply the rod of discipline upon Israel (cf. Ezek. 20:37–38), the prophet also reminds them with all certainty that the people of Israel will continue to exist. Other nations will experience destruction from God's hand, but not His people Israel.

Jeremiah also assured the preservation of Israel immediately after the revelation of the New Covenant (Jer. 31:31–34). The implication of the New Covenant is that it would last forever. To assure its eternality, God also promised that the parties to the covenant (Israel and Judah) would also be eternal. Hence, the Lord gives Israel a promise through His prophet, found in Jeremiah 31:35–37,

> This is what the LORD says:
> The One who gives the sun for light by day,
> the fixed order of moon and stars for light by night,
> who stirs up the sea and makes its waves roar—
> the LORD of Hosts is His name:
> If this fixed order departs from My presence—
> this is the LORD's declaration—
> then also Israel's descendants will cease
> to be a nation before Me forever.

> This is what the LORD says:
> If the heavens above can be measured
> and the foundations of the earth below explored,
> I will reject all of Israel's descendants
> because of all they have done—
> this is the LORD's declaration.

These verses offer two areas of evidence to support the eternal nature of the Jewish people. First, God assures Israel's preservation by pointing to the fixed order of nature. Just as God has ordained the sun, moon, and stars, as well as the waves of the sea, so He has ordained the permanence of Israel. Only if the natural order can be overturned, "then . . . Israel's descendants will cease to be a nation before me forever" (31:35–36). The second evidence refers to the measuring the heavens and searching the foundations of the earth—both impossibilities. Yet, if these impossible conditions could be met, only then God would "reject all of Israel's descendants" as His people" (31:37). There is no plainer support in Scripture for the preservation of the Jewish people as a promise of God. In a sense, this is a statement of God's foreign policy.

Author and teacher Arnold Fruchtenbaum has frequently given guest lectures in a variety of venues on the subject, *How to Destroy the Jewish People*. Not surprisingly this is always quite controversial. Generally this lecture draws supporters of Hamas as well as Neo-Nazis, both of whom are genocidal in their views of the Jewish people and would certainly like to know how to destroy them. Also, there are protesters, assuming that the Fruchtenbaum is actually advocating the destruction of the Jewish people. Yet, Fruchtenbaum's text is Jeremiah 31:35–37, and his lecture uses this passage as the proof from Scripture. He shows that it is impossible to destroy the Jewish people, anymore than someone could stop the sun, moon, and stars from shining or measure the heavens or explore the core of the earth. God's foreign policy promises the preservation of His people.

The intentional, determined, and repeated efforts throughout history to destroy the Jewish people make their preservation an even more remarkable evidence of the truth of God's Word. In biblical history, Pharaoh attempted to commit genocide by murdering Israelite male babies (Ex. 1:15–16); Balak attempted to curse the Jewish people through Balaam (Num. 22:4–8); And Haman laid plans for the genocide of all the Jewish people in the known world (Est. 3:8–10). Later on the Jewish people faced the destructive power of Babylon, a defeat from which it seemed there could be no recovery. After their return to the land (539 BC), Jewish people experienced two horrific defeats at the hands of the Romans (AD 70 and 135) in which nearly 2 million Jewish residents in the land of Israel died. From the Middle Ages to the modern period, the Jewish people endured murders at the hands of Crusaders and Cossacks. They suffered pogroms and persecution, and ultimately the Nazi Holocaust, when Adolf Hitler and the Third Reich attempted to destroy all of Jewry. The Nazis were tragically effective, murdering six million Jewish people, a number so large it is difficult to grasp. Perhaps the scope of the Holocaust is easier to comprehend by personalizing it. For example, I grew up having few family members, since Hitler murdered most of them, including both my maternal and paternal grandparents, seven of my aunts and uncles, my four half-brothers, and one half-sister. Nevertheless, the Nazis did not succeed in destroying all the Jewish people of the world, or even Europe.

The Yiddish expression—"So many Hamans, but only one Purim"—is not quite true. Although Purim seems to be the only time that a genocidal murderer was stopped before the Jewish people could suffer any harm, nevertheless, in every other persecution, God ultimately did deliver the Jewish people. For this reason, we Jewish people sing, "*Am Yisrael Chai*" (The People of Israel Live). Faithful to His word, God has always preserved the Jewish people. The liturgy of the Passover Haggadah recognizes this with the song, *V'Hee Sh'amdah* (This Promise):

> This promise made to our fathers holds true also for
> us. For more than once they have risen up against us
> in their attempts to destroy us; throughout all genera-

tions they rise against us and seek our destruction. But the Holy One, Blessed be He, always delivers us from their hands.[7]

The late Israeli Prime Minister, Menachem Begin, made a similar point, speaking at the Western Wall in Jerusalem as part of the closing ceremonies of the first World Gathering of Jewish Holocaust Survivors on June 18, 1981. Specifically addressing the question of faith in God in light of the Holocaust, Begin reminded his audience, some 10,000 survivors, how close Hitler and Nazi Germany came to winning World War II. Begin pointed out that had Hitler been successful, it would have meant the murder of not six million Jewish people, but the deaths of some 10 million European Jews. It could likely have led to the murder of virtually all the Jewish people around the globe. Then he went on to state that, although many Jewish people wonder why God did not act to save them in the Holocaust, Jewish people need to be assured that God did intervene and delivered the Jewish people before it was too late. Then, with passion, he begged his audience of Jewish Holocaust survivors to believe in the God of Israel, who "always delivers us from their hands."[8]

The famous, "Your majesty, the Jews" anecdote presents God's faithful preservation of the Jewish people as evidence of the truth of Scripture. In one version, "Fredrick II, King of Prussia (1740–1786) asked Joachim von Zieten, General of the Hussars, whom he esteemed highly as a Christian for his plain and uncompromised views, "Give me proof for the truth of the Bible in two words!" To which Zeiten replied, 'Your majesty, the Jews!'"[9] S. R. Haynes cynically notes that the same essential anecdote is told of a variety of rulers.[10] In the unlikely event that this story actually happened, with some ruler at some time, it so lost in legend, that the original characters in it are impossible to determine. Regardless of its apocryphal nature, the story is still significant because it captures a genuine truth—that despite persecution, pogroms, and programmatic genocide, God, faithful to His Word, has preserved His people. Hence, Charles Feinberg, commenting on Jeremiah 31:35–37, is correct: "The survival of Israel through the centuries can be explained only on supernatural grounds." God's preservation of the Jewish people provides a strong evidence of the truth of Scripture.

The Restoration to the Land of Israel

In addition to the preservation of the people of Israel, the Jewish people also provide a second, significant evidence of the proof of Scripture. That is, that against all likelihood, after two thousand years of exile, God restored the Jewish people to the land of Israel in fulfillment of predictions of the biblical prophets.

Since their world-wide exile nearly two millennia ago, Jewish people have daily prayed that they would be restored to the land of Israel. Moreover, the Hebrew prophets foretold a day when God would draw His people back to their promised land. Throughout church history, Christians for the most part could not conceive of a literal fulfillment of this promise so they interpreted these prophecies figuratively or historically. However, some believers in the 19th century did indeed take the promise of a return literally and therefore began to anticipate a Jewish return to the land of Israel.[11]

Bible believers frequently ask how the unprecedented reborn State of Israel fits with Bible prophecy. For several reasons, it appears that the best explanation is that the modern state of Israel seems to be a dramatic work of God in fulfillment of the Bible's predictions of a Jewish return to the land of Israel.

First, the Bible predicts that Israel would return to the land in unbelief, meaning without first having experienced a national spiritual regeneration as predicted (Zech. 12:10; 13:1; Rom. 11:25–26). Biblical prophecy indicates that the Jewish people will turn to God only *after* returning to the land of Israel. One passage that supports this is Ezekiel 36:24–26. It begins with the promise of return, "For I will take you from the nations, gather you from all the lands, and bring you into your own land" (NASU). The following two verses (36:25–26) indicate chronology," *Then* I will sprinkle clean water on you and you will be clean; I will cleanse you from all your filthiness and from all your idols. Moreover, I will give you a new heart and put a new spirit within you; and I will remove the heart of stone from your flesh and give you a heart of flesh." Note that the spiritual regeneration of Israel follows the restoration of the Jewish people to the land of Israel. Israel has been reborn as a secular state by secular Jews. This is the precursor to the day when the entire nation turns in faith to the Messiah Jesus.

Second, the Bible predicts that Israel would return to the land of Israel in stages. Ezekiel 37 contains the vision of a valley of dry bones. The bones come to life in stages, first sinews on the bones, then flesh, then skin, and finally, the breath of life (37:6–10). Then God tells Ezekiel that "these bones are the whole house of Israel (37:11)" and that their restoration is a picture of the way God will bring them "into the land of Israel (36:12)." So the regathering of Israel is not an event that will occur instantaneously, in one single event. Rather, it is a process that culminates in the nation receiving the breath of life by turning to Messiah Jesus.

In this passage, the dry bones represent Israel in exile, without any hope. The process of the bones coming together with sinew, flesh, and skin refer to the waves of immigration before Israel's rebirth. This is precisely how the Jewish people have returned to the land of Israel. There were the five separate *aliyot* (immigration waves), from 1881 to1939, returning Jewish people from Europe to the Promised Land. Then, after the birth of Israel in 1948, some one million European Jewish survivors came to Israel. Not long after that, some 800,000 Jewish people were driven from the Arab world and came home to the land of Israel. More recently, in the 1990s, some 1½ million Jewish people fled the former Soviet Union and immigrated to Israel. These immigration waves demonstrate that the Jewish people have returned in stages. The body without breath represents unbelieving Israel today, restored but not yet regenerated. Finally, according to this passage, the final step will be when God breathes the breath of life on these bodies, representing the day when the entire nation of Israel turns in faith to Messiah Jesus.

Third, the Bible predicts that Israel would return to her land through persecution. God says of Israel through the prophet Jeremiah, "I will return them to their land that I gave to their ancestors (Jer. 16:15)." In the next verse, God says that He will use "fishermen" and "hunters" to pursue His people back to their land (16:16). This metaphor for persecution has been literally fulfilled in the rebirth of Israel. Since the birth of modern Zionism, the primary motivation for return to the land of Israel has been anti-Jewish persecution. In the last 100 years, God has used Czarist pogroms, Polish economic discrimination, Nazi genocide, Arab hatred, and Soviet repression to drive Jewish people back to their homeland. Economic success and religious freedom in the Diaspora keeps Jewish people complacent about returning; so God uses "fishermen" and "hunters" to drive them back to the Promised Land.

Fourth, the Bible predicts that Israel would return to the land to set the stage for end-time events. Daniel 9:27 speaks of a firm covenant between the future world dictator and the Jewish people, which will unleash the final events before Messiah Jesus' return. This prophecy assumes a reborn State of Israel. The Jewish State had to be restored so this prediction (and many others) can take place. There needs to be a reborn state of Israel for this treaty to be signed, for the temple to be rebuilt, for Jerusalem to be surrounded by the nations during the battle of Armageddon, even for Jesus to return to deliver the Jewish people from their enemies (Zech. 14:3). Since Israel has returned in unbelief, in stages, through persecution, it is likely that the modern the State of Israel fulfills the predictions of the ancient Hebrew prophets . . . and sets the stage for events yet to come.

Although the prophets foresaw God's restoration of Israel as an eschatological work, for the most part, throughout Church history, Christian interpreters have either historicized or allegorized their predictions. For example, 19th century commentator Adam Clarke, in explaining Ezekiel 37, interpreted it historically, seeing its fulfillment at "the restoration of that people from the Babylonish captivity, and their resettlement in the land of their forefathers." He also noted the process described in the passage but saw the stages fulfilled at the edict of Cyrus

(Ezra 1:2–3), the edict of Darius (Ezra 4:23–24), and the orders of Artaxerxes to Nehemiah (Neh. 2:7).[12]

An alternative approach has been to interpret the prophecies of the return allegorically. An example of this is Martin Luther's lectures on the book of Genesis. Luther was fascinated by the promises made to Abraham's descendants in Genesis 12. When Luther asked who those descendants might be, He looked at the Jewish people of his day and concluded that they could not possibly be the descendants to which the Scriptures referred. Thus, he wrote, "If the Jews are Abraham's descendants, then we would expect to see them back in their own land. We would expect them to have a state of their own. But what do we see? We see them living among us scattered and despised."[13] To him, the idea that God would actually fulfill His promises literally and return the Jewish people to the land was unthinkable. As a result, Luther's immediate view was that the Abrahamic promises, including the promise of return, had been transferred to the church. According to him, Abraham's seed was figurative for the Church. Therefore, the restoration of the Jewish people to the land of Israel was, according to Luther, to be understood allegorically.

Yet, there were exceptions to these historical and allegorical perspectives. For example, English restorationists, saw the prophecies of Israel's return to the land of Israel, and took them literally. As a result, they became the first modern advocates of a Jewish return to the land of Israel, with the full expectation that this would fulfill Bible prophecy.[14]

So, in fulfillment of the Scriptures, God brought the Jewish people back to the land of Israel. First, Jewish pioneers returned and rebuilt the land. Then, in 1947, the United Nations partitioned Palestine into a Jewish state and an Arab state. And finally, the Jewish people declared statehood on May 15, 1948.[15] The return to Zion is a powerful evidence of the proof of Scripture. It is beyond remarkable that God would restore a dispersed people, despised throughout history as "wandering Jews," and in literal fulfillment of biblical prophecy, bring them home to their land after 2,000 years of exile.

The Salvation of the Remnant of Israel

Besides the preservation of the people of Israel and their restoration to the land of Israel, the Jewish people provide yet another evidence of the truth of Scripture. This confirmation of the Bible pertains to Jewish believers in Jesus, namely, the salvation of the remnant of Israel.

The Hebrew Prophets predicted that, when the Messiah came, the entire nation of Israel, would know the Lord. For example, the prophet Isaiah foretold that in the future, "then all your children will be taught by the LORD, their prosperity will be great, and you will be established of a foundation of righteousness" (Isa. 54:13–14). This indicates that when God's kingdom would come to the earth, all of the Jewish people, including their children will know the Lord and be founded on righteousness.

Additionally, in Jeremiah 31:31–34, the statement of the New Covenant, God promises, "I will be their God, and they will be My people. No longer will one teach his neighbor or his brother, saying: Know the LORD, for they will all know Me, from the least to the greatest of them"—the LORD's declaration. "For I will forgive their wrongdoing and never again remember their sin" (Jeremiah 31:33b–34). This is saying that it will not be just be a remnant of Jewish people that come to know the Lord as part of the New Covenant, but the whole nation will know the Lord and experience divine forgiveness.

With this expectation, it is understandable that when Israel's leadership refused to recognize Jesus as the Messiah, causing the majority of the Jewish people to reject Him as well, this brought great sorrow to those who anticipated the national redemption of Israel. Paul expressed this sorrow when he wrote, "I have intense sorrow and continual anguish in my heart. For I could wish that I myself were cursed and cut off from the Messiah for the benefit of my brothers, my countrymen by physical descent. They are Israelites . . ." (Rom. 9:2–4a). Paul is so grieved, that if possible (and it is not), he would be willing to be separated from the Messiah Jesus, if only his people would believe. Paul's grief was a result of his anticipation, that when Messiah came, all Israel would know the Lord. It would seem that Israel's rejection would demonstrate that perhaps God did not keep His promises and therefore, would actually be an argument that the Scriptures cannot be trusted.

In response to this faulty idea, Paul will explain how the Scriptures can indeed still be trusted despite Israel's unbelief. After reiterating the benefits and covenant privileges God granted to Israel (Rom. 9:4–5), Paul directly addresses the problem of Israel's unbelief in light of this scriptural promise. He states, "But it is not as though the word of God has failed" (Rom. 9:6a). Despite Israel's national rejection of the Messiah Jesus, God's word is still true. Paul's proof is found in the righteous remnant of Israel, the Jewish believers in Jesus. He speaks of them when he says, "For not all who are descended from Israel are Israel" (Rom. 9:6b). Although some have taken this to mean that God has expanded Israel into a spiritual Israel, consisting of both Jewish and Gentile believers, that is not what Paul means. Rather, he is speaking of a sub-group within Israel, the Jewish believers. Jewish believers are Abraham's descendants by both physical and spiritual descent, and so they are the true Israel. The context argues for a reference here to a narrowing of Israel, referring to Jewish believers, rather than an expansion, referring to Jewish and Gentile believers together in the Church. Robert Saucy expresses it well:

> But consideration of the context makes it much more plausible that Paul has reference to a division *within* Israel. Having introduced this major section by declaring his concern for "those of my own race, the people of Israel" (9:3–4), the apostle goes on to elaborate God's elective purpose *within* the physical descendants of Abraham (cf. 9:7–13). The point of the entire section is that while the promises of God to Israel may appear to have failed when one looks at the totality of Israel, which is predominantly unbelieving, there is a remnant within Israel, "an 'Israel' within ethnic Israel."[16]

In addition to the contextual argument, there is a lexical argument for interpreting Romans 9:6–8 of Messianic Jews. Fruchtenbaum has done an extensive word study, reviewing each of the 73 uses of "Israel" in the New Testament. In each case, it refers to physical descendants of Abraham, Isaac, and Jacob.[17] It seems extremely unlikely that Paul would use the word "Israel" to include Gentiles here when it so unusual. This is particularly true because interpreting both this passage as speaking of Jewish followers of Jesus fit its context far better.

Hence, Paul characterizes Messianic Jews as the true Israel by virtue of their physical descent and their appropriation of God's promises by faith in Messiah. A good paraphrase of Romans 9:6 would be, "God's word is true—there is a faithful, believing Israel within collective Israel, the faithful remnant." Thus, according to Paul, God keeps His promises to the Jewish people through the true Israel, the Jewish followers of Messiah Jesus.

Paul gives yet another proof that God has kept faith with His promises to Israel in Romans 11:1–6:

> I ask, then, has God rejected His people? Absolutely not! For I too am an Israelite, a descendant of Abraham, from the tribe of Benjamin. God has not rejected His people whom He foreknew. Or do you not know what the Scripture says in the Elijah section—how he pleads with God against Israel? Lord, they have killed Your prophets, torn down Your altars; and I am the only one left, and they are trying to take my life! But what was God's reply to him? I have left 7,000 men for Myself who have not bowed down to Baal. In the same way, then, there is also at the present time a remnant chosen by grace.

Paul's point is that God has not rejected Israel as His people, citing as his proof, the faithful remnant of Israel. He argues that he himself, as a Jewish man who believes in Jesus, demonstrates that God has kept faith with Israel. Moreover, he shows from Scripture, in the story about Elijah, the prophets of Baal, and the 7,000 of Israel who did not bow to Baal (1 Kings 19:10–18), God has always worked through a faithful remnant in Israel. Paul concludes with the assertion that there remains in his own day (and the present one as well) a remnant of faithful Jewish believers in Jesus, chosen by God's grace. The remnant is proof that God has not rejected His people.

So how do these references to the remnant of Israel provide evidence that God is faithful to His Word? It is because the remnant, the true Israel, is designed to be the earnest that God has given that one day God will fulfill the promise that "all Israel will be saved" (Rom. 11:26–27). Arguing that today, Israel's rejection of the Messiah Jesus is only partial ("a partial hardening has come to Israel") and temporary ("*until* the full number of the Gentiles has come in"). But, in the future, when the Liberator comes from Zion, the entire nation will believe and then all Israel will know the Lord.

There has always been a remnant of Jewish believers in Jesus. According to Paul, Jewish believers in Jesus are proof that God is faithful to His promises. Yet consider how unlikely it is for any Jewish person to believe in Jesus, given the Church's terrible history of persecution of the Jewish people and its false representation of the Messiah Jesus by allegedly acting in Jesus' name. Furthermore, Jewish people have been led to believe that turning to Jesus is a form of cultural suicide. Nevertheless, as unlikely as it is for a Jewish person to believe in Jesus, by God's grace, He opens Jewish hearts to believe. In the last generation there has been a surge of Jewish believers, numbering in the hundreds of thousands. And these are Jewish people not seeking to reject or hide their Jewish identity but celebrate it and thank God for it. They are evidence that God is faithful to His Word.

Moreover, Messianic Jews today function as a down payment, an earnest, of the seemingly more unlikely event—that one day the entire nation of Israel, at the return of Jesus the Messiah, will turn to Him in faith, and experience the New Covenant. Then they will all know the Lord, from the least to the greatest of them, just as Scripture foretold.

This chapter has maintained that the preservation of the people of Israel, their restoration to the land of Israel, and the salvation of the remnant of Israel all function as evidences of the truth of God's word. In light of this, what would some fitting responses be? Here are three suggestions.

First, God's people should give glory to God because He is faithful to the Scriptures. In particular, this is Paul's response to his explanation of Israel's unbelief (found in Rom. 9–11). Having revealed God's work through a remnant of Jewish believers, and the ultimate salvation of all Israel at the return of the Messiah, Paul concludes Romans 9–11 with a doxology, declaring,

Oh, the depth of the riches both of the wisdom and knowledge of God! How unsearchable His judgments and untraceable His ways! For who has known the mind of the Lord? Or who has been His counselor? Or who has ever first given to Him, and has to be repaid? For from Him and through Him and to Him are all things, to Him be the **glory** forever. Amen

God should be glorified because He is so faithful to His Word.

Second, God's people should trust God's Word, the Bible. Sometimes, when looking at the promises of Scripture, God's people may think that God will not keep His promises. They doubt that "all things work together for the good of those who love God: those who are called according to His purpose" (Rom. 8:28). But look at the history of Israel. With all the difficulties Jewish people faced throughout history, it did not appear that God would preserve them, or restore them to their land, or even save a remnant of them. Yet, God was always faithful to His promises to Israel as found in the Bible. His children should observe how faithfully God kept His promises to Israel and then trust His word, because He will be just as faithful to them.

Third, God's people should stand with the Jewish people. If anything, the passages cited in this chapter show how near and dear Jewish people are to God's heart. Standing with the Jewish people can be done in many ways, but two are particularly significant. First, standing with the Jewish people requires communicating the Messiah Jesus to them in loving way. The greatest kindness that can be shown to the Jewish people is to let them know that the Messiah of Israel has come and forgiveness is available by faith in Him. Second, followers of Messiah Jesus can stand with the Jewish people by resisting the hatred of Jewish people. Anti-Semitism has not faded away but is resurgent and even growing. Followers of Jesus should use every influence to stand against the hatred and the persecution of the Jewish people.

Conclusion

This chapter ends where it began. Mark Twain wrote: "All things are mortal but the Jew; all other forces pass, but he remains. What is the secret of his immortality?" The answer to his question lies not in the Jewish people themselves but in the God who chose them. The answer is found in God's faithfulness to His covenant and to His own Word. God has preserved the people of Israel, He restored them to their land, He redeemed a remnant in anticipation of redeeming the entire nation in the future. God's faithfulness to Israel is evidence of the truth of Scripture. As the apostle Paul would say, "The word of God has not failed!"

Study Questions

1. Why does the preservation and influence of the Jewish people present problems for secularists?

2. Where in Scripture does God assure the eternal preservation of the Jewish people? Discuss each passage and determine its meaning in context.

3. Why does God (in Scripture) assure the eternal preservation of the Jewish people?

4. What makes God's preservation of the Jewish people so remarkable?

5. What makes the expression "so many Hamans but only one Purim" partially inaccurate?

6. Many people recognize that God would bring the Jewish people back to the land of Israel in the end of days but only after the nation trusts in Jesus as their Messiah. Since the modern state of Israel was established as a secular state, make a case that this is or is not a fulfillment of Bible prophecy.

7. Why should some passages in Jeremiah and Ezekiel, which speak of a regathering to the land of Israel, be understood as referring to an eschatological return and not the return from Babylon?

8. Why did interpreters throughout Church history interpret passages about the return to Zion as either historical or allegorical?

9. What did the Hebrew Bible anticipate for the spiritual status of the Jewish people when the Messiah would establish His kingdom? How was this a problem for New Testament believers, particularly Paul?

10. How does Paul explain this difficulty? What does he mean when he writes, "For not all who are descended from Israel are Israel" (Rom. 9:6)?

11. How does the remnant of Israel function as an evidence of the truth of Scripture?

12. Explain what "And in this way, all Israel will be saved" means? How does this prediction provide an evidence of the truth of Scripture?

13. What response should followers of Messiah have in response to the people, the land, and the future of Israel functioning as proofs of Scripture?

Conference Video

chosenpeople.com/rydelnik

Interview with Dr. Michael Rydelnik

chosenpeople.com/rydelnik-interview

ISRAEL AND JEWISH EVANGELISM TODAY

Dr. Mitch Glaser

Glaser, in his chapter *Israel and Jewish Evangelism Today*, argues for a connection between the salvation of the Jewish remnant and the establishment of a future kingdom where the Messiah reigns from David's throne. The biblical depiction of a national future for Israel has fueled a passion for Jewish evangelism in the past. Glaser shows the link between the salvation of the Jewish people at Jesus' return and believes this link will stir hearts for the cause of Jewish evangelism.

Paul writes to the Romans that the Gospel is for the "Jew first" (Rom. 1:16), giving some type of priority to Jewish evangelism. Paul's sense of urgency for the salvation of Jewish people arose from his understanding that the salvation of the Jewish remnant in the last moments of the last days initiates the return of the Messiah.

This national Jewish repentance leads to Jesus' return (Matt. 23:37–39; Acts 3:19–21). Even the prophets show the relationship between Jewish forgiveness and a literal messianic kingdom (Zech. 12:10). God has not forgotten His people, because He will not allow His promise to be destroyed (Rom. 11:29). Israel will experience the full blessings of the Abrahamic Covenant when she returns to God (Gen. 12:1–3).

Glaser states, "the eschatological argument for the priority of Jewish evangelism is founded upon our understanding of the unique role the Jewish people play in the plan of God." Since the salvation of Israel leads to Messiah's return, Jewish evangelism must be a priority for the Church.

Introduction

I believe that Jewish people need to consciously accept Jesus in order to have a place in the age to come (John 14:6; Acts 4:12). This *saving* faith grows out of a Spirit enlightened understanding of the Gospel and need to embrace Yeshua as the Messiah (John 3:16–17, John 16:8).[1]

I do not believe that God's promise, of establishing a future kingdom where the Messiah Jesus rules on the throne of David and the ensuing season of Messianic Shalom that fills the earth, assures individual Jewish people of a place in the age to come (Isaiah 2:1–5, 9:6–7, 11:6–10, Jeremiah 31:31–36).

A distinction must be made between the national promises to the nation of Israel and the personal salvific fate of individual Jewish people (Romans 2:12–16, 25, 9–23, 27–28, Ephesians 2:8–9).

Therefore, believing that the Scriptures describe a national future for Israel should not dampen our enthusiasm to share the Gospel with Jewish people today or tomorrow. In fact, knowing this kingdom is close and that the salvation of the Jewish remnant is linked to the second coming should fire our passion for Jewish evangelism today.

As Apostle Paul writes in Romans 11:25–27,

> For I do not want you, brethren, to be uninformed of this mystery—so that you will not be wise in your own estimation—that a partial hardening has happened to Israel until the fullness of the Gentiles has come in; and so all Israel will be saved; just as it is written, The Deliverer will come from Zion, He will remove ungodliness from Jacob. This is My covenant with them, When I take away their sins.

The purpose of this chapter is to help us understand the power of this *eschatological argument for Jewish evangelism* as when Christians accept this position it tends to fuel efforts to bring the Gospel to the Jewish people. Linking the end-time "conversion" of the Jewish remnant with the return of Jesus is a powerful motivation for Jewish evangelism

Conversely, when this understanding of the Scriptures is not accepted or minimized, the importance of Jewish evangelism is often diminished.

The Eschatological Motivation in Mission History
The Early Pietist Missionaries

The eschatological motivation for Jewish mission has historically been the key to encouraging the church to reach Jewish people with the Gospel. There is significant evidence that this was the key motivating factor for Jewish evangelism amongst the early church fathers, the medieval, pre and post Reformation periods and even more so in the early eighteenth century rise of the modern missions movement.

This understanding of understanding Israel's role in the last days moved the early Moravian missionaries to prioritize missions to the Jews.

Lutz Greisiger suggests the following in an essay entitled, "Israel in the Church and the Church in Israel":[2]

> The hope for the conversion of Israel, as a pivotal stage in the eschatological drama, was probably the motive par excellence for the Jewish missionary enterprises of the eighteenth century. Chapter 11 of the letter to the Romans had given a clear schedule: "... a hardening has come upon part of Israel, until the full number of Gentiles come in" (Rom. 11:25)— only then will Israel be converted and redeemed. The "teachers" of the "Church in Israel" reversed this sequence: here Israel appears as the avant-garde of the Kingdom of Christ, from which the conversion not merely of the Gentiles but even of the Gentile Christians will come! Thus, it is inevitable that the unity of Israel is preserved until the whole people will have converted and be able to fulfill its salvation-historical mission. The "Church in Israel" constitutes in this process the nucleus, so to speak, of the future "Orthodox" People of God.[3]

The eschatological motivation gave impetus to the rise of Jewish missions in the early part of the eighteenth century. The wide acceptance of this eschatological motivation for Jewish mission was also broadly understood among the Churches of Scotland and the British and Scandinavian Christian Zionists.

This position caught the attention of Christians in the United States through the book titled *Jesus is Coming Again*, written by Methodist layman, William E Blackstone.[4]

This theological argumentation for Jewish evangelism was an improvement over less flattering characterizations of the Jewish people as "destitute" and enslaved by both "wooden" Orthodoxy and Kabbalistic superstition, living in the *miserable* ghettos of Eastern Europe, which was reflective of anti Jewish prejudice at the time.

In the late nineteenth century—many believed the Jewish people were conspiring to take over the world's banking and political systems as portrayed in books like the *Protocols of the Elders of Zion*.[5] A common rationale for Jewish missions was then viewed as follows; if Christians were successful in bringing the Gospel to the Jewish people, the church would be able to transform the moral core of society and those Jews who were a potentially negative influence on American and culture and values would be converted to Christianity and therefore no longer a threat.

So, winning the Jews to Jesus was a way of transforming and purifying *Christian* society.

In the twentieth century, the Jewish people engendered Christian pity after enduring the horrors of the Holocaust and the establishment of modern Israel. The Jewish people were viewed as *underdogs* and the worldwide Christian community viewed the Jewish people favorably. This positive attitude towards the Jewish people led to greater emphasis on Jewish missions.

Today, the Jewish people and Jewish evangelism has somewhat fallen out of favor, as Israel and the Jewish people are not as noticeably needy. In more recent days, many Western Christians have sided politically with Palestinians, viewing Israel and the Jewish people more negatively, and directed their "mission impulse" towards social justice issues and towards evangelizing Arabs and Muslims in particular.[6]

This shift in sympathies is now commonplace in the United Kingdom, Northern and Central Europe, and is rising in America. It is fueled by the growing acceptance of the viewpoints of the *new Supersessionists*,[7] the drifting of the American church from pre-millennialism, and a seemingly *compassion-driven* acceptance of the Palestinian historical narrative and political agenda.

We must help believers find theological motivation for Jewish evangelism that will lead to increased witness, prayer, and financial support. This is why the "eschatological motivation for Jewish Missions" is critical and needs to be understood and taught. It is clear, unchanging, compelling and simple to articulate. It is understandable by most Christians whether they live in United States, Europe, Asia, or Africa.

I recognize that not every Christian is going to be persuaded by the theological arguments presented in this chapter due to differing hermeneutics or theological systems. However, one does not need to be pre-millennial or even believe in a literal future for national Israel to accept the eschatological argument for Jewish missions. In other words, the theological motivation that links the second coming of Christ with the end time repentance of the Jewish people transcends most theological systems and is powerful as motivation for Jewish outreach in itself.

The Critical Passages

There are a number of critical passages, besides Romans 11:25–27, which point to the eschatological motivation for Jewish missions. The first passage to be reviewed is not often viewed eschatologically, but should be understood in light of Romans chapters 9–11.

To the Jew First (Romans 1:16)

For I am not ashamed of the gospel, for it is the power of God for salvation to everyone who believes, to the Jew first and also to the Greek. (Romans 1:16). Those engaged in Jewish evangelism are well familiar with this passage and understand its importance in motivating the church towards Jewish evangelism. This brief verse has been interpreted in a number of different ways,[8] but more often than not, is shown to emphasize the importance of Gentile Christians reaching Jewish people with the gospel.

For example, well know contemporary New Testament scholar, N.T. Wright, comments on the link between Romans 11:13ff. and 1:16,

> But all these things, so far from meaning that Gentile Christians are now the truest sort of covenant members, means rather that Gentile Christians owe the Jews an incalculable debt, cognate indeed with the debt they owe the Messiah himself, the Jew par excellence whose casting away meant reconciliation for the world. And the debt must be discharged in terms of the continuing mission to unbelieving Israel; the very Gentile mission itself has this is one of its sidelong purposes.[9]

It is my intention to help us see Romans 1:16 in light of the entirety of the Book of Romans, which should be viewed eschatologically.

I would suggest that the reason the Apostle Paul believes the Gospel, in one way or another should go to the Jewish people first, is founded upon his understanding of the events of the *eschaton*. When Romans 1:16 is viewed eschatologically the urgency of Jewish evangelism becomes evident.

Paul is not suggesting that the Roman believers withhold the Gospel from the Gentiles until every Jewish person in the world is reached. Neither is the Apostle implying that the Gospel has already come to the Jewish people first and therefore preaching the Gospel to the "Jew first" no longer has any particular application to the mission of the church today. Romans 1:16 is written in the present tense. Therefore, if the Gospel is still the power of God "for" salvation and is still for "everyone who believes," then the Gospel is still "to the Jew first."

The Greek word used by Paul and translated first is "proton" (ιουδαιω τε πρωτον).[10] It implies a priority, rather than a sequential order of events.[11] The word is also used in Matthew 6:33 where the Lord Jesus reminds us to *Seek first the kingdom of God*. The kingdom of God should always be sought as a priority in our lives, even as we seek other things. In a similar way, reaching Jewish people with the Gospel must be a priority concern for all who know the Lord Jesus as their Savior, but not to the exclusion of non-Jews.[12]

Paul, the apostle to the Gentiles, focused his ministry on reaching non-Jews with the Gospel message. But, this did not lessen his concern for the salvation of the Jewish people. Wherever Paul went in his ministry among the Gentiles he also preached the gospel to the Jewish people living in that area (Acts 13:13–52; 14:1–5; 18:7–11; 19:8–10). He would make sure that this was his first evangelistic effort to reach a particular city before he spoke to the Gentiles. The salvation of the Jewish people was an ever present concern for Paul and his actions in the Book of Acts reveal his understanding of what he penned in Romans 1:16.

Why—"To the Jew First"?

One cannot fully understand Romans 1:16 without understanding Paul's conclusion in Romans 11, where he speaks about the end time repentance of the remnant of Israel and their reception of Jesus as Savior. In fact, the priority described in Romans 1:16 is founded on Romans 11:25–27 (and more completely on 11:11–29) and must be viewed in light of the role the Jewish people play the second coming of Christ.

The Apostle's argument may be summarized be as follows, *if Jewish people are successfully evangelized then Jesus the Messiah will return.* The Apostle had no idea when this would take place as he probably thought the Lord would come within his own lifetime. Therefore, there was an *eschatological urgency* in the tone of his preaching and in his letter to the Roman believers encouraging them to prioritize the evangelization of the Jewish people. His theology was enacted in his own strategy for mission. And this is why we should follow suit. In effect, Paul argued that if the church desired to witness the second coming of Christ, the Jewish people must be evangelized.

Based upon the above, the church cannot think of Jewish evangelism as just simply evangelizing "another people group." The Jewish people have been tagged with a theological import unlike other peoples. This needs to be respected and therefore Jewish evangelism could never become the great omission of the great commission and the church must make Jewish evangelism a priority in light of Romans 1:16.

Genesis 12:1–3

The core of God's plan and purposes for the Jewish people was revealed through the unconditional covenant He made with Abram in Genesis 12. In this passage the Lord promises the patriarch that his descendants would become a nation, inhabit the Promised Land, and become a blessing to the whole world.

> [1] Now the Lord said to Abram, Go forth from your country, And from your relatives And from your father's house, To the land which I will show you; [2] And I will make you a great nation, And I will bless you, And

make your name great; And so you shall be a blessing; [3] And I will bless those who bless you, And the one who curses you I will curse. And in you all the families of the earth will be blessed (Genesis 12:1–3).

The lineage of promise then passed through two of their sons; Isaac and Jacob.[13]

The nation of Israel became the object of God's love and sovereign choice. As Moses wrote,

For you are a holy people to the Lord your God; the Lord your God has chosen you to be a people for Himself, a special treasure above all the peoples on the face of the earth. The Lord did not set His love on you nor choose you because you were more in number than any other people, for you were the least of all peoples. (Deuteronomy 7:6–7).

Assuming then, that God created and called the Jewish people for His holy purposes—what are these purposes? What is the divine raison d'être for the existence of Israel and the Jewish people?

God created the Jewish people to be a blessing to the world, to be a holy people, Kingdom of Priests and a witness of the one true God.[14] Israel was chosen and called to reveal the glory of God to the nations of the world and ultimately to lead the world to the Messiah.

This is foundational to the eschatological argument for Jewish evangelism. It may be said, based upon the Abraham covenant that God created and chose the Jewish people for the sake of the Gentiles. The penultimate purpose of God for the Jewish people was to use His chosen nation as His instruments in turning the nations to the God of Israel through the Messiah Jesus.

However, this would be impossible without the people of Israel returning to the God who chose them. In other words, for the Jewish people to fulfill the purpose for which they were created—the turning of the nations—they would themselves need to be turned. And so this great theme of Israel's return to the God of Abraham, Isaac, and Jacob is woven like a fine golden thread throughout the tapestry of the Bible.

The Scriptures teach that after years of straying from covenant faithfulness, the Lord would bring His people back to Himself—through his Son, at which time the Jewish people would fulfill their appointed destiny to bless the world through the rule of the Messiah in His Messianic kingdom. In fact, the return of the Jewish people to the God of Israel is the means by which the Jewish people experience the full blessings of the Abraham covenant. And whereas the Christology is not fully realized in these Old Testament passages,[15] the predicted repenting, returning, and planting of the Jewish people in the Land of promise is a well established theme throughout the Bible.

The following four passages, built upon the hope of the Abrahamic covenant, will detail how this plan will unfold and provide a logical, step-by-step illustration of the *eschatological argument* for Jewish evangelism. There are a number of other passages of Scripture in both Old and New Testaments that could be used to illustrate this final path to redemption for Israel and the Jewish people, but these few have been selected for their clarity.

Matthew 23:37–39

Matthew chapter 23 is a pivotal passage in understanding the logic of the argument.[16]

> [37] Jerusalem, Jerusalem, who kills the prophets and stones those who are sent to her! How often I wanted to gather your children together, the way a hen gathers her chicks under her wings, and you were unwilling. [38] Behold, your house is being left to you desolate! [39] For I say to you, from now on you will not see Me until you say, Blessed is He who comes in the name of the Lord!

Every effort of Jesus to turn the hearts of the Jewish people was thwarted by the Jewish leaders throughout His earthly ministry who rejected His person and message. Finally, the Savior comes to the heartbreaking conclusion that He is going to be a rejected by his own people (Isaiah 53:3, John 1:11). This poignant passage should be viewed as a lament, which reflects the heart of the Messiah for His people. He portrays Himself as a *hen wanting to gather her chicks under her wings* which is a very moving image of the Savior's love for His chosen people and unwillingness to completely reject them for rejecting Him.

It is a passage characterized by great pathos; mourning is tempered by hope and it is upon this hope that the *eschatological argument* for Jewish evangelism is founded.

Yeshua pronounces two judgments upon the Jewish people in this passage. After recounting the history of rejecting the prophets and ultimately Himself, He states that the Temple will be destroyed and the He is going to depart from Israel. It is well known that the word, "your house"[17] refers to the Temple, in this case Herod's Temple, which was the symbol of religious identity for the Jewish people. Jesus predicts that the house will be left desolate and destroyed. We understand that this prophecy was fulfilled through the Roman general Vespasian, who destroyed the Temple in AD 70.

The second judgment is the departure of Jesus[18] from the Jewish people, once again affirming that He was unwilling to establish his promised kingdom on earth without the full faith and participation of His people. Therefore, if His people would not return to the God of Abraham, Isaac, and Jacob He would have to leave until the time came when they were willing to repent and return to the Lord.

This all seems fairly dismal, yet embedded within this judgment is the hope of redemption. As Yeshua tells the Jewish leaders He is leaving He adds the phrase;

> For I say to you, from now on you will not see Me until you say, Blessed is He who comes in the name of the Lord!

The Jewish people will see Jesus again, but that would be preceded by their saying; "Blessed is He comes in the name of the Lord." The passage turns on the article, translated "until."[19] The Jewish people would not see Jesus again until they believe that He is the promised Messiah, which is described in the above phrase. Some suggest that this is reminiscent of the statement a rabbi makes when the groom approaches the wedding canopy in order to receive his bride. Therefore, by saying, *Blessed is He who comes in the Lord*, Israel is portrayed as recognizing that Jesus as their groom and acknowledging they are the bride.

So in this instance, we see the Jewish people finally turning back to the Lord and the Messiah returning to His chosen people and the world for which He died. Clearly, this links the repentance of the Jewish people with the second coming of Jesus.

Acts 3:19–21

> [19] Therefore repent and return, so that your sins may be wiped away, in order that times of refreshing may come from the presence of the Lord; [20] and that He may send Jesus, the Christ appointed for you, [21] whom heaven must receive until the period of restoration of all things about which God spoke by the mouth of His holy prophets from ancient time.

The healing of the lame man in the Temple provides a perfect opportunity for the Apostle Peter to preach the gospel to thousands of Jewish people crowded into the Temple area for worship. This is traditionally viewed as his second sermon in the Book of Acts and after rehearsing a brief portion of Jewish history, Messianic prophecy and focusing on the rejection of Jesus, the Apostle concludes with the above appeal.

Speaking as an Old Testament prophet, the Apostle calls upon the Jewish people to both repent and return to the Lord. The result according to Peter would be, *that your sins may be wiped away, in order that times of refreshing may come from the presence of the Lord. . . .*

If Peter's words are taken literally, then it is fair to conclude that the Apostle expected, based upon the Jewish people's repentance and return, that their sins would be forgiven and that "times of refreshing," which in his mind refers to all that the Old Testament promised about the Messianic kingdom, would come through the return of Jesus. This presumes that the phrase *the presence of the Lord* be taken literally.

The Apostle Peter, as with all the Apostles, expected the Lord to return within his own lifetime. He did not think about some faraway and distant Messianic hope nor did he *allegorize* the presence of the Lord as the Holy Spirit indwelling believers—which, though true, was not his evident understanding. Peter was expecting the messianic king to come and the messianic Kingdom to be established, precipitated by the repentance and return of the Jewish people to the Lord.

In summary, Peters appeals to the Jewish people to repent and return and if the Jewish people did this, then their sins would be forgiven and God would send Jesus to rule and reign. Again, this links the salvation of Israel with the second coming of Jesus.

Zech. 12:10 (Zech. 12:1–9; Zech. 13:1; Zech. 14: 3–4, 16–19)

> [9] And in that day I will set about to destroy all the nations that come against Jerusalem. [10] I will pour out on the house of David and on the inhabitants of Jerusalem, the Spirit of grace and of supplication, so that they will look on Me whom they have pierced; and they will mourn for Him, as one mourns for an only son, and they will weep bitterly over Him like the bitter weeping over a firstborn.

The prophet paints a graphic scene of Israel's final days. Unless heavenly intervention emerges quickly, the Jewish people and the promises of God would be destroyed. The nations of the earth, though we do not know exactly which ones, have surrounded Jerusalem and Israel with the intention of destroying the Jewish people. It will be at this final and most drastic moment that the Lord remembers his promises to his chosen people and pours out His spirit upon them. As a result, the Jewish people who have now experienced God's presence and power through his Spirit, literally turn to the One whom they have pierced. This turn sets off a series of cataclysmic events that ultimately result in the second coming of Christ and the establishment of the messianic kingdom.

It is important to see the chronology of these events. The following presents these critical events in a sequential manner, taking into consideration passages from Zechariah chapters 12, 13, and 14.

- The Jewish people are surrounded by their enemies (Zech. 12:3,9).
- The Lord determines to destroy the enemies of His chosen people (Zech. 12:9).
- God pours out his spirit upon the house of David and the inhabitants of Jerusalem (Zech. 12:10).
- Those who receive His Spirit, the Jewish remnant, turn to the One they have pierced (Zech. 12:10).
- The Jewish people begin mourning as a nation; person by person, family by family, tribe by tribe (Zech. 12:11–13).
- A fountain is opened for the forgiveness of sin (Zech. 13:1).
- The Lord battles against the enemies of the Jewish people (Zech. 14:1–2).
- The Lord returns and stands on the Mount of Olives (which is split in half) and then continues to battle the enemies of Israel (Zech. 14:3–4).
- He establishes his Messianic kingdom over all the earth with His capitol in Jerusalem (Zech. 14:9–11ff.).
- The Lord calls upon those nations that survived His judgment to pay homage to Him as their King by coming up to Jerusalem for the Feast of Tabernacles. There's an impending threat of drought if the nations disobey (Zech. 14:16–21).

In summary, the nations of the world surround the Jewish people to seek her destruction but God takes the initiative and pours out His spirit. As a result, the nation looks to Jesus, recognizes their role in the crucifixion, at which point the nation repents and begins mourning for their sin. A fountain *filled with blood* [20] is opened for the forgiveness of sin and those nations that came to destroy the Jewish people are themselves destroyed when the returning Savior brings judgment upon Israel's enemies. He established His throne in Jerusalem and the nations who remain come to Jerusalem to observe the Feast of Tabernacles and to worship the Messianic king.

Once again, we see that the second coming of Jesus is precipitated by the end time repentance of the Jewish people and their recognition that Jesus is the crucified and atoning Messiah (Zech. 12:10). The passage makes it clear that the end time repentance of the Jewish people and their subsequent forgiveness of sin leads to the establishment of a literal messianic kingdom with Jerusalem as the Messiah's throne.

Evidently, the totality of these events have not yet taken place even though the New Testament writer does indicate that the crucifixion of Jesus was predicted in Zechariah 12:10 (John 19:37). This prophecy could not possibly have been totally fulfilled at the cross as there are many additional elements what would need to transpire from the perspective of Zechariah's prophecy.

Dr. Charles Feinberg, in his commentary on Zechariah, writes the following about the context of this passage:

> The actual events, world embracing in character, which are presented include the world confederacy against Jerusalem: the conviction of Israel nationally by the Spirit of God; the presentation of Christ as their rejected Messiah; the National Day of Atonement; the cleansing of the hearts of the nation; the purging of the land from idolatry; the crucifixion of the Messiah, the time of Jacob's trouble, the partial success of the nations invading Palestine (Israel) and besieging Jerusalem; the appearance of the Messiah for His people; their rescue and his coming with his saints; the changed and renovated Holy Land; the Feats of Tabernacles and more![21]

The events described are clearly future to our day. The nations of the earth have surrounded the Jewish people and Jerusalem is about to fall. But, instead of succumbing to the hostility of the nations, God intervenes and sends His Son to save His chosen people.

Romans 11:11–29

The final passage is found in Romans 11 where the Apostle Paul argues that God has not cast off his people Israel, despite their rejection as a nation of Jesus, their Messiah. His final argument that God isn't finished with Israel is that "all Israel will be saved" (Rom. 11:25–27).[22]

He writes,

> For if their being cast away is the reconciling of the world, what will their acceptance be but life from the dead? (Romans 11:15).

It is reasonable to juxtapose Romans 11 with Zechariah chapter 12 as in effect, the remnant among ethnic Israel recognize their mistake in rejecting Jesus and repent and turn to Him—Yeshua is sent from heaven to cleanse the nation from sin, defeat the enemies surrounding the nation and to establish the kingdom on earth. It is important to note that God takes the initiative in pouring out His Spirit—as He is the One who promised that the Jewish people would be both nationally and spiritually restored. (Gen. 12:1–3, Jer. 31:31–35, Ezek. 37:13–14, Rom. 11:25–26)

The solution to Israel's impending doom would not be implemented by weapons made by man's hand, as earlier the prophet stated, "Not by might, not by power, but by My Spirit says the Lord" (Zechariah 4:6). The answer to mankind's weakness, failure, and sin is the Holy Spirit, who leads us to repentance at the feet of Jesus.

In effect, Romans 11:25–26 paints a more developed picture of the redemption promised in Zechariah 12:10. Paul describes the end of an era in which the Jewish people are estranged from God because the Jewish leaders rejected Jesus at his first coming. However, based upon Paul's argument in Romans 9–11, it becomes clear that God has not rejected the Jewish people (Romans 11:1) and has rather preserved a remnant within the nation (Romans 11:5), until the day, when the remnant becomes the nation. In this passage, the apostle tells us, that in the end, God will save "all Israel," which refers to the entirety of the nation of Israel alive at that time.

This cataclysmic end time event takes place after what Paul describes as the *fullness of the Gentiles*— has come in. It is evident from this passage that prior to the salvation of national Israel and the end of days there will be a season/era, where God is working among the Gentiles in a special way—grafting numerous wild olive branches into the olive tree as described in Romans 11:16–24.[23]

Paul tells us that the salvation of Israel leads to the fullness of redemption described further in Romans 11:12,

> Now if their fall is riches for the world, and their failure riches for the Gentiles, how much more their fullness.

In summary, the Jewish people will return to the God of their Fathers by accepting the Messiah and the Abrahamic promises will be fulfilled. The nations will then witness the return of the Lord. The Lord will not reject His people (Romans 11:29), because He is always faithful to His promises and the very existence of the Jewish people today is a powerful argument for the truth of the Bible and evidence for the existence and power of the God of Abraham, Isaac, and Jacob. God will not allow His promises or people to be dismissed and destroyed.

Conclusion

The eschatological argument for the priority of Jewish evangelism is founded upon our understanding of the unique role the Jewish people play in the plan of God. Reaching Jewish people with the gospel must become a priority concern for all Christians as ultimately, the salvation of the future remnant is the final step in the process of Jesus' second coming and brings about the fullness of God's blessings to the world.

This end time remnant will have their hearts prepared through hearing the Gospel (Romans 10:9–14) and we are God's instruments today in preparing the hearts of those who will come to faith today and become part of the remnant of tomorrow.

As Paul writes,

> I say then, have they stumbled that they should fall? Certainly not! But through their fall, to provoke them to jealousy, salvation has come to the Gentiles (Rom. 11:11).

Gentiles within the Body of Messiah are called to reach Jewish people for Jesus and missions to the Jews must help in this great work.

There is a wonderful story about the relationship between John Wilkinson, a Gentile missionary who founded the Mildmay Mission to the Jews, and J. Hudson Taylor, founder of the China Inland Mission (now OMF). Every January, Taylor would send Wilkinson a gift with a note attached, "To the Jew first." Wilkinson would then send the same amount back as gift to Taylor for his work among the Chinese with a note that read, "And also to the Gentiles."

We can prioritize reaching Jewish people because of God's choice of Abraham's seed according to the flesh, and still reach the world as commanded by our Messiah prior to His ascension.

It begins with you! Through your prayers, giving and witnessing to your Jewish friends—making them jealous—the plan of God will go forth in power! We cannot allow Jewish evangelism to become the Great Omission of the Great Commission.

In fact, it is part of the Chosen People Ministries organizational mission statement, the organization I lead, "to help empower and equip our brothers and sisters in the church to evangelize and disciple Jewish people."

Chosen People Ministries hopes to encourage, provide materials, and to build strategic bridges with Gentiles in the Body of Messiah—many of whom are missionaries on our staff—to fulfill this mandate in the twenty-first century. In fact, it might be through the testimony of Gentile believers that the end time Jewish remnant are prepared to call upon the One whom they have pierced and witness the second coming of the Lord.

Study Questions

1. Can you describe an opportunity you had sharing the Gospel with a Jewish person? What questions did they ask and how did you respond? What objections did you find hard to answer, and upon reflection how would you have responded differently?

2. What is your understanding of Romans 1:16, and how does this passage impact the Jewish evangelism today? What is your view on what Paul meant by "to the Jew first"?

3. Does your church have any type of involvement in Jewish missions—if so, can you describe?

4. In your own words, describe what Dr. Glaser meant by the eschatological motivation for Jewish missions. Do you have any thoughts about this idea?

5. What, in your opinion, is the reason why God chose the Jewish people. What is the purpose of the nation and how do you see this purpose fulfilled historically, today and in the future?

6. Does the Abrahamic covenant include the promise of the Land of Israel? Can you reflect for a moment on this promise in light of the current political climate in Israel?

7. In your own words, please summarize the importance of the key passages cited in the chapter: Matthew 23:37–39, Acts 3:19–21, Zechariah 12:10 and Romans 11:25–29?

8. What do you think about this line of reasoning and how should this impact your own personal ministry to Jewish people and that of your local congregation?

9. What other passages of Scripture in either the Old or New Testaments do you find important passages that might motivate a disciple of Jesus to share the Good News with Jewish people?

10. What acts of kindness do you think you and your church or congregation might initiate on behalf of the state of Israel, your local Jewish community, or for Jewish people you know and love that might open hearts for the Gospel?

Conference Video

chosenpeople.com/glaser

Interview with Dr. Mitch Glaser

chosenpeople.com/glaser-interview

16

ISRAEL AND THE LOCAL PASTOR

PASTOR DAVID EPSTEIN

E pstein, in his chapter *Israel and the Local Pastor,* discusses why he, as a pastor, has such a great love for both the Jewish people and the nation of Israel. He tells his own personal story to share why his love for the Jewish people is personal. His name speaks of his great-grandfather's Jewish heritage, but it also reminds him of how his father was the victim of ruthless anti-Semitism. Through the witness of his family, Pastor Epstein placed his faith in the Messiah, Jesus.

Epstein's love for the Jewish people has led him to consistently encourage members of his congregations to, in turn, encourage Jewish people to discover the Jewish Messiah.

Epstein lives and serves in a very Jewish city, New York. He offers many anecdotes of his interaction with Jewish neighbors and colleagues. His love for the Jewish people and for Israel has opened innumerable doors to share his faith.

Introduction

The greatest spiritual influence in my life growing up was my mom, who not only prayed for me like no one ever prayed for me, but she also modeled for me a great love for the Jewish people, the land of Israel, and biblical history and prophecy. She visited Israel seven times and returning on one trip from Tel Aviv she said to the Israeli seated next to her, "I just want you to know how much I love Israel and the Jewish people." The Israeli was pleasantly surprised and asked, "Why do you love us?" And my mom answered, "Because you have given the world the Messiah, my Lord Jesus." She then proceeded to share the gospel with him.

In New York City, where I have pastored for the past seventeen years, within a few blocks of my church and apartment are the offices of my Jewish doctor, my Jewish barber (whom sadly, I no longer need), and my Jewish chiropractor, with whom I have had a number of interesting spiritual discussions, and who has attended a Passover Seder at my church. One day he said to me, "Dave, do you know what one of my professors actually said to our entire class one day? He said, 'Ladies and gentlemen, chiropractic is the greatest gift ever given to the human race!' What do you think about that?" And I said, "Did he *really* say that? That's interesting, but I believe that the greatest gift ever given to the human race is the Messiah, Jesus Christ." And then I paused for effect, and stretching my back in a dramatic way said, "But on days like today, I think the second greatest gift ever given to the human race is chiropractic!"

Jesus said to the influential Jewish leader and teacher Nicodemus, "For God so loved the world that he gave his one and only Son, that whoever believes in him shall not perish but have eternal life" (John 3:16).

Paul, the Jewish Christian apostle, formerly the religious terrorist Saul, in writing to the Roman Christians said:

> For I am not ashamed of the gospel, because it is the power of God that brings salvation to everyone who believes: **first to the Jew**, then to the Gentile. For in the gospel the righteousness of God is revealed—a righteousness that is by faith from first to last, just as it is written: "The righteous will live by faith" (Rom. 1:16–17).

There are many reasons why I, as a pastor, love Israel and the Jewish people:

It's Personal (it's *my* thing)

My name, David Paul Epstein, offers the first glimpse of why it's personal. My paternal great grandfather was a Russian Jew. He and his family were victims of the pogroms, harassed and driven from their home by hate-filled anti-Semites. Like Tevye in *Fiddler on the Roof*, I'm sure that my great grandfather occasionally asked God, "Why couldn't you have chosen somebody else?" But by God's grace, he was able to come to America. So out of the crucible of suffering there emerged new life. By law, those immigrants were required to legally adopt the name of the individual who sponsored them—in my family's case, that was a German Jewish businessman named Epstein. To this day we are not quite sure of our original family name—only God knows.

In America, my Jewish grandfather was born and married my grandmother, a Gentile. They had five children including my dad, Aaron Leon Epstein. Tragically, while my dad was still a boy, his father walked away and abandoned them. Growing up, my dad experienced the pain, not only of a father's rejection, but also the same ugly anti-Semitism. Many times he was called a "Christ-killer" by other children, whose hearts and minds had been polluted by the ignorant, vicious example of their parents. But in spite of it all, my dad grew strong and thrived. My grandmother sent him to church, where he put his faith in Jesus the Messiah. My dad had lost his earthly father, but had been found by his heavenly Father—Abba Father.

My dad excelled in sports, becoming a Maryland State track champion in high school, whose records stood for years. December 7, 1941—Pearl Harbor: My dad was a seventeen-year-old high school student, who with some of his friends, the very next day went to the military recruiting office and enlisted in the Navy. By the time he was eighteen he was fighting the Nazis.

He did exceptionally well in the military, becoming the youngest enlisted man up until that time to become a Chief Petty Officer. After the war he was invited to join General Eisenhower's staff in Paris—SHAPE Headquarters—the Supreme Headquarters of the Allied Powers in Europe. Unfortunately, there was still no earthly father to be proud of him, pray for him, and brag about him.

Dad married my mom and had three kids—me and my sisters, Kathie Lee and Michie. Then something happened that changed our family forever. While I was a teenager in the 1960s, my dad received a phone call from his dad who had abandoned the family decades earlier. My grandfather, who I had never met nor would ever meet, was dying in a Baltimore hospital and asking his children to please come and be with him. Only my dad went to his bedside. He told us later that his dad lay dying with tubes everywhere, and looked up at my dad and said, "Son, please forgive me." And my dad said, "I forgive you Pop." This one act of forgiveness opened the floodgates of God's mercy. My mom and sisters trusted Jesus, my grandmother and other family members came to the Messiah, and God even saved me after I had put my family through five years of hell on earth. The chain of bitterness and unforgiveness that had enslaved our family for years was broken. We began to walk with God. The prophecy of

Isaiah concerning the liberating ministry of the coming Messiah was fulfilled in our midst:

> The Spirit of the Sovereign LORD is on me, because the LORD has anointed me to proclaim good news to the poor. He has sent me to bind up the brokenhearted, to proclaim freedom for the captives and release from darkness for the prisoners, to proclaim the year of the LORD's favor (Isaiah 61:1–2).

My dad was the finest man and the best businessman I ever knew. He had invested his soul and life in the Jewish Messiah—he invested wisely! At the end of his life, suffering with dementia and Parkinson's disease, we would ask him, "Dad, do you know what's happening to you?" And he would say, "Yes, my brain is dying." And we would say, "Are you afraid?" And he would say, "No—I'm going to see Jesus."

Jesus says it's important to build our lives on the solid rock—to have a piece of the Rock:

> Everyone who hears these words of mine, and puts them into practice is like a wise man who built his house upon the rock. The rain came down, the streams rose, and the winds blew and beat against that house; yet it did not fall, because it had its foundations upon the rock (Matthew 7:24–25).

It's Moral (it's the *right* thing)

For eight years I was a college professor of Biblical Studies and History, and one of my most memorable encounters was with an elderly Jewish lady who had come by the college and was wandering the faculty hallway, apparently looking for someone. I said, "Ma'am, can I help you?" She answered, "Young man, who teaches theology around here?" (I remember thinking, "Thank God I don't teach theology around here!") I replied, "I don't teach theology, but I do teach biblical studies—can I help you?" She said, "Young man, follow me into the chapel." (Apparently she had done some scouting ahead of time!) So I obediently followed her. Then she looked at me and said, "Young man, I want you to look me in the eyes and tell me that my family who were murdered at Auschwitz went to hell because they were Jews." I was stunned, and in that instant, not having a clue what to say, I breathed a prayer to God and began to respond slowly, "Ma'am, I can't even imagine your pain. What was done to your family was evil—it was obscene—and there will be a day of perfect justice. But no one knows what your family was thinking or trusting in during those last moments—so there is hope. The Bible teaches that no one is justified by their own suffering—but there is one who has suffered for us, because he loves us—and he is Jewish—Jesus, the Messiah." And I stopped, not knowing how she would react. But she remained quiet, thoughtful. Then she said, "Young man, thank you for taking the time to talk with me—I would like to come back and talk with you again." And I said, "I would like that." But she never did. I will look for her in glory.

The Holocaust, the Crusades, and the Inquisition continue, understandably so, to be a major stumbling block for our Jewish friends, relatives, coworkers, and neighbors to the gospel of Jesus Christ. The church has committed horrendous crimes against the Jewish people.

Consider the complex example of Martin Luther, a great man of faith used by God in the Reformation to recover and restore the biblical gospel that had been neglected and perverted by the church for over a thousand years. Martin Luther proclaimed salvation by faith alone in Jesus Christ; the authority of Scripture alone; and the priesthood of all believers. He was a giant of the faith! Tragically, in his later years, instead of continuing to glorify God, Luther dishonored him terribly because of his hatred and persecution of the Jews. He even inspired Hitler four hundred years later, who in *Mein Kampf* honored Luther as a great reformer (clearly more impressed with Luther's anti-Semitism than with his theology). Martin Luther, in his tracts against the Jews, slandered them as "venomous, bitter worms, and disgusting vermin."[1] Luther encouraged the German people to "set fire to Jewish synagogues and schools in honor of our Lord Jesus and in honor of Christendom. . . . I also advise that Jewish houses be destroyed and their prayer books and Talmudic writings, in which such idolatry and lies and cursing and blasphemy are taught, be taken from them; that their rabbis be forbidden to teach under threat of death; that safe conduct in the highways be denied the Jews and that all cash and treasures of silver and gold be taken from them and be set aside for safekeeping."[2] Hitler, of course, was inspired and loved it!

The horrific impact of Martin Luther on the Jewish people right up until our day cannot be over estimated! Dr. Erwin Lutzer, a personal friend, historian, and the pastor of the great Moody Church in Chicago, in his Medallion award winning book, *Hitler's Cross*, tells us that:

> In Luther's last days, when the irritability of age and disease took over he said many things that would have been best left unsaid, whether it was regarding the papacy or the Anabaptists or the Jews. Luther always spoke in colorful and condemning language and his comments were despicable and anti-Christian. . . . No wonder Jewish people today are kept from serious investigation of the merits of Christ and often pray, "Oh God, turn out to be anybody but Jesus."

They believe that to accept Christ as the Messiah is not only to deny the Jewish religion but to deny their heritage, their family, their culture—to accept Christ is to embrace an enemy.[3]

I have seen the impact Luther has on the Jewish religious leadership in New York City. I meet regularly with a number of evangelical leaders and some of New York City's leading rabbis. It is a tremendous opportunity to get to know each other, to love each other, and to sometimes take action as religious leaders who care about our city and our world. Our most recent topic was *The Theology of Corruption and the Theology of Reconciliation*. One of the group, a Jewish lawyer, said, "Some of the things that I read in the Bible that Jesus said hit me like a ton of bricks. It really gets to me. For instance, how Jesus said, 'Put others first, love others, and prefer them before yourself.' I really like his ethics and how realistic Jesus is. I think it was in John's gospel where it says, 'Jesus was not entrusting himself to the people around him because they were corrupt.' That's why Martin Luther disappoints me so much. He did so much to fight corruption in the Catholic Church but then out of his own corruption, he hated the Jews and encouraged his countrymen to hate and destroy them also."

As I left the synagogue that day I was struck by how this Jewish lawyer was so attracted to Jesus and so repulsed by Martin Luther. I was also struck by a memorial wall in the synagogue with special lights and an inscription which read: "These do I remember and my heart is grieved. This lamp burns perpetually as a memorial to our six million Jewish brethren, innocent victims of the unspeakable Nazi brutality whose sacred memory is enshrined in our hearts. May their tragic fate be a grim reminder of the horror wrought by blind hatred, a stern warning to all men against silence in the face of tyranny and a solemn admonition that we must never forget them."

Christian views on prophecy have played a major role in the way the Christian church has treated the Jewish people over the centuries. What you believe about the end times really does make a difference. Hal Lindsey in his insightful book *The Road to Holocaust* makes some powerful points in supporting this contention:

> It is tragic that even the great reformer Martin Luther was finally seduced by all the anti-Jewish propaganda of his times. . . . the *Encyclopedia Judaica* rightly comments about Luther's tract: "Short of the Auschwitz oven and extermination, the whole Nazi holocaust is pre-outlined here." Is it any wonder that Hitler and Julius Streicher quoted Martin Luther as justification for their murderous "Final Solution For the Jews?"

The fact that such a great man of faith in the scriptures as Luther could be seduced by Satan to write such a monstrous thing proves two things:

First, the anti-Jewish propaganda within the Church and society in general was virulently and thoroughly embedded in the culture.

Second, the original false interpretation of prophecy, which Luther obtained from Augustine, was a powerful blinding force that kept even the great reformer, who was an otherwise brilliant and literal interpreter of the Scriptures from grasping what God's Word literally and unconditionally taught: that the Jews are still His elect people with a definite future in His plan.[4]

It's Political (it's the *smart* thing)

Islamic terrorists attacked the symbols of America's financial and military strength when they targeted the World Trade Center and the Pentagon on 9/11. In reality, their greatest hatred is reserved for our political freedom, our religious faith expressed in our Judeo-Christian heritage, and our friend and ally, the nation Israel.[5]

In Islamic terrorism today:

- There is the conviction that Islam is supreme and destined to world dominance through jihad for Allah's glory.
- There is an intense hatred of Israel and the Jews and a total commitment to their utter destruction.
- There is a willful corruption of the history of Israel and the Middle East.
- There is the brutal use of the Palestinians as political pawns.
- There is the grotesque offering of their own children as "*martyrs*" and homicide/suicide bombers.[6]

In the March 6, 2010 edition of the *Wall Street Journal*, in the Weekend Interview, Matthew Kaminski spoke with Mosab Yousef, the author of *Son of Hamas*, a follower of Jesus, whose father is a Hamas leader imprisoned in the West Bank. Kaminski asked Mr. Yousef:

"Do you consider your father a fanatic?

"He's not a fanatic," says Mr. Yousef. "He's a very moderate, logical person. What matters is not whether my father is a fanatic or not—he's doing the will of a fanatic God. It doesn't matter if he's a terrorist or a traditional Muslim. At the end of the day a traditional Muslim is doing the will of a fanatic, fundamentalist, terrorist God. I know this is harsh to say. Most governments avoid this subject. They don't want to admit this is an ideological war."

"The problem is not in Muslims," he continues. "The problem is with their God. They need to be liberated from their God. He is their biggest enemy. It has been 1,400 years they have been lied to."[7]

Over the past few years, I have met regularly with a small group of evangelical leaders and some of New York City's most influential rabbis. One reason the Jewish leaders originally agreed to the dialogue was because of their curiosity about the evangelicals, who, although they long for the rabbis to embrace Jesus as their Messiah, also stand with Israel and the Jewish people in a time of increasing worldwide anti-Semitism. In one meeting, as we discussed the world community's accelerating attack on Israel, I said, "Israel and the Jewish people have only two friends left in the world—the United States and the evangelical church. Much of the world hates you, and no one else supports you—not the Arabs, the Catholic Church, the liberal protestant church and the National and World Council of Churches, the European Union and certainly not the United Nations, which is virulently anti-Israel and anti-America. You have two friends left and the Bible says that one day 'all the nations of the earth' will attack Israel (Zech. 12:3)—and this will include the United States—we are already seeing an erosion of American support under the Obama administration." It was very quiet in the room—but no one seemed to disagree.

The United Nations began well. It was under UN auspices that Israel became a nation in 1948 in the aftermath of World War II. In the greatest conflict in the history of mankind, in which 50 million people died, out of the ashes of the Holocaust—Israel was reborn as a nation! The UN played a significant role in devising a two-state solution which respected the national aspirations of both Jews and Palestinians. The Jewish people would receive a homeland called Israel; and the Palestinians would receive a homeland called Palestine. It would also establish Jerusalem as an international city, with two capitals. It was a noble effort. But on the very day that Israel became an independent nation—*on that very day*—the military forces of six Arab nations attacked Israel immediately. From the north came Syria and Lebanon—from the east came Iraq and Jordan—from the south came Saudi Arabia and Egypt. The UN had a plan, but there weren't enough statesmen, there weren't enough leaders to actually implement the plan. But God says—my Messiah is coming and my plan will succeed where all others have failed.

For to us a child is born, to us a son is given, and the government will be on his shoulders. And he will be called Wonderful
Counselor, Mighty God, Everlasting Father, Prince of Peace.
Of the greatness of his government and peace there will be no
end. He will reign on David's throne and over his kingdom,
establishing and upholding it with justice and righteousness
from that time on and forever. The zeal of the Lord Almighty
will accomplish this (Isaiah 9:6–7).

Over the years the UN has accomplished some good things and at
times has been well motivated. However, their credibility and effective-
ness are now severely compromised.

Israeli Prime Minister Netanyahu's in his address to the United
Nations General Assembly said it best (on Sept. 24, 2009):

Nearly 62 years ago, the United Nations recognized
the right of the Jews, an ancient people 3500 years old,
to a state of their own in their ancestral homeland. I
stand here today as the Prime Minister of Israel, the
Jewish state, and I speak to you on behalf of my country and my people.

The United Nations was founded after the carnage of
WWII and the horrors of the Holocaust. It was charged
with preventing the recurrence of such horrendous
events. Nothing has undermined that central mission
more than the systematic assault on the truth.

Yesterday, the President of Iran stood at this very podium, spewing his latest anti-Semitic rants. Just a few days
earlier, he again claimed that the Holocaust is a lie.

Yesterday, the man who calls the Holocaust a lie spoke
from this podium. To those who refused to come here
and to those who left this room in protest, I commend
you. You stood up for moral clarity, and you brought
honor to your countries.

But to those who gave this Holocaust denier a hearing
I say on behalf of my people, the Jewish people, and
decent people everywhere: Have you no shame? Have
you no decency?

A mere six decades after the Holocaust, you gave le-
gitimacy to a man who denies that the murder of six

million Jews took place and pledges to wipe out the Jewish state. What a disgrace! What a mockery of the charter of the United Nations. . . .

Ladies and Gentlemen, the jury is still out on the United Nations.

We want peace. I believe such a peace can be achieved, but only if we roll back the forces of terror, led by Iran, that seek to destroy peace, eliminate Israel, and overthrow the world order. The question facing the international community is whether it is prepared to confront those forces or accommodate them.

In the spirit of the timeless words spoken to Joshua over three thousand years ago, "Let us be strong and of good courage." Let us confront this peril, secure our future and, God willing, forge an enduring peace for generations to come.[8]

Peace in the Middle East will only come from the God of Peace and His Son Jesus Christ, who loves the Jews and the Arabs, who loves Abraham and Sarah, and also loves Hagar and Ishmael.[9]

It's Biblical (it's *God's* thing)

Occasionally we have had a number of our Orthodox Jewish neighbors protest in front of Calvary Baptist Church in New York City, where I have pastored these past seventeen years. The reason often given for the protests is that we work together with Jewish Christian ministries such as Jews for Jesus, Chosen People, and Word of Messiah to offer the gospel to Jewish people. We are often accused of deception because we invite Jewish people to receive Jesus as their Messiah and assure them that they don't stop being Jewish when they become followers of Yeshua Hamashiach, Jesus the Messiah. On one particular day, I was discussing the Old Testament prophets with one of the Jewish rabbis who is a leader in the counter-missionary movement. As we talked, his rabbinical students were listening, even as the rabbis prepared for a press conference on a New York City sidewalk, right in front of my church. I said, "Rabbi, your prophets in the Bible tell us that the Messiah will be born to a virgin, and do miracles, and live a sinless life, and die for mankind's sins and rise from the dead—and Yeshua fulfilled all the Scriptures." And the rabbi, without hesitation, in front of all his students, shouted out to me, "I don't care what the Bible says—I care what the rabbis say!" The rabbi had brought his students to picket our church, and as the crowd grew, and the press conference was about to begin, the students held up their signs which said—*Stop Converting Jews* and *We Don't Need Saving*. During the press conference the rabbi literally accused us as Christians of stealing Jewish children from their mothers and said that if a Jewish person trusted in Jesus, that person ceased to be Jewish! So I asked the rabbi, "Are you still looking for the hope and consolation of Israel?" And he said, "Yes, I am." And so I asked him, "And when Messiah comes—will you believe in Him?" And he said, "Yes, I will." And so then I asked, "So rabbi, when Messiah comes and you believe in him—will you cease to be Jewish?" The rabbi was silent. Then he said, "No, I will not cease to be Jewish." So I asked him, "Then why do you insist that those Jews who believe in Yeshua as Messiah cease to be Jewish?" And the rabbi had no answer. This is just one example of the mindset and attitude present in every religion, when corrupt religious tradition is allowed to override and veto biblical truth!

Ironically, during my very first meeting with the rabbis, which took place at a New York City synagogue, we were all sitting around a table introducing ourselves, when one of the rabbis looked across the table at me and said, "Pastor Epstein, for the sake of full disclosure, I need to acknowledge that I was one of the rabbis who picketed your church." So I responded, "I hope our people treated you well." He said, "Oh yes, they were very gracious, showing us hospitality and offering us water." When it came time for me to introduce myself and say a word, I told them the story of my great grandfather, the Russian Jew persecuted during the pogroms whose family found new life in America. The room was very quiet, but there was an amazing sense of solidarity because of the shared suffering. Walls began to be broken down. Recently, in another meeting where we discussed the nation Israel, two of the rabbis asked me, in front of all the other leaders, about a series of messages I had preached on the prophet Ezekiel entitled "The Coming War against Israel." They asked for the church website, expressing an interest in listening to the messages. And of course, I was delighted! It was very cool. God is working.

God makes some strange choices. If you are a Christian today, God chose you. He also chose the poor. And God chose the Jews.

> For you are a people holy to the LORD your God. The LORD your God has chosen you out of all the peoples on the face of the earth to be his people, his treasured possession (Deut. 7:6).

The world tends to agree with poet William Norman Ewer who said, "How odd of God to choose the Jews."

But there must be a method to God's "madness."

When considering Israel and the Middle East, one of the books that has informed and challenged me the most is *Heritage: Civilization and the Jews* by the renowned Israeli statesman and scholar Abba Eban. He writes from a secular, humanistic perspective, which provides a valuable insight into the modern Israeli mind. The historical chronicle and insights are powerful, but when it comes to the prophetic element, by necessity, it is painfully absent. Abba Eban ends his narrative with a fascinating examination of the *mystery* of the Jews: The mystery of their preservation, resonance, suffering, renewal and future.

And yet, the Bible sheds light on every mystery that Abba Eban rightly identifies—and the beginning of the answer to each mystery is: *God chose the Jews.*

The Mystery of Jewish Preservation (survival)

"How did this people manage to preserve its identity in dispersion and exile, without a territorial base or political institutions, in conditions under which no other people has ever survived?"[10]

Because God chose the Jews!

This is what the LORD says, he who appoints the sun to shine by day, who decrees the moon and stars to shine by night, who stirs up the sea so that its waves roar— the LORD Almighty is his name: "Only if these decrees vanish from my sight," declares the LORD, "will Israel ever cease being a nation before me."

This is what the LORD says: "Only if the heavens above can be measured and the foundations of the earth below be searched out will I reject all the descendants of Israel because of all they have done," declares the LORD (Jer. 31:35–37).

The Mystery of Jewish Resonance (influence)

"Why do so few people have so large a voice, so that whatever men do and think and say to this very day has been profoundly affected by the Jewish experience? Religion, philosophy, law, drama, science, art, political systems, social institutions, moral ideas—these have all been profoundly agitated by the currents of the Jewish mind."[11]

Because God chose the Jews!

The Lord had said to Abram, "Go from your country, your people and your father's household to the land I will show you. I will make you into a great nation, and

I will bless you; I will make your name great, and you will be a blessing. I will bless those who bless you, and whoever curses you I will curse; and all peoples on earth will be blessed through you" (Genesis 12:1–3).

If you fully obey the Lord your God and carefully follow all his commands I give you today, the Lord your God will set you high above all the nations on earth. All these blessings will come on you and accompany you if you obey the Lord your God. . . . (Deut. 28:1–2).

The Mystery of Jewish Suffering

"There is the mystery of suffering, a mystery that passes all understanding and defies all parallel."[12]

Because God chose the Jews!

However, if you do not obey the Lord your God and do not carefully follow all his commands and decrees I am giving you today, all these curses will come on you and overtake you. . . . Then the Lord will scatter you among all nations, from one end of the earth to the other. There you will worship other gods—gods of wood and stone, which neither you nor your ancestors have known. Among those nations you will find no repose, no resting place for the sole of your foot. There the Lord will give you an anxious mind, eyes weary with longing, and a despairing heart. You will live in constant suspense, filled with dread both night and day, never sure of your life. In the morning you will say, "If only it were evening!" and in the evening, "If only it were morning!"—because of the terror that will fill your hearts and the sights that your eyes will see (Deut. 28:15–16; 64–67).

The Mystery of Jewish Renewal

"And finally, there is the mystery of renewal, the ability to take a language, land, and people separated for centuries and bring them back together again in a new birth of independent life."[13]

Because God chose the Jews!

"For I will take you out of the nations; I will gather you from all the countries and bring you back into your own land. I will sprinkle clean water on you, and you will be clean; I will cleanse you from all your impurities and from all your idols. I will give you a new heart and put a new spirit in you; I will remove from you your heart of stone and give you a heart of flesh. And I will put my Spirit in you and move you to follow my decrees and be careful to keep my laws. Then you will live in the land I gave your ancestors; you will be my people, and I will be your God. . . . " (Ezek. 36:24–28).

The Mystery of the Jewish Future

Abba Eban concludes his fascinating history by asserting: "As we come now to the end of the twentieth century, the Jewish future is uncharted; there are no certainties ahead."[14] But there are!

Because God chose the Jews!

The Jewish prophet Zechariah agrees:

On that day the LORD will shield those who live in Jerusalem. . . . On that day I will set out to destroy all the nations that attack Jerusalem. "And I will pour out on the house of David and the inhabitants of Jerusalem a spirit of grace and supplication. They will look on me, the one they have pierced, and they will mourn for him as one mourns for an only child, and grieve bitterly for him as one grieves for a firstborn son (Zech. 12:8–10).

On that day a fountain will be opened to the house of David and the inhabitants of Jerusalem, to cleanse them from sin and impurity (Zech. 13:1).

Then the LORD will go out and fight against those nations, as he fights on a day of battle. On that day his feet will stand on the Mount of Olives, east of Jerusalem, and the Mount of Olives will be split in two from east to west, forming a great valley, with half of the mountain moving north and half moving south. You will flee by my mountain valley, for it will extend to Azel. You will flee as you fled from the earthquake in the days of Uzziah king of Judah. Then the LORD my God will come, and all the holy ones with him (Zech. 14:3–5).

The Jewish Messiah Jesus agrees:

> For as lightning that comes from the east is visible even in the west, so will be the coming of the Son of Man. . . . Then will appear the sign of the Son of Man in heaven. And then all the peoples of the earth will mourn when they see the Son of Man coming on the clouds of heaven, with power and great glory. And he will send his angels with a loud trumpet call, and they will gather his elect from the four winds, from one end of the heavens to the other (Matt. 24:27–31).

The Jewish apostle Paul agrees:

> I do not want you to be ignorant of this mystery, brothers and sisters, so that you may not be conceited: Israel has experienced a hardening in part until the full number of the Gentiles has come in, and in this way all Israel will be saved. As it is written: "The deliverer will come from Zion; he will turn godlessness away from Jacob. . . . And this is my covenant with them when I take away their sins" (Rom. 11:25–27).

Conclusion

To love Israel and the Jewish people is a privilege and responsibility given to the world by God. Sadly, at times, the world and even the church have been slow to respond to God's invitation—and so we forfeit God's blessing.

Right after 9/11, while our church was helping to train 1,200 lay counselors and ministering to hundreds of hurting, frightened people, an elderly Jewish couple came in one day and said to me, "Pastor, we're Jewish, but our synagogue is far away, and we really want to pray—can we pray here?" I was deeply moved that God would bring them by and said, "Of course—you are welcome here." It reminded me again of the word of God spoken through Isaiah the prophet and Jesus the Messiah, "My house will be called a house of prayer for all nations" (Isa. 56:7; Mark 11:17).

One Sunday after the morning services, a Jewish couple who live in our midtown neighborhood but had never attended our church approached me with an interesting question, "Pastor Epstein, we walk by Calvary Baptist Church regularly and have asked each other more than once, 'How does a man named David Epstein end up pastoring a Baptist church?' Could you tell us your story?" And of course, I was more than happy to oblige!

Just another New York City divine appointment with the gospel!

To love Israel and the Jewish people is personal (it's my thing); it's moral (it's the right thing); it's political (it's the smart thing); and ultimately, it's biblical (it's God's thing).

"And as many as walk according to this rule, peace and mercy be upon them, and upon the Israel of God" (Gal. 6:16).

Soli Deo Gloria!

Study Questions

1. Is the gospel today still "first for the Jew"?

2. In the author's explanation of his love for Israel and the Jewish people, he offers personal, moral, political and biblical reasons. Which ones impact you the most? The least?

3. Why would Martin Luther, a giant of the Reformation, encourage such hatred and hostility towards the Jewish people? How is Luther a cautionary tale?

4. Is the historical mistreatment of the Jewish people by the Christian church, culminating in the Holocaust, the greatest hindrance to Jewish people believing in God? In Jesus?

5. Is radical Islam's total commitment to destroy Israel and the Jews primarily a political or a religious motivation? Is Iran Israel's greatest threat?

6. Do you agree or disagree with the author's contention that the United Nations is virulently anti-Israel and anti-America?

7. Is America's support for Israel eroding?

8. Why would Abba Eban, as brilliant as he was, contend that the mystery of the Jews and their future is unknowable?

9. How does our understanding of the last days impact our treatment of the Jews and our attitude toward Israel?

10. Why does the Jewish leadership and community have such an ambivalent attitude towards the evangelicals? How can understanding this inform and reform our witness?

11. How do we explain the Bible's uncanny accuracy in explaining and prognosticating the mystery of the Jews and their future?

12. Is loving the Jewish people really a privilege and responsibility given to the world and the church by God? What are the personal and global implications?

Conference Video

chosenpeople.com/epstein

Interview with Pastor David Epstein

chosenpeople.com/epstein-interview

17

A SURVEY OF POSITIONS ON ISRAEL CURRENTLY TAUGHT AT THEOLOGICAL SCHOOLS

Dr. Gregory Hagg

Hagg, in his chapter *A Survey of Positions on Israel Currently Taught at Evangelical North American Theological Schools*, presents a summary of a survey he conducted of approximately seventy different Christian educational institutions across the United States, examining the shift in theological perspectives in American seminaries concerning Israel over the last two decades. He has observed a waning of support and interest in Israel.

Hagg sent a list of ten questions to seventy institutions and does an excellent job of summarizing the results of the survey, supplying both analysis and some excellent suggestions for how pastors, seminary professors, and leaders within the church might help motivate those they lead to engage in Jewish evangelism and prayer for the Jewish people.

From this chapter, you will gain insights into the direction of the Body of Christ especially in North America and hopefully it will challenge you to find ways to support the work of bringing the Good News of the Gospel to the Jewish people.

Unfortunately, it seems that when the role of the Jewish people in God's plan is under appreciated Jewish evangelism diminishes. Further, when modern Israel is vilified, Jewish evangelism is often neglected in its wake.

Introduction

How is it possible that in just over two decades there has been such a significant shift in the theological perspective on Israel in our churches? Many have noted that there are fewer and fewer churches that teach about Israel, whether the past, present, or future. Many pastors are suggesting that there can be no consensus on the future of God's ancient Chosen People, so it is far better to avoid the issue than to run the risk of dogmatically proclaiming what, they say, is shrouded in mystery. There are just too many views on eschatology out there

Not only is there confusion, but there is also ridicule. Who wants to be characterized by old style Dispensational charts and graphs and timelines? To be lumped together with those who have popularized a certain eschatology and then skewered by critics is not desirable.

The burden of this chapter is to present a simple survey of the role Israel and the Jewish people might have in the theological thinking of Christian academic institutions in the United States. Could it be that the shift in the pulpit has come from a shift in the classroom? Are there observable trends in the theological education within some of the most prominent seminaries in America?

Methodology

This survey was prepared by one who affirms the consistent theological perspective that is represented in this volume. The data collected comes from two primary sources: the stated curricula for each of the seminaries surveyed and the personal responses to a survey by leaders in those institutions.

Originally, the study was to be limited to the most evangelical of the seminaries in North America, but after further consideration, the list was expanded to include approximately seventy schools. This assured a fairly good cross section of institutions which would be traditionally thought of as conservative and evangelical. However, the list also included some schools not known for their commitment to evangelical positions.

The academic deans of each of the seventy institutions (or individuals who were delegated by them in a few cases) were asked to participate in this survey, the details of which will follow. The other primary source of information came from the official websites of each of these seminaries. Such key words as the following were used to search those sites:

- Israel
- Palestine
- Palestinian Christians
- Doctrinal Statement
- Jewish Christians
- Arab Christians
- Christ at the Checkpoint

- Jewish evangelism
- Arab evangelism
- Faculty trained in Jewish studies
- Faculty trained in Arab studies

Generally speaking, many seminaries provided tours to Israel and other Middle Eastern lands for the purposes of studying historical geography or archaeology. Very few websites contributed to the discussion at hand—how American seminaries view the People, the Land, and the Future of Israel. Likewise, courses listed in the curricula usually focused on the biblical history of Israel rather than current events. In self-described premillennial schools, courses were listed as having to do with the role of Israel in the coming kingdom, but details of precisely how the nation is viewed by the professors or discussed in the courses was not available. In future studies of this nature, an examination of the syllabi of these courses would prove beneficial. Such detail, however, was beyond the purview of this chapter. Unfortunately, therefore, reviewing these websites yielded little information on the topics.

However, the academic leaders of a few of the seminaries were willing to give personal opinions along with their answers to the questions posed. While all of them requested that they not be quoted directly, they all gave permission to use the data collected, which give a picture of what is transpiring in some of the seminaries. It was rather disappointing that only fourteen of the seventy schools contacted responded to the survey. After asking several deans what they thought would be the best way to conduct such a survey, it was concluded that a brief emailed survey should be sent at an optimum time for assuring a response. Telephone surveys might be less time consuming but also less accurate. Anyone involved in seminary education knows that there is no optimum time. Summer vacations were ruled out along with the beginnings of semesters when most administrative work is at its peak. Likewise, time is at a premium during the last weeks of a semester. However, it was hoped that the end of the fall semester, just prior to and during the Christmas/New Year's break, would be that optimum time. A twenty-percent return may not be the ideal response, but the following results may provide a glimpse into the subject at hand.

The Survey

1. Have you observed a change in attitude among your faculty members concerning the Jewish people, the land of Israel, and the future of Israel over the past five to ten years?

    a. Less Supportive
    b. More Supportive

c. Highly Critical
d. Somewhat Critical
e. About the Same

This first question focused on any observable change in attitudes over the past decade concerning the Jewish people. The question is based upon the assumption that there has been a trend away from general support for the nation of Israel as mentioned above. Of the fourteen responses, only two (14%) indicated that there has been a "more supportive" attitude toward Israel among the faculty members. This was from two schools that are generally regarded to hold to a strong premillennial eschatology as indicated in their doctrinal statements, reputations, and this survey.

It was apparent that an increase in support has not occurred among the faculty of other schools as ten of the fourteen (71%) said that this attitude remained the same. Of these schools nine of the ten (90%) were labeled by the respondent as premillennial in a following question. Only one was said to be amillennial in orientation, one did not respond, and one checked "other" on that question.

It was the latter seminary that also said the faculty had changed to a "highly critical" view of Israel. It is interesting to note that the one who responded to these questions provided additional comments at the end of the survey indicating that the general views of his school did not really represent his own personal positions. The school was characterized as a "mainline institution" which would not have an official policy on the issues raised in the survey. He also implied that while most of the faculty members are pro-Palestinian, they kept this to themselves rather than teaching a political view in class.

The respondent also reported that, in his opinion, the faculty lost interest in contemporary Judaism and Israel and their ethical reflections inevitably conclude that the plight of the Palestinians is due to a "gross injustice perpetrated by the State of Israel" and the larger Jewish community. For his own part, in his teaching he attempts to engage either Israel or Judaism in the discussion, and he presents a more complex view in class. While the seminary and the respondent shall go unnamed, it is helpful to mention that this was not one of the institutions that are affiliated with the Evangelical Theological Society. So, this opinion could likely be found in many such schools which were included in the request to take the survey but did not respond.

Before leaving this first question, it is instructive to summarize the comments of the dean of one of the schools who said that while the seminary's denomination had done much church planting in Israel to reach the Jews as a lost people group, the seminary does not give attention to the people of Israel as a theological or eschatological entity. Again, this school was characterized as having a faculty whose members were "mostly amillennial." Additionally, this dean remarked on what is apparent on the website, namely that the school has a robust interest and programs designed to study the connections between Judaism of the first century and the writing of the New Testament by Jewish people.

Of the two schools, which were reported to have seen an improvement in the faculty's attitude toward Israel, "more supportive," one of them conducts frequent study tours to Israel. His conclusion was that these trips have helped significantly improve the attitude of the students and faculty toward Israel. Only one seminary was said to have become "less supportive" of Israel, and this school has historically been ardently premillennial and was labeled as such on the following questions.

One wonders, however, if this is symptomatic of a similar trend in other premillennial schools which did not participate in the survey. Some private conversations with various academic leaders would support the notion.

2. If your seminary sponsors trips to Israel, do the participants visit Arab territories (i.e. Gaza, West Bank, Bethlehem)? If so, has this altered the views of seminary leaders with regard to Israel's right to the Land?

   a. Yes, most feel Israel has no right to the Land
   b. No, most support Israel's right to the Land
   c. It is done to be sure we present a balanced view to students

The second question had to do with trips to Israel, especially those that included Arab territories, with a view to determining whether or not such visits changed the perspectives of the faculty. This question was based on the premise that both Israel and the Palestinians have well developed public relations efforts that seek to influence the opinion of the rest of the world, not the least of which is the American church.

Once again, the responses were predictable. Only twelve seminary deans answered this question, with six (50%) stating that the majority of their professors "support Israel's right to the Land" in spite of visits to the Arab territories. It should be noted that each of these institutions holds to a premillennial eschatology, according to the survey as well as website doctrinal statements.

One of the deans expressed his regret that such trips are not scheduled at the present time. Another dean said that his seminary sponsors trips to places like the West Bank and Bethlehem, but they are designed as historical studies and archaeological research rather than exploring current political issues.

This latter view probably represents the majority of all seminary tours to Israel. If political views are considered, they are minimized by the professors. One dean, whose seminary has no official position on the future of ethnic Israel or a specific doctrinal stance on eschatology, remarked that there is no agreed basis on what constitutes a "right" to land. Therefore, his faculty focuses on the claims to the land and how they have changed over the years. Notice that there is no attempt to suggest that the Bible has any relevance to this discussion.

Even among those seminaries that are known for their evangelical stance, four (33%) of them responded in the same way to this question. They said that whenever their seminaries conduct tours to these areas "it is done to be sure they present a balanced view to students." This, of course, means that they want to avoid political statements. One dean commented that while there is a briefing on the political situation, the leaders do not take a position on the government of Israel or the theological right to the land claimed by the Jews or the Palestinians.

The same dean remarked that on-campus teaching does address these issues. He, himself, covers topics like dispensationalism versus covenant theology along with the views of Christian Zionism versus replacement theology.

Finally, as expected, the seminary that most likely would be characterized as least conservative (another non-ETS school) has a faculty that feels "Israel has no right to the Land." This dean reported no specific treatment of Romans 9–11 in the curriculum, yet believed that Israel, as an ethnic people, has a future. It is uncertain whether this refers to the Jewish people of today or a regathered nation in the future. It seems that there was considerable confusion in these responses, which reflects a degree of uncertainty among those schools which do not study these issues as part of their biblical or theological curriculum in their schools.

3. Do you have courses in your curriculum that address the interpretation of Romans 9–11 with regard to the future of Israel and the Jews? If so, which basic view is embraced by *most* of your faculty?

    a. Premillennial
    b. Amillennial
    c. Postmillennial
    d. Other

    Furthermore, which of the following specific views do you believe is held by *most* of your faculty? (We want your opinion, even if it seems to be a generalization.)

    a. Israel as an ethnic people has a future.
    b. Israel as a nation has a future in a land that is their own.

c. Israel's unbelief has meant she has forfeited any future blessing.
d. Future blessing is found only in the church, and Israel has no future.

The third question was meant to explore the attitude in the seminaries toward a key passage in the discussion, Romans 9–11. As just illustrated, there are seminaries which might not even address the Biblical content. It is no surprise that schools considered premillennial seminaries replied that they offer at least one course that studies Romans 9–11. So eleven (85%) of the respondents apparently teach that the future of the Jews is related to this passage. The deans who responded to this question also felt the majority of their faculty members would answered two follow-up questions in the affirmative: "Israel as an ethnic people has a future, and Israel as a nation has a future in a land that is their own." Even the self described amillennial school and the two schools not affiliated with ETS have faculties that believe the first proposition to be true; however, it would be a stretch for them to say that the nation will have a "land that is their own" someday! Oddly enough, however, one of them answered in the affirmative.

Not one of the deans suggested that Israel's unbelief resulted in the forfeiture of any future blessings. This would suggest that the concept of punitive supersessionism may not be held by as many professors in American seminaries as thought.

The additional comments from the deans were particularly helpful on this question. It was striking to learn that although the denominational position of one of the seminaries was premillennialism, the faculty was predominantly amillennial. One would expect faculty would try to be fair but be more convincing of their own convictions, even if the denomination or seminary has an historical theological position which is otherwise. Students would be influenced by the teaching of those professors, regardless of how fair-minded they attempt to be. Perhaps this simple admission from one dean provides enormous evidence for the shift in attitudes among many churches that once were more inclined to support Israel's right to possess the land.

In a similar vein, one of the seminaries requires the faculty to hold a premillennial position, but the dean said that the interpretation of what this means was broad. One individual reported that most of the faculty would not see "Biblical Israel" as a theologically relevant construct in relation to the modern nation of Israel. One of the seminaries most committed to the idea that "Israel as a nation has a future in a land that is their own" believes the nation his faculty has in mind is the "Israel of God" or Paul's new Israel. This is the belief that the Jewish people only have a place in God's future plans when they accept God's Messiah. The faculty generally believes that genetics and ethnicity have nothing to do with the promises of God or the election of Israel. This, of course, is a complicated issue, but the preceding position seems to equate Jew and Gentile in the Body of Messiah with reference to the land promises in the same way that they are related with reference to salvation promises. Is it possible that there is a difference? Salvation levels the playing field dramatically so that Paul could say, "There is neither Jew nor Greek, there is neither slave nor free man, there is neither male nor female; for you are all one in Christ Jesus" (Galatians 3:28, NASB). Most Christians would agree that there is no future for Israel apart from faith in the Messiah, but could it be that the promises concerning the land are dependent upon God's election of an ethnic people?

Another response echoes the same sentiment; namely that the Israel of the New Testament does not refer to a political entity with a government, a military, a legislature, (or dare say a Knesset and a Temple). It could not refer to the State of Israel according to this view. This respondent says, of course, God has a sovereign plan for all nations, but there is no future for the current member of the UN called Israel. A further comment from the same dean underscores the idea that most of his faculty would limit the nation to "messianic Judaism" or the Jews who have come to believe that Jesus is the Messiah. Ethnic Israel's theological future, therefore, is only possible among Jews who believe. His view supports Jewish believers who choose to live as Jews in contradistinction to those secular Jews who do not. It is interesting to note that this comment comes from the same academic leader who considers his faculty amillennial in a premillennial denomination!

4. Does your seminary have a position on the future of ethnic Israel? If so, does this view refer to the Jewish people of today or a regathered nation in the future?

   a. Ethnic Israel of today
   b. Ethnic Israel of the future
   c. Ethnic Israel has no future

The fourth question seeks to drill a bit deeper in the same area. Although it may sound redundant, the intent is to flesh out more specific attitudes toward the nation of Israel as it exists today. Almost all of those who responded to the previous question indicated that their faculty believes there is a future for ethnic Israel, even in a land of their own (twelve, or 86%, with two not responding), but when it comes to identifying which "ethnic Israel," several wanted to qualify their answers. Of the fourteen responses to this question, four (29%) said that their seminary had no position on this question. Of those who said their seminaries did have an official position on this issue, four (25%) said "ethnic Israel of today," while six (60%) said "ethnic Israel of the future."

It almost goes without saying that a relatively small number of those seminaries consulted believe that the current nation of Israel is likely the ethnic Israel which is to receive the promises of God with regard to the Land. Even among those who say it is the "ethnic Israel of today" one academic leader states that we do not know with certainty the time of fulfillment. His conclusion is that the nation of Israel today may or may not be the final regathered nation. The time of fulfillment may belong to a future regathered people. The academic leader of another seminary in this category stated that we cannot distinguish between the "today" Israel and the "future" Israel. Today's Israel *could* be the Israel which experiences the ultimate promise of Romans 11.

These viewpoints seem to create apathy toward to the current State of Israel, especially when that government is accused of acting with questionable morality. How could God be supportive of a nation which does not behave in a godly manner? How could God have this current Jewish nation in mind for blessing when it is a secular state filled with agnostic leaders and a population divided by the very secular and ultra-religious Jewish People?

Among the seminaries that speak only of an "ethnic Israel of the future," one academic leader said the faculty would not believe Israel's future is linked to ethnic Israel today. One of these requires faculty to be premillennial, but not all faculty members see the future for ethnic Israel tied to the current Jewish State. Another premillennial seminary which does not have a position on this topic, has faculty members who have declared that ethnic Israel has no future. Once again, it seems that faculty members have academic freedom and are able to teach what they wish, even if the official position of the school or denomination differs. The question that begs an answer is, "What support is offered for the current State of Israel based upon biblical principles?" Perhaps this volume will clarify the issue by declaring "the gifts and the calling of God are without repentance," (Romans 11:29). Disobedience and disbelief are disciplined by God, but the election of Israel is secured by the promises of God.

5. If your faculty is predominantly Premillennial in their thinking, which of the following positions would you say most of your faculty hold?

   a. Historic Premillennial
   b. Covenant
   c. Dispensational
   d. Realized Eschatology
   e. Progressive Dispensational
   f. Other

The fifth question of the survey has been referred to in previous discussion, but it may be of interest to note that the major subcategories of premillennialism are represented. Five (36%) faculty of the schools were thought to be "historic premillennial" while four (29%) were "dispensational" and six (43%) listed "progressive dispensational" as the predominant view. Three of the respondents checked each of the above, so the figures are skewed a bit. No one checked "realized eschatology," and one respondent commented that this view is incompatible with any form of premillennialism. Similarly, one of the academic leaders pointed out that both "covenant" and "historic" were one and the same.

There was no response from those seminaries that seem to have little evangelical connection. Perhaps the information from this question merely indicates that basically all of the schools responding to the questions were premillennial. Other than the one amillennial seminary (in the premillennial denomination, described above), no self-described amillennial school responded. However, the list of seventy included many that have historical roots in amillennial theology. One can only speculate whether or not the nature of the survey questions discouraged participation.

6. In your *personal* opinion, would you say that the present Modern State of Israel has any Biblical, political, or ethical claim to the Land of Israel?

   a. Yes
   b. No
   c. Perhaps
   d. Not sure

This question was designed to discover the personal opinion of academic leaders. Of course, the amount of influence the academic deans have over their faculty members will vary from institution to institution, but their personal convictions must play some role in the views espoused by others. Surprisingly, eight (73%) of those who responded said "yes" concerning the Modern State of Israel's right to the Land. One dean said "no" with regard to the present national entity, one said "perhaps," one said "not sure," and one did not respond at all. Perhaps the strongest statement from a dean was that the land was given to Israel by God long ago and forever. He referred to a presentation at the most recent ETS meeting by Dr. Michael Vlach, a contributor to this book, who argued that the present state of Israel has a legal and a political right which dates to 1948 and perhaps earlier than that. Interestingly, another academic leader said that the biblical claim is debatable, but the political and ethical claim is strong. Usually, the Bible is used in the argument for a claim to the Land while current socio/political events have been used by many to argue against the right of Israel to possess the Land.

A similar sentiment was registered by one who questioned the use of the generic term Land of Israel and suggested that the issue is really speaking of the West Bank and Gaza strip. The Modern State of Israel, he said, has some political and moral claim to these areas, but no biblical claim in its current composition. If, on the other hand, genuine revival occurs and messianic Judaism becomes more prominent, the newly configured population might resemble the "future ethnic Israel" of a previous question. This view clearly requires the nation to be obedient to the gospel in order to have legitimate claim to the Land. It begs the question of whether or not the Land belonged to disobedient Israel in ancient history. The nation was not allowed to control the Land during times of rebellion against God and expulsion from the Land, but the ownership was part of a promise by God to the elect people of Israel. The history is replete with examples of back and forth sovereignty over the Land, but once again, the promises were and are irrevocable.

7. Does your seminary address the current Arab-Israeli Conflict in any courses? If so, what approach is more likely to be used in the courses?

   a. Lectures by Pro-Arab Palestinians
   b. Lectures by Pro-Israel Jewish Christians
   c. A Mix of Lecturers
   d. Other

Essentially, nine (65%) seminary leaders said that a "mix of lecturers" or "other" methods were used to address this issue on their campuses. There were three (21%) who said only "lectures by pro-Israel Jewish Christians" took place in their schools. Each of these was dispensational and premillennial. One respondent, who is also a professor, stated that the Arab-Israeli conflict comes up in classes and on trips to Israel. In the classroom the professor tries to give a fair and balanced presentation using YouTube clips from both sides of the issue. One other dean was not certain, but he assumed that a balanced perspective was given in classes. One of the clearly less conservative seminaries stated that this is not a major issue on their campus. It seems obvious from these responses that the attempt is being made to give both sides in most schools.

8. Are there specific courses in your degree program (specifically the M.A., Th.M., or M.Div.) which emphasize Jewish and/or Arab evangelism?

a. Jewish Evangelism
b. Arab Evangelism
c. Both
d. Neither

This question was intended to survey the type of evangelistic training that is available. Only two (17%) schools offer courses in "Jewish evangelism" without offering courses in "Arab evangelism," one of which has a concentration in Messianic Judaism. There were six (50%) who said that both "Jewish evangelism" and "Arab evangelism" are taught in courses on campus, one of whom commented that his seminary emphasizes evangelism and discipleship for all nations and peoples. Two of the deans sought to clarify the question in that Muslim was a better term to use than "Arab." Regardless of the term used, however, most would agree that in the narrower discussion of the Arab-Israeli conflict, it is important for pro-Israel groups to emphasize the loving evangelization of Palestinians. Surprisingly, four (33%) of those who answered this question said that their schools emphasized "neither." Two of them were staunch premillennial seminaries, and two were the ones not related to the Evangelical Theological Society and assumed to be far less interested in evangelism in general.

9. Does your seminary have extracurricular presentations, activities, or clubs related to Israeli Jews or Palestinian Arabs? Are there groups on campus that promote either or both?

a. Yes, related to Israeli Jews
b. Yes, related to Palestinian Arabs
c. Yes, both
d. No, none

This question is designed to explore the efforts made to treat these issues through extracurricular events on the campuses. Only one seminary (7%) mentioned having a group related to the support of Israeli Jews, but no comment was given about the nature of it, whether it was a fellowship of students who were Israeli Jewish believers, or a group that might promote the causes of Israeli Jews such as the right to possess disputed land. Another seminary (7%) mentioned a group for Palestinian Arabs. This dean explained in personal comments that this fellowship was the result of having an international worker who makes presentations related to outreach among Muslims in Israel. It is a temporary club connected with the short term assignment of the worker. Thus, there is no ongoing club that "promotes" Palestinian Arabs.

The dean of one seminary, which happened to be least likely connected to a strong evangelical tradition, reported that there were clubs for both Israeli Jews and Palestinian Arabs. The question in the survey implies that the groups exist to promote the causes of each; however, no specific comment clarified the response. One could easily surmise that these might provide opportunities for debating the political, moral, and biblical arguments on the issues.

A total of ten (71%) of the seminaries reported that there were no extracurricular presentations, activities, or clubs for either group. This is somewhat surprising given the highly charged nature of the issues at hand. Of course, if this question is geared toward determining how politically oriented a seminary might be, it is not unusual that conservative, evangelical schools would not encourage such things on their campuses. Unity would be stressed.

One dean remarked that there had been a recent conference on Messianic Judaism on his campus, and a chapel was scheduled where the theme of Jesus in the Passover would be presented. Also, this seminary devoted a chapel service to the viewing of the film *O Little Town of Bethlehem*, followed by discussion. Another of these deans admitted that their school's undergraduate program held a conference which advocated a one-sided approach considered to be pro-Arab.

10. Would you describe your institution as one looking forward to the fulfillment of the unfulfilled prophecies given to Israel, those which seem more concretely and ethnically tied to historical, physical Israel?

   a. Yes
   b. No
   c. Mixed (50%)
   d. Mixed (75% Yes)
   e. Mixed (75% No)

The final question of the survey was intended to give an "institutional" summary in that the deans were asked to characterize their seminaries with reference to biblical prophecies about Israel. While previously, the emphasis was upon the faculty members, now the emphasis is upon the institution. Although the majority of individual members of the teaching staff might more likely self-describe as premillennialists, could the seminary be described otherwise? Likewise, the reverse could be true. An historically premillennial seminary could conceivably have a majority of its faculty members holding another view.

Of the thirteen seminary leaders who responded, five (38%) stated "yes" to the question. Four of the five seemed true to form since they also indicated earlier that the faculty members were premillenni-al (and dispensational or progressive dispensational). One school's re-spondent, however, earlier said the school was amillennial, based upon a preponderance of faculty who held this view. But in this question the institution is described as "looking forward to the fulfillment of the unfulfilled prophesies given to Israel, those which seem more con-cretely and ethnically tied to historical, physical Israel." Again, faculty and institutional reputation seem to be at odds. If this one seminary represents a similar disposition in others, there could be mixed signals being given elsewhere. Furthermore, in a comment on the question, it becomes clear that the "unfulfilled promises" were not related to things like temple worship, land resettlement, Torah observance, or a Davidic throne in Jerusalem. Rather, the promises refer to worldwide preach-ing of the gospel and/or Jewish confession of the messiahship of Jesus, items that hardly require the "historical, physical Israel."

Admittedly, this question, as one leader commented, would have to include the views of the entire campus community, students as well as faculty, and if there were an undergraduate component, that would have to count as the "institution," as well. With this in mind, another five (38%) said that it was a 50/50 call for their schools. A couple schools indicated that the institution would be mixed with three-quarters of the "institution" looking forward to the fulfillment of the unfulfilled prophecies given to Israel. One seminary said ninety-five percent of the school would be so inclined. The comment of one dean reflects the burden of this book when he said that his school's conviction is that the literal fulfillment of prophecy must take place. It is the bibli-cal pattern. Prophecy not yet literally fulfilled will still be fulfilled in the future. All those who hold this high view of Scripture will confess that this principle holds true for every aspect of the Word of God's commentary on the People, the Land, and the Future of Israel.

Study Questions

1. Where do most pastors get the basic framework for their theology?

2. How do the media influence one's views of the Modern State of Israel and the circumstances surrounding the Palestinian question?

3. What is the predominant position held by the leadership in your own church concerning the People, the Land, and the Future of Israel?

4. Has there been an observable change over the past decade or so in the attitudes of your family, school, business, or church toward the support of Israel as a nation?

5. Is it surprising to you that the results of the research in this chapter reveal a weakening support for Israel as a legitimate political entity in the Middle East?

6. How would you explain the growing anti-Israel or pro-Palestinian stance among faculty members in schools that have traditionally been thought of as evangelical institutions?

7. Do you think a professor's political bias should be part of his Bible teaching?

8. From the information provided in this chapter, what role does a tour of Israel play in forming the theological perspectives of the faculty member of seminaries?

9. What biblical, political, or ethical evidence exists for the Modern State of Israel to claim that it has a right to possess any or all of the Land?

10. What role has political propaganda played in the attitude of seminary faculties toward Israel and the Palestinian question?

CONCLUSION

Dr. Darrell L. Bock

The People, the Land, and the Future of Israel is not just a book about a people. It is about the work and promises of the living God. How God treats Israel is a reflection of His character and His commitment to His own Word. It shows that God loves us by His grace and goes to every length to draw people to Him. This concluding chapter considers why the future of national Israel matters to all of us. When one looks at all of these chapters and considers a biblical theology of national Israel, five key points consistently surface. Let's look at them one at a time to see what the biblical text is telling us.

Five Points Emerging from the Biblical and Historical Survey

1. God made promises to national Israel about an earthly kingship of shalom centered in Jerusalem and He will be faithful to them.

Starting in Genesis and extending to Revelation, God made covenantal promises to humanity, Abraham, and the people of Israel to be a blessing to the world through them. He never veers away from that promise. In all the essays on the teaching of the Hebrew Scripture, we see this affirmed again and again in very concrete and earthly terms. The picture is of nations streaming to Zion and Jerusalem to experience the peace God has brought through His kingdom. That shalom is for everyone, and Israel is its focal point. Not because Israel stands in contrast to the nations at this point, but because the hub of God's activity streams out to the world through the one God chose to bring the promises He made. Jesus blesses the world in the context of this specific history before there is a new heaven and earth for eternity.

Whether one considers the foundations laid in the Pentateuch (Merrill's essay), looks at how the writings develop that promise to focus on a king (Kaiser's essay), or reflects upon what the prophets say about the end of exile (Chisholm's essay), a consistent theme arises. It is that the kingdom on earth comes through the one who is connected to Israel and the nations stream to him. The very return of Jesus to complete those promises is affirmed in Matthew (Wilkens' essay), Luke–Acts (Bock's essay) and in Revelation 19–22, in line with the Romans 9–11 hope (Vanlaningham's essay) that one day all Israel will be saved. Even the general epistles, which often are not brought into this discussion at all, have indications of this overall perspective (Evans' essay). The hermeneutics (Blaising and Vlach's essays) and overview of the biblical story (Saucy and Feinberg's essays) make the point. It is in this light that the book of Revelation needs to be read. National Israel and her king are at the center of the biblical plan of redemption that is blessing for the world. At the hub, stands Jesus the Christ. One day all is resolved in and through Him as heavenly shalom fills the earth.

The history of discussion and Jewish history also show the heartbeat for this hope from the Jewish side (Rydelnik, Leventhal, and Brown's essays). All of this has an immense impact on Jewish evangelism and to lose this theme is to lose a rationale for an aspect of the Great Commission, which started from Jerusalem (Glaser's essay) and remains something of value from a pastor's perspective (Epstein's essay). That does not mean there is no debate and discussion on these questions (Hagg's essay). It is a tragic fact that a church that became more Gentile came to lose its heart for Israel and struggled in the face of massive Jewish rejection of Jesus. That sad history, however, does not change what the biblical text called for—and calls for even today. It is a heart that beats with hope for the Jewish people, as Paul's heart does in Romans when he holds out great hope for their return to blessing through Messiah.

2. The future of Israel and the land is a matter of God's word, faithfulness, and grace. All judgments on Israel are temporary and will be ultimately reversed when the remnant of the last days turn to the One who was pierced.

Do we really take God at His word? His commitments are a reflection of His unchanging character. He couched these commitments in covenants and undertook the burden of bringing them to pass. He holds His chosen people accountable throughout history as the Scriptures describe exile and judgment results from covenant unfaithfulness, yet never suggest a total abandonment of this people.

The picture of Hosea and the declarations of prophet after prophet say God will not decisively turn His back on those with whom he made covenant. Jesus taught that Israel's house was and would be desolate until she responded. Peter echoed that promise and looked back to what the Hebrew Scriptures declared, saying God would do what He promised. The ultimate biblical story is not about a failure of Israel that disqualified her, but about the faithfulness of God that never lets her go. This is why the New Testament points to temporary judgment and always holds out hope for the Jewish people.

3. Gentile inclusion does not require Israel's exclusion.

Other readings of Scripture argue for and rightly emphasize the hope of Jesus for the world, including Gentiles. These other views often come with an implicit dismissal of a future for the Jewish people in line with her ancient hopes, saying that God has reconfigured how to understand *His people*. This Christocentric focus locates the delivery of the promise squarely and only on Jesus. That point is well made and well taken. But what it risks ignoring are two points: (1) Jesus the king continued to hope for the turning of His people, even praying for them on the cross that the people's role in His death one day meet with forgiveness, and (2) the fact that including others in blessing need not mean the original recipients are excluded once God leads them back to the promised one. That is exactly what texts like Zechariah and Romans declare. As the Apostle Paul writes, *"for the gifts and the calling of God are irrevocable"* (Romans 11:29).

4. Fulfilling these promises to Israel does not express favoritism nor should it cause disunity among the people of God as Israel's blessing will bring benefit, reconciliation and ultimate shalom at Jesus' return.

As these essays show, all this can be affirmed without dividing the church. Nor does it reflect a favoritism that inclines in that direction. After all, the election of the Jewish people was God's doing and not man's. As Paul writes, the Gospel is *"to the Jew first and also to the Greek."* The salvation he discusses in Romans and in Galatians for that matter, blesses both Jew and Gentile, and does so allowing all ethnicities to remain who they are, affirming the power of a deeper and more profound reconciliation available through the Messiah.

This is the heart of the cross. This reconciliation and worldwide shalom occurs when Jesus rules on earth as both the nations and Israel worship him in Jerusalem. They will sing together in a sacred city; they will enjoy together in the presence of their common Lord. This ultimate unity is the goal of the cross and expresses the fullness of the gospel.

5. What the New Testament adds to previous covenant promises does not cancel what the Old Testament has already affirmed, but complements it. Any other reading of the Scriptures leads to spiritualizing the promises of the Old Testament, vacating the original meaning of these texts, and lacks full coherence with the teaching of

Scripture. Such a defective approach ignores the many biblical texts that refer to the nation and the land, and so reduces the full scope of our future hope.

Here is the issue where the key differences among believers on this topic lie. How does one put the entire package of Scripture's teaching together in a unified whole? Our essays as a whole contend that a more unified, comprehensive picture and theology emerges when the New Testament completes what the Old Testament began. The impact of excluding national Israel from our reading of the Old Testament texts minimizes our hope and diminishes the full extent of our future shalom.

We offer these essays with the prayer that Jesus may be seen as the one true hope for both Jews and Gentiles. And that knowing Him might lead us to take Him at His word, affirming the hope that burns within our souls that He will return to literally fulfill His promises for Israel and the nations. This can only lead us to exclaim in wonder, along with the Apostle, *"For from Him and through Him and to Him are all things. To Him be the glory forever. Amen"* (Romans 11:36).

NOTES

Chapter 1: Israel according to the Torah

1. The two terms do occur synonymously, but usually in semi-poetic texts where a match must be found for one or the other (Deut. 4:6; 4:33–34; 26:5; 2 Sam. 7:23; 1 Chron. 17:21; Isa. 1:4; 9:3; 51:4; Jer. 2:11; 33:24; Ezek. 37:22–23; Zeph. 2:9; Hag. 2:14).

2. "Nation" presupposes such features as (1) consanguinity; (2) common language; (3) definable boundaries; (4) a strong central government; (5) a bureaucratic establishment; (6) a sense of political, social, and military cohesion; and (7) a sense of history and destiny as a socio-political entity. See TDOT 2:426–433. Gottwald distinguishes between the two by suggesting that '*am* is "a chiefly social and cultural term and *gôy* [is]a chiefly political term." Norman Gottwald. *The Tribes of Yahweh*. Maryknoll, NY: Orbis, 1979, p. 241.

3. The Septuagint (LXX) renders the name *Ebraios* and the Latin Vulgate Hebraeus; hence, English Hebrew, French *Hbreu*, German Hebräer, Italian Ebreo. The Israelites never called themselves Hebreu "Hebrews" except in situations of shame or in the presence of foreigners who knew them by that name. See Ex. 2:13; 3:18; 5:3; 7:16; 10:3; 21:2; Deut. 15:12; Jer. 34:14; Jonah 1:9.

4. As for the language of the Eberites, nothing can be known since their places of residence and cultural/historical environment are likewise unknown. One might suppose that Sumerian, Old Akkadian, or even Amorite or some other Northwest Semitic dialects were in play. This would certainly have been the case with Abraham who clearly was at home in Sumerian, Old Babylonian, and Amorite. The diversity of language at the time is reflected well in Genesis 10:31: "These are the sons of Shem by their clans (*mišpāḥôt*) and languages (*lĕšōnôt*), in their territories ('*ărāṣōt*) and nations (*gôyî'm*)."

5. The primacy of Shem is suggested by (1) his being named first though he clearly was not Noah's firstborn son (Gen. 10:21; cf. Gen. 5:32; 6:10; 9:18; 10:1; 1 Chron. 1:4); (2) only Shem's genealogy is traced after the tower of Babel narrative (Gen. 11:10–32); and (3) Noah blessed Yahweh as "the God of Shem" (Gen. 9:26), suggesting thereby that Shem would occupy an important role in service to Yahweh. Moreover, though the offspring of the eldest son Japheth would be large in number, they would "dwell in the tents of Shem" (v. 27). Likewise, Canaan (here representing his father Ham) would become subservient to Japheth, thus also in the tents of Shem (vv. 25–27). To dwell in the tent suggests both protection and dominion. See Victor P. Hamilton, *The Book of Genesis Chapters 1–17*. NICOT. Grand Rapids: Eerdmans, 1990, p. 326, n. 19; Kenneth A. Mathews, *Genesis 1-11:26*. NAC 1A. Nashville: B&H, 1996. For the chronological order of the sons, see Eugene H. Merrill, "Chronology," *Dictionary of the Old Testament: Pentateuch*. Ed. T. Desmond Alexander and David W. Baker. Downers Grove, IL: InterVarsity, 2003, p. 116. Delitzsch correctly under-

stands the ultimate fulfillment in that Gentile Christians are for the most part Japhethites dwelling in the tents of Shem. Franz Delitzsch, *A New Commentary on the Book of Genesis.* Vol. I. Trans. Sophia Taylor. Edinburgh: T. & T. Clark, 1888 (repr. Klock & Klock, 1978), p. 298.

6. "Likeness" translates *děmût*, the same term used in the creation account in Genesis 1:26. It is essentially synonymous to *şelem*. Thus A. H. Konkel, NIDOTTE 1:969. Cf. Genesis 1:26–27; 5:1, 3.

7. The root underlying the name Noah is *nwḥ*, "rest," here in the noun form *nōaḥ*, which does not derive from this verb but sounds much like it (assonance), thus Lamech's choice of the name. The technical root of the name most likely is *nûaḥ*, "to be quiet." HALOT, 685.

8. The root *nḥm* (here *yěnaḥămēhû*), "he will bring us comfort;" cf. the exhortation of Isaiah who, speaking of the re-gathering of Israel, says, *naḥămû nāḥ ămû 'ammîm*, "comfort, comfort my people" (Isa. 40:1).

9. "Toil, difficulty, hardship" translates *'işşābôn* both here and in Genesis 3:17. The idea is onerous labor with reference to both the woman and the man, and not physical pain. Women will generally have many children ("I will multiply [*hērōnēk*] your pregnancy") but also a great deal of physical labor as a result. Her having many children will be stressful ("with emotional stress [*bě'eşeb*] she will bear children") by the very fact of having to care for them, thus adding to a woman's already burdensome life. Thus (convincingly) C. Meyers, TDOT 11:280.

10. This is clear from the various narratives which leave no space for unmentioned ancestors. Thus, Abraham is the direct father of Isaac (Gen. 21:1–3), Isaac the father of Jacob (Gen. 25:21–26), and Jacob the father of Judah (Gen. 29:34–35). Abraham died in 1991 BC and Judah was born ca. 1910. Only eighty years passed between these two events. Eugene H. Merrill, "Fixed Dates in Patriarchal Chronology," BSac 137/547 (1980): 241–251.

11. For a less expansive description of the role of Judah, see Moses' blessing in Deuteronomy 33:7.

12. The terms used here are *šēbeṭ* and *měḥōqēq*. The former (perhaps a homonym) can also be translated "tribe," an interesting paronomasia in light of Judah's privileged place among the tribes. The latter term derives from a verb meaning "enact," so the image is that of a ruler who has absolute authority HALOT, 347.

13. This translation is preferable to the enigmatic but common "until Shiloh comes." The name Shiloh occurs nowhere else in the Bible except with reference to the first permanent location of the Mosaic Tabernacle and cultus after the Conquest (Josh. 18:1). This can hardly be the referent here because a place cannot come in the normal sense of the verb here (*bō'*). For the proposal that the word Shiloh should be understood as "the one to whom it belongs" (*š+lě+ô*), see Eugene H. Merrill, "Rashi, Nicholas de Lyra, and Christian Exegesis," WTJ 38 (1975): 66–79.

14. Zedekiah is listed last in the biblical narratives (2 Kings 24:18–20; Jer. 52:1–11; 2 Chron. 36:11–16) and in the genealogy of Chronicles (but not Matthew; 1 Chron. 3:17), but Jehoiachin re-emerged as Judah's king many years after his exile and was considered the last of David's royal house (Matt. 1:11; 2 Kings 25:27–29). For the problem regarding Jehoiachin's being rejected by Yahweh and cursed with childlessness (Jer. 22:24–30; cf., however, 1 Chron. 3:15), see Holladay, *Jeremiah 1*, p. 611: "the point of course is since he will see no son of his upon the throne of Judah, he is childless in the only meaningful way for a king."

15. Eugene H. Merrill, *Haggai, Zechariah, Malachi.* Chicago: Moody, 1994, p. 58. For extra-biblical testimony to this merciful act by Evil-Merodach, successor to Nebuchadnezzar, see ANET, p. 308.

16. See, e.g., William J. Dumbrell, *Covenant and Creation: A Theology of Old Testament Covenants.* Nashville: Thomas Nelson, 1984, pp. 31–33; Eugene H. Merrill, *Everlasting Dominion: A Theology of the Old Testament.* Nashville: B&H, 2006, pp. 278–281; Peter J. Gentry and Stephen J. Wellum, *Kingdom through Covenant.* Wheaton, IL: Crossway, 2012, pp. 611–618.

17. The grammatical form of both "eat" and "die" is the emphatic infinitive absolute (respectively *'ākōl, tō'kēl,* and *môt tāmût*). They may certainly and freely eat but they surely will die.

18. The form for "curse" here is the piel infinitive of *qll,* a term rarely used in covenant contexts; the usual word is *'rr* (cf. Gen. 3:17).

19. F. J. Helfmeyer (TDOT, 1:181–182) points out that this is the first of three covenants confirmed by a sign, the other two being the Abrahamic, whose sign is circumcision, and the Mosaic, whose sign is the Sabbath. God needs no reminder of anything, of course, but the sealing of covenants by some sign or other was so much a part of the tradition of covenant relationship in the ancient Near East that it would be expected here even if unnecessary. See Hermann Gunkel, *Genesis.* Trans. Mark E. Biddle. Macon, GA: Mercer University Press, 1997, pp. 150–151; Theodor H. Gaster, *Myth, Legend, and Custom in The Old Testament.* Vol. 1. New York: Harper & Row, 1975, pp. 130–131, 140–148.

20. The curse on Canaan rather than Ham has been a crux interprens from ages past. For various viewpoints, see U. Cassuto, *Commentary on Genesis II.* Jerusalem: Magnes, 1984, pp. 167–170. Cassuto understands Canaan's subjugation to both Shem and Japheth to refer to the invasion of the kings of the East against the cities of the plain in the story of Lot (Gen. 14). His arguments here are very convincing.

21. Von Rad proposes that 'What Shem is and the advantage he has over others does not consist in special human merits. But Shem's portion is Yahweh!" Gerhard von Rad, *Genesis.* OTL. London: SCM, 1961, p. 133.

22. See the following important treatments: Gary N. Knoppers, "Ancient Near Eastern Royal Grants and the Davidic Covenant: A Parallel?" JAOS 116 (1996): 670–697; Dennis J. McCarthy, *Old Testament Covenant.* Richmond: John Knox, 1972; George E. Mendenhall, "Law and Covenant in Israel and the Ancient Near East," BA 17 (1954): 50–76; Eugene H. Merrill, "The Covenant with Abraham: The Keystone of Biblical Architecture," JDT (2008): 5–17; J. A. Thompson, "Non-Biblical Covenants in the Ancient Near East and Their Relevance to Understanding the Covenant Motif in the Old Testament," ABR 8 (1960): 38–45; Moshe Weinfeld, "The Covenant of Grant in the Old Testament and in the Ancient Near East," JAOS 90 (1970): 184–203.

23. A few exegetical comments regarding Genesis 12:1–3 must suffice: (1) Yahweh's promise is to make Abraham's seed not a people but a nation (*gôy*); (2) Abraham and his seed are commanded to be a blessing (qal impv *hĕyēh*; it is not optional (v. 2); the verb translated "be blessed" in v. 3 is a niphal (*nibrĕkû*) whose sense is usually reflexive ("will bless themselves"). However, Genesis 22:18 and 26:4 render as a hithpael (*hitbĕrĕkû*). Thus, the niphal in v. 3 should (and can) be construed as a passive, "be blessed." See WO, 23.2.2; NIDOTTE, 759–760.

Chapter 3: Israel according to the Prophets

1. See Ezekiel 20:39–44; Hosea 1:11; 11:11; Joel 3:1–2; Amos 9:14–15; Micah 7:12; and Zephaniah 3:19–20.

2. The language echoes the words of Moses (Deut. 4:25–31; 30:1–10) and of Solomon in his temple dedicatory prayer (1 Kings 8:46–53). See especially (a) "seek" in Deuteronomy 4:29; (b) "return" in Deuteronomy 4:30; 30:2, 10; 1 Kings 8:47–48; (c) "do evil" in 1 Kings 8:47; (d) "show compassion" in Deuteronomy 4:31; 30:3; 1 Kings 8:50; and (e) "forgive" in 1 Kings 8:50.

3. Robert B. Chisholm, Jr., *From Exegesis to Exposition: A Practical Guide to Using Biblical Hebrew* (Grand Rapids: Baker, 1998), 176.

4. Ibid.

5. Ibid., p. 174.

6. For this methodological approach and insight, I am indebted to D. Brent Sandy, *Plowshares and Pruning Hooks* (Downers Grove, IL: InterVarsity, 2002). See his chapter "How Have Prophecies Been Fulfilled?" (pp. 129–54).

7. Taking a redactional critical approach, Cogan proposes that there were two traditions about the circumstances of Ahab's death. In dealing with the apparent contradiction between the prophecy and the account of its fulfillment, Cogan theorizes that 1 Kings 22:38 reflects an "alternate tradition . . . that was not harmonized with the Elijah tales." Mordechai Cogan, *I Kings*, AB (New York: Doubleday, 2001), 495.

8. See Leviticus 4:24, 33; 6:18 (English v. 25); 7:2; 14:13; Numbers 9:17; 2 Samuel 15:21; Jeremiah 22:12; Ezekiel 21:35 (English v. 30); Hosea 2:1 (English 1:10). For syntactical analysis of the use of a relative pronoun and clause after a construct noun, see E. Kautzsch, ed., *Gesenius' Hebrew Grammar* (tr. A. E. Cowley; 2nd ed.; Oxford: Oxford University Press, 1910), 421 (paragraph 130c).

9. Indeed Cogan and Tadmor state, "these words of Huldah remain a striking example of unfulfilled prophecy." Mordechai Cogan and Hayim Tadmor, *II Kings*, AB (New York: Doubleday, 1988), 295.

10. In the Chronicler's version of Josiah's death, the king cries out, "I am seriously wounded" (2 Chron. 35:23). This is incongruous with dying "in peace," for dying "in peace" is the antithesis of dying by the sword, as Jeremiah 34:4–5 makes clear.

11. In this regard, Andersen and Freedman state: "If Micah 5:1–5 is an eighth-century prophecy that the outcome of menacing imperialism would be the fresh creation of David's empire, then it was never fulfilled. Israel never conquered Assyria. Such a prophecy could retain its vitality in later interpretation only by postponing it to the end-time. . . . In this later setting Assyria has now become an archetypal symbol." Francis I. Andersen and David Noel Freedman, *Micah*, AB (New York: Doubleday, 2000), 481.

12. In response to those who want to date the oracle to preexilic times, Merrill argues that such a view is "insensitive to the particular lexicography of eschatological prophecy." He adds: "What must be done is to recognize that Egypt and Assyria here represent the universal distribution of the exiles of all ages. The combination or juxtaposition of Egypt and Assyria had become a cliché long before Zechariah's time. By far Israel's most persistent and hostile foes, these two nations epitomized bondage and exile throughout the OT tradition." He then compares Zechariah's use of these symbols with that of Isaiah 19:23–25. E. H. Merrill, *Haggai, Zechariah, Malachi* (Chicago: Moody, 1994), 278.

13. For another example of a long-range fulfillment of a prophecy, see 1 Kings 16:34, which records the fulfillment (approximately five hundred years later) of Joshua's curse on Jericho (Josh. 6:26). 1 Kings 16:34 characterizes this curse as prophecy by referring to it as "the word of the LORD."

14. For the New Testament evidence, see Robert B. Chisholm, Jr., *Handbook on the Prophets* (Grand Rapids: Baker, 2002), 280.

15. Ibid., 281.

16. For more on this point, see ibid., 285–86.

Chapter 4: The People and Land of Israel in Jewish Tradition

1. For clarity's sake, I will follow this usage in this chapter.

2. For a convenient outline of this Talmudic statement in context, see http://www.dafyomi.co.il/pesachim/points/ps-ps-113.htm.

3. For a convenient online explanation of the phrase, see http://www.myjewishlearning.com/holidays/Jewish_Holidays/Passover/The_Seder/Conducting_a_Seder/After_the_Meal/Next_Year_in_Jerusalem.shtml.

4. http://dovbear.blogspot.com/2010/10/what-was-significance-of-doves-olive.html

5. S. R. Driver, *The Book of the Prophet Jeremiah* (London: Hodder and Stoughton, 1906), xxxix-xli.

6. For a broad overview, with references, see Michael L. Brown, *Real Kosher Jesus: Revealing the Mysteries of the Hidden Messiah* (Lake Mary, FL: Frontline, 2012).

7. Cf. David B. Barrett, George Thomas Kurian, and Todd M. Johnson, eds., *World Christian Encyclopedia: A Comparative Survey of Churches and Religions in the Modern World* (2nd ed; New York/Oxford: Oxford Univ. Press, 2011).

8. Emil Schürer, rev. and ed. By Geza Vermes, Fergus Millar, and Matthew Black, *The History of the Jewish People in the Age of Jesus Christ* (Edinburgh: T&T Clark, 1979), 2:514–547, with extensive documentation.

9. Note that replacement theologians like Rev. Stephen Sizer err greatly in their quotation of verses like Hebrews 11:10, 16, as if the children of Israel in the Bible didn't care about having a homeland—the one promised by God. For my debate with Dr. Sizer on "How Christian Is Christian Zionism?", go to http://www.youtube.com/watch?v=22jgGE4hELI.

10. See, conveniently, Yaakov Elman and Moshe Schapiro, editors and translators, *The Living Nach: Later Prophets* (New York/Jerusalem: Moznaim, 1995), 31.

11. Ibid., 147.

12. Ibid., 150–151.

13. See Michael L. Brown, *Answering Jewish Objections to Jesus. Vol. 2: Theological Objections* (Grand Rapids: Baker, 2000), 169–186.

14. *Living Nach*, 451.

15. Ibid.

16. D. A. Carson, "Matthew," in Tremper Longman III and David E. Garland, eds., *The Expositor's Bible Commentary* (rev. ed.; Grand Rapids: Zondervan, 2010), 9:481; see there for further references.

17. A. T. Robertson, *Word Pictures in the New Testament* (Nashville: Broadman Press, 1933), 3:46–47.

18. As noted by Craig S. Keener, *A Commentary on the Gospel of Matthew* (Grand Rapids: Eerdmans, 1999), 558, and with reference to Matthew 23:39, "Perhaps as in some early Jewish teaching (cf., e.g., Ezek. 36:33; Amos 9:8–12; Tob. 13:6; Jub. 1:15–18; Rom. 11:25–27; b. Sanh. 97b), Israel's repentance was the goal of history, and her salvation was contingent on her repentance. . . ."

19. For the question of whether traditional Judaism believed in "original sin," see Brown, *Answering Jewish Objections to Jesus*, 198–208.

20. Cf. b. Chagigah 12a; Rashi to b. Baba Batra 75a.

21. See http://www.jewishencyclopedia.com/articles/758-adam.

22. *Living Nach*, 616.

23. See Andrew Bonar, ed., *Memoir and Remains of Robert Murray M'Cheyne* (repr., Carlisle, PA: Banner of Truth, 1966), 192.

Chapter 5: Israel according to the Gospels

1. For expansions on much of the following material, see Michael J. Wilkins, *Matthew*, NIVAC (Grand Rapids: Zondervan, 2004), and the forthcoming Michael J. Wilkins, A *Theology of Matthew*, Biblical Theology of the New Testament (Grand Rapids: Zondervan, forthcoming).

2. Unless otherwise noted, all translations are from the ESV.

3. For an overview of terminology and use in Matthew, see Terence L. Donaldson, *Jews and Anti-Judaism in the New Testament: Decision Points and Divergent Interpretations* (Waco: Baylor University Press, 2010), esp. 12–25, 30–54. For a wider study, see Michael J. Vlach, *Has the Church Replaced Israel?: A Theological Evaluation* (Nashville: B&H, 2010).

4. E.g., Ulrich Luz, *Matthew 21–28: A Commentary* (trans. Wilhelm C. Linss; Hermeneia; Minneapolis: Augsburg Fortress, 2005), 42–44.

5. For overviews of the issues in John's gospel, see Reimund Bieringer, Didier Pollefeyt and Frederique Vandecasteele-Vanneuville, eds. *Anti-Judaism and the Fourth Gospel* (Louisville: Westminster John Knox, 2001); Ruth Sheridan, "Issues in the Translation of οἱ Ἰουδαῖοι in the Fourth Gospel," *JBL* 132.3 (2013): 671–695.

6. E.g., Anthony Saldarini, "Reading Matthew Without Anti-Semitism," in *The Gospel of Matthew in Current Study*, ed., David E. Aune (Grand Rapids: Eerdmans, 2001), 166–184; esp. 170–173.

7. For historical overviews, see Ronald E. Diprose, *Israel and the Church: The Origin and Effects of Replacement Theology* (Bucks, U.K.: Authentic Media, 2004), esp. 175–192.

8. Those who contend that Israel has a national future, in some way, are quite diverse; see e.g., David L. Turner, "Matthew 21:43 and the Future of Israel," *BibSac* 159 (January–March 2002): 46–61; Craig A. Blaising, "The Future of Israel as a Theological Question," *JETS* 44, 3 (September 2001): 435–450. The general theme of the restoration of Israel is important for E. P. Sanders, *Jesus and Judaism* (Philadelphia: Fortress, 1985) and N. T. Wright, *Jesus and the Victory of God* (Minneapolis: Fortress, 1997), although it differs significantly. See also Matthias Konradt, *Israel, Kirch und die Völker im Matthäusevangelium*, WUNT 2/215 (Tübingen: Mohr Siebeck, 2007), e.g., 203, 393ff., who emphasizes that Israel retains its place as God's elect people, but also shares in God's salvation through the unique and necessary death and resurrection of Jesus.

9. E.g., M. Daniel Carroll R., "Blessing the Nations: Toward a Biblical Theology of Mission from Genesis," *BBR* 10.1 (2000): 17–34; Richard J Erickson, "Joseph and the Birth of Isaac in Matthew 1," *BBR* 10.1 (2000): 35–51; James Hamilton, "The Seed of the Woman and the Blessing of Abraham," *TynBull* 58.2 (2007): 253–73.

10. See Andreas J. Köstenberger, "Matthew," in *Salvation to the Ends of the Earth: A Biblical Theology of Mission*, Andreas J. Köstenberger and Peter T. O'Brien, NSBT 11 (Downers Grove, IL: InterVarsity, 2001), 89–90.

11. Cf. Scot McKnight, "Jesus and the Twelve," in *Key Events in the Life of the Historical Jesus: A Collaborative Exploration of Context and Coherence*, edited by Darrell L. Bock and Robert L. Webb, WUNT 2/247 (Tübingen: Mohr Siebeck, 2009), 181–214; Karl H. Rengstorf, "δώδεκα," *TDNT* 2:326.

12. Cf. John P. Meier, *Companions and Competitors*, vol. 3 of *A Marginal Jew: Rethinking the Historical Jesus*, ABRL (New York: Doubleday, 2001), 251–252.

13. J. Julius Scott, "Gentiles and the Ministry of Jesus: Further Observations on Matt. 10:5–6; 15:21–28," *JETS* 33.2 (1990): 161–169; David L. Turner, *Matthew*, BECNT (Grand Rapids: Baker, 2008), 264.

14. D. A. Carson, "Matthew," *The Expositor's Bible Commentary*, rev. ed. (Grand Rapids: Zondervan, 2010), 9:240.

15. Charles H. H. Scobie, "Israel and the Nations: An Essay in Biblical Theology," *TynBul* 43.2 (1992): 283–305, esp. 293–94; Carson, "Matthew," 240.

16. Cf. Klyne R. Snodgrass, *Stories with Intent: A Comprehensive Guide to the Parables of Jesus* (Grand Rapids: Eerdmans, 2008), 172–173.

17. See F. Gerald Downing, "The Woman from Syrophoenicia, and Her Doggedness: Mark 7:24–31 (Matthew 15:21–28)," *Women in the Biblical Tradition*, George J. Brooke, ed., Studies in Women and Religion 31 (Lewiston: Edwin Mellen, 1992), 129–149.

18. Gene R. Smillie, "Even the Dogs": Gentiles in the Gospel of Matthew," *JETS* 45.1 (March 2002): 73–97.

19. For somewhat similar, yet differently nuanced views, see Turner, *Matthew*, 518–519; Grant R. Osborne, *Matthew*, ZECNT (Grand Rapids: Zondervan, 2010), 790–794.

20. Robert H. Smith, "Mt 27:25—The hardest verse in Matthew's gospel," *Currents in Theology and Missiology* 17 (6, 1990): 421.

21. For discussion of these and other views, see Carson, "Matthew," 290–93, who holds to the latter.

22. Craig L. Blomberg, *Matthew*, NAC (Nashville: Broadman, 1992), 176; W. D. Davies and Dale C. Allison, *A Critical and Exegetical Commentary on the Gospel According to Saint Matthew*, 3 vols., ICC (Edinburgh: T&T Clark, 1991) 2:189–90

23. Turner, *Matthew*, 562.

24. E.g., Stephen Hre Kio, "Understanding and Translating 'Nations' in Mt 28:19," *The Bible Translator* 41.2 (1990), 230–239; Douglas R. A. Hare, *The Theme of Jewish Persecution of Christians in the Gospel According to St. Matthew* (Cambridge: Cambridge University Press, 1967).

25. E.g., see Davies and Allison, *Matthew*, 3:684; Craig S. Keener, *The Gospel of Matthew: A Socio-Rhetorical Commentary*, new edition (Grand Rapids: Eerdmans, 2009), 719–20.
26. E.g., R. T. France, *The Gospel of Matthew*, NICNT (Grand Rapids: Eerdmans, 2007), 910–928; Blomberg, *Matthew*, 357–59.
27. E.g., Davies and Allison, *Matthew*, 3:344; Robert H. Gundry, *Matthew: A Commentary on His Handbook for a Mixed Church under Persecution* (1982; Grand Rapids: Eerdmans, 1994), 485.
28. Cf. Sanders, *Jesus and Judaism*, 103; David C. Sim, "The Meaning of *palingenesia* in Mt 19.28," *JSNT* 50 (1993): 3–12.
29. Carson, "Matthew," 426; cf. George R. Beasely-Murray, *Jesus and the Kingdom of God* (Grand Rapids: Eerdmans, 1986), 275–276.
30. Cf. Robert L. Saucy, *The Case for Progressive Dispensationalism* (Grand Rapids: Zondervan, 1993), 267–69.

Chapter 6: Israel in Luke–Acts

1. Gary M. Burge, *Jesus and the Land: The New Testament Challenge to "Holy Land" Theology* (Grand Rapids: Baker, 2010).
2. See esp. Burge, *Jesus and the Land*, 56.
3. By Israel, we mean the Jewish people in a very literal sense, inclusive of the Land promises and not simply a reference to the modern state of Israel. More specifically we are referring to the role Israel plays in the program of God for the ages and that arguing the nation no longer has a role in God's purposes is not biblically defensible as this entire volume seeks to demonstrate.
4. For a wider study of this theme, see Richard Bauckham, "The Restoration of Israel in Luke-Acts," in *Restoration: Old Testament, Jewish and Christian Perspectives* (ed. James M. Scott; Leiden: Brill, 2001), 435–87. Bauckham's study focuses on seven themes, while I will address specific passages. His themes are: (1) Elijah restores the people (Luke 1:16–17, 76b–77), (2) Messiah delivers the people from oppression (Luke 1:68–73, 78–79), (3) Israel's consolation as light to the nations (Luke 2:25–38), (4) the redemption of Jerusalem and return from the diaspora (Luke 2:31–32, 38), (5) Messiah reigns forever (Luke 1:32–33; 69–71, 78–79), (6) God exalts the lowly and humbles the exalted (Luke 1:46–55), and (7) Messiah is opposed and divides Israel (Luke 2:34–35). To these we add (1) a look at the Spirit as marker of the new era and (2) the sequencing and cause for Israel being set aside and then renewed. I shall not examine Bauckham's theme 1, but the rest we shall treat to one degree or another.
5. Peter Gentry and Stephen Wellum, *Kingdom through Covenant: A Biblical Theological Understanding of the Covenants* (Wheaton: Crossway, 2012).
6. See Darrell L. Bock, *Luke 1:1–9:50* (Grand Rapids: Baker 1994), 14–18; Darrell L. Bock, *Acts* (Grand Rapids: Baker, 2007), 23–28; Darrell Bock, *A Theology of Luke and Acts: God's Promised Program Realized for All Nations* (Grand Rapids: Zondervan, 2012), 99–148.
7. I. Howard Marshall, *The Gospel of Luke: A Commentary on the Greek Text* (Grand Rapids: Eerdmans, 1978), 67.
8. Darrell L. Bock, *Proclamation from Prophecy and Pattern: Lucan Old Testament Christology* (Sheffield; Sheffield Academic Press, 1987); Mark Strauss, *The Davidic Messiah in Luke-Acts: The Promise and Its Fulfilment in Lukan Christology* (Sheffield: Sheffield Academic Press, 1995).
9. Frederick W. Danker, *Jesus and the New Age: A Commentary on Luke* (Philadelphia: Fortress, 1988), 38; Robert F. O'Toole, *The Unity of Luke's Theology: An Analysis of Luke-Acts* (Wilmington: Michael Glazier, 1984), 18, who says it means Christians.
10. Marshall, *The Gospel of Luke*, 68; Grundmann, *TDNT* 9:569 n. 483.
11. Beyer, *TDNT* 2:764.
12. David Ravens, *Luke and the Restoration of Israel* (Sheffield: Sheffield Academic Press, 1995), 38.
13. Bock, *Luke 1:1–9:50*, 123–24, 127–28.

14. Bock, *Luke* 9:51–24:53, 1251.
15. E. Earle Ellis, *The Gospel of Luke* (Greenville, S.C.: Attic, 1974), 245.
16. James M. Scott, "'And Then All Israel Will Be Saved' (Rom. 11:26)," in *Restoration: Old Testament, Jewish and Christian Perspectives* (ed. James M. Scott; Leiden: Brill, 2001), 489–527.
17. Richard J. Dillon, *From Eye-Witnesses to Ministers of the Word: Tradition and Composition in Luke 24* (Rome: Pontifical Biblical Institute, 1978), 129–30.
18. Danker, *Jesus and the New Age*, 392.
19. On *apokathistēmi* (restore), see Mal. 3:23 LXX (4:6 Eng.), where it is an eschatological technical term, and Dan. 4:36 LXX. Acts 3:21 will return to this idea.
20. John R. W. Stott, *The Message of Acts* (Downers Grove, IL: InterVarsity, 1990), 41.
21. Hilary LeCornu and Joseph Shulam, *A Commentary on the Jewish Roots of Acts* (vol. 1; Jerusalem: Academon, 2003), 15.
22. Michael E. Fuller, *The Restoration of Israel: Israel's Re-gathering and the Fate of the Nations in Early Jewish Literature and Luke-Acts* (Berlin: DeGruyter, 2006), 242.
23. Pace Ernst Haenchen, *The Acts of the Apostles: A Commentary* (trans. B. Noble and G. Shinn; Oxford: Blackwell, 1987), 143.
24. Bauckham, "The Restoration of Israel in Luke–Acts," 477, says this speech "is full of restoration terminology."
25. Kremer, EDNT 1:95.
26. BAGD 63; BDAG 75; Schweizer, *TDNT* 9:664.
27. Schweizer, *TDNT* 9:664.
28. I have developed this imagery in my *The Real Lost Gospel: Reclaiming the Gospel as Good News* (Nashville: Broadman & Holman, 2010), 23–37.
29. Fuller, *The Restoration of Israel*, 239.

Chapter 7: The Jewish People according to the Book of Romans

1. These scholars are sometimes called "replacement" theologians or "supersessionists" because they are often characterized as teaching that "the Church replaces and supersedes Israel." They object to the label, however, and claim that those of us who use it are employing loaded language. I will label them "fulfillment theologians" to avoid the accusation. "Fulfillment" seems to be the more neutral term they prefer.
2. These points are drawn from Michael J. Vlach's *The Church as a Replacement of Israel: An Analysis of Supersessionism* (Edition Iserlogie, vol. 2) (Frankfurt: Peter Lang, 2009), 83–94, 121–32. See also Vlach's, *Has the Church Replaced Israel? A Theological Evaluation* (B & H Academic, 2010); and "Has the Church Replaced Israel?: A Current Evaluation of Replacement Theology," An Unpublished Paper Submitted to the Evangelical Theological Society, November 19–21, 2013, accessible at http://www.mikevlach.citymax.com/f/Replacement_Theology_for_ETS_DSG2.pdf (accessed 11/24/13). See also the helpful chapter by Craig A. Blaising in this book.
3. In what follows on the Abrahamic Covenant, Abraham's seed, the nations, and God's blessings, I am heavily indebted to the fine work of Mark Forman, *The Politics of Inheritance in Romans* (SNTSMS 148) (Cambridge: Cambridge University Press, 2011).
4. Forman, *Politics of Inheritance*, 76–77.
5. Ibid., 77–78, 87.
6. Israel's "mediatorial role" is revelational, but not salvific. In other words, it is God, not Israel, who will save and bless the world. But He uses Israel as a means to connect with the world, like a priest among his people, to reveal His grace and might and to attract the nations.
7. For this material from Early Judaism, see Gerhard H. Visscher, *Romans 4 and the New Perspective on Paul: Faith Embraces the Promise* (Studies in Biblical Literature, vol. 122) (New York: Peter Lang, 2009), 198–99 n. 197.
8. N. T. Wright recognizes that many OT and Early Judaism texts propound Israel's possession of the nations while still having a stake in its own land, but concludes "this is not Paul's view." "[I]n Paul's thought ethnic, national Israel

will not rule the world. . . . Paul's development of the 'inheritance' theme, so important in Genesis 15 and elsewhere in the Pentateuch, here takes a decisive turn" ("Romans," in *The New Interpreter's Bible*, vol. 10, ed. Leander E. Kleck *et al.* [Nashville: Abingdon, 2000], 495–96.

9. Sizer, *Zion's Christian Soldiers? The Bible, Israel and the Church* (Downers Grove, IL: InterVarsity, 2007), 95.

10. John Piper rightly notes that the force of the present tense "are" in 9:4 confounds attempts to relegate Israel's privileged position strictly to the past. See Piper's *The Justification of God: An Exegetical and Theological Study of Romans 9:1-23* (Grand Rapids: Baker, 1993), 24–25. It is unbelieving Israelites in Paul's day, and ours, who *are* the holders of these privileges, *contra* Sizer, *Zion's Christian Soldiers?*, 165–67.

11. Suggested by Richard H. Bell, *The Irrevocable Call of God: An Inquiry into Paul's Theology of Israel* (WUNT, vol. 184) (Tübingen: Mohr Siebeck, 2005), 381.

12. O. Palmer Robertson, *The Israel of God: Yesterday, Today, and Tomorrow* (Phillipsburg, NJ.: P & R Publishing, 2000), 173.

13. The *fullness* probably refers to "the full number" of Jewish people who are saved. Paul discussed numbers of individual people groups throughout Romans 11 (see "the rest," 11:7; "save some of them," 11:14; the "fullness of the Gentiles," 11:25; "all Israel," 11:26). In addition, in secular Greek, when referring to people, *fullness* was used to denote the entire citizenry of a Greek city (for the ancient references, see Gerhard Delling, *Theological Dictionary of the New Testament*, ed. Gerhard Friedrich, trans. Geoffrey W. Bromiley, vol. 6 (Grand Rapids: Eerdmans, 1968), 299. For more evidence, see Paul Jewett, *Romans: A Commentary* (Hermeneia) (Minneapolis: Fortress, 2007), 677–78.

14. See Wright's *The Climax of the Covenant* (Minneapolis: Fortress Press, 1991), esp. 231–67; "The Paul of History and the Apostle of Faith," *Tyndale Bulletin* 29 (1978): 83; "Romans and the Theology of Paul," in *Society of Biblical Literature 1992 Seminar Papers*, ed. Eugene H. Lovering, Jr. (Atlanta: Scholars Press, 1992), 184–213; "Romans and the Theology of Paul," in *Pauline Theology, Volume III: Romans*, ed. David M. Hay and E. Elizabeth Johnson (Minneapolis: Fortress, 1995), 56–62 (these last two works are distinguished in my article by their dates); "Romans," *The New Interpreter's Bible*, ed. Leander E. Keck, *et al.* (Nashville: Abingdon, 2002), vol. 10, 687–93; *The New Testament and the People of God* (Minneapolis: Fortress, 1992), 236–46. For a similar approach, see also Ralph P. Martin, *Reconciliation: A Study of Paul's Theology* (Grand Rapids: Zondervan, 1989), 134–35.

15. For a more detailed summary of Wright's position and an evaluation of it, see Michael G. Vanlaningham, "An Evaluation of N.T. Wright's View of Israel in Romans 11," *BibSac* 170 (April–June, 2013): 179–193.

16. "Romans and the Theology of Paul," 1992, 186–187. Similarly, Burge, *Jesus and the Land*, 90.

17. Ibid., 195, 197, 202. See, in addition, G. K. Beale, *A New Testament Biblical Theology* (Grand Rapids: Baker, 2011), esp. 704–27 where he treats the relevant texts from Paul's epistles.

18. *Climax*, 240. Similarly, see Carl E. Olson, *Will Catholics Be "Left Behind"?* (San Francisco: Ignatius, 2003), 215–21, in his discussion of the nature of the Church and Israel. This is also Sizer's position (*Zion's Christian Soldiers?*, 57–61, 171) and Robertson's (*The Israel of God*, 188–91).

19. See his "Romans," 690. Wright cites Galatians 3:28–29 ("There is neither Jew nor Greek . . . for you are all one in Christ Jesus.") and Philippians 3:3–4 ("for we are the true circumcision") as additional support for redefining "all Israel" to include more than Jewish believers.

20. In his comments on Romans 9:31; 10:19, 21, where "Israel" occurs, Wright ascribes to the word the English gloss "Israel" with full-fledged ethnic Jews as its referent, and does not appear to see "Israel" broadened to include Gentiles (see "Romans," 648–49 for his comments on 9:31, and 669–70 for those on 10:19 and 21). For further evidence against Wright's understanding, see Peter Stuhlmacher, *Paul's Letter to the Romans: A Commentary* (Louisville: Westminster/John

Knox Press, 1994), 160–61; and R. B. Hays, *Echoes of Scripture in the Letters of Paul* (New Haven: Yale University Press, 1989), 163–64.

21. "Romans," 690. See also Robertson, *The Israel of God*, 187–90. Though he ultimately rejects the idea, Jack Cottrell offers the suggestion that in 9:24–26 Paul might conceive of the remnant as consisting in both Jews and Gentiles, which would support Wright's understanding (*Romans* [The College Press NIV Commentary] [Joplin, MO: College Press, 1998], 2:283).

22. For a full critique of this third point, see, once again, Vanlaningham, "Evaluation," 186–91.

23. Thomas R. Schreiner, *Paul, Apostle of God's Glory in Christ: A Pauline Theology* (Downers Grove: InterVarsity, 2001), 477–78.

24. See "Romans and the Theology of Paul," 1992, 204, 207. Robertson maintains that Israel's hardening continues even after the fullness of the Gentiles has come in, so that there cannot be a full-orbed salvation of all ethnic Jews in the future (*Israel of God*, 179–80). For a critique of his view, see Vanlaningham, *Christ, the Savior of Israel*, 187–90.

25. Dongsu Kim ("Reading Paul's [and thus all Israel will be saved, Rom. 11:26a] in the Context of Romans," *Calvin Theological Journal* 45 [2010]: 326) maintains wrongly that "will be saved" is a gnomic future and thus has no true future reference. Regarding the characteristics of the gnomic future, Daniel B. Wallace writes, "The future is very rarely used to indicate the likelihood that a *generic* event will take place. The idea is not that a particular event is in view, but that such events are true to life" (*Greek Grammar Beyond the Basics: An Exegetical Syntax of the New Testament* [Grand Rapids: Zondervan, 1996], 571, emphasis his). But "all Israel will be saved" hardly denotes a *generic*, non-particular, true-to-life act. If the salvation of all Israel were to take place throughout the Church age, and even during Paul's day, then Paul might have used the present tense more advantageously, aspectually viewing this salvation as an unfolding process.

26. For a helpful, detailed discussion of "all Israel" in the LXX, see the fine discussion by James M. Scott, "'Und So Wird Ganz Israel Gerettet Werden' (Röm 11,26)," in *Christen, Juden und die Zukunft Israels: Beiträge zur Israellehre aus Geschichte und Theologie* (Edition Israelogie, vol. 1) (Berlin: Peter Lang, 2009), 55–95.

27. Similarly Bell, *The Irrevocable Call of God*, 381. *Contra* Chapman, *Whose Promised Land?*, 229.

28. For a fuller discussion of the implications of these two passages as they relate to the timing of Israel's salvation, See Michael G. Vanlaningham, *Christ, the Savior of Israel: An Evaluation of the Dual Covenant* and Sonderweg *Interpretations of Paul's Letters* (Edition Israelogie, vol. 5) (New York: Peter Lang, 2012), 133–39.

29. Christopher R. Bruno, "The Deliverer from Zion: The Source(s) and Function of Paul's Citation in Romans 11:26–27," *Tyndale Bulletin* 59 (2008): 124–25.

30. Several caveats are in order regarding Bruno's observations, but space will not permit discussion of them here. See Vanlaningham, *Christ, the Savior of Israel*, 229–30.

31. For more connections between Isaiah 59:20–21 and Paul in Romans 11:26b–27a, see J. Ross Wagner, *Heralds of the Good News: Isaiah and Paul in Concern in the Letter to the Romans* (Leiden: Brill, 2002), 276–94.

32. Again, see Wagner, *Heralds of the Good News*, 284.

33. Matt Waymeyer, "The Dual Status of Israel in Romans 11:28," *The Master's Seminary Journal* 16 (Spring 2005): 57–71.

34. Waymeyer, "Dual Status," 71.

35. So says Bell, *The Irrevocable Call of God*, 379. *Contra* Robertson, *The Israel of God*, 38, and Wright, "Romans," 693, who aver that 11:29 is solely about God's redemptive grace.

36. Burge (*Jesus and the Land*, 90–91), after arguing for the irrevocability of the gifts and calling of God for Israel, then quite inexplicably, writes, "Paul's bold treatment of the law, Jerusalem and even the Temple all point to an implicit rejection of Jewish territoriality. . . . Moreover God's promise to Abraham is

not for Judea and its restoration but for the world. An ethnocentric territoriality anchored to ancestral theological claims cannot survive Paul's fresh rearrangement of God's saving purposes in Christ."

37. BDAG, 53.
38. Regarding the recurrence of "now" in 11:30–31, see Vanlaningham, *Christ, the Savior of Israel*, 257–61.
39. Mark A. Seifrid, "Romans," in *Commentary on the New Testament Use of the Old Testament*, eds. G. K. Beale and D. A. Carson (Grand Rapids: Baker, 2007), 687.
40. For the details of the meaning of the OT verses in their contexts and how Paul applies them to the Messiah, see Seifrid, "Romans," 688–91.
41. Seifrid, "Romans," 688, and Wagner, *Heralds of the Good News*, 316–26.
42. Bell, *The Irrevocable Call of God*, 379. *Contra* the fulfillment advocates who maintain that Jesus fulfills the promises of Israel and thereby deny the Jewish people of realization of *all* the promises God made to them.

Chapter 8: Israel according to the Book of Hebrews and the General Epistles

1. L. T. Johnson, *Hebrews: A Commentary* (Louisville: Westminster John Knox Press, 2006) 43–44.
2. See the concise summary of parallels in S. McKnight, *The Letter of James* (Grand Rapids: Eerdmans, 2011) 24–26.
3. Among others, see J. Painter, *Just James: The Brother of Jesus in History and Tradition* (Minneapolis: Fortress, 1999); B. D. Chilton and C. A. Evans (eds.), *James the Just and Christian Origins* (Leiden: Brill, 1999); B. D. Chilton and J. Neusner (eds.), *The Brother of Jesus: James the Just and His Mission* (Louisville: Westminster John Knox, 2001).
4. In addition to McKnight's commentary, see also L. T. Johnson, *The Letter of James* (Garden City: Doubleday, 1995); D. J. Moo, *The Letter of James* (Grand Rapids: Eerdmans, 2000).
5. See the discussion in P. H. Davids, *The First Epistle of Peter* (Grand Rapids: Eerdmans, 1990) 3–7; P. J. Achtemeier, *1 Peter* (Minneapolis: Fortress, 1996) 1–9.
6. For a very helpful study of letter-writing in late antiquity, see E. R. Richards, *Paul and First-Century Letter Writing: Secretaries, Composition and Collection* (Downers Grove, IL: InterVarsity, 2004). One should remember what Josephus says about the composition of his own works. At the beginning of *Jewish Wars*, he states that he translated his Hebrew (or Aramaic?) account into Greek (*J.W.* 1.3). But in the later *Against Apion*, Josephus acknowledges, in reference to *Jewish Wars*, that "with the aid of some assistants for the sake of the Greek. . . . I committed to writing my narrative of the events" (*Ag. Apion* 1.50). Thanks to these and other assistants all of Josephus' surviving works were written in good quality Greek, but this in itself does not tell us how well Josephus himself could speak or write Greek. The quality of the Greek of 1 Peter tells us about the scribe and/or composer; it tells us nothing about Peter's facility with the Greek language.
7. More than 20 *Enoch* and related scrolls were found at Qumran. Indeed, at Qumran *Enoch* is better represented than many of the books of Scripture.
8. Peter's "she" is not his wife, who did travel with him (1 Cor. 9:5; Matt. 8:14); it is the church, the *ecclesia*, as in 2 John 1, 13. Rightly Davids, *First Epistle of Peter*, 201–2.
9. The adjective *isotimon* occurs only here in the New Testament. The word occurs five times in Josephus (e.g., *Ant.* 12.119: the king gave the Jews "privileges equal to those of the Macedonians and Greeks") and almost three dozen times in Philo (e.g., *Sacrifices of Abel and Cain* 8: "God accounts a wise man as entitled to equal honour").
10. See the discussion in P. H. Davids, *The Letters of 2 Peter and Jude* (Grand Rapids: Eerdmans, 2006) 161–62.
11. On the Promised Land as the place of God's "rest," see Deut. 3:20; 12:9–10; 25:19; Josh. 1:13, 15; 21:44; 22:4. As Israel was about to cross the Jordan River

and begin the conquest of the Promised Land, Joshua commands: "Remember the word which Moses the servant of the Lord commanded you, saying, 'The Lord your God is providing you a place of rest, and will give you this land'" (Josh. 1:13). The Promised Land is the place of rest.

12. See the discussion in M. E. Tate, *Psalms 51–100* (Dallas, TX: Word, 1990) 502–4.

Chapter 9: Israel and Hermeneutics

1. For an introduction to biblical hermeneutics, see William W. Klein, Craig L. Blomberg, and Robert L. Hubbard, Jr., *Introduction to Biblical Interpretation* (Dallas: Word Publishing, 1993); Walter C. Kaiser, Jr., and Moisés Silva, *An Introduction to Biblical Hermeneutics: The Search for Meaning* (Grand Rapids: Zondervan, 1994); Grant R. Osborne, *The Hermeneutical Spiral: A Comprehensive Introduction to Biblical Interpretation* (Downers Grove: IVP, 1991); G. B. Caird, *The Language and Imagery of the Bible* (Philadelphia: Westminster Press, 1980). On aspects of literary hermeneutics, see Robert Alter, *The Art of Biblical Narrative* (New York: Basic Books, 1981; rev. ed. 2011); idem, *The Art of Biblical Poetry* (New York: Basic Books, 1985; rev. ed. 2011); Tremper Longman III, *Literary Approaches to Biblical Interpretation*, Foundations of Contemporary Interpretation 3 (Grand Rapids: Zondervan, 1987); V. Phillips Long, *The Art of Biblical History*, Foundations of Contemporary Interpretation 5 (Grand Rapids: Zondervan, 1994). On the broader field of hermeneutics, including philosophical hermeneutics, see Anthony C. Thiselton, *The Two Horizons: New Testament Hermeneutics and Philosophical Description with Special Reference to Heidegger, Bultmann, Gadamer and Wittgenstein* (Exeter: Paternoster, 1980); idem, *New Horizons in Hermeneutics* (Grand Rapids: Zondervan, 1992). For a recent symposium covering different aspects of the field, see Stanley E. Porter and Beth M. Stovell, *Biblical Hermeneutics: Five Views* (Downers Grove: IVP, 2012).

2. On Supersessionism, see Kendall Soulen, *The God of Israel and Christian Theology* (Minneapolis: Fortress, 1996); Michael J. Vlach, *Has the Church Replaced Israel? A Theological Evaluation* (Nashville: B&H, 2010); Calvin L. Smith, ed. *The Jews, Modern Israel and the New Supersessionism* (Lampeter, UK: Kings Divinity Press, 2009); Barry Horner, *Future Israel: Why Christian Anti-Judaism Must Be Challenged* (Nashville: B&H, 2008). As an example of the debate in terms of *literal* vs. *spiritual* hermeneutics, see the discussions of interpretation in John F. Walvoord, *The Millennial Kingdom* (Grand Rapids: Zondervan, 1959); J. Dwight Pentecost, *Things to Come: A Study in Biblical Eschatology* (Grand Rapids: Zondervan, 1958); and Oswald T. Allis, *Prophecy and the Church* (Philadelphia: Presbyterian and Reformed, 1945).

3. W. D. Davies, *The Gospel and the Land: Early Christianity and Jewish Territorial Doctrine* (Berkeley: University of California Press, 1974. See also his *The Territorial Dimension of Judaism: With a Symposium and Further Reflections* (Minneapolis: Fortress, 1991.

4. Ibid., 368.

5. See for example, Gary M. Burge, *Whose Land? Whose Promise? What Christians Are Not Being Told about Israel and the Palestinians* (Cleveland: Pilgrim Press, 2003); idem, *Jesus and the Land: The New Testament Challenge to 'Holy Land' Theology* (Grand Rapids: Baker, 2010); Philip Johnston and Peter Walker, eds. *The Land of Promise: Biblical, Theological, and Contemporary Perspectives* (Downers Grove: IVP, 2000); P. W. L. Walker, ed. *Jerusalem Past and Present in the Purposes of God*, 2nd ed. (Grand Rapids: Baker, 1994); P. W. L. Walker, *Jesus and the Holy City: New Testament Perspectives on Jerusalem* (Grand Rapids: Eerdmans, 1996).

6. Geerhardus Vos, *The Pauline Eschatology* (Grand Rapids: Baker, 1930); idem, *Biblical Theology: Old and New Testaments* (Grand Rapids: Eerdmans, 1948); O. Palmer Robertson, *The Christ of the Covenants* (Phillipsburg, NJ: P&R, 1980).

7. William J. Dumbrell, *The Search for Order: Biblical Eschatology in Focus* (Grand Rapids: Baker, 1994); Graeme Goldsworthy, *According to Plan: The Unfolding*

Revelation of God in the Bible (Downers Grove: IVP, 1991); idem, *Christ-Centered Biblical Theology: Hermeneutical Foundations and Principles* (Downers Grove: IVP, 2012); T. Desmond Alexander, *From Eden to the New Jerusalem: An Introduction to Biblical Theology* (Grand Rapids: Kregel, 2008); idem, *From Paradise to the Promised Land: An Introduction to the Pentateuch*, 2nd ed. (Grand Rapids: Baker, 2002).

8.   See Richard Davidson, *Typology in Scripture: A Study of Hermeneutical TUPOS Structures*, Andrews University Seminary Doctoral Dissertation Series 2 (Berrien Springs, MI: Andrews University, 1981). See also, Stephen J. Wellum, "Hermeneutical Issues in 'Putting Together' the Covenants," in Peter J. Gentry and Stephen J. Wellum, *Kingdom through Covenant: A Biblical-Theological Understanding of the Covenants* (Wheaton: Crossway, 2012), 81–126.

9.   David L. Wolfe, *Epistemology: The Justification of Belief* (Downers Grove, IVP, 1982), 50–55.

10. G. K. Beale, *A New Testament Biblical Theology: The Unfolding of the Old Testament in the New* (Grand Rapids: Baker, 2011).

11. Ibid., 710.

12. Michael E. Fuller, *The Restoration of Israel: Israel's Re-gathering and the Fate of the Nations in Early Jewish Literature and Luke-Acts* (Berlin: Walter de Gruyter, 2006). A better book is edited by James Scott, *Restoration, Old Testament, Jewish and Christian Perspectives* (Leiden: Brill, 2001). Although necessarily limited in the texts that it examines, it does feature studies on Romans 11:26 and Acts 1–3. The articles by Richard Baucham ["The Restoration of Israel in Luke-Acts," 435–87] and James Scott ["'And then all Israel will be saved' (Rom 11:26)," 489–527] on these texts are excellent.

13. The use of the web metaphor for logical systems can be found in W. V. O. Quine, *From a Logical Point of View*, 2nd ed. (New York: Harper, 1961). See the discussion in Wolfe, *Epistemology*, 44–45.

14. J. L. Austin, *How to Do Things With Words* (Oxford: Univ. Press, 1962); John Searle, *Speech-Acts: An Essay in the Philosophy of Language* (Cambridge: Univ. Press, 1969).

15. See for example, Richard Briggs, *Words in Action* (Edinburgh: T&T Clark, 2001); Thiselton, *New Horizons in Hermeneutics*; Kevin Vanhoozer, *Is There a Meaning in This Text?* (Grand Rapids: Zondervan, 1998).

16. Richard Briggs, "Speech-Act Theory," in *Dictionary for Theological Interpretation of the Bible*, ed. Kevin J. Vanhoozer (Grand Rapids: Baker, 2005), 763.

17. For the terminology of new creation eschatology in relation to what I call *spiritual vision eschatology*, see Craig A. Blaising, "Premillennialism," in *Three Views on the Millennium and Beyond*, ed. Darrell L. Bock (Grand Rapids: Zondervan, 1999), 160–81. Some who have affirmed this type of eschatology include N. T. Wright, *Surprised by Hope: Rethinking Heaven, the Resurrection, and the Mission of the Church* (New York: HarperOne, 2008); idem, *New Heavens, New Earth: The Biblical Picture of the Christian Hope*, Grove Biblical Series B11 (Cambridge: Grove Books, 1999); Jurgen Moltmann, *The Coming of God: Christian Eschatology*, trans. Margret Kohl (Minneapolis: Fortress, 1996); J. Richard Middleton, *A New Heaven and a New Earth: Reclaiming Biblical Eschatology* (Grand Rapids: Baker, forthcoming); Donald Gowan, *Eschatology in the Old Testament* (Philadelphia: Fortress, 1986); Douglas Moo, "Nature in the New Creation: New Testament Eschatology and the Environment," *Journal of the Evangelical Theological Society* 49 (2006): 449–88.

18. Paul's words on the future glory of the present creation in Romans 8 also point the a renovation of the present creation rather than an annihilation and re-creation *de novo*.

19. N. T. Wright, *Surprised by Hope*.

20. A redefinition of Israel lies at the heart of Wright's literary project. See for example, N. T. Wright, *The Climax of the Covenant: Christ and the Law in Pauline Theology* (Minneapolis: Fortress, 1991), 29, 61–62, 240, 250; idem, *The New Testament and the People of God*, Christian Origins and the Question of God, vol. 1 (Min-

neapolis: Fortress, 1992), 457–58; idem, *Jesus and the Victory of God*, Christian Origins and the Question of God, vol. 2 (Minneapolis: Fortress, 1996), 446, 471.
21.   Craig A. Blaising, "The Future of Israel as a Theological Question," *Journal of the Evangelical Theological Society* (2001): 435–50, republished in *To the Jew First: A Case for Jewish Evangelism in Scripture and History*, ed. Darrell L. Bock and Mitch Glaser (Grand Rapids: Kregel, 2008), 102–21.

Chapter 10: Israel as a Necessary Theme in Biblical Theology

1.   Elmer Martens, "Tackling Old Testament Theology," JETS 20 (1977), 123, cited in Paul R. House, "Biblical Theology and the Wholeness of Scripture," *Biblical Theology* (ed. Scott J. Hafemann; Downer's Grove: IVP, 2002): 267–279.
2.   See Edward W. Kink III and Darian R. Lockett, *Understanding Biblical Theology* (Grand Rapids: Zondervan, 2012).
3.   For example: William Dumbrell, *The Search for Order* (Eugene, OR: Wipf and Stock, 1994); and specific to our topic—C. Marvin Pate, J. Scott Duvall, J. Daniel Hays et al. *The Story of Israel* (Downers Grove: Intervarsity Press, 2004).
4.   G. K. Beale, *The Temple and the Church's Mission* (NSBT 17; Downers Grove: IVP, 2004); and John Sailhammer, *The Pentateuch as Narrative* (Grand Rapids, IL: Zondervan, 1992).
5.   James Chukwuma Okoye, *Israel and the Nations* (ASMS 39; Maryknoll, NY: Orbis 2006), 24–34; and Roy E. Ciampa, "The History of Redemption," in Scott J. Hafemann and Paul R. House (eds.) *Central Themes in Biblical Theology* (Grand Rapids: Baker, 2007), 259–263.
6.   Bruce K. Waltke, *An Old Testament Theology* (Grand Rapids: Zondervan, 2007), 194–203.
7.   Dan J. McCartney, "Ecce Homo: The Coming of the Kingdom As the Restoration of Human Viceregency," *WTJ* 56 (1994), 1–21.
8.   Waltke, *OT Theology*, 143–169.
9.   Ibid., 181–183.
10.   Erich Sauer, *The King of the Earth* (London: Paternoster, 1962), 92–100.
11.   McCartney, "Ecce Homo," 8.
12.   Dumbrell, *Creation and Covenant*, 26–27.
13.   Ibid., 42.
14.   The language of Gen. 12:3—in you all of the "families" of the earth will be blessed (or make themselves blessed)—is soon put in terms of the "nations" in Genesis 49:10.
15.   Daniel Isaac Block, *The Gods of the Nations: Studies in Ancient Near Eastern National Theology*, ETSM 2 (Winona Lake, IN: Evangelical Theological Society, 1988). Block sees the fundamental elements of a nation as common ethnicity, territory, theology, politics, and language.
16.   Merrill, Everlasting Dominion, 298.
17.   Martin Buber, *The Kingship of God* (New York: Harper, 1967), 124 ff.
18.   David B. Torrance, *Israel God's Servant* (Carlisle, UK: Paternoster, 2007).
19.   Norman H. Snaith, *The Distinctive Ideas of the Old Testament* (London: Epworth, 1944), 102.
20.   Dumbrell, *Creation and Covenant*, 87.
21.   See on this Stephen Dempster, *Dominion and Dynasty* (NSBT 15; Downers Grove, IL: IVP, 2003), 47–53.
22.   I. Howard Marshall, *New Testament Theology* (Downers Grove: IVP, 2004), 719n10. The irony is that Marshall himself in this major work addresses the new covenant only in a footnote!
23.   Principle passages of the new covenant include: Jer. 24:7; 32:38–40; 50:5; Ezek. 16:60; 34:25; 36:27–28; 37:26; Isa. 42:6; 49:8; 54:10; 55:1–5; 59:21; 61:8; Mal. 3:1; cf. 2:1–9.
24.   Dumbrell is correct to note in this how the prophet has predicted the coming obsolescence of his own office and the entire Temple cult (William Dumbrell, *The End of the Beginning Revelation 21–22 and the Old Testament* (Eugene, OR: Wipf and Stock, 2001), 92–93.

25. Walther Eichrodt, *Theology of the Old Testament* (2 vols; Philadelphia: Westminster, 1961), 2:59.
26. See here Andreas Köstenberger and Peter T. O'Brien, *Salvation to the Ends of the Earth* (NSBT 11; Downers Grove: IVP, 2001), 42–49, 252–53.
27. For example, N. T. Wright, *Jesus and the Victory of God* (Minneapolis: Fortress, 1997).
28. Peter Walker, *The Land of Promise* (Downers Grove, IL: IVP, 2000), esp. 81–120.
29. Andrio Konig, *The Eclipse of Christ in Eschatology* (Grand Rapids: Eerdmans, 1989).
30. Scot McKnight, *A New Vision for Israel* (Grand Rapids: Eerdmans, 1999).
31. Sauer, *King of the Earth*, 98–99.
32. Hermann Ridderbos, *Paul: An Outline of His Theology* (Grand Rapids: Eerdmans, 1975), 44ff.
33. J. I. Packer considers "Father" as the *Christian* name for God. The personal intimacy of 'Abba' was not a knowledge Israel had of the divine love (J. I. Packer, *Knowing God* [Downer Groves, IL: IVP, 1973], 182, 183; cf. Donald Guthrie, *New Testament Theology* [Downers Grove, IL: InterVarsity, 1981], 77, n. 5.).
34. D. J. Antwi, "Did Jesus Consider His Death to Be an Atoning Sacrifice?" *Int* 45 [1991]: 17–28.
35. Scott J. Hafemann, "The Covenant Relationship," in *Central Themes in Biblical Theology* (Scott J. Hafemann and Paul R. House eds; Grand Rapids: Baker, 2007), 59.
36. This section adapted from Robert L. Saucy, "Is Christ the Fulfillment of National Israel's Prophecies? Yes and No!" unpublished presentation at national meeting of the Evangelical Theological Society, 2010.
37. David Van Drunen, *Living in God's Two Kingdoms* (Wheaton, IL: Crossway, 2010).
38. See Craig Blaising in *Three Views of the Millennium and Beyond* (Zondervan, 1993), 214–215.
39. 2 Bar. 29.1–30.5; 4 Ezra 6–7; Sib. Or. 5.414–30; Ascen. Isa. 4.1–18; Justin, Dial. 81.3–4.
40. Richard Bauckham, *The Theology of the Book of Revelation* (Cambridge, UK: Cambridge University Press, 1993), 69.
41. Allan J. McNicol, *The Conversion of the Nations in Revelation* (LNTS 438; London: T& T Clark, 2011), 46.
42. McNicol, *Conversion of the Nations*, 59.
43. Ibid., 66.

Chapter 11: Israel in the Land as an Eschatological Necessity?

1. Perhaps some may wonder why I employ an indirect argument if there are direct proofs to establish Israel's right to possess the land. The reason is that if a theological conviction is true, there should be Scriptures which directly support it, but the doctrine must also fit with other biblical and theological teachings we know to be true. In other words, doctrines cannot be true in their own right and yet contradict one another. My approach in this essay is to note biblical truths about the end times (but not about Israel's return to and possession of the land *per se*) that must be fulfilled and to ask whether these trues confirm or disconfirm the notion that Israel not only will but must possess the land as a national entity. My contention is that Israel's possession of the land and control of her own political, military and religious life does fit with these other end-time events I shall discuss. In fact, if Israel does not possess the land in the way just mentioned, these other end-time prophecies cannot be fulfilled.
2. Here the point is that each day of a literal week stands for a year. Hence, one week (seven literal days) stands for seven years. The prophecy, then, predicts that there will be seventy groups of weeks, that is, seventy of these groups of seven years, or four hundred ninety years. For an excellent, thorough discussion of Daniel 9:24–27 see Paul D. Feinberg, "An Exegetical and Theological Study of Daniel 9:24–27," in John S. and Paul D. Feinberg, eds., *Tradition and*

Testament: Essays in Honor of Charles Lee Feinberg (Chicago: Moody Press, 1981).
3. Here I suspect that this passage connects with the image of the beast that is given life to talk, mentioned in Rev. 13:15. This cannot be conclusively confirmed, but what Revelation 13 says, if done in the temple, would certainly desolate and desecrate it!
4. Some may object that Daniel 9:27 can be fulfilled by some non-Jewish nation that controls Jerusalem and Israel. However, this is highly unlikely for several reasons. The making of a peace treaty with the willful king assumes that the nation wants to maintain some sort of political sovereignty over itself. But, if the nation is run by non-Jews, why not capitulate to the willful king and let him run the nation? Moreover, if Israel is basically non-Jewish during the seventieth week, why would sacrifices be made in the Temple? What other major religion would require such sacrifices, and what evidence is there that a country with that religion would gain control over Israel for the seventieth week? However, most problematic with this alternate interpretation of verse 27 is that if it is true, then the first sixty-nine of Daniel's seventy weeks are about Israel, while the seventieth week is not about her at all. This is problematic because Daniel is told that all seventy weeks are about his people, the Jews. So, while it is imaginable that Daniel 9:27 is about an Israel filled and controlled by non-Jews, the evidence against that idea is overwhelming!
5. Charles L. Feinberg, *God Remembers: A Study of the Book of Zechariah* (New York: American Board of Missions to the Jews, 1965), p. 249.

Chapter 12: Israel in Church History

1. For a detailed discussion of Replacement Theology/Supersessionism see Michael J. Vlach, *Has the Church Replaced Israel? A Theological Evaluation* (Nashville, TN: B & H Academic, 2010); Barry E. Horner, *Future Israel: Why Christian Anti-Judaism Must Be Challenged* (Nashville, TN: B & H Academic, 2008).
2. This is not a statement that unbelieving Israelites will experience the blessings of the covenants and promises. One must express faith for that to occur. But it does reveal that the covenants and promises to the nation Israel have not been forfeited.
3. Justin declared, "For the true spiritual Israel, and descendants of Judah, Jacob, Isaac, and Abraham . . . are we who have been led to God through this crucified Christ." Justin Martyr, *Dialogue with Trypho* 11, *The Ante-Nicene Fathers*, eds. Alexander Roberts and James Donaldson (Grand Rapids: Eerdmans, 1950–51), 1:200. Hereafter all references to this set will be *ANF*.
4. Jeffrey S. Siker, *Disinheriting the Jews: Abraham in Early Christian Controversy* (Louisville, KY: Westminster/John Knox, 1991), 195.
5. Ibid.
6. Lee Martin McDonald, "Anti-Judaism in the Early Church Fathers," in *Anti-Semitism and Early Christianity: Issues of Polemic and Faith*, eds. Craig A. Evans and Donald A. Hagner (Minneapolis: Fortress, 1993), 230.
7. Tertullian, *An Answer to the Jews* 1, *ANF* 3:151.
8. Clement, *The Instructor* 2.8, *ANF* 2:256.
9. Tertullian, *An Answer to the Jews* 1, *ANF* 3:152.
10. Cyprian, *Three Books of Testimonies Against the Jews, ANF* 5:507.
11. Carl F. Ehle, Jr., "Prolegomena to Christian Zionism in America: The Views of Increase Mather and William E. Blackstone Concerning the Doctrine of the Restoration of Israel," Ph.D. Dissertation, New York University, 1977, 31.
12. Justin Martyr, *Dialogue with Trypho*, 80, *ANF*, 1:239.
13. Tertullian, *On Modesty*, 8, *ANF*, 4:82.
14. Origen, *The Song of Songs, in Ancient Christian Writers*, eds. Johannes Quasten and Joseph C. Plumpe (Westminster, MD: The Newman Press, 1957), 26:252.
15. Jeremy Cohen, "The Mystery of Israel's Salvation: Romans 11:25–26 in Medieval and Patristic Exegesis," *Harvard Theological Review* 98 (2005): 263.
16. Ibid., 260.
17. St. Jerome, *Commentary on St. Matthew*, 2. St. Jerome, *Commentary on St. Mat-*

thew, 2, quoted in Dennis Fahey, *The Kingship of Christ and the Conversion of the Jewish Nation* (Kimmage, Dublin: Holy Ghost Missionary College, 1953), 108.

18. Augustine, *City of God, 29 NPNF¹*, 2:448.
19. Walter Zander, *Israel and the Holy Places of Christendom* (London, Weidenfeld & Nicolson, 1971), 7.
20. John Y. B. Hood, *Aquinas and the Jews* (Philadelphia: University of Pennsylvania Press, 1995), 3.
21. Thomas Aquinas, "Super Epistolam Ad Romanos"; II.2, http://www.tacalumni.org/Aquinas/TOMA_075.txt. Accessed January 25, 2004. Translation by John Y. B. Hood.
22. Robert E. Lerner, "Millennialism," in *The Encyclopedia of Apocalypticism*, eds. John J. Collins, Bernard McGinn, and Stephen J. Stein. (New York: Continuum, 2000), 2:353.
23. Thomas Ice, "Lovers of Zion: A Brief History of Christian Zionism," *Voice* (March/April 2005).
24. Regina Sharif, *Non-Jewish Zionism, Its Roots in Western History* (London: Zed, 1983).
25. Martin Luther, "On the Jews and Their Lies," in *Luther's Works*, American Edition (55 vols.; ed. Jaroslav Pelikan and Helmut T. Lehmann; Philadelphia: Muehlenberg and Fortress, and St. Louis: Concordia, 1955–86), 47:138–39.
26. Luther's strongest statements against the Jews are found in his 1543 tract, "Concerning the Jews and Their Lies." He referred to the Jews as a "miserable and accursed people." Luther's intolerance toward the Jews is also evident in the following statement: "What shall we Christians do with this rejected and condemned people, the Jews? Since they live among us, we dare not tolerate their conduct, now that we are aware of their lying and reviling and blaspheming." See *Luther's Works*, 47:137.
27. Willem VanGemeren, "Israel as the Hermeneutical Crux in the Interpretation of Prophecy," *Westminster Theological Journal* 45/1 (1983):142.
28. Clark M. Williamson, *A Guest in the House of Israel: Post-Holocaust Church Theology* (Louisville: Westminster/John Knox, 1993), 131.
29. John Calvin, "Commentary on the Book of the Prophet Isaiah," in *Calvin's Commentaries* 8:269.
30. Geneva Bible (n.p.: London, 1581).
31. Ian Murray, *The Puritan Hope: Revival and the Interpretation of Prophecy* (Banner of Truth, 1971), 43
32. Thomas Brightman, *A Revelation Of The Apocalypse*, 1615
33. Sir Henry Finch, *The World's Great Restauration, or Calling of the Jews, and with them of all Nations and Kingdoms of the Earth to the Faith of Christ*, 1921.
34. Murray, *The Puritan Hope*, 42.
35. Reiner Smolinski, "Israel Redivivus: The Eschatological Limits of Puritan Typology in New England," in *The New England Quarterly*, Vol. 63, No. 3 (September, 1990): 363.
36. Wilhelmus à Brakel, *The Christian's Reasonable Service*, IV, 530–531.
37. Petrus Serrarius, *An Awakening Warning to a Wofull World* (Amsterdam, 1662), 27, 29.
38. Jonathan Edwards, *The Works of Jonathan Edwards*, (Carlisle, PA: Banner of Truth Trust, reprint, 1976), 1:607.
39. Charles Haddon Spurgeon, "The Harvest and the Vintage," in *The Metropolitan Tabernacle Pulpit*, 50:553–54.
40. Ibid.
41. Spurgeon, "The Restoration and Conversion of the Jews," in The Metropolitan Tabernacle Pulpit, 10:426.
42. Dennis M. Swanson, "Charles H. Spurgeon and the Nation of Israel: A Non-Dispensational Perspective on a Literal National Restoration." See http://www.spurgeon.org/misc/eschat2.htm. 2000. Accessed December 7, 2013. For more information on Spurgeon's views on eschatology and Israel see also, Dennis M. Swanson, "The Millennial Position of Spurgeon," *The Master's Seminary Journal*, 7/2 (Fall 1996): 183–212.

43. Ronald E. Diprose, *Israel in the Development of Christian Thought* (Rome: Istituto Biblico Evangelico Italiano, 2000), 1.
44. Peter Ochs, "Judaism and Christian Theology," in *The Modern Theologians*, ed. D.F. Ford (Malden, MA: Blackwell, 1997), 618.

Chapter 13: Israel in Light of the Holocaust

1. Rachmiel Frydland, *When Being Jewish Was a Crime* (Nashville: Thomas Nelson Inc., Publishers, 1978). See another Holocaust survivor who also found his way back to Israel, Eliezer Urbach, with Edith S. Weigand, *Out of the Fury: The Incredible Odyssey of Eliezer Urbach* (Charlotte, NC: Chosen People Ministries, Inc., 1987). For another graphic look at the Holocaust and the establishment of the Nation of Israel in 1948, see the historical novel of Leon Uris, *Exodus* (New York: Bantam Books, A Division of Bantam Doubleday Dell Publishing Group, Inc., 1958, 1959); also, in the same historical fiction, see Larry Collins and Dominique Lapierre, *O Jerusalem!* (New York: Simon & Schuster and Pocket Books, 1972, 1973).
2. Frydland, *When Being Jewish Was a Crime*, 13.
3. Zola Levitt, in *When Being Jewish Was a Crime*, 9.
4. Frydland, *When Being Jewish Was a Crime*, 76–79, 83–84.
5. Ibid., 121–122.
6. Ibid., 122.
7. Emil L. Fackenheim et al., "Jewish Values in the Post-Holocaust Future: A Symposium," *Judaism* 16 (Summer 1967): 282; also see Elie Wiesel, *The Gates of the Forest*, trans. Frances Frenaye (New York: Avon Books, 1966), 192; and of course, see Wiesel's classic Holocaust autobiography *Night* (New York: Avon Books, A Division of The Heart Corporation, 1958, 1960).
8. Elie Wiesel, "Telling the Tale," *Dimensions* 2 (Spring 1968): 10.
9. Michael Berenbaum, "Teach It to Your Children," *Sh'ma* 11 (1 May 1981): 100–101.
10. Charles Krauthammer, *Things That Matter: Three Decades of Passions, Pastimes and Politics* (New York: Crown Forum, 2013), 2–3.
11. Abba Eban, *My People: The Story of the Jews* (New York: Behrman House, Inc., 1968), 430.
12. For detailed rabbinic (Jewish religious) responses to the Holocaust, see Robert Kirschner, *Rabbinic Response of the Holocaust Era* (New York: Schocken Books Inc., 1985); Irving J. Rosenbaum, *The Holocaust and Halakhah*, The Library of Jewish Law and Ethics (New York: Ktav Publishing House, Inc., 1976); H. J. Zimmels, *The Echo of the Nazi Holocaust in Rabbinic Literature* (New York: Ktav Publishing House, Inc., 1977); etc. For other Jewish scholars wrestling with the evil of the Holocaust, see Fred E. Katz, *Ordinary People and Extraordinary Evil: A Report on the Beguilings of Evil* (Albany, NY: State University of New York Press, 1993); Oliver Leaman, *Evil and Suffering in Jewish Philosophy*, Cambridge Studies in Religious Traditions 6 (Cambridge, UK: Cambridge University Press, 1995); etc.; and from a Christian perspective on evil, see Henri Blocher, *Evil and the Cross*, trans. David G. Preston (Downers Grove: InterVarsity Press, 1990); D. A. Carson, *How Long, O Lord? Reflections on Suffering and Evil* (Grand Rapids: Baker Book House, 1990); Norman L. Geisler, *If God, Why Evil?* (Minneapolis: Bethany House Publishers, 2011); Os Guinness, *Unspeakable: Facing Up to the Challenge of Evil* (New York: HarperCollins Publishers, 2005); etc. For other Jewish scholars wrestling with the problem of suffering in general, including the Holocaust, see Shalom Carmy, ed., *Jewish Perspectives on the Experience of Suffering*, The Orthodox Forum Series (Northvale, NJ: Jason Aronson Inc., 1999); David Kraemer, *Responses to Suffering in Classical Rabbinic Literature* (New York: Oxford University Press, 1995); etc. And from among the many historical works on the Holocaust, see Raul Hilberg, *The Destruction of the European Jews* (Chicago: Quadrangle, 1967); Nora Levin, *The Holocaust: The Destruction of European Jewry 1933-1945* (New York: Schocken Books, 1968); etc.

13. Seymour Cain, "The Question and the Answers After Auschwitz," *Judaism* 20 (Summer 1971): 263.
14. Zimmels, *The Echo of the Holocaust in Rabbinic Literature*, xxi.
15. Robert L. Wilkin, *The Land Called Holy: Palestine in Christian History and Thought* (New Haven, CT: Yale University Press, 1992), xiii–xiv. Among some of the more recent literature on Israel, the Middle East, and the historical involvement of Jews, Christians, and Muslims, see Michael B. Oren, *Power, Faith, and Fantasy: America in the Middle East, 1776 to the Present* (New York: W. W. Norton & Company, 2007); and Simon Sebag Montefiore, *Jerusalem: A Biography* (New York: Alfred A. Knopf, 2011).
16. See note #22.
17. Mark Hitchcock, *The Amazing Claims of Bible Prophecy* (Eugene, OR: Harvest House Publishers, 2010), 96.
18. Randall Price, "The Divine Preservation of the Jewish People," World of the Bible Ministry Update, October 1, 2009 at http://www.worldofthebible.com/update.htm, quoted in Hitchcock, The Amazing Claims of Bible Prophecy, 97.
19. Stanley A. Ellisen, "God, Satan, Man: Three Worlds" in *Conflict: The High Drama of Bible Prophecy* (Sisters, OR: Multnomah Publishers, 1998), 149; id., *Biography of a Great Planet* (Wheaton, IL: Tyndale House Publishers, Inc., 1975), 147.
20. J. Rufus Fears, *The Wisdom of History* (Chantilly, VA: The Great Courses, 2007), 114–115.
21. Chaim Herzog and Mordechai Gichon, *Battle of the Bible* (New York: Random House, 1978), 12–14. For a historical atlas that details the various periods of war and peace in Israel, see Moshe Aumann, Shlomo Ketko, and Lorraine Kessel, *War and Peace: Carta's Atlas of Israel, Antiquity to Present* (Jerusalem: The Israel Map and Publishing Company, Ltd., 2012); in addition, see Martin Gilbert, *Jewish History Atlas*, rev. ed. (New York: Macmillan Publishing Co., Inc., 1969, 1976); id., *Jerusalem History Atlas* (New York: Macmillan Publishing Co., Inc., 1977); and more specifically, id., *The Macmillan Atlas of the Holocaust* (New York: Macmillan Publishing Co., Inc., 1982).
22. Monroe Rosenthal and Isaac Mozeson, *Wars of the Jews: A Military History from Biblical to Modern Times*, Hippocrene Jewish History Series (New York: Hippocrene Books, Inc., 1990), 13–14.
23. Abraham Joshua Heschel, *Israel: An Echo of Eternity* (New York: Farrar, Strauss Giroux, 1967, 1968, 1969), 66–67.
24. Michael L. Brown, *What Do Jewish People Think about Jesus? And Other Questions Christians Ask about Jewish Beliefs, Practices and History* (Grand Rapids: Chosen Books, A Division of Baker Publishing Group, 2007), 139–140.
25. Michael L. Brown, *Answering Jewish Objections to Jesus: General and Historical Objections* (Grand Rapids: Baker Books, 2000), 193; on Isaiah's Messianic Suffering Servant and His relationship to the Jewish people, see my chapter, "Why I Believe Jesus Is the Promised Messiah," in *Why I Am a Christian*, rev. ed., ed. Norman L. Geisler and Paul K. Hoffman (Grand Rapids: Baker Books, 2001, 2006), 221–238.
26. Theodor Herzl, *The Jewish State* (New York: Dover Publications, Inc., 1946, 1988 [first published as a pamphlet in Vienna, in 1896, titled: *Der Judenstaat*]), 72, 96.
27. Michael B. Oren, *Six Days of War: June 1967 and the Making of the Modern Middle East*, A Presidio Press Book (New York: The Random House Publishing Group, 2002, 2003), 2.
28. Ibid., 2, 3, 16.
29. Jakob Jocz, *The Jewish People and Jesus Christ After Auschwitz: A Study in the Controversy Between Church and Synagogue* (Grand Rapids: Baker Book House, 1981), 7–8; id., *The Jewish People and Jesus Christ: The Relationship Between Church and Synagogue*, 3rd ed. (Grand Rapids: Baker Book House, 1949, 1979).
30. Martin Gilbert, *Israel: A History* (New York: William Morrow and Company, Inc., 1998), 3, 14, 186.
31. Quoted by Martin, 7.
32. For the new identity of the Jewish people as a result of the Holocaust, see my

chapter, "The Holocaust and Jewish Identity," in *Jewish Identity and Faith in Jesus*, ed. Kai Kjaer-Hansen (Jerusalem: Caspari Center, 1996), 137–148.

33. Irving Greenberg, "Cloud of Smoke, Pillar of Fire: Judaism, Christianity, and Modernity after Auschwitz," in *Auschwitz: Beginning of a New Era? Reflections on the Holocaust*, ed. Eva Fleischner (New York: KTAV Publishing House, Inc., 1977), 43, 48, 50.
34. Abraham R. Besdin, "Reflections on the Agony and the Ecstasy," *Tradition* 11 (Spring 1971): 23.
35. Nachum L. Rabinovitch, "The Religious Significance of Israel," *Tradition* 14 (Fall 1974): 24.
36. Marc E. Samuels, "In Praise of Doubt," *Judaism* 20 (Fall 1971): 458.
37. Eliezer Berkovits, *Faith after the Holocaust* (New York: KTAV Publishing House, Inc., 1973), 152–153, 156–157.
38. Eliezer Berkovits, *God, Man and History: A Jewish Interpretation*, 2nd ed. (Middle Village, NY: Jonathan David Publishers, Inc., 1965), 153–154.
39. Eliezer Berkovits, "Crisis and Faith," *Tradition* 14 (Fall 1974), 14–15.
40. Jacob Neusner, *The Way of Torah: An Introduction to Judaism*, 2nd ed., The Religious Life of Man Series, ed. Frederick J. Streng (Encino, CA: Dickenson Publishing Company, Inc., 1974), 92–93.
41. Berkovits, *Faith after the Holocaust*, 70, 136.
42. Jacob L. Talmon, "European History as the Seedbed of the Holocaust," in *Holocaust and Rebirth: A Symposium*, trans. Efraim Zuroff (Jerusalem: Yad Vashem, 1974), 70.
43. Greenberg, "Cloud of Smoke, Pillar of Fire: Judaism, Christianity, and Modernity after Auschwitz," 33.
44. Jacob B. Agus, "God and the Catastrophe," *Conservative Judaism* 18 (Summer 1964): 14.
45. Emil L. Fackenheim, Richard H. Popkin, George Steiner, and Elie Wiesel, "Jewish Values in the Post-Holocaust Future: A Symposium," *Judaism* 16 (Summer 1967): 287.
46. Emil L. Fackenheim, "The People Israel Lives," *The Christian Century* 87 (6 May 1970): 567.
47. Emil L. Fackenheim, "The Human Condition after Auschwitz," in *Understanding Jewish Theology: Classical Issues and Modern Perspectives*, ed. Jacob Neusner (New York: KTAV Publishing House, Inc., 1973), 172.
48. Fackenheim et al., "Jewish Values in the Post-Holocaust Future: A Symposium," 272; Fackenheim is using this so-called "614th Commandment" as a reference to the rabbinic count of the 613 commandments in the Mosaic Law. In addition, see his *The Jewish Return into History: Reflections in the Age of Auschwitz and a New Jerusalem* (New York: Schocken Books, 1978).
49. To understand how this kind of Holocaust siege mentality played itself out in Israel, until recently, see my chapter, "The Masada Suicides: The Making and Breaking of a Cultural Icon," in *Suicide: A Christian Response*, ed. Timothy J. Demy and Gary P. Stewart (Grand Rapids: Kregel Publications, 1998), 269–283. In this chapter, I examine how young Israeli military recruits used to take their oath of allegiance on the top of this first century desert rock-fortress called Masada; in the sacred site of Masada, these young recruits, both boys and girls, swore, "Masada will never fall again! Never again! Never again!"
50. See Aristotle, *Physics* II 3; 194 b 17–20; also *Posterior Analytics* 71 b 9–11; 94 a 20; *Metaphysics* V 2; 107b, 29–31; 1046 b, 5–6; 1048 a, 8 *et passim*; 1049b; etc.
51. *The Merriam Webster's Deluxe Dictionary*, The Tenth Collegiate Edition (1998).
52. Ibid.
53. The Instrumental Cause was developed by philosophers after Aristotle.
54. On Winston Churchill's commitment to the Jewish people in general, as well as his specific commitment to the establishment of the modern State of Israel, see Oskar K. Rabinowicz, *Winston Churchill on Jewish Problems* (New York: Thomas Yoseloff, Publisher, 1960).
55. John F. Walvoord, *Israel in Prophecy* (Grand Rapids: Zondervan Publishing House, 1962), 26.

56. What I am calling the "Trespass-Exile-Return" pattern has also been detailed by other scholars, sometimes using different terminology; e.g., the "Sin-Exile-Return" pattern (S-E-R) in Mark Adam Elliott, *The Survivors of Israel: A Reconsideration of the Theology of Pre-Christian Judaism* Grand Rapids: William B. Eerdmans Publishing Co., 2000), 75, 360, 366–367, 370–371, 381, 384, 628; Elliott also discusses the "Destruction-Preservation Soteriology" (D-P), 575–637, plus 345, 443, 640; also, the "Sin-Exile/Punishment-Return" Pattern (S-E-R/P) in Graham N. Stanton, *A Gospel for a New People: Studies in Matthew* (Louisville: Westminster/John Knox Press, 1992), 247–255; and the "Sin-Judgment-Grace" Pattern (S-J-G) in Mark Strom, *The Symphony of Scripture: Making Sense of the Bible's Many Themes* (Downers Grove, IL: InterVarsity Press, 1990), 24–43; etc. For the Exile as a major ongoing biblical image, see *Dictionary of Biblical Imagery*, ed. Leland Ryken, James C. Wilhoit, and Tremper Longman III (Downers Grove, IL: InterVarsity Press, 1998), s.v. "Exile."

57. On the eternal nature and provisions of the Abrahamic Covenant, see Gen. 12:1–3; 13:14–17; 15:1–21; 17:1–27; 22:15–18; 26:1–11; 28:10–22; 32:24–32; 35:1–15; etc. Also see David Baron, *Israel's Inalienable Possessions* (New York: The American Board of Missions to the Jews, Inc., 1943, 1968); Paul N. Benware, *Understanding End Times Prophecy: A Comprehensive Approach*, rev. ed. (Chicago: Moody Publishers, 1995, 2006), 35–54ff.; Stanley A. Ellisen, *Who Owns the Land?: The Arab-Israeli Conflict*, rev. ed. (Wheaton: Tyndale House Publishers, Inc., 1991, 2003), 7–11, 132–138, 145, 151; Charles L. Feinberg, *Premillennialism or Amillennialism?* rev. ed. (New York: The American Board of Missions to the Jews Inc., 1916), 34–37ff.; Arnold G. Fruchtenbaum, *Israelology: The Missing Link in Systematic Theology*, rev. ed. (Tustin, CA: Ariel Ministries Press, 1989, 1992), 334–344ff., 570–581ff., 628–631ff., 799–802; J. B. Hixson and Mark Fontecchio, *What Lies Ahead: A Biblical Overview of the End Times* (Brenham, TX: Lucid Books, 2013), 85–99ff.; Hal Lindsey, *The Everlasting Hatred: The Roots of Jihad* (Washington, D.C.: WND Books, 2011), 16–55; J. Dwight Pentecost, *Things to Come: A Study in Biblical Eschatology* (Grand Rapids: Dunham Publishing Co., 1958), 65–94ff.; Michael Rydelnik, *Understanding the Arab-Israeli Conflict: What the Headlines Haven't Told You* (Chicago: Moody Publishers, 2004), 111–124, 137–149; Charles C. Ryrie, *The Basis of the Premillennial Faith* (Neptune, NJ: Loizeaux Brothers, 1953), 48–75ff.; also Walvoord, *Israel in Prophecy*, 27–79; id., *The Millennial Kingdom* (Grand Rapids: Dunham Publishing Co., 1959), 139–193ff.; plus, *The Coming Millennial Kingdom: A Case for Premillennial Interpretation*, ed. Donald K. Campbell and Jeffrey L. Townsend (Grand Rapids: Kregel Publications, 1997), *et passim*; etc.

58. Among many authors on this concept of a Deuteronomistic history, see Walter C. Kaiser, Jr., *Toward an Old Testament Theology* (Grand Rapids: Zondervan Publishing House, 1978), 63–66, 122–124ff., 136–137, 144–152; also by Kaiser, Toward Old Testament Ethics, Academie Books (Grand Rapids: Zondervan Publishing House, 1983), 302–304.

59. The Deuteronomistic theology was played out and recorded in the Deuteronomistic history, that is, the historical books of Joshua through 2 Kings. For a popular summary of the Deuteronomic History, see John H. Sailhamer, *The NIV Compact Bible Commentary* (Grand Rapids: Zondervan Publishing House, 1994), 175–178; for a more detailed development, see Robert B. Chisholm Jr., *Interpreting the Historical Books: An Exegetical Handbook*, Handbooks for Old Testament Exegesis Series (Grand Rapids: Kregel Publishers, 2006), 128–131; David M. Howard, Jr., *An Introduction to the Old Testament Historical Books* (Chicago: Moody Press, 1993), 77–78, 102, 145, 179–182; Hermann Austel, "The United Monarchy: Archaeological and Literary Issues," in *Giving the Sense: Understanding and Using Old Testament Historical Texts*, ed. David M. Howard Jr. and Michael A, Grisanti (Grand Rapids: Kregel Publishers, 2003), 169–177; and Richard D. Patterson, "The Divided Monarchy: Sources, Approaches, and Historicity," in *Giving the Sense: Understanding and Using Old Testament Historical Texts*, ed. David M. Howard Jr. and Michael A, Grisanti (Grand Rapids: Kregel Publishers, 2003), 183–186. On the historical and

theological purposes of the Book of Deuteronomy, see Gleason L. Archer, Jr., *A Survey of Old Testament Introduction*, rev. ed. (Chicago: Moody Press, 1964, 1974, 1994, 2007), 226–236; R. K. Harrison, *Introduction to the Old Testament* (Grand Rapids: William B. Eerdmans Publishing Co., 1969), 635–662; Paul R. House, *Old Testament Theology* (Downers Grove, IL: InterVarsity Press, 1998), 42, 170–171, 198–199, 299–300, 322–323; Earl S. Kalland, "Deuteronomy," in *The Expositor's Bible Commentary*, vol. 3, ed. Frank E. Gaebelein (Grand Rapids: Zondervan Publishing House, 1992), 3–235; Samuel J. Schultz, *The Old Testament Speaks: A Complete Survey of Old Testament History and Literature*, 5th ed. (New York: HarperOne Publishers, 1960, 1970, 1980, 1990, 2000), 43, 85–87; and Herbert Wolf, *An Introduction to the Old Testament Pentateuch* (Chicago: Moody Press, 1991), 19, 73, *et passim*; and more specifically on the historical setting of the Book of Deuteronomy, see Eugene H. Merrill, *Kingdom of Priests: A History of Old Testament Israel* (Grand Rapids: Baker Book House, 1987), 24–25, 80–82, 91, 444; id., *An Historical Survey of the Old Testament*, 2nd ed. (Grand Rapids: Baker Book House, 1991), 28, 129–130, 193; on the Book of Deuteronomy at a popular level, see Louis Goldberg, *Deuteronomy*, Bible Study Commentary Series (Grand Rapids: Lamplighter Books, Zondervan Publishing House, 1986; and Samuel J. Schultz, *Deuteronomy: The Gospel of Love*, Everyman Bible Commentary Series (Chicago: Moody Press, 1971); also id., *The Message of the Old Testament* (San Francisco: Harper & Row, Publishers, 1986); etc.

60.   It should be noted that *the best* that the Mosaic Covenant could do for the nation Israel was to grant her temporal prosperity and victory of her enemies. On the other hand, *the worst* that the Mosaic Covenant could do for the nation Israel was to bar her from any temporal prosperity, played out in defeat from her enemies, and finally exile or dispersion into foreign nations (her enemies). In other words, in regard to *eternal* matters, the Mosaic Covenant/Law could in no way deal with either the nation Israel or the individual Israelite (cf. Rom. 3:19–31; 5:20; 7:7; Gal. 3:19–25ff.; 1 Tim. 1:8–11; etc.). Whereas the nation Israel is guaranteed an unconditional and therefore eternal relationship with God (through the Abrahamic Covenant; cf. Gen. 12:1–3; 15:1–21; etc.), the *eternal* destiny of any individual Israelite was, and is, based on faith and faith alone in the progressively revealed Messiah, the Lord Yeshua (cf. Gen. 15:6; Rom. 3:21–26; 4:3, 20–22; Gal. 3:6; Eph. 2:1–22; James 2:23; etc.).

61.   It must also be remembered that the so-called blessings of the Mosaic Covenant/Law are no longer in effect. Two-thirds of the Mosaic Law was bound up with the Temple, the levitical priesthood, and the sacrificial system, etc. When the Romans destroyed the Temple in Jerusalem in AD 70, all of these legal requirements became null and void. The Lord Yeshua had predicted the destruction of the Temple and Jerusalem, but He permitted one generation to pass before His prophecies were fulfilled, allowing for the Jewish leadership to repent of its rejection of His Messiahship (cf. Matt. 23:37–39; Luke 21:20–24; the Book of Hebrews, etc.). In other words, the moment that the Lord Yeshua, the Lamb of God, died for the sins of the world, every animal sacrifice in the Temple (*commanded* by God; cf. Lev.; etc.) became at best redundant and at worst blasphemous (cf. John 1:29, 36; 19:30; etc.). Oh the patience of God that (ideally) leads to salvation (cf. 2 Pet. 3:15; etc.)! On the Mosaic Law and its relationship to the divinely-ordained sacrificial system, see Louis Goldberg, *God, Torah, Messiah: The Messianic Jewish Theology of Dr. Louis Goldberg*, ed. Richard A. Robinson (San Francisco: Purple Pomegranate Productions, 2009), *et passim*; also Arnold G. Fruchtenbaum, *Hebrew Christianity: Its Theology, History, and Philosophy* (Tustin, CA: Ariel Ministries Press, 1983), 81–89; and id., *Israelology*, 373–380, 588–601.

62.   On "the latter [last, end of] days" [*acharith hayamim*] as a technical term pointing forward to the future eschatological period of judgment (i.e., the temporal curses) and enrichment (i.e., the temporal blessings), see Gen. 49:1; Deut. 4:30; 31:29; Num. 24:14; and more specifically in the prophets, Isa. 2:2

NOTES

// Mic. 4:1; Jer. 23:20; 30:20; 48:47; 49:39; Ezek. 38:16; Dan. 2:28; 10:14; Hos. 3:5; also Matt. 25:31–46, esp. 34, 41, 46; etc.).

63. To be in Exile, outside of the protective hand of God in the Promised Land, was to experience the worst of God's temporal judgments [disciplines] (see Lev. 26:33, 38–41; Deut. 4:23–28; 28:36, 48, 63–68; also Daniel; Jeremiah; Ezekiel; plus Pss. 42–23; 74; 79; 80; 85; 126; 137; etc.); also see John Claeys, *Apocalypse 2012: The Ticking of the End Time Clock—What Does the Bible Say?* (Sisters, OR: VMI Publishers, 2010), 41–64, 73–150, 161–208ff.

64. Heschel, *Israel: An Echo of Eternity*, 67–69.

65. For further development of this final two-fold return, see David Baron, *The Visions and Prophecies of Zechariah: "The Prophet of Hope and Glory"* (Fincastle, VA: Scripture Truth Book Co., 1962 [repr., 1918]), 358–359; David L. Cooper, *Messiah: His Final Call to Israel* (Los Angeles: The Biblical Research Society, 1962), 68–122; Arnold G. Fruchtenbaum, *The Footsteps of the Messiah: A Study of the Sequence of Prophetic Events*, rev. ed. (San Antonio, TX: Ariel Ministries, 1982, 2003), 409–449ff.; Walter C. Kaiser, Jr., "The Land of Israel and the Future Return: Zechariah 10:6-12)" in *Israel, The Land and the People: An Evangelical Affirmation of God's Promises*, ed. H. Wayne House (Grand Rapids: Kregel Publications, 1998), 216–218; Lindsey, *The Everlasting Hatred*, 34–36; Tom McCall, "Who Owns the Land?" in *The Gathering Storm: Understanding Prophecy in Critical Times*, ed. Mal Couch (Springfield, MO: 21st Century Press, 2005), 146–147; plus in the same book, Andy Woods, "Jeremiah 30: Birth Pangs, Tribulation, and Restoration," 155–157; also, Randall Price, *Jerusalem in Prophecy* (Eugene, OR: Harvest House Publishers, 1998), 199–220; Harold A. Sevener, *Israel's Glorious Future: The Prophecies and Promises of God Revealed* (Charlotte, NC: Chosen People Ministries, Inc.,1996), 7–58ff.; etc.

66. The Final Return of the Believing Remnant of Israel, in belief [faith], will take place in the following sequence: the Regeneration of Israel, the Regathering of Israel, the Possession of the Land, the Reuniting of the Two Tribes, and the Reestablishment of the Davidic Throne and the Messianic Kingdom [the Millennium: the Thousand Year Reign] (cf. 2 Sam. 7 // 1 Chron. 17 // Ps. 89; Ps. 83; Isa. 2; 11; 60–66; Jer. 30–33; Ezek. 33–39; 40–48; Dan. 2; 7; 9:24–27; Hag. 2; Zech. 6:12–13ff.; 8–14; Mal. 3:1–6; 4:1–6; Matt. 24–25; Mark 13; Luke 21; John 11; 14; Rev. 13; 19–22; etc.); for more on these prophecies, see Rachmiel Frydland, *What the Rabbis Know About the Messiah*, 2nd ed., ed. Elliot Klayman (Cincinnati: Messianic Publishing Co., 1991, 1993), 107–109; Elwood McQuaid, *For the Love of Zion* (Bellmawr, NJ: The Friends of Israel Gospel Ministry, Inc., 2007), 197–214; Renald E. Showers, *What on Earth Is God Doing? Satan's Conflict with God*, rev. ed. (Bellmawr, NJ: The Friends of Israel Gospel Ministry, Inc., 1973, 2003), 121–125.

67. The Jews of Poland are a painful example of the few who survived: Of the three million Jews in Poland before World War II, only fifty thousand survived the horrors of the Holocaust; cf. *Encyclopaedia Judaica*, vol. 8, s.v. "Holocaust" (Jerusalem: Keter Publishing House Jerusalem Ltd., 1972), 889–890.

68. Louis Goldberg, *Turbulence Over the Middle East: Israel and the Nations in Confrontation and the Coming Kingdom of Peace on Earth* (Neptune, NJ: Loizeaux Brothers, 1982), 204–205.

69. *Dictionary of Biblical Imagery*, s.v. "Exodus, Second Exodus."

70. See Eugene H. Merrill, "Pilgrimage and Procession: Motifs of Israel's Return," in *Israel's Apostasy and Restoration*, ed. Avraham Gileadi (Grand Rapids: Baker Book House, 1988), 261–272; Kaiser, "The Land of Israel and the Future Return (Zechariah 10:6–12)," 209–227; id., *Toward Rediscovering the Old Testament*, Academie Books (Grand Rapids: Zondervan Publishing House, 1987), 46–58; and J. Alva McClain, *The Greatness of the Kingdom* (Chicago: Moody Press, 1959), 151–152, 198–200.

71. Although the State of Israel was born in 1948, there has always been a Jewish presence in the Promised Land, from the time of David to the present. In fact, even before 1948, there were at least two modern *Aliot* [pl. of *Aliyah*; i.e., *Aliyahs*. So, *Aliyah* is a "going up" or "ascent"; the Law of the Return that allows

for any Jew in the world to return to the modern Zionist State of Israel and establish citizenship]. The First *Aliyah* is dated at 1882; and the Second *Aliyah* is dated at 1905–1914. It should also be remembered that the city of Jerusalem alone has survived under the most horrific conditions: destroyed twice, besieged twenty-three times, attacked fifty-two times, recaptured forty-four times, etc. On the various *aliyot*, see Rydelnik, *The Arab-Israeli Conflict*, 63–71, 79–82, 118–119. On Jerusalem's place in history and prophecy, see Price, *Jerusalem in Prophecy*; Hugh Kitson, *Jerusalem: The Covenant City* (West Sussex, U.K.: Hatikvah Ltd, 2000); etc.

72. H. L. Ridderbos, "The Future of Israel," in *Prophecy in the Making: Messages Prepared for Jerusalem Conference on Biblical Prophecy*, ed. C. F. H. Henry (Carol Stream, IL: Creation, 1971), 316, quoted in Michael J. Vlach, *Has the Church Replaced Israel? A Theological Reflection* (Nashville: B&H Academic, of B&H Publishing Group, 2010), 69. Ridderbos is responding to the long-standing Christian theological doctrine called Replacement Theology or Supersessionism, in which the Jewish people, having rejected Jesus as Messiah, are no longer the people of God, and so have forever been replaced by the Church in God's program. For a detailed refutation of Replacement Theology, see Barry E. Horner, *Future Israel: Why Christian Anti-Judaism Must Be Challenged*, NAC Studies in Bible & Theology (Nashville: B&H Academic, of B&H Publishing Group, 2004); plus, Ronald E. Diprose, *Israel and the Church: The Origin and Effects of Replacement Theology* (Rome, Italy: Instituto Biblico Evangelico Italiano, 2000); and from a historical perspective on Replacement Theology, see Peter Richardson, *Israel in the Apostolic Church*, Society for New Testament Studies Monograph Series 10 (Cambridge: Cambridge University Press, 1969).

73. Jocelyn Hellig, *The Holocaust and Antisemitism: A Short History* (Oxford: Oneworld Publications, 2003), 101, 105.

74. Heschel, *Israel: An Echo of Eternity*, 70.

75. Price, *Jerusalem in Prophecy*, 303.

76. Frydland, *When Being Jewish Was a Crime*, 134.

Chapter 14: The Jewish People: Evidence for the Truth of Scripture

1. Arnold J. Toynbee, *A Study of History*, 12 Volumes (Oxford: Oxford University Press, 1934–61), Vol 1, Section VII, 135–39.

2. Mark Twain, "Concerning the Jews," *The Complete Essays of Mark Twain*, Charles Neider, Ed. (Cambridge, MA: Da Capo Press, 2000), 249–50.

3. *Olam* (eternal, everlasting) is used three times in describing the Abrahamic covenant (17:7; 13; 19) and once of the covenant's land grant (17:8). V. P. Hamilton notes that this is done to emphasize that although God may have expectations of Abraham (cf. 17:1–2), this restatement is by no means to indicate that the unconditional, unilateral covenant of Genesis 15 has now become bilateral, dependent on Abraham walking blamelessly before God. (*The Book of Genesis* in the New International Commentary on the Old Testament, Ed. R. K. Harrison [Grand Rapids, MI: Eerdmans, 1990], I:465). Rather, it remains unconditional, and therefore, everlasting as God Himself.

4. G. Wenham, *Genesis 16–50* in Word Biblical Commentary, Eds. D. Hubbard and G. W. Barker (Dallas: Word Books, 1994), 22.

5. Jeremiah 25:8–14 predicts a seventy-year captivity to Babylon before God would restore Judah to their land.

6. The eschatological perspective of Jeremiah 30 is derived from several factors. First, the oracle begins by saying "the days are certainly coming" (30:3), a phrase Jeremiah frequently associates with the end of days (16:14–16; 23:5–6; 31:27, 31). Second, the passage anticipates the "time of trouble for Jacob" (30:7), a time that does not refer to the Babylonian captivity but the events of the day of the Lord. Third, the passage anticipates the restoration of Israel under "David their king" (30:9), depicting the future, eschatological, reign of the Messiah Jesus (cf. Hos. 3:4–5 which describes Israel seeking "the LORD their God and David their king" and returning to God's goodness "in the last

days."). Finally, Jeremiah looks towards the day when God will fully restore Israel spiritually, when the Lord says to the nation "you will be My people and I will be your God" (30:22), a transformation that was not fulfilled at the return from Babylon but will occur at the end of days.

7. Personal translation of the traditional liturgy as found in Nathan Goldberg, *Passover Haggadah*, Based on the Haggadah by Z. Harry Gutstein (New York: Ktav, 1984), 12.

8. Personal recollection. I was present at the conference and at the Western Wall that evening.

9. Randall Price, "Is the Modern State of Israel Prophetically Significant?" Unpublished paper, delivered at the 13th Annual Pre-Trib Research Center Conference in Dallas, TX, December 6–8, 2004.

10. These include Frederick II and his physician, Frederick the Great and a courtier, Queen Victoria and Benjamin Disraeli, the Kaiser and Otto Von Bismarck, and Louis XIV and Blaise Pascal. In yet other versions, the rulers mentioned are Peter the Great and Napoleon. S. R. Haynes, *Reluctant Witnesses: Jews and the Christian Imagination* (Louisville, KY: Westminster, 1995), 59–60.

11. This section about the prophecies of the return to the land of Israel is adapted from my book, *Understanding the Arab Israeli Conflict*, Revised (Chicago: Moody Publishers, 2007), 132–34.

12. Adam Clarke, *Clarke's Commentary: The Holy Bible Containing the Old and New Testaments with a Commentary and Critical Notes*. 6 vols. (Nashville, TN: Abingdon, 1856), IV:525–26. The difficulty with holding that Ezekiel's prophecy pertains to the historical return from Babylon is the expectation that (a) the entire nation of Israel will experience spiritual regeneration (Ezek. 37:13–14), something that decidedly did not happen at the post-exilic return; (b) when Israel comes to know the Lord they will be led by "one Shepherd," the messianic son of David (37:24); (c) when Israel returns to the land of Israel, they will never be driven from the land again (37:25). (d) all the nations would know that the Lord set Israel apart (37:28). None of these were fulfilled in the 5th and 6th Centuries BC but await an eschatological fulfillment.

13. As cited in Halvor Ronning, "The Land of Israel: A Christian Zionist View," *Immanuel* 22/23 (1989): 132.

14. See Donald M. Lewis, *The Origins of Christian Zionism* (New York: Cambridge University Press, 2010).

15. For a summary of this history, see Rydelnik, *Understanding the Arab Israeli Conflict*, 75–106.

16. Robert L. Saucy, "Israel and the Church: A Case for Discontinuity" in *Continuity and Discontinuity: Perspectives on the Relationship between the Old and New Testaments*, edited by John S. Feinberg (Westchester, IL: Crossway, 1988), 245.

17. Arnold G. Fruchtenbaum, *Israelology: The Missing Link in Systematic Theology* (Tustin, CA: Ariel Ministries Press, 1993), 684–90. Some have argued that the one New Testament exception is Paul's use of the "Israel of God" in Galatians 6:16. But this verse also speaks of Jewish believers within Israel (see Hans Dieter Betz, *Galatians*, Hermeneia—A Critical and Historical Commentary on the Bible (Philadelphia: Fortress, 1979), 320–23; Walter Gutbrod, "Israel, k.t.l.," *Theological Dictionary of the New Testament*, III:387–88.

Chapter 15: Israel and Jewish Evangelism Today

1. I do not believe that a Jewish person is capable of keeping the Law to the extent that their human efforts would in some way satisfy God's demands for righteousness—enabling the individual Jewish person to enter heaven on their own merit (Gal. 2:15–16, 3:23–25, Romans 10:2–4 ff.).

2. Part of a larger volume entitled, *Chiliasts and Judentzer Eschatology and Mission to the Jews in German Protestantism Between the 17th and 18th Century*.

3. The full title of the chapter is, *Israel in the Church and the Church in Israel: The formation of Jewish Christian communities as a proselytizing strategy within and outside the German Pietist mission to the Jews of the eighteenth century and*

the book, Lutz Greisiger, 'Chiliasten und "Judentzer"—Eschatologie und Juden-
mission im protes-tantischen Deutschland des 惧憹. und 惧憹. Jahrhun-
derts,' Kwartalnik historii Zydów / Jewish History Quarterly 惗俺俺憱, vol. 峥
(惗惗俺), 憯博憯–憯懷憯.)

4. William Blackstone, Jesus is Coming Again, New York: Fleming H Revell,
1908. Also found online in full at http://www.jesus-is-savior.com/Books,%20
Tracts%20&%20Preaching/Printed%20Books/JIC/jic-chap_03.htm

5. http://archive.org/search.php?query=protocols%20of%20the%20elders%20
AND%20mediatype%3Atexts

6. Anglican theologians Colin Chapman, Stephen Sizer and American New Testament scholar, Gary Burge have done much to shape the views of main
line Evangelicals on both sides of the Atlantic towards Israel and the Jewish
people. Chapman's Whose Promised Land? and Whose Holy City are both published by Baker Academic and Sizer's, Christian Zionism and Zion's Christian
Soldiers, published by Intervarsity Press have profoundly influenced the opinions of Christians, both theologically and politically. Burge, who teaches at
Wheaton College, has done much the same through two major books as
well as numerous articles on the subject. His first work, Whose Land? Whose
Promise?: What Christians Are Not Being Told About Israel and the Palestinians
and his latest book, Jesus and the Land: The New Testament Challenge to "Holy
Land" Theology, published by Baker Academic Press.

7. Supersessionists today continue to generally affirm that the Church has either replaced, subsumed, or otherwise fulfilled God's intended purposes for
Israel and that the nation of Israel, as usually defined, has been "permanently
set aside" by God for her disobedience, both in our current day and in the
future

8. Charles Hodge suggests, The term proton relates to time and sequences, rather than specialty or priority. Therefore, he promotes the view that the Gospel
came to the Jewish people first—they rejected it—and now the Gospel is to
go primarily to the Gentiles. (To the Jew First, 196)

9. Pauline Theology, Volume III, Editors David M. Hay and E. Elizabeth Johnson,
1995, pp. 30–67. Minneapolis: Fortress, 11 (Also see Romans and the Theology
of Paul, http://ntwrightpage.com/Wright_Romans_Theology_Paul.pdf)

10. In summary, then, proton has the meaning of "first," and this includes "first
in time, and place, in order, and importance." Applying this verse to the
great commission, the Gospel, whenever and by whatever means it goes out
from a local church, must go to the Jew first. This is the biblical procedure
for evangelism regardless of the method. Since most believers in local assemblies participate in the great commission may lead to monetary giving, is to
require giving to the Jew first. This is true of the individual believers both of
the local assembly in the mission's budget. What is true of the local church
is also true the missionary in the field you must first take the gospel to any
Jews who may be in a field where he is working. Regardless of the particular
place of calling, his obligation is to seek out the Jews and present them to the
gospel. Where there is already a command, no special leading is necessary
(To the Jew First, 207).

11. See Ernst Käsemann, Commentary on Romans, trans. and ed. Geoffrey Bro-
miley (Grand Rapids: Eerdmans, 1980), 23; William R. Newell, Romans
Verse by Verse (Chicago: Moody, 1938), 22. For a helpful discussion of this
subject, see the essay by Wayne A. Brindle, "'To The Jew First': Rhetoric,
Strategy, History, or Theology?" BSac 159 (2002): 221–33. Darrell L. Bock,
Walter C. Kaiser, and Craig A. Blaising, Dispensationalism, Israel and the
Church (Zondervan, 1992).

12. A wonderful story is told of the relationship between John Wilkinson, a Gentile missionary to the Jews who founded the Mildmay Mission to the Jews
and of J. Hudson Taylor founder of the China Inland Mission—now OMF. It
seems that every January Taylor would send Wilkinson a check for a sum of
money with a note attached, "to the Jew first." Wilkinson would then the
amount back to Taylor with a note that read, "And also to the Gentiles."

13. Abraham, Genesis 17:1–14, 15:1–5, 22:15–18, Isaac, Genesis 17:9–22, 21:1–7, 26:1–5; Jacob, Genesis 25:19–28, 35:9–15.
14. Exodus 19:3–6; Isaiah 43:8–15
15. Deut. 4:25–31; Jer. 31:31–34; Ezek. 37:21–28
16. Though this is a common teaching within Dispensational circles, I am personally indebted to Dr. Arnold Fruchtenbaum who first alerted me to the truths of this magnificent text.
17. ο οικοσ, "House of God" in Jesus and the Gospels. The NT uses both *oikos* and *oikia*, but usually links tou theou to oikos, reserving the phrase for the temple (or the Christian community, Heb. 3:6; 1 Peter 4:17). Jesus speaks about the house of God in Mark 2:26 and in Mark 11:17 (based on Isa. 56: 7), where the temple is holy because it is a house of prayer for the nations (cf. John 2: 16, which recalls Zech. 14:21). Theological Dictionary of the New Testament: Abridged in One Volume Hardcover—Abridged by Gerhard Kittel (Editor), Gerhard Friedrich (Editor), Geoffrey W. Bromiley (Editor)
18. Oftentimes, God's removal of Himself from His people is viewed as a judgment. (See Ezek. 10:18–19 and Rom. 1:24–27.)
19. εωσ αν
20. See http://www.hymnsite.com/lyrics/umh622.shtfor full lyrics to the hymn.
21. Feinberg, Charles, *The Prophecies of the Prophet Zechariah*, Chicago, Ill: Moody Press pg. 219
22. O Palmer Robertson, "Is there a distinctive future for ethnic Israel in Romans 11?" *Perspectives on evangelical theology* (1979): 209–227. Pieter W. van der Horst, "'ONLY THEN WILL ALL ISRAEL BE SAVED': A SHORT NOTE ON THE MEANING OF...IN ROMANS 11:26.," *Journal of Biblical Literature* 119, no. 3 (Fall 2000 2000): 521. Michael G. Vanlaningham, "Romans 11:25–27 and the future of Israel in Paul's thought," *Master's Seminary Journal* 3, no. 2 (Fall 1992): 141–174. Toby Ziglar, "Understanding Romans 11:26: Baptist perspectives," *Baptist History and Heritage* 38, no. 2 (Spr. 2003): 38–51. Christopher Zoccali, "'And so all Israel will be saved': competing interpretations of Romans 11.26 in Pauline scholarship," *Journal for the Study of the New Testament* 30, no. 3 (March 2008): 289–318. "The mystery of Israel's salvation: a re-reading of Romans 11:25–32 in light of the Dead Sea scrolls," *Flores Florentino* (2007): 653–666. For a further helpful discussion of this subject, see the essay by Wayne A. Brindle, "'To The Jew First': Rhetoric, Strategy, History, or Theology?" *BSac* 159 (2002): 221–33.
23. See the video of the event sponsored by the Carl Henry Center focusing on this passage; including the author Doug Moo and others. http://www.youtube.com/watch?v=keVxUdvYZe4
24. Mark Twain, "Concerning the Jews," *Harper's Magazine*, March 1899.

Chapter 16: Israel and the Local Pastor

1. David A. Rausch, *A Legacy of Hatred* (Chicago: Moody Press, 1984), 29.
2. Martin Luther, *On the Jews and Their Lies* (1543), trans. Martin H. Bertram, in *Luther's Works, The Christian in Society*, ed. Franklin Sherman and Helmut T. Lehmann (Philadelphia: Fortress Press, 1971), 47:268.
3. Erwin Lutzer, *Hitler's Cross* (Chicago: Moody Press, 1995), 86–87.
4. Hal Lindsay, *The Road to Holocaust* (New York: Bantam, 1989), 23–24.
5. David Epstein, *A Time for Hope* (ANM Publishers, 2011), p4.
6. *A Time for Hope*, 90.
7. Matthew Kaminski, *Wall Street Journal*, Weekend Interview: Mosab Yousef, March 6, 2010.
8. NYPOST, Post Opinion, Friday Sept. 25, 2009, 35.
9. *A Time for Hope*, 113–118.
10. Abba Eban, *Heritage: Civilization and the Jews* (Summit Books, NY, 1984), 338.
11. Ibid.
12. Ibid.
13. Ibid.
14. Ibid.

MORE ENDORSEMENTS

"Few things are more important in our day than having an accurate—and scriptural—understanding of the essential issues addressed in this comprehensive and challenging work. Editors Darrel L. Bock and Mitch Glazer have done a masterful job putting together the ideas and insights of some of this generation's most gifted and dedicated teachers, ministers, scholars, and theologians. Yet, the result is not an academic exercise meant only for the seminarian, but a workbook for any serious student of the Bible, lover of history, or astute observer of current events. How blessed we are to have such an inspiring and indispensable resource available to us 'at such a time as this.' I could not recommend it more highly!"

Marty Goetz, messianic music minister and recording artist

"Yes, the church is the new Israel, but does that mean the promises to the old Israel no longer need be kept? If God breaks his promises to Israel, then how can the church trust God? We live in an age of increasing anti-Semitism, anti-Zionism and confusion—even in the church. This book thoroughly surveys what the Bible says is God's plan for the children of Israel, their land, and their future. And it upholds God's covenant relationships with Israel and the church. Pastors and layman alike will profit from reading this book."

Mike McClure, former Chair of the Department of Bible and Theology, John Wesley College

"Our merciful, loving, and faithful God has not turned his back on the Jewish people. There are great things ahead: God will fulfill the promises he gave to the Jewish people (including his promises regarding the land), there will be a massive number of Jews turn to *Yeshua* as *ha-Mashiach* (Jesus the Messiah), and Israel will truly become a blessing to the nations. This book presents a solid and convincing case regarding the future of Israel and the Jewish people. Because this topic has been so neglected by our churches in recent years, this book needs to be at the top of your reading list."

Clinton E. Arnold, Dean and Professor of New Testament,
Talbot School of Theology

"The church is in desperate need of this book, but not everyone will agree with it. Unfortunately, even in some parts of the evangelical world, it is becoming politically correct to deny Israel's right to exist as a nation in the land and paint them as the villain in Middle Eastern and world politics. On the other side are those for whom Israel can do no wrong. In light of the importance of Israel as God's covenant people, their connection to the land in the Bible, and the long history of the Jewish struggle for survival from the first century to the twenty-first, this book deserves a serious reading by all believers.

"This book engages well with the biblical, theological, and historical issues. Yes, the Gentiles have been very much a part of God's redemptive program from the start, but 'Gentile inclusion does not mean Israel's exclusion,' whether then or now. The church does not 'replace' Israel. And thankfully, even in the midst of all this debate about the interpretative and political issues, the writers keep in the forefront of the discussion the need to love Jew and Palestinian alike, and the core priority of evangelism that both might put their faith and life in the hands of *Jeshua Hammashiach*."

Richard E. Averbeck, Professor of Old Testament and
Semitic Languages, Trinity Evangelical Divinity School

"*The People, the Land, and the Future of Israel* is a welcome scholarly, yet wonderfully readable, assessment of one of the vexing questions of modernity. What does the Bible say about the Jews? Brim full of insight, armed with a keen sense of the socio-political contours of the present age, and fully prepared with Scriptural truth, this long-needed handbook, with a practical response to the quagmire in the Middle East, has been penned by a coterie of scholars. This book begged for publication for the benefit of the church and Israel alike."

Paige Patterson, President,
Southwestern Baptist Theological Seminary